International Financial Services

(formerly *International Trade Finance*)

Gary Collyer

Paul Cowdell

Peter McGregor

GLOBAL
professional
publishing

This edition published by Global Professional Publishing 2008

Global Professional Publishing

European Innovation Centre, Fitzroy House

11 Chenies Street

London WC1E 7EY

United Kingdom

Email: publishing@gppbooks.com

ISBN: 978-1-906403-19-5

Printed in the United States by International Book Techologies

Gary Collyer has previously been technical adviser to the International Chamber of Commerce (ICC) and has chaired the Working Groups for the development of ISP 98, the revision of UCP 500 and the UCP 600 Drafting Group.

Editor of six ICC opinion publications, Gary is also an editorial board member of *Documentary Credit Insight* and *Documentary Credit World*. In April 2006, Gary established Collyer Consulting LLP with the aim of providing banks with consultancy services that would include the development of training material, review of legal documentation and the provision of consistent, accurate and up-to-date information relating to existing offerings, new initiatives and developments in international trade. Until October 2006, Gary remained corporate director and global head of traditional trade services, trade finance and product delivery for the Transaction Banking Group at ABN AMRO Bank NV.

Paul Cowdell has worked for many years at Midland Bank dealing with the international trade needs of corporate clients. Paul was a tutor on Midland Bank's staff training courses related to international trade facilities for corporate clients. Now a Principal Lecturer at Sheffield Hallam University in Risk Management, Corporate Treasury Management and Derivatives, Paul has authored and co-authored several texts and articles on international trade facilities and foreign currency risk exposure management.

Peter McGregor. With a successful career in banking at both Midland Bank Ltd (now part of HSBC Bank UK) and Nedbank Ltd, South Africa, Peter went on to pursue a career in academia.

Peter joined Sheffield City Polytechnic (now Sheffield Hallam University) in 1989, and has taught at all levels from professional through to undergraduate and postgraduate Masters' degrees. His main areas of teaching expertise are financial services, lending and risk management, international trade finance, corporate treasury management, banking and financial services law and regulation. In addition to his teaching commitments, Peter also undertakes consultancy work and is a Fellow of the Chartered Institute of Bankers (CIB). Peter was awarded the CIB's Diploma in Financial Services in 1989 and in 2007 was also made a Fellow of the Higher Education Academy.

Contents

Preface

This first edition of *International Financial Services* is intended to assist all students and practitioners who seek to acquire the necessary background information to gain an understanding of the finance of international trade, foreign exchange and support services provided for exporters, importers and merchants by London's financial institutions. The text incorporates all relevant developments up to 1 January 2008.

It concentrates in particular on the needs of students studying for the International Financial Services module within the Institute of Financial Services Foundation degree programme.

The text is in five parts.

♦ Part I consists of a single introductory topic which sets out the rationale for the development and growth of international trade.

♦ Part II discusses the determination of spot and forward foreign exchange rates and interest rates. It then analyses the practical applications of hedging techniques, both internal and external, for foreign exchange and interest rate exposures and finally covers foreign exchange and settlement procedures, with coverage of the issue of fraud, money laundering and terrorist financing.

♦ Part III assesses the role of documents used in international trade and then analyses the way that documents are linked inexorably and logically with the shipping and payment terms agreed between importer and exporter.

♦ Part IV then examines the implications of the various financial and non-financial services from the point of view of exporters.

♦ Finally, Part V analyses documentary credits from the applicant's point of view, and then evaluates the benefits and drawbacks of various specialist forms of documentary credit, such as transferable and back- to- back credits, together with services and facilities for importers. There is a final topic covering facility letters and loan agreements, choice of law, jurisdiction and exchange controls.

For easy reference a list of learning objectives appears at the beginning of each unit. In addition, there are appendices, which include copies of various International Chamber of Commerce (ICC) rules covering documentary collections and documentary credits.

The aim of this text is to help readers acquire a sound understanding of relevant theoretical and practical concepts, coupled with an ability to apply the principles in a given practical situation.

Foreign exchange rates fluctuate; therefore the reader should be aware that the rates used in the numeric examples should be considered as indicative only.

Acknowledgements

Much of the material herein draws heavily on *International Trade Finance*, 8th edition. The publishers, therefore, wish to acknowledge the contributions of Alastair Watson, Paul Cowdell and Derek Hyde to this edition.

The authors and the **ifs** *School of Finance* would like to thank HSBC Bank plc and the International Chamber of Commerce for their kind permission to reproduce various documents and articles.

The authors also wish to thank Walter 'Buddy' Baker of Atradius, Martin Jay of Amlin Transit and Peter Salmon of Wright Kerr Tyson Ltd for providing valuable input to this publication.

Finally, the authors wish to acknowledge the advice and support of George Fullerton, Business Development Executive at Sheffield Chamber of Commerce and Industry, Dr David Goacher and Derek Hyde of Sheffield Hallam University, Gary Slawther, Head of Treasury at Jarvis plc and Andrew Cantrill, formerly of HSBC Sheffield.

ifs SCHOOL OF FINANCE
MODULE SPECIFICATION

1.	Title	**International Financial Services** (working title)
2.	**Start date**	Courses of study commencing in May 2008
3.	**Level of module**	I (within QAA Framework for Higher Education) Subject benchmark: General Business & Management
4.	**Number of credits**	30 credits
5.	**Status**	Option module
6.	**Recommended prior modules**	♦ Organisational Management in Financial Services ♦ The Commercial Environment
7.	**Programmes of study to which module contributes**	Foundation Degree in Financial Services Management

Date of production/revision	13 June 2006	
Date of approval	**ifs** Programme & Validation Committee	
	ifs Academic Board	
	University of Kent	

8.   Purpose/rationale/positioning

International Financial Services is an option module within the Foundation Degree programme and is aimed students that are either working in an international environment at present, or aspire to do so.

This module provides students with an understanding of the principles and practices of international trade payments and finance. This includes an appreciation of the importance of international trade, the types of risks involved, including those arising from interest and exchange rate fluctuations, and the range of methods available to manage them. Students will have the opportunity to gain an understanding of the international legal and regulatory framework within which international trade has to be conducted, but the emphasis is on the practical, operational nature of this subject area.

Through the assessment, students will be able to demonstrate their ability to apply their technical knowledge to practical situations, specifically for customers trading internationally in a variety of different circumstances. This will include demonstrating an understanding of customer needs, the ability to compare and contrast the different products available to customers and to explain why a particular product or solution may be appropriate. Students will also be expected to explain the advantages and disadvantages of different options and solutions effectively and with authority in customer- facing situations.

| 9. | **Intended subject specific learning outcomes and, as appropriate, their relationship to programme learning outcomes** |

On completion of this module, students will be able to:

1. Explain the importance of international trade and why it differs from domestic trade.
2. Understand the nature of international banking and the correspondent relationships.
3. Analyse, identify risks and suggest mitigation techniques appropriate to:
   - Interest and exchange rate exposure
   - Relevant legal and regulatory issues
   - Payment methods
   - Contract bonds and guarantees
4. Explain the determination of interest and exchange rates and understand the implications for foreign trade.
5. Explain payment settlement and clearing systems in sterling and foreign currency including Chaps, Target and the use of nostro and vostro accounts.
6. Examine commercial terms, specifically INCOTERMS, used in the delivery of goods.
7. Explain a range of foreign currency hedging strategies and mechanisms.
8. Discuss methods of payment including letters of credit and documentary collections and the ability to apply underlying international rules governing those methods of payment.
9. Explain financial crime and the regulatory environment.
10. Discuss finance alternatives including protection against credit and political risks.

These intended module learning outcomes contribute to the following programme learning outcomes: A1, A3, A4, A5, A9, A10, A11 and A13 together with the generic programme skills set out in section B- D of the programme specification.

| 10. | **Intended generic learning outcomes and, as appropriate, their relationship to programme learning outcomes** |

On completion of this module students will be able to demonstrate achievement of the following generic learning outcomes:

1. Ability to learn through reflection on practice and experience
2. Ability to undertake detailed research on a particular area and work with complex material
3. Ability to analyse problems, identify appropriate solutions and make decisions
4. Ability to work and study independently and utilize resources effectively
5. Ability to communicate effectively in a manner appropriate to the context and audience

These intended generic learning outcomes contribute to the generic programme skills set out in section B- D of the programme specification.

11. Methods of delivery

Students are required to follow an approved course of study that provides them with learning support. There are two distinct modes of study:

1. At approved Academic Centres authorised by *ifs* to provide tuition for the programme.
2. On a distance learning basis with tutorial support being provided by *ifs'* network of distance learning tutors.

Each student enrolled on the programme will have access to the My*ifs*ILE environment and the *ifs* KnowledgeBank learning resources.

Students may opt to pursue the module by either of the above modes of study, and will undertake their learning for each module within designated study sessions that will culminate with a final assessment.

Study hours:

The module is the equivalent of 300 notional learning hours. This learning may be acquired in a variety of ways:

♦ via the support offered by Academic Centres or *ifs* distance learning provision;
♦ by private study;
♦ by completing formative assignments;
♦ by learning acquired and applied in the work environment; and
♦ by reflecting on and utilising previous learning.

12. Assessment

Achievement of the learning outcomes for each option module is assessed in two ways:

♦ Via a written examination; and

♦ Via a summative coursework assignment. This assessment uses the underpinning subject knowledge assessed in the examination as the framework within which to assess the achievement of the intellectual, subject specific and transferable skills summarised in the module specification. It is recommended for each module that the summative assignment should not be submitted for marking until the associated formative assignments have been submitted and tutor feedback has been received.

Examination:

Examination questions will be practical, application-based and be focused at an operational level. According to the nature of the subject matter, a variety of question styles and approaches will be included in the examination. Questions might be based on case study materials and require a discursive answer, a business report or a series of shorter answers. Students will typically be required to explore and compare the technical aspects of an issue or topic or to apply their understanding to, for example, solve a problem or provide a recommended solution for a customer.

The question paper will be structured as follows:

♦ Two compulsory 20-mark questions; and

♦ One 10-mark question from a choice of two.

The pass mark for this component is 40%.

Time allowed: Two hours.

Summative coursework assignment:

This component will contribute 50% of the overall assessment and will be based upon the submission of one assignment at the end of the course but prior to the examination. The assignment will take the form of case study questions based on stimulus material. Students will be expected to collect information, undertake research, etc., and the assignment will allow the opportunity to reflect on or analyse comparative perspectives, e.g. different cultures, countries, organisations, etc. Feedback will not be provided on this component.

At regular intervals during the course of study, students will be expected to submit three short formative assignments. These assignments, which will take the form of developmental learning activities towards the assessed coursework and unseen examination components, will be integrated within the study plan and will provide students both with opportunities to reinforce their learning as they progress through the course of study and the opportunity to prepare for both the summative assignment and unseen examination.

Whilst these formative assignments will not contribute to the overall assessment, students are strongly advised to take the opportunity to complete them, as feedback will be provided from their tutor on their progress through the course of study.

The pass mark for this component is 40%.

---

13. Syllabus overview

This module has been designed to provide students with a knowledge and appreciation of the many aspects of providing financial services to customers trading, or based, overseas.

Students are firstly provided with a background introduction to the growth and importance of international trade and finance. The module especially focuses upon the additional risks that need to be taken into consideration by customers when trading internationally and by financial institutions when providing payment services and finance, together with the methods that can be used to mitigate or reduce the potential impact of these risks.

Students will then have the opportunity to explore the importance and influence of interest and exchange rates, how they are determined and to what extent they are interdependent. The module then examines in detail the methods of payment, performance bonds, guarantees and financing options that are used and the legal and regulatory framework within which they have to operate. This includes international rules and commercial terms governing various aspects of international trade.

---

14. Syllabus

1. The continuing growth, context and importance of international trade and finance, and international banking

This section of the syllabus has been designed to provide students with a background understanding of the nature and importance of international trade, the role of financial institutions in financing such trade and the workings of correspondent banking relationships.

Its focus is learning outcomes 1 and 2 covers the following issues:

- Nature of trade
- Nature of international banking
- The importance of correspondent relationships: bank support generally:
  - Advice and support
  - Trade promotion

2. Risk

In many ways, one of the key differentiators between international and domestic trade and banking can be seen as substantially increased risk in various forms. This section of the syllabus has been designed to provide students with the opportunity to focus on the sorts of risks inherent in trading across borders.

Its focus is learning outcomes 3, 7 and 10 and covers the following issues:

- Credit risks
- Financial risks
- Legal risks
- Country risks
- Interest and exchange rate exposure risks
- Payment risks

3. Interest and Exchange Rates

Understanding the role that interest rates play within a financial system is critical to this module. They influence the dynamics of financial flows in the economy and the profitability of particular groups of financial institutions. This section of the syllabus has therefore been designed to help students recognise that there are a range of interest rates that exist within the economy and to be able to explain the relationships between, and determinants of, such rates. In an era of globalisation, a significant amount of financial risk comes from exchange rate uncertainty. This section therefore also helps students to understand some of the principle determinants of exchange rates and the different types of exchange rate systems.

Its focus is learning outcomes 4 and 7 and covers the following issues:

- Determination
- Exchange rate systems, e.g. fixed, floating, adjustable peg
- Euro
- Parity relationships

4. Risk mitigation

Once the risks have been identified, as in Section 2 above, these risks need to be mitigated or reduced in some way. This section of the syllabus has been designed to provide students with an insight into the methods that financial institutions can use to reduce their own risks or introduce them to their customers for their use. (Note: this section is concerned with general awareness of the types of instrument and basic calculations only.)

Its focus is learning outcomes 7 and 10 and covers the following issues:

♦ Hedging strategies
♦ Forwards and options
♦ Currency accounts and borrowing
♦ SWAPS and derivatives (general overview only)

5. Legal and Regulatory Framework

When dealing in an international context, it is absolutely crucial that both the customer and the service provider are aware of the legal context within which they are operating. This section of the syllabus enables the student to study the rationale behind the law applicable to the contract and the country where any actions will be taken on default. The international aspect of regulation is also covered.

Its focus is learning outcomes 6, 8 and 9 and covers the following issues:

♦ Choice of law
♦ Jurisdiction
♦ Exchange controls
♦ Fraud
♦ Money laundering
♦ Terrorist financing

6. Methods of payment

Companies involved in international trade need to understand the range of products available to be able to select the most appropriate payment method considering, amongst other things, speed, security and cost both to remitter and the beneficiary. This section of the syllabus enables students to be able to explain the features of each payment method and recommend the most appropriate to meet customers needs.

Its focus is learning outcomes 3, 5 and 8 and covers the following issues:

♦ Open account/clean payments, payment settlement systems, e.g. nostro/vostro, euro
♦ Collections URC
♦ Credits UCP
♦ INCOTERMS
♦ Credit insurance
♦ e- banking

7. Contract bonds and guarantees

This section of the syllabuses focuses upon the several types of bonds and guarantees that a domestic seller may be called upon to provide for a foreign buyer. A third party gives these security undertakings so that the buyer has an undertaking, in the case of non-performance or fraud, giving him a right of recall without resorting to the courts. Students will also gain an understanding of the rights and obligations under contract bonds and guarantees.

Its focus is learning outcomes 3 and 8 and covers the following issues:

- Performance bonds/guarantees
- Standby letters of credit
- Rights and obligations

8. Financing

This section of the syllabus focuses upon methods of providing short to medium-term finance (longer-term and specialist finance, such as syndicate loans, are not included in this module). The terms and conditions contained within a facility letter and events of default are also covered in this section.

Its focus is learning outcomes 8 and 10 and covers the following issues:

- Overdraft
- Bill finance/forfaiting
- Factoring
- Invoice discounting
- Buyer and supplier credit – Government supported export credit schemes
- Facility letters and loan agreements
- Events of default

Part I

Introduction

Part I of the text is intended to provide an overview of international trade. It analyses the rationale for the growth of international trade.

Topic 1

International trade: an introductory overview

On completion of this topic the student should be able to:

- understand why and how domestic trade and international trade differ;
- understand the concepts of absolute and comparative advantage, and how these concepts, in general, tend to support arguments for increasing the volume of international trade; and
- appreciate the role played by GATT, WTO and SMP in promoting the growth of trade.

1.1　How international trade differs from domestic trade

Domestic trade has the following characteristics, which apply to both parties:

- a common language and culture;
- the same laws;
- an absence of customs formalities;
- usually relatively simple documentation;
- a single currency;
- relatively simple formalities to transport goods from buyer to seller.

International trade is much more complex in that, generally speaking, it has the opposite characteristics to those listed above.

Completing a sale of goods overseas can be much more costly than a domestic sale in terms of marketing efforts, coping with customs formalities, dealing with different legal requirements and organising relatively complex transport arrangements. Further risk is involved if settlement is in a foreign currency, because there is no guarantee of the value in domestic currency terms at the time that settlement and conversion are effected. In addition to the risk of buyer default, which can obviously apply in domestic business but which may be more acute with an unknown buyer from overseas, there can be default caused by the overseas government's actions. As an example, one government imposed restrictions on payments during the Asian Financial Crisis of 1998.

The immediate reaction to all of this is to ask why anyone would wish to trade internationally when domestic trade is so much more simple. The purpose of this book is to explain the theoretical reasons that support the growth of international trade and then to show how organisations such as banks, the International Chamber of Commerce (ICC) and credit insurers can overcome the additional problems posed by cross border trade.

1.2   Why do countries trade?

This question can best be considered by analysing the relationship between consumption and work. People may possibly be able to produce everything they need through their own labour, but this will not be appeal to most people because they would find their consumption confined to a narrow range of goods. Thus individuals in modern economies do not try to produce exactly what they consume; instead, individuals work for money, which is then used for consumption purposes.

A person's work may help to produce only a small range of goods, but the wages paid for that work help that person to obtain access to a much wider range of goods and services. The well- known economic concepts of specialisation and division of labour, under which people specialise in the production of certain items and then obtain other goods through trade, evolved from the above concepts. Trade is therefore necessary if the full benefits of specialisation are to be enjoyed.

Even towns and cities are not normally completely self- sufficient. Those cities that might technically be capable of such self- sufficiency would be worse off without trade because the variety and quality of goods would be reduced if trade did not take place.

Because people gain by trading between each other, trade will take place naturally without the need for any encouragement. Trade also takes place naturally between countries, because it would be illogical to expect gains from trade to stop at national boundaries.

In recent times, the increase in the importance of services, the political impetus from the development of free trade areas such as the North America Free Trade Agreement (NAFTA) and the European Single Market Programme (SMP), and pressure from organisations such as the World Trade Organization (WTO), which assumed the functions of the General Agreement on Tariffs and Trade (GATT), have resulted in an ever- increasing amount of trade in goods and services between different countries.

1.3   The concepts of absolute advantage and comparative advantage in international trade

1.3.1   Absolute advantage

Absolute advantage is an imperfect explanation for the reasons for international trade, but it paves the way for the more cogent argument of comparative advantage, which can be found below.

Let us consider a very simple hypothetical example to illustrate absolute advantage. A country is said to have an absolute advantage in the production of a commodity if it uses fewer resources than another country to produce a given quantity. Thus for a commodity with only one factor of production – say labour, for example – if one country uses less labour than another to make a given amount of the commodity, that country has an absolute advantage. This concept of absolute advantage assumes that one hour of labour in one country has the same characteristics as one hour in another country.

1.3.1.1   Example 1.1

Table 1.1 illustrates this by comparing the hypothetical examples of wheat and car production in Canada and Ireland. It assumes that the only factor of production is hours of labour and that an hour of labour in one country is identical to an hour of labour in another country. It also assumes that there are only two countries, only two commodities, and that the goods are of the same standard and quality in each country.

Table 1.1

	WHEAT *Hours to produce one ton*	*CARS* *Hours to produce one*
Ireland	300 hours	150 hours
Canada	200 hours	250 hours

Relying solely on the information above, it is clear that Canada has an absolute advantage in the production of wheat, because it takes fewer hours of labour in Canada to produce a ton of wheat, but the opposite applies to cars, in relation to which Ireland has an absolute advantage. In addition, 450 hours of labour in either country will produce one car and one ton of wheat.

What happens if trade were to take place and Canada to exchange one ton of wheat for one car from Ireland?

Canada would save 250 hours by obtaining one car from Ireland and not having to produce it itself, and it could use those 250 hours to produce 1.25 tons of wheat. Thus 450 hours of labour, after the trade shown above, would leave Canada with one car and 1.25 tons of wheat. This is a net benefit to Canada of one quarter of a ton of wheat.

Conversely, Ireland would obtain a ton of wheat from Canada and would then use the 300 hours saved to produce two cars, thus obtaining a net benefit of one car.

This phenomenon arises with international trade because each country specialises in producing the commodity in which it has an absolute advantage. In Canada, 450 hours are devoted to wheat, producing 2.25 tons of wheat, one of which is traded for a car. In Ireland, 450 hours are devoted to producing three cars, one of which is exchanged for a ton of wheat. Thus specialisation and division of labour, whether on the part of individuals, towns or countries, will lead to a greater total output of goods and services.

The prices at which the trade is arranged will determine how the gains from trade are split between the two parties. From the point of view of Ireland, the minimum amount of wheat required to break even in exchange for one car is 0.5 tons, because 150 hours of labour produce 0.5 tons of wheat or one car in Ireland. From the point of view of Canada, the maximum amount of wheat it can give in exchange for one car and still break even is

1.25 tons, because in Canada, the 250 hours it takes to produce one car could be used to produce 1.25 tons of wheat. Thus the expected exchange value of one car exported from Ireland to Canada would be somewhere between 0.5 and 1.25 tons of wheat. The exchange value between these two parameters that is actually applied will determine the split of the benefits of the trade between Ireland and Canada.

1.3.2   Comparative advantage

While Example 1.1 made it clear that, in principle, two countries can gain from trade when one has an absolute advantage in the first commodity and the other has an absolute advantage in the second commodity, this section will show how trade is beneficial in a two- good, two- country economy even when one country has an absolute advantage in both commodities. A country is said to have a comparative advantage in a good if its opportunity cost of producing the good is lower than that of other countries. Likewise, if the opportunity cost of producing the good is higher than that of other countries, a country is said to have a comparative disadvantage in that good. In principle, a country should export goods in which it has a comparative advantage and import goods in which it has a comparative disadvantage.

1.3.2.1   Example 1.2

Let us look at the following simplified example, in which Canada is assumed to have an absolute advantage in the production of both wheat and cars.

Table 1.2

	WHEAT *Hours to produce one ton*	**CARS** *Hours to produce one*
Ireland	400 hours	375 hours
Canada	200 hours	300 hours

Here Canada has an absolute advantage in both goods because it requires fewer hours of labour to produce both cars and wheat in Canada. The opportunity cost of producing these goods can be shown in Table 1.3.

Table 1.3

	WHEAT *one ton*	**CARS** *one*
Ireland	1.07 cars	0.94 tons of wheat
Canada	0.67 cars	1.50 tons of wheat

Explanation: if Ireland uses 400 hours to produce cars instead of wheat, it will produce 400/375 of a car, ie 1.07 cars.

From the above, we can conclude that Canada has a comparative advantage in wheat production, having a lower opportunity cost than Ireland, but Ireland has a comparative advantage in the production of cars due to the lower opportunity cost of car production in Ireland.

Similar principles to those shown in Example 1.1 above will apply in the determination of the exchange value of one car – but if we assume for the moment that one car can be traded for one ton of wheat, what will happen if Canada exchanges one ton of wheat for one car from Ireland?

Canada will utilise 500 hours of labour to produce 2.5 tons of wheat, and after exchanging one ton for one car, will have a total of 1.5 tons of wheat and one car. Thus Canada benefits by 0.5 tons of wheat.

What about Ireland under this transaction? Ireland will utilise 775 hours in producing 2.07 cars. One car will then be exchanged for one ton of wheat resulting in a net gain for Ireland of 0.07 cars.

1.3.3   Comparative advantage with money inputs

1.3.3.1   Example 1.3

Let us retain the two commodities, two countries, one factor of production model already used, but let us assume that the hourly rate of pay for labour is Can$40 in Canada and 20 in Ireland. On this basis, and excluding any profit element, the price of the goods from our comparative advantage example is shown in Table 1.4.

Table 1.4

	WHEAT (per ton)	Per CAR
Ireland	€8,000	€7,500
Canada	Can$8,000	Can$12,000

If the rate of exchange between the Canadian dollar and the euro is Can$1.5 = 1, the cost in euro terms of wheat produced in Canada is 5,333.33 per ton (ie 2666.67 cheaper than Ireland- produced wheat), and the cost of a car produced in Ireland in terms of Canadian dollars is Can$11,250 (ie Can$750 below the cost of a car produced in Canada).

Much, of course, depends on the rate of exchange between the two currencies and on the hourly wage rates in the two countries. It can be seen, however, that the Canadian dollar equivalent of the Irish hourly wage is Can$30 at the stated rate of exchange, whereas the actual hourly rate in Canada is Can$40. The explanation for this could lie in the fact that the Canadian worker was, in this hypothetical example, more efficient than the Irish worker and thus earned a greater hourly rate. In practice this efficiency might be an illusion because the Canadian worker may be better supported by capital equipment.

Whatever the reasons, traders will wish to buy wheat in Canada to sell in Ireland and to buy cars in Ireland to sell to Canada, ignoring transaction costs of the deal.

1.3.4   Further comments on the implications of comparative advantage for international trade

The purpose of the preceding examples was to demonstrate, in general terms, that there is a gain from trade when countries export goods in which they have a comparative advantage and import goods in which they have a comparative disadvantage. If these 'rules' are followed, there is a total gain from international trade, because the total quantity of goods available expands as a result of more efficient resource allocation.

There are, however, practical difficulties that can arise from the implementation of a policy of trade based on the principle of comparative advantage. When imports are suddenly allowed, there are immediate practical problems for the importing country:

- home- based producers could go into liquidation, with resultant unemployment;
- alternatively, home- based producers will reduce wages to compete;
- other sectors of the home economy which relied upon the defunct firms for their income will also suffer.

Logically, the unemployment and loss of trade caused by allowing imports will not last forever, because labour and resources will be moved into other industries with a comparative advantage, but there is considerable argument as to the size and duration of the immediate losses caused when imports are allowed. In general, countries that have liberalised trade have seen economic growth (the 'tiger economies' of the Far East, for example), but there are massive short- term problems when home industry is first exposed to external competition, as can be seen from previous events in Eastern Europe. The analysis of absolute advantage and comparative advantage ignores these issues, as well as the more obvious difficulties of whether goods produced in different countries are identical, the effects of transaction costs of trade and the implications of exchange rate movements.

This book is not the place for a full in- depth analysis of the various facets of the theory of comparative advantage as a driver of international trade; the purpose here is simply to demonstrate that international trade should normally result in economic growth due to more efficient resource allocation.

1.4   The General Agreement on Tariffs and Trade (GATT), the World Trade Organization (WTO) and the European Single Market Programme (SMP)

1.4.1   Introduction

Now that we have studied the theoretical concept of comparative advantage as the basis of international trade, we shall look at how the GATT, the WTO and the SMP have begun to overcome the obstacles to trade that exist in practice.

The General Agreement on Tariffs and Trade (GATT) was first signed in 1948 and, since that time, it has been subject to various sets of negotiations (known as 'Rounds') to try to reduce or, ideally, eliminate tariff and non- tariff barriers with a view to encouraging economic growth through world trade. The final GATT Round, known as the Uruguay

Round, began in 1986 and was successfully completed in 1995, at which time the World Trade Organization (WTO) came into existence.

1.4.2 The Uruguay Round of GATT

The negotiators' initial target was to reduce tariff barriers by at least a third within five years, but the world's major trading countries finally agreed to more substantial cuts. As a result, the final level of tariffs for industrialised countries fell from an average of 5% to 3.5%. The European Union (EU) reduced customs duties from 6.8% to 4.1% and the USA from 6.6% to 3.4%. Before the first GATT negotiations in 1947, average tariffs stood at a far higher 40%.

As far as the EU is concerned, the concessions affected exports valued at around £8.5bn and EU imports valued at around £5.5bn. More than 40% of EU imports are now duty- free.

The Uruguay Round also sought to reduce or eliminate non- tariff barriers by examining various rules and procedures that can lead to delays, extra costs and frustration in international trade. These cover such technical questions as customs valuation, pre- shipment inspection and procedures for securing import licences. The changes were aimed at making information on the various requirements more readily available, at keeping paperwork to a minimum and at ensuring that documents are processed speedily.

In addition, the negotiations covered sanitary and phytosanitary regulations as well as technical standards to ensure these are not used for protectionist purposes. The WTO also established a more efficient procedure for handling trade disputes among WTO member countries.

Before the Uruguay Round, services such as banking, consulting and telecommunications were subject to very different national rules. Now, governments must, in effect, apply the same conditions to both domestic and foreign suppliers. As a result of the General Agreement on Trade in Services (GATS) negotiated as part of the Uruguay Round, a wide range of banking, securities and insurance activities are now answerable to multilateral rules. World exports in services came close to $2.8trn in 2006.

Finally, the Uruguay Round saw the successful negotiation of multilateral disciplines on trade related aspects of intellectual property rights, through the so- called TRIPs Agreement.

1.4.3 Multilateral trade agreements: the World Trade Organization (WTO)

Multilateral agreements are agreements to which the bulk of the international community subscribe and their effect is felt in most of the world. Bilateral agreements are agreements between a relatively small number of countries and apply in a particular region (for example, the EU).

The World Trade Organization is an example of a multilateral agreement.

The WTO came into existence in January 1995. It enjoys equal status with the International Monetary Fund (IMF) and the World Bank, and its membership has grown to

151 member countries at the time of writing. While GATT focused only on trade in merchandise goods, the WTO has responsibility over trade in goods (including agriculture), services and intellectual property.

On its website, the WTO describes itself as a 'rules- based, member- driven organization – all decisions are made by the member governments, and the rules are the outcome of negotiations among members.'

The website describes the functions as:

- administering WTO trade agreements;
- forum for trade negotiations;
- handling trade disputes;
- monitoring national trade policies;
- technical assistance and training for developing countries;
- co- operation with other international organisations.

One of the WTO's key roles will be to administer the new procedures for settling disputes between its members. Now, strict deadlines are set for each stage of the process, non- confidential evidence is made public for the first time, interested parties such as consumer groups can give evidence and no single member can block the decision of the new dispute settlement mechanism.

In the years following the conclusion of the Uruguay Round and building on its success, the WTO successfully negotiated additional agreements to further liberalise multilateral trade, notably in telecommunications, financial services and information technology.

After a failed attempt at initiating a new round of WTO negotiations in Seattle in 1998, the WTO succeeded in launching the Doha Development Agenda in November 2001 in the Qatari capital of Doha. The overarching objective of this latest round of multilateral trade negotiations is to improve the integration of developing countries in the world economy by ensuring that trade plays its full part in fostering economic development.

Due to be completed by the end of 2004, despite successive WTO ministerial conferences in Cancún (2003), Hong Kong (2005) and even a suspension of the negotiations between July 2006 and February 2007, the Doha Round (as it is also called) is still under negotiation at the time of writing. The Doha Round includes negotiations across a broad range of trade issues including agriculture, goods, services (including financial services), trade rules (including subsidies, anti- dumping and regional trade agreements) and trade facilitation.

While incremental progress has been achieved across all areas of the negotiations, making the current potential Doha package quite substantial in terms of yielding greater trade liberalisation, agreement on liberalising agricultural trade and trade in industrial products is proving a very challenging task, particularly between industrialised countries and large emerging economies. An important difference between the Uruguay and Doha Rounds is that tariff reductions under the Uruguay Round allowed WTO members to pick and choose which tariffs they would reduce, and by how much, to achieve an overall reduction in bound tariffs expressed in percentage terms; Doha Round tariff reductions will be made according to a 'Swiss formula' that will give countries less flexibility to pick and choose, cutting highest tariffs the most and resulting in a narrower band of final bound tariffs.

1.4.4 Bilateral trade agreements: the European Single Market Programme (SMP)

Up to the mid- 1980s, cross- border trade in the EU was subject to the same obstacles as cross- border trade outside the EU.

Examples of such obstacles include that:

- all goods were stopped and checked at frontiers;
- most products had to comply with different laws in different member States;
- services, such as banking, transport and telecommunications, were largely insulated from competition from other EU member States.

The SMP began with an agreement by member States, signed in February 1986, containing around 270 measures to create a single market. The measures currently adopted relate in the main to:

- the liberalisation of public procurement, which involved making the rules on works and supplies contracts more transparent, stepping up checks and extending the rules to important new areas such as transport, energy and telecommunications;
- the harmonisation of taxation, which meant aligning national provisions on indirect taxes, VAT and excise markets, and financial services;
- recognition of the 'equivalence of national standards' harmonisation of safety and environmental standards;
- the removal of technical barriers;
- the creation of an environment that encourage business co- operation by harmonising company law and approximating legislation on intellectual and industrial property;
- the removal of the automatic need for customs clearance when goods cross EU boundaries, although customs authorities have a right to check goods if there are any suspicious circumstances.

According to its website, the SMP claims to have brought about the complete opening up of transport and telecommunication services, a significant opening up of other 'public service' sectors (electricity, gas and postal services), supervision of mergers and the protection of biotechnological inventions.

The SMP website suggests that the Internet market should eventually culminate in a fully integrated market on national lines. This would have a single currency, a harmonised tax system, and a legal system to enable businesses to operate effectively throughout the market.

It should be noted that the SMP is only one example of a bilateral free trade agreement. Today, there are many examples of bilateral free trade agreements around the world, including, for example, the North American Free Trade Agreement (NAFTA), which covers Canada, the USA and Mexico.

Part II

Introduction

Part II of the text provides an appreciation of the key factors driving foreign exchange markets and then shows how businesses can manage foreign exchange exposures.

There then follows an analysis of the factors that determine movement in interest rates, together with coverage of how businesses can manage interest rate exposures.

Finally, this part explains the processes and principles relating to international money transfers and alerts the reader to the ever- present danger of fraud.

Topic 2

The foreign exchange market: spot markets, forward markets, different exchange rate regimes, and the euro

On completion of this module, the reader should be able to:

- distinguish between the various exchange rate regimes;
- understand the broad significance of the developments concerning the single European currency, the euro;
- evaluate the factors that affect foreign exchange rate movements in the spot market;
- understand that the basic operations of the foreign exchange market and its participants;
- distinguish between telephone/paper-based dealing systems and computer based systems;
- analyse the relationship between spot, forward and relative interest rates and relative inflation rates;
- appreciate the size of the foreign exchange markets.

2.1 The various exchange rate regimes and their benefits and drawbacks

Many organisations, such as businesses, banks and speculators, wish to exchange one currency for another from time to time. A rate of exchange is, in effect, the price of one currency in terms of another. For example, if a business exchanges US$100,000 for sterling at a rate of US$1.50 = £1, then the business will receive £66,666.66 in exchange for its dollars. On the other hand, if the rate of exchange is $US2- £1, then the business will receive £50,000 sterling in exchange for its dollars. As can be seen from the above, the US dollar is weaker in terms of sterling when the rate is US$2= £1, as opposed to when the rate is US$1.50 = £1, because more dollars are required in exchange for £1, or alternatively £1 is worth more dollars when the rate is US$2= £1.

The term 'spot rate' is used for a rate of exchange for a transaction that is to take place today, or within two working days. The term 'forward rate' is used for a rate of exchange quoted today for a transaction that is to be settled at a known future date or within two known future dates. Spot and forward rates are discussed in more detail later in this topic.

Exchange rates can fluctuate from minute to minute or even from second to second and the factors that affect exchange rates depend on the type of exchange rate regime in force.

In theory, there are many different forms of exchange rate regimes that may be operated. At one extreme, exchange rates may be left to float cleanly, with no deliberate official interference, so that the market forces (ie supply and demand) determine the exchange rates. This regime is known as a 'clean floating' regime.

At the other extreme, there is the rigidly fixed exchange rate regime, within which currencies are given fixed parities by an administrative edict. (In this case the normal exchange market mechanism is bypassed entirely). An example of a fixed rate regime was the European Exchange Rate Mechanism (ERM), which the UK joined in 1990 and left in 1992. At that time the single European currency did not exist, and the various European countries each, in the main, had their own currency. Thus, for example, France had the French Franc and Germany had the Deutsche Mark. Under the ERM the rate of sterling against various other European currencies, in particular the German currency, was fixed within a narrow band, with the various governments being committed to the maintenance of the fixed parities.

Between the two extremes there are many variants of the basic forms, each involving differing degrees of official exchange market intervention.

2.1.1 Clean floating exchange rates

The advocates of clean floating exchange rates, within which market forces alone determine the spot rates, argue that a country's monetary and fiscal policies should not be constrained by the need to defend a fixed exchange rate. They believe that exchange rates should be determined by the supply of, and the demand for, currencies in the free market.

The main disadvantages of **clean floating** are that:

- it can cause uncertainty in relation to business transactions;
- time lags in adjustment may make the balance of payments situation worse in the short run (ie when home currency has depreciated, relative export and import prices alter before relative quantities of goods traded. This results in the J- curve effect, in that the balance of payments current account initially deteriorates and only subsequently moves into surplus);
- domestic inflationary pressures may be generated as import prices rise from a depreciation of home currency;
- official financial discipline may be undermined, because there will be no requirement to curb inflationary expectations to protect the exchange value of home currency.

The main advantages of a **freely floating currency** are that:

- it provides an automatic adjustment mechanism for dealing with balance of payments problems. Thus, in theory, a surplus on the balance of payments should result in an appreciating exchange rate, which will then cause a rise in relative export prices resulting in the surplus being eroded. Leaving aside the problems of elasticity of demand and the J- curve effect, however, it must be remembered that there are many factors other than the balance of payments position that cause exchange rate movements;

- there should be no need for the imposition of restrictive measures by the authorities to interfere with trade because of the need to defend a fixed rate;

- at least in theory, international currency reserves are no longer required (except for occasional stabilisation of the exchange rate), because the government no longer has to choose the exchange rate that it believes to be 'correct'.

2.1.2   The adjustable peg system (the Bretton Woods system)

From the end of the Second World War until the early 1970s, most countries were on the 'adjustable peg' system (often referred to as the 'Bretton Woods' system). The basic notion was that a fixed parity exchange rate system would provide a stable basis for international economic activity, but that allowance must be made for the occurrence of fundamental changes in the underlying real economic positions of countries participating in the scheme. Thus, although countries agreed to intervene in the foreign exchange market and to implement appropriate economic policies in order to hold the value of their currencies to within a narrow band around fixed dollar par values, in the event of a 'fundamental disequilibrium' on the balance of payments, they were allowed to adjust their exchange rates.

The problem with the adjustable peg system stems from:

- the difficulty in defining what is meant by 'fundamental disequilibrium';

- deciding when and by how much to adjust the exchange rate;

- the risk of retaliation (including competitive devaluation when one currency has been adjusted downwards in value to try and improve the balance of payments position);

- speculative pressure, which can also make the problem worse.

The benefits of the adjustable peg, which were certainly apparent in the less volatile economic conditions prior to the 1970s, are that this type of 'fixed' rate system may encourage international trade (through the reduction of exchange rate risks) and longer term business planning is made easier. Governments are also encouraged to pursue sound economic and financial policies (especially in respect of inflation) in order to support the existing exchange rate.

2.1.3   Managed floating

Since 1972, with the exception of the period October 1990 to September 1992, the UK has followed a regime of 'managed floating'. The Bretton Woods system had proved to be too inflexible, particularly when confidence was lost in its base, the US dollar. Initially, it was hoped that floating would be only temporary, until an alternative basis for a worldwide fixed rate system could be found. Managed floating has, however, worked reasonably well and is widely used throughout the world. A serious practical problem with clean floating is that exchange rates may become unstable and financial uncertainty may be created. With managed floating, the authorities intervene to iron out short- term fluctuations, leaving market forces to determine long- term trends; the problem here is in deciding when a movement is short term. Furthermore, there are limits to the extent to which the authorities are able to intervene, because their stock of foreign currency reserves is finite.

2.1.4 Fixed exchange rate systems

The European Monetary System (EMS) was the precursor to the single European currency and operated in the late 1980s and for most of the 1990s. Sterling was a member of the Exchange Rate Mechanism (ERM) from 1990 to 1992.

The benefits of this fixed rate system for the UK were generally stated as being that:

- the EU accounts for over a half of all of the UK's overseas trade, so a more stable relationship between sterling and other EU currencies should help both exporters and importers in their business planning and pricing decisions;

- if UK producers were no longer able to rely upon a depreciating value for sterling in order to maintain their international competitiveness, they would be under greater pressure to hold down wage and price rises, in the face of generally modest inflation rates within the rest of the EU (failure to hold down UK inflation rates relative to other ERM members could have dire consequences for UK output and jobs, assuming that devaluation of sterling was not seen as an acceptable option).

Some critics of the ERM argued that:

- its operation had tended to undermine economic growth within the participating countries. Immediately prior to September 1992, there was a strong body of opinion within the UK supporting a reduction in interest rates to stimulate economic growth to offset the effects of the recession. In order to keep sterling at its agreed central parity (commonly known by the German Deutsche Mark rate of 2.95), however, UK interest rates had to be kept relatively high;

- in order to achieve exchange rate stability in the longer term, it would have been necessary that the economic performances of the countries involved should be broadly similar. In practice, the UK has often seemed to be at a different stage of the business cycle from its EU partners;

- the successful operation of the ERM required the subordination of domestic policies within individual countries for the purpose of harmonising economic performance. That co-ordination of policies would be directed towards bringing inflation rates in member States to similar low levels, reducing interest rate differentials between the respective countries and limiting the extent of balance of payments imbalances in the medium term. While these objectives may command support, convergence of economic conditions is not easy to achieve in practice;

- when sterling was put into the mechanism in October 1990, there was much controversy over the parity chosen. Indeed, the fears that, because of sterling's importance in international trade and investment, its entry into the ERM might generate instability within the mechanism (especially relative to the German Mark) and thus require excessive exchange market intervention, proved to be well-founded.

Excessive speculation against sterling caused it to be withdrawn from the ERM in September 1992. This had a damaging effect on the economic credibility of the UK government at the time.

2.2 The single European currency (the euro)

2.2.1 Background

The Maastricht Treaty envisaged that there could be irrevocable fixing of exchange rates within the EU, as the precursor to the introduction of a single EU currency. On 1 January 1999, the single European currency came into being and the 'irrevocable fixing' of exchange rates within participating members of the EU took place.

An important aspect of the Maastricht Treaty was the establishment of a European Central Bank (ECB). It was intended that the ECB would be politically independent and would have as its main objective the maintenance of price stability within the EU.

A member State's own central bank is still maintained as part of the European System of Central Banks (MSCB), and these national central banks are expected to support the ECB in the implementation of agreed policy. Each individual central bank will also be required to be politically independent of its own country's government. The responsibilities of the ECB include the conduct of EU monetary policy, foreign exchange market operations, the holding and management of member States' foreign exchange reserves and the promotion of the smooth operation of EU payments systems.

Some have questioned the wisdom of having a single interest rate covering countries at different stages of economic development. A single interest rate could be set too low for countries in which demand needs to be adjusted downwards to offset inflationary pressures, while in other parts of the EU, the single rate of interest might be too high, because lower rates are needed to stimulate economic activity. Currently, countries such as Germany are thought to prefer higher interest rates to control inflation, while other countries would prefer lower interest rates to stimulate exports by lowering the value of the euro.

2.2.2 Which countries are participating member States?

The European Union now consists of 27 member States, as follows: Austria; Belgium; Bulgaria; Cyprus (the Greek speaking part); Czech Republic; Denmark; Estonia; Finland; France; Germany; Greece; Hungary; Ireland; Italy; Latvia; Lithuania; Luxembourg; Malta; the Netherlands; Poland; Portugal; Romania; Slovakia; Slovenia; Spain; Sweden; the United Kingdom.

There are three 'candidate' countries, which have started negotiations to join: Croatia; the Former Yugoslav Republic of Macedonia; Turkey.

Croatia and Macedonia are expected to complete entry negotiations within two or three years, but Turkey's entry is not expected until some time after that.

Thirteen of the European Union countries currently use the euro as their domestic currency: Austria; Belgium; Finland; France; Germany; Greece; Ireland; Italy; Luxembourg; the Netherlands; Portugal; Spain; Slovenia.

Malta and Cyprus (the Greek- speaking part) joined these countries in using the euro as domestic currency on 1 January 2008.

Denmark and UK have opt-out clauses, which means that they are not obliged to adopt the euro, and Sweden is also not a participating country

2.2.3 What are the implications of the euro for Europe's foreign exchange markets?

- The euro has replaced the Deutsche Mark as a reserve currency for central banks.

- Foreign exchange markets between participating currencies have ceased to exist.

- The government bonds of participating countries, both those in existence as at 1 January 1999 and those subsequently issued, are now all denominated in euros. There will be a common basis for interest, that of the euro, but the different credit quality of the various governments will ensure that there is some difference in bond yields of participating governments.

- The UK already has the largest US dollar foreign exchange dealings of all of the EU countries and it appears that a great deal of euro-denominated business between non-UK parties is carried out on the London market.

2.2.4 Implications of the euro for UK financial services

Some believe that London could be perceived as an 'offshore' centre, which was cut off from the financial hub of Frankfurt where the European Central Bank is situated. As yet, however, there is little evidence of such a development. Thus, the euro on its own would not seem to be a major source of competitive disadvantage for the UK financial services industry. Other factors, such as the relative cost savings, efficiencies of the various IT systems, different tax regimes, different labour flexibilities, and different legal and regulatory systems may prove more significant factors in determining the relative competitive position of London and Frankfurt.

Obviously, the single currency, together with the Single Market Programme (see Topic 1) should mean that there is greater scope for competition across Europe between banks. Such developments take time and students must monitor the position by reading the financial press.

2.2.5 The Single European Payments Area (SEPA)

Article 3 of the EC Regulation on cross-border payments in euro was adopted in December 2001 and should be fully operational in all EU countries by 1 January 2008. The rules are that all small value (up to €50,000) cross-border non-cash payments in euros should cost no more in bank commission than a corresponding domestic payment. Because most countries' banks currently make no charge for domestic transfers, then qualifying euro-currency transfers will also attract no charges. Cash and paper cheque transactions are excluded from the rules and will probably continue to be charged for. The savings on transfer charges will give an added competitive advantage to those businesses trading in euros throughout the EU. For customers to benefit from this, banks are insisting that all transfers must include full and clear beneficiary bank and account details. These are known as Bank Identifier Code (BIC) and International

Bank Account Number (IBAN) details, and are usually quoted at the head of the bank statements of current account holders in the EU.

2.2.6 Are the advantages and disadvantages of a country joining a fixed rate exchange system, such as the Exchange Rate Mechanism, equivalent to those of joining a single currency system, such as the euro?

The benefits and drawbacks of joining a fixed exchange rate system are not the same as those of joining a single currency such as the euro.

- With a fixed- rate system, the country retains the right to manage its domestic interest rates and money supply. Leaving the system is always a possibility if circumstances dictate this. This is what happened to sterling when it left the ERM in 1992.

- None of the above is possible with a single currency. There is one interest rate and one policy on money supply (set by the European Central Bank), which may not suit countries at different stages of the economic cycle. Although it is possible to leave a single currency, the political and economic ramifications would be much greater than those involved in leaving a fixed rate regime.

- In a single currency, there will be the same exchange rate for every participating member against non- participating members. This is not the case with a fixed rate regime, although arbitrage will ensure that the rates are not too far apart except at times of strong speculative pressure.

- If the devaluation option is removed, then there could be pressure from euro participating countries with relatively high domestic inflation to be helped to lower their export prices by way of EU subsidies.

- Some writers feel that a single currency can only succeed if there is a single government throughout the area in which the currency operates, because domestic policies such as taxation need to be harmonised to make the single currency succeed.

- There are restrictions on government deficits imposed on participating members of the euro. From time to time, there is speculation that the European Commission will impose fines under the 'excessive deficits procedure' on some participating members for breaching the stability pact. This can cause resentment as, for example, when Romano Prodi, formerly the European Commission's president, was quoted as describing the stability pact as 'stupid'.

2.3 The factors that affect foreign exchange rate movements, to the extent that government intervention does not reduce their impact

A rate of exchange is the price of one currency in terms of another. A spot rate is a rate of exchange for a transaction that is to be settled today, or within two working days. Banks quote bid and offer spot rates. The bid–offer principle will be familiar to anyone who goes into a travel agent to purchase foreign currency before going on holiday. The travel agent offers two rates: the bid rate, at which it will purchase unused foreign currency from returning holidaymakers, and the offer rate, at which it will sell the foreign currency to those going on holiday. The offer rate is the one that makes the foreign currency more valuable and the bid rate is the one that makes it less valuable. The spread is the difference between the two rates, which represents one part of the travel agent's profit margin. Banks and other market makers also quote bid–offer rates and the spread is part of their profit margin.

For the sake of clarity, the remainder of Section 2.3 will ignore bid–offer spreads in the explanation of the factors that affect exchange rate movements.

The factors that affect exchange rate movements, unless counteracted by government intervention, are shown below. Each factor is considered in isolation, but in practice, one factor may impact on another. The basic principle is that if a rate of exchange is the price of one currency in terms of another, then any factor that affects supply or demand for that currency must also affect the exchange rate.

2.3.1 Relative levels of short- term interest rates

In the short term, the most important factor affecting exchange rates is usually the relative levels of interest rates, or rather the anticipated short- term changes therein. For example, at the times when the UK Monetary Policy Committee (MPC) reduces UK interest rates, sterling tends to weaken. Similar effects have been seen in the USA, especially during Autumn 2007. The Federal Reserve reduced US interest rates and this was followed by a weakening of the US dollar. Obviously, there could have been many factors other than changes in interest rates that caused the change in the value of the currency, but the fact remains that, in 'normal 'circumstances, short- term interest rate differentials play an important part in the determination of short- term foreign exchange rate movements. The reason for the importance of interest rates is that *other things being equal*, if interest rates rise in one country and remain unchanged in another, then international investors will switch deposits into the currency with the higher interest rates.

2.3.2 Other factors affecting spot rates

Obviously, at times such as when sterling was ejected from the Exchange Rate Mechanism in September 1992, speculative pressures rather than factors such as relative interest rates (and expectations of changes therein) affected the short- term value of the pound. To the extent that exchange rates are allowed to float freely, then any factor that affects the component parts of the current account and/or capital account of the balance of payments, and hence which affects the supply and demand conditions on the currency markets, may potentially influence the pattern of currency exchange rates.

The major factors affecting international trade and capital flows include:

- real economic variables, eg consumer tastes, real income levels and technological innovation;
- relative inflation rates;
- relative interest rates, which must be viewed in real terms with expectations of inflation rates taken into account;

- non- economic factors, eg the social and political environment;
- government policies, which may often affect the balance of payments indirectly.

2.3.3 The theory of purchasing power parity (PPP)

Purchasing power parity (PPP) offers an explanation of movements in currency exchange rates in the long run. The theory states that the equilibrium exchange rate between any two currencies is that rate which equalises the domestic purchasing powers of the two currencies. For example, if a bundle of goods has a price of £5 in the UK and US$10 in the USA, then, according to the theory the equilibrium exchange rate is £1 = US$2. Trade flows will bring about this value by altering the supplies of and demands for currencies.

There are major problems with the theory:

- it ignores the existence of international capital flows, as well as the transport and transactions costs associated with trade;
- it fails to recognise the fact that many goods and services are not traded internationally;
- the role of news is not considered. In the real world, major unpredicted events often occur and these unexpected events are often referred to as 'news'. Exchange rates respond very quickly to new information, so news can often have an immediate impact on spot rates – but prices of goods normally change much less quickly as a result of news, so the relevant price indices do not adjust as quickly as the spot rates.

2.3.4 Studies of PPP

A study by R. MacDonald (1988), *Floating Exchange Rates Theories and Evidence* (Unwin Hymen) reviewed 14 empirical studies of the purchasing power parity theory. Ten rejected the PPP as a long- run predictor of exchange rates, while four showed the PPP as being valid in the long term. The general consensus is that there are substantial deviations from the PPP in the short run, but the case is less clear in the long term.

On the other hand, *The Economist* uses the McDonalds hamburger as a 'light hearted' benchmark for assessing the validity of the PPP, on the basis that this is a standard product that is sold in most countries. In July 2007, *The Economist* 'reported that the average American price of a 'Big Mac' was US$3.41, whereas the price in the UK was £1.99. The PPP implied rate of exchange between the pound and dollar was US$1.71 whereas the spot rate on 2 July was $2.01, a difference of 18%. For the eurozone, the comparison was 3.06 against US$3.41, with a PPP implied rate of exchange of US $1.11. The spot rate on 2 July was US$1.36, a difference of 22%. Those who believe that the PPP holds and who are satisfied that the 'Big Mac' represents an adequate basket of goods would have concluded that the euro and pound sterling were overvalued against the US dollar at the time of the survey.

It must be emphasised that *The Economist* itself takes a light- hearted view of what it calls 'burgernomics', commenting that it does not 'cut the mustard', that hamburgers cannot be traded across borders, that prices can be distorted by taxes and different costs of rents. Nevertheless, the survey concludes that 'over the long run, purchasing power parity – including the Big Mac PPP – is a fairly good guide to exchange rate movements'.

2.3.5 Conclusion on PPP

Surveys of the foreign exchange markets have shown that the majority of spot transactions do *not* arise as a result of underlying trade transactions; instead, many transactions occur from the actions of banks balancing their books as a result of derivatives- based transactions, such as forward contracts (examples of these transactions are shown in Section 2.6). This phenomenon was confirmed by the Bank of England news release dated 25 September 2007, 'BIS Triennial Survey of Foreign Exchange and Over- the- Counter Derivatives Markets in April 2007 - UK Data'.

Because every foreign exchange transaction should have some effect on supply and demand and hence may affect the spot rate, and because the majority of foreign exchange transactions are not trade related, it is reasonable to conclude that factors other than the balance of payments and purchasing power parity theory can influence spot rate changes.

It is therefore suggested that the main relevance of the PPP is when trading partners' inflation rates differ. In such cases, it is likely that the exchange rate of the country that is experiencing the highest rate of inflation will depreciate in the long run.

2.3.6 Key factors that may influence exchange rates in 2008

Students must keep abreast of developments by reading good quality newspapers, because major and sometimes unexpected changes can take place at any time. At the time of writing, the key speculation concerns the weakness of the US dollar. The twin US deficits on current account and budget, coupled with fears of economic problems due to the 2007 sub- prime crisis, have lead to speculation that countries such as Saudi Arabia might follow Kuwait and abandon the peg between their currencies and the US dollar. In addition, there is speculation that Asian countries such as China might reduce their holdings of US dollar denominated Treasury bills, which could cause a dramatic fall in the value of the US dollar. Finally, there is speculation that Organization of the Petroleum Exporting Countries (OPEC) members could change their pricing policies so that the price of oil is denominated in euros instead of being denominate in US dollars.

The weakness of the US dollar has caused difficulties for the euro. Exporters from Europe feel that the weakness of the US dollar has given US exporters a competitive advantage. Within the eurozone, however, Germany has managed to maintain low domestic inflation, thereby keeping its prices down and is less badly affected by the weak US dollar. Other countries within the eurozone have not been so successful in curbing domestic price rises and their exporters are finding it difficult to compete on price with their US competitors. This could lead to tension because Germany might want higher interest rates to curb inflation, whereas other eurozone countries might want lower interest rates to stimulate their economies, reduce the value of the euro and make their exports more competitive.

As ever, nothing is certain in foreign exchange rates. In November 2007, Robert Mundell, a Nobel prize economist and currency expert, was quoted as saying: 'The dollar will remain the anchor of the world's currency system unless the US makes some catastrophic errors. The dollar has problems, but the euro also has problems and these are structural. Germany has been able to cope with the dollar crisis through a strong export recovery. But the situation is critical in France and Italy'. At the same time, Stephen Jen, currency analyst at Morgan Stanley, gave an opinion that the US current account deficit was narrowing fast and that this would pave the way for a major rebound in the US dollar in 2008.

It is difficult to know how sterling will be affected by these developments and readers should follow the issue by reading good quality press articles.

2.4 The basic operations of the foreign exchange market and its participants

These markets have no physical form, in the sense of there being an actual marketplace in which dealers in currencies meet, rather, the markets exist through a sophisticated network of communications, involving telephone, telex and computer links. London is the world's largest foreign exchange market, largely due to the business generated from other financial activities relating to products such as insurance and Eurobonds, and to shipping, commodities and banking. In addition, London benefits from its geographical location and a time zone that enables trade to take place with Europe throughout the day, with Japan, Hong Kong and Singapore in the morning and with the USA after 1 pm.

The markets in different countries are closely associated and exchange market activity today is a truly international occupation. Further, it is often suggested that the foreign exchanges constitute almost perfect markets, with the prices of currencies (exchange rates) responding immediately to the finest changes in demand and supply conditions.

The main participants in the foreign exchange markets are central banks, commercial and investment banks, hedge funds, corporations and private speculators.

- Corporations use the market because they require foreign currency in connection with their cross- border business. Some corporations deal directly with other corporations to bypass the market and avoid the banks' bid- offer spreads. (See Section 2.5 for bid- offer spreads.)

- Hedge funds will undertake complex transactions to profit from arbitrage opportunities. Alternatively, they will undertake 'carry trade', eg they borrow Japanese yen at low interest rates, convert yen to US dollars or other currencies that pay higher interest rates, and subsequently convert the currencies back to yen to repay the original borrowing, thereby making a profit from the interest rate differentials. As long as the yen does not appreciate during the operation, there is a guaranteed profit from the transactions. Currently, there is some doubt as to whether the interest differentials will justify the exchange rate risks of carry trade. There are reports that hedge funds may well try and sell dollars short to gain from the weakness of the US dollar. Selling dollars short involves borrowing US dollars and immediately selling them, perhaps for sterling, at the current rate of exchange. When the time comes to repay the original US dollar borrowing, the hedge fund will sell sterling and buy the dollars back and repay the US dollar obligation. If the dollar has become weaker, then the sterling cost of buying back the dollars will be less than the amount of sterling originally received and the hedge fund will make a sterling denominated profit on the transaction. Obviously, if the US$ strengthens, then the hedge fund will lose on the short selling transaction.

- Commercial banks act as market makers who undertake at all times to quote buy and sell rates for foreign exchange transactions. Market makers profit from the spread between their buy and sell rates (bid- offer rates), but they must be ready to adjust prices very quickly to avoid being short of a rapidly appreciating currency or being over- stocked with a rapidly depreciating one. Banks deal with customers, and with other banks and hedge funds.

- Brokers act as intermediaries and make their profit from commissions. Brokers have dedicated communication links with banks (telephones, telex and computer- based links), and they should be aware at any given time of the trends in the market makers' prices and which market makers currently offer the best deal for their clients' needs.

2.5 Distinguishing between telephone/paper- based dealing systems and computer- based systems

Dealings in the market may be 'spot' (under which transactions take place at current market prices with settlement being within two business days of the deal being contracted) or 'forward' (under which a price is agreed for currency to be delivered at a future date, with settlement being more than two business days after dealing). The following explanation is based on the information in The Bank of England fact sheet (April 2000), which gives the following example of how a telephone based deal might be carried out.

To execute a *spot* deal a broker could contact a market maker and ask for the rate, for example, 'sterling- dollar' (ie US dollars to the British pound, for an underlying sterling amount of £10m). Here the broker is acting on behalf of a price taker and the market maker is a price maker. The implications of this will be shown in the example below.

The market maker normally quotes a two- way price - that is, it stands ready to bid for or offer up to some standard amount. Let us assume in this case that the £10m is within the standard amount and let us also assume that the rate for pounds against the dollar is quoted by the market maker as £1 = US$1.6315- 25. This would mean that the market maker bids for pounds at US$1.6315 and offers them at US$1.6325. The *spread* is the difference between these two prices and favours the market maker against the price taker to whom the quote has been made. Thus, the two- way price quotes shown above mean:

- when the market maker is receiving US dollars and paying out £10m sterling to the price taker, the market maker will receive US$1.6325 for every £1 paid to the price taker. Thus the market maker will pay £10m to the price taker and will receive US$16,325,000 from the price taker in exchange;
- when the market maker is receiving £10m sterling and paying out US dollars, the market pays out US$1.6315 for every £1 received from the price taker. Thus, the market maker pays US$16,315,000 to the price taker and receives £10m in exchange.

From the above, it can be seen that the market maker gains from the spread between the bid–offer rates.

This aspect will be covered in more detail in Topic 3 when we shall refer to the 'buy high/sell low' rule in more detail.

During interbank trading in which participants know the 'big figures' (ie dollars and cents, pounds and pence) the market maker might quote only the *points* (the last two figures of the price). For example, if the rate for pounds against the US dollar was £1 = US$1.6315- 25, then the market maker would quote 'fifteen- twenty five': the bid is for pounds at US$1.6315 and the offer is at US$1.6325.

If the caller wishes to deal, they will *hit* – that is accept – one side of the price.

Confirmation of this oral contract will be exchanged in writing and instructions concerning payment given, and passed on to the settlements staff who ensure that the respective currency amounts are transferred into the designated accounts on the value date.

The system described above is the traditional telephone- based system and this system is still the major dealing technique for large- scale transactions. But there are now computer based dealing systems that have benefits and drawbacks compared to the more traditional dealing processes.

Note: the authors are indebted to the Bank of England (2000), *The Foreign Exchange Market Fact Sheet*, April, for the material on how the market operates.

2.5.1 Drawbacks of the traditional paper- based and telephone- based trading in foreign exchange

For an international business, the processing cycle consists of:

- deciding that the company needs to enter into a foreign exchange transaction, for example, if an exporter needs to convert foreign currency receipts to home currency or if an importer needs to obtain foreign currency in exchange for home currency to meet a commercial obligation;
- obtaining competitive quotes from banks;
- executing the deal;
- formally confirming the deal;
- recording the deal in the company's accounting system and in any other internal records;
- settling the deal.

Paper- based systems are cumbersome. For example, in transactions of large amounts, corporates may call up a number of banks to obtain competing quotes and this process can take time, sometimes up to 15 minutes. The problem then arises that if the best quote came from the bank that the corporate had called at the start of the process – perhaps 11 am – then that bank's price could have changed by 11.15 am. An alternative method of obtaining competitive quotes for large transactions, which can be used by larger corporates is for three or four of the corporate's authorised staff to make simultaneous phone calls from the same office for quotes from the different banks. The different banks will be asked to 'hold the line' while a senior person from the corporate writes down the different bank quotes on a flip chart. This senior person will then indicate which quote to accept. The process avoids the time delay, but is very staff- intensive and staff may be unavailable at the crucial time.

In addition, the deal may be recorded incorrectly when it is copied from paper records onto electronic systems. A survey by the International Swaps and Derivatives Association (ISDA) found a 24% error rate in the processing of paper/telephone- based transactions. Such errors can be very costly in terms of the time taken to correct the accounting entries, additional queries from internal and external auditors, and market risk due to a misunderstanding of the true nature of the position.

Finally, it is difficult to construct an audit trail with paper- based systems. For example, details of rejected quotes are often not recorded, so it is difficult to keep an accurate record of what quotes were actually available at the time that the deal was made.

2.5.2 Why are banks keen to offer computer- based systems?

The banks are very keen to develop electronic dealing facilities for foreign exchange transactions for a client. The benefits to banks are the usual IT benefits of reduced costs. It has been estimated that the administration cost to a bank for a telephone-based foreign exchange deal could be in the region of £50, whereas the administration cost for a computer based deal would be nearer to £12. The administration cost is virtually the same whatever the size of the deal.

Some banks offer modem- based facilities whereby corporate treasurers have to access them via their own computer terminals; others offer Internet based facilities. Banks have built in 'firewall' and other procedures to help to allay fears about the security of Internet- based facilities. It must also be remembered that banks cannot afford any bad publicity about computer- based dealing facilities, because such delivery channels are central to banks' cost cutting strategies.

2.5.3 Benefits to clients in computerised dealings.

While the benefits of computerised delaings to banks may be obvious, there are also benefits for the customers such as:

- the ability to employ straight through processing (STP) systems. This means that the details of the deal will be captured in a single input, so that all future operations such as confirmation and settlement, will automatically contain the same deal data. This avoids costly mistakes, such as the transposition of figures or confirming a 'buy' as a 'sell';
- STP means that there will be a single audit trail to track the deal, and that the accounting entries can flow automatically from the single initial input;
- STP means that the status of the various foreign exchange deals can be shown in 'real time' as opposed to the more usual once- a- day report that is generated for paper systems;
- STP saves on administration costs for the company and results in lower bid-offer spreads from banks, which pass on some, but not all, of their cost savings;
- simultaneous quotes can be obtained electronically and the best quote will automatically be accepted;
- the enhanced accuracy of electronic systems reduces the internal scrutiny required from internal and external audit and enhances the confidence of the treasury staff and senior managers in the treasury function.

2.5.4 Possible drawbacks of electronic banking systems for corporates

- There can be complex code words and security procedures that may delay the setting up of the deal. Such delays could be very costly in volatile markets and the larger the underlying amounts, the greater this risk.
- Tight internal security is needed over code words and access to prevent fraud or error for the clients.
- If the system goes wrong, there can be costly mistakes, especially if there is no back up system as part of a contingency plan.

2.5.5   In what circumstances are electronic systems more appropriate from a corporate's point of view?

Electronic systems are particularly applicable when there are large volumes of relatively low value payments. If there are a relatively small number of high value transactions, however, then the traditional dealer access methods can be more suitable. Access to dealers can 'shave' margins for large deals, whereas, for smaller deals, the corporate is usually simply a price taker. The savings on bid–offer spreads or option premiums can justify the extra administration costs when the individual deals are large.

2.5.6   The development of multi- bank foreign exchange portals

A number of multi- bank foreign exchange portals have been developed. The investments in IT infrastructure are huge, with figures of around US$150m being quoted for one venture that was abandoned.

There are two types of portal. One type, which will be largely owned by banks in a joint venture, enables non- bank corporates who are linked to the system to trade with banks with whom they have a relationship. The corporate will input its requirements and the system will automatically match the corporate's request with the relationship bank that offers the best quote. The other type of portal is owned by non- banks and corporates linked to that type of site will have automated access to the best quote from any bank within the system. FXAll is a portal owned by banks such as HSBC, Bank of America, JP Morgan, and Goldman Sachs. Currenex is an example of non- bank- owned trading site.

Ultimately, these non- bank owned portals might accept non- bank corporates as fully participating members. This could mean, for example, one non- bank corporate doing a deal directly with another non- bank corporate, which would amount to a form of disintermediation in foreign exchange.

It should be noted that there are nowadays many more large non- bank players in the forex markets, offering very competitive rates, often much better than those of the banks. This has made the market very competitive and continues the trend towards disintermediation of the banks in foreign exchange.

The movement of non- bank players into the foreign exchange market was aided by the fact that foreign exchange was one of the few areas of finance that did not require Financial Services Authority regulation and banking status.

Until recently, it was common for customers wanting to use conventional banking procedures for the transfer of funds abroad in foreign currency to deal with two separate departments of the bank:

- the dealing section agreed a rate of exchange; and
- the money transfer section provided details of the beneficiary and how the funds were to be transferred.

Obviously this caused difficulties, especially in the event of any problems, when the customer was not sure which part of the bank to deal with.

The non- bank participants were able to offer a 'one- stop' service, which made the process much quicker and simpler for the customer. Banks are now offering a single one- stop service to mid- cap corporates as well as to FTSE100 companies, to counter non- bank competition.

2.6 Factors that influence the forward rates in foreign exchange

Sometimes an exporter may obtain a commercial contract whereby payment is to be made in foreign currency at a specified future date. Alternatively, an importer may enter into a commercial contract whereby payment is to be made in foreign currency at a specified future date. At the time that the commercial contract is entered into, neither the exporter nor the importer will know the amount to be received or paid in home currency terms.

A forward exchange contract is one method that can be used to overcome the uncertainty about the home currency amounts of future receipts or payments in foreign currency. The detailed benefits, drawbacks and discussion on whether a business should or should not use foreign exchange contracts are covered in subsequent topics of this part of the text. In this topic we shall confine ourselves to examining the factors that influence forward exchange rates.

2.6.1 Introductory example

A forward deal is an agreement between two parties (usually a market maker and a customer) to set a rate at the outset for a deal (covering a set amount of foreign currency) which is to be settled at a future date (or between two set future dates).

2.6.1.1 Example 2.1

Let us first consider a highly simplified example to illustrate the principles that lie behind the relationship of the forward rate to the spot rate. Suppose a UK exporter, who expects to receive US$1m in one year's time, asks a UK bank for a forward rate. The following process could take place, given the following information:

Spot rate £1 = US$ 1.5

Eurodollar one- year fixed interest rates 6%

Eurosterling one- year fixed interest rates 10%

The euro currency interest rates for convenience can be considered as the wholesale rates of interest.

The action taken by the bank

- At the outset, the bank will agree a forward rate of 1.4455 (after calculating the consequences of the actions shown below). This rate will ensure that the bank is not at risk from any subsequent exchange rate movements, provided that the delivery of the US dollars takes place to restore the bank's position to the status quo.

- Today the bank will borrow US$943,396.23 and convert it to sterling £628,930.82 at the spot rate of 1.5.

- The bank will pay debit interest of 6 % on the US dollar funds, but will receive credit interest of 10% on its new sterling balances.

- In one year's time, the sterling balances will total £691,823.90 (with interest).

- In one year's time, the US dollar debit balance will amount to US$1m (with interest).

- At the end of the year, the exporter will deliver US$1m and the bank will pay £691,823.90.

- The bank will then use the customer's US$1m to repay its own dollar advance.

- Thus the forward rate will have been calculated at the outset as:

$$\frac{1,000,000.00}{691,823.90} = 1.4455$$

The purpose of the above example is to illustrate the general principle that the forward rate is derived from the spot rate and relative interest rate differentials. It does, however, make several simplifying assumptions that do not apply in practice:

- it ignores the spread between the bank's bid and offer rates for foreign exchange transactions. In practice, these spreads apply to both spot and forward rates;

- it ignores the difference between deposit and lending rates of interest;

- it ignores transaction costs;

- it assumes that the above is the only transaction by the bank in the forward dollar market. In practice, there is endless scope for the bank to match its positions by other deals and by transactions in other markets such as futures;

- it assumes that there are no government restrictions or tax distortions on such funds transfers.

Note on use of a swap to cover the position of the bank.
In practice, the bank would almost certainly have covered its potential liability under the forward contract by a swap, rather than by borrowing US dollars. Thus the bank would have 'swapped '(ie paid over to the another, possibly US, bank) £666,667 in exchange for US$1m. At the end of the year, the principals would have been swapped back (ie the transaction would have been reversed), with the UK bank's exporter customer funding the US$1m and the US Bank providing sterling that would be used to fund the purchase of the dollars from the customer. The two banks would have agreed at the outset an interest payment to cover the fact that the US Bank was gaining interest from its increased sterling balances. The interest payment calculation would be based on the differential between the interest rates on dollar and sterling.

A summary of the swap is as follows.

- Today, as soon as the forward contract has been agreed, the UK bank and US banks swap. The UK bank pays £666,667 to the US bank and receives US$1m in exchange.

- The two banks agree to reverse the transaction in one year, with the US bank to make an additional payment to the UK bank to compensate the UK bank for losing out on the higher sterling interest rates.

- In one year's time, the following transactions take place:

- The UK bank receives US$1m from its exporter customer and pays it over to the US bank.

- The US bank pays the UK bank £666,667, plus interest as follows:

$$\frac{666,667 \times 0.04}{1.06} = £25,157,$$

thus the total sterling paid is £691,824,

- thus the forward rate would be agreed as

$$\frac{1,000000}{691,824} = 1.4455$$

which is the same result as for currency borrowing.

- for banks this method is more convenient than currency borrowing. In practice, the interest rate differential on the swap might be finer than for straight conventional currency borrowing.

Further details of currency swaps can be found in Topic 8, Section 8.1.9.

2.6.2 Simplified explanation of why arbitrage will support the forward rate shown in Example One

2.6.2.1 Example 2.2

If the one- year forward rate had been agreed at a different figure – for example 1.60 – and assuming that a large UK corporate could borrow and deposit at the rates shown in the above example, there would have been scope for a risk- free profit as follows.

1. The UK customer could have borrowed, for exmple, US$1m for one year, and agreed a forward contract for the bank to sell US$1.06m (the balance plus interest) at 1.60 one- year forward.

2. The US dollars would have been converted to sterling immediately at 1.5, giving a sterling equivalent of £666,666.67, which would have been deposited at 10%.

3. The US dollar advance to be repaid after one year's interest would be 1,060,000.

4. At the end of the year, the sterling balances would have amounted to £733,333.34 and only £662,500 would have been used to acquire the US$1,06m at the agreed forward rate of 1.60.

5. Thus there would have been a risk free profit of £70,833 for the customer.

6. Obviously if a forward rate of 1.60 was on general offer in such circumstances, there would be an immediate demand by customers for US dollar borrowing which would tend to raise the US dollar interest rate, and there would be a demand for spot sterling, which would tend to make spot sterling appreciate. Thus, by a process known as 'arbitrage', market forces would tend to remove this anomaly, moving the forward rate back to its logical interest rate parity figure.

7. Likewise, if the forward rate had been set at 1.40, a profit could be made by customers from borrowing £1m sterling, converting it to dollars, covering forward at 1.40, investing the dollars at 6% and then converting dollar principal

in one year of US$1.59m back to sterling. The resultant sterling sum of £1,135,714 would have exceeded the sterling advance of £1.1m (including interest).

2.6.3   The determination of forward rates, by way of premium, or discount

When a forward currency is more valuable than spot currency, then the forward rate is said to be 'at a premium'. In the example above. the forward dollar rate would have been at a premium to spot rate because it required fewer dollars (US$1.4455 at the one year forward rate) in exchange for £1 than the US$1.50 required in exchange for £1 in spot deals.

We shall see in Topic 3 that the forward premium is deducted from the spot rate when calculating the forward rate.

The acronym **LIP** can be used to determine when a forward currency is likely to be at a premium to spot (**LIP** (The forward currency with the **L**ower **I**nterest rates will be at a **P**remium to its **S**pot value)).

If we look at the above hypothetical example of the US dollar spot being at 1.50 and the one year forwards being at 1.4455, we can see that the reason behind this is that the US dollar interest rates are lower than sterling. Thus, in the course of the operation to cover (or hedge) its position under the forward contract, the bank 'gains' by borrowing at 6% in dollars, but investing the sterling proceeds at 10%. Hence, ignoring bid–offer spreads, the bank can afford to pay out more sterling against one- year forward dollars than against spot dollars. If there is more forward sterling than spot sterling against a given amount of dollars, then forward sterling is weaker and conversely the forward dollar is stronger. Hence the forward dollar is said to be at a premium to spot.

Conversely, when the forward currency is weaker than the spot, it is said to be at a discount to spot. Had the forward rate been at 1.60 at the time that the spot rate was 1.50, then it would have required more one- year forward dollars than spot dollars in exchange for one pound. Thus the forward dollar would have been at a discount to spot in £:US$ deals.

We shall see in Topic 3 that a discount is added to spot rates in calculations of forward rates.

The acronym **HID** can be used to decide when a forward rate is at a discount to spot. (**HID** (The forward currency with the **H**igher **I**nterest rates will be at a **D**iscount to its spot value).)

If eurodollar interest rates had been higher than eurosterling (for example, 10% and 6% respectively) in the above example, the bank would have had to pay 10% interest on its US dollar borrowing and would have received only 6 % on the sterling deposit. Thus the bank would have wished to pay out less sterling to its customer under the forward contract than it would have paid out at spot rates. If there is less forward sterling than spot sterling against a given amount of dollars, then the forward pound is stronger than the spot pound and the forward dollar is weaker than the spot dollar in £:US$ deals.

Please refer back to the examples above and you will see that the forward US$ is at a premium to spot in £:US$ transactions when the US interest rate is lower (6%) than the UK rate (10%).

2.6.4 Example of the use of premiums and discounts to calculate a forward rate

For convenience, forward rates are not quoted outright (eg 1.4455 in Example 2.1 above); what is quoted is the differential between the spot and the outright forward (the premium or discount). Premiums and discounts are subject to much less fluctuation than spot rates, so quoting differentials requires far fewer changes to any published forward rates.

Most writers show the forward premium or discount to be determined by means of the following general equation:

$$\frac{\text{Spot rate x interest differential x time in days}}{360 \times 100}$$

When the forward period is for less than a year, the number of days can complicate the calculation because some countries calculate interest on the basis of a 360- day year, whereas for sterling the number of days is taken to be 365. In any event, to be strictly accurate the effects of compounding should be taken into account for periods of less than one year. In addition, this equation requires adjustment to take account of whether the banks bid or offer rate is used.

Let us for convenience repeat the details of the original hypothetical example

Spot rate	US$1.50 – £1
One-year fixed eurodollar interest rate	6%
One-year fixed eurosterling interest rate	10%
One-year forward rate	US$1.4455 = £1

Because the forward dollar is at a premium to spot as a result of the nature of the interest differential, the above formula could be used, without concerning ourselves about the number of days because the period is one whole year) to calculate a premium of

$$\frac{1.50 \times 4}{100} = 0.06$$

The premium will then be deducted from the spot to show an outright forward rate of 1.44.

To be strictly accurate, the formula could be rewritten to calculate the premium as:

$$\frac{\text{Spot rate x interest differential time in days}}{(1+i) \times 360 \times 100}$$

Thus the premium to be deducted from the spot (ignoring the complexities of periods below one year) to show an outright forward rate is calculated as:

$$\frac{1.50 \times 0.04}{1.10} = 0.0545$$

The outright forward rate would then be 1.5000

Less one-year forward premium $\quad \frac{0.0545}{1.4455}$

When the forward rate is at a discount, the lower interest rate should be applied to the denominator of the above formula and the resultant discount would be added to the spot rate to calculate the outright forward.

Let us use the formula to demonstrate the position when the interest rate position is the opposite way round:

Spot rate US$ 1.50 = £1
One-year fixed eurodollar interest rates: 10%
One-year fixed eurosterling interest rates: 6%

The forward discount would be:

$$\frac{1.5 \times 0.04}{1.06} = 0.0566 \text{ discount}$$

So the one-year forward rate would be 1.50 + 0.0566 = 1.5566.

If the rate of exchange has a direct quote – that is, a number of home currency units is equal to one unit of foreign currency – then the formula will have to be adjusted to take account of this change in quote.

2.6.5   The premium or discount as a percentage of spot

Simply by rearranging the above formulae, the premium or discount as a percentage of spot can be calculated. This percentage should equate to the interest rate differentials in the two centres, subject to the caveats expressed concerning the above calculations.

2.7   The relationship between spot, forward and relative interest rates and relative inflation rates

2.7.1   Interest rates and inflation

There are many theories that explore the factors that determine the level of interest rates. For the purposes of this topic, we are only concerned with the link between inflation, real rates of interest and nominal rates.

The nominal rate is the rate actually quoted in a transaction and the real rate is the nominal rate adjusted to take account of inflation. For new transactions, the nominal rate will incorporate the real rate and an allowance for anticipated inflation over the relevant period of the transaction to provide the lender with an anticipated real rate of return. This effect is often called the 'Fisher Effect', after Irvine Fisher, one of the pioneers of the theory of interest rate determination.

2.7.2 Interest rate parity

We have demonstrated in the examples above that there is a link between the spot rate and relative interest rate differentials, and the forward rate for a given future period. If we then assume that real rates of interest are the same internationally, then the difference in the rates of interest on deposits of different currencies with equally creditworthy banks would arise solely from different inflationary expectations.

2.7.3 The link between interest rates, inflation, forward and spot rates

When Fisher's link between inflationary expectations and interest rates holds, when real rates of interest are equalised between countries and when interest rate parity holds, then spot and forward rates are linked to interest rates and anticipated levels of inflation in the two countries concerned.

There are many obvious limiting assumptions to this general principle, among which are:

- the effects of transaction costs;
- the possibility of government restrictions on funds transfer;
- the possibility of government intervention in the markets;
- differential taxation treatment of the transactions in different countries.

2.7.4 The forward rate as an unbiased predictor of the future spot rate

The forward rate is generally found to be an unbiased predictor of the future spot rate for the relevant period. 'Unbiased predictor' means that if the forward rate is used to predict the future spot rate at the end of the equivalent period of time, then, in the long run, the sum of the gains will equal the sum of the losses. Empirical evidence has, however, shown that, in the short term, the forward rate has consistently undervalued the future spot rate when the spot rate has been rising strongly and, conversely, the forward rate has consistently overvalued the future spot rate when the spot rate has been falling rapidly.

2.8 Market size

Students need to have a sense of the sheer size of the foreign exchange markets and so we will now look at one interesting source of information.

In April 2007, 54 central banks and monetary authorities participated in the triennial central bank survey of foreign exchange and derivatives market activity. The Bank of England conducted the UK survey, which covers the business of institutions operating within the UK in these markets.

All comparisons are with the previous survey in 2004 and are expressed in US$bn, unless otherwise stated. The following information from the survey is extracted from the Bank of England News Release dated 25 September 2007 'BIS Triennial Survey of Foreign Exchange and Over- the- Counter Derivatives Markets in April 2007 - UK Data'.

- Foreign exchange market turnover in the UK increased by 80% from April 2004 to April 2007.

- The UK remains the single largest centre of foreign exchange activity with 34.1% of global turnover in April 2007, increasing from 31.3% in 2004.

- Average daily turnover in foreign exchange was US$1,359bn during April 2007, 80% higher than the US$753bn per day recorded for April 2004, or a rise of 73% at constant 2007 exchange rates. This growth continues the upward trend seen in 2004 results.

For details of a worldwide comparison of foreign exchange markets, readers may wish to consult the Bank for International Settlements website at http://www.ecb.int/press/pr/date/2007/html/pr070925.en.html.

Topic 3

Spot rates and forward rates

On completion of this topic the student should be able to:

- define a rate of exchange and appreciate how rates are quoted;
- differentiate between the bank's buy and sell rates;
- understand the difference between fixed forward exchange contracts and option forward exchange contracts;
- calculate fixed forward rates and option forward rates using the spot as a base and adjusting for the premium or discount.

3.1   Rates of exchange and how they are quoted

A rate of exchange is the price of one currency in terms of another. In the UK, rates of exchange are normally quoted as the number of foreign currency units that are equivalent to one pound sterling. This method of quotation is termed the **indirect quote**. By contrast, most EU currencies are quoted as the number of units of home currency that are equivalent to one unit of overseas currency. This is termed the **direct quote**. In this book we concentrate on the indirect quote method.

Bank dealers normally quote two rates of exchange: the **buying** rate and the **selling** rate. Because the bank wishes to make a profit on the 'turn' (ie the difference between the two rates), it will use the higher rate for buying and the lower one for selling. Thus, if the rate quoted for the US dollars is 1.8525- 1.8535, the bank will buy at US$1.8535 and sell at US$1.8525. The reason for this is quite logical: the bank wants to receive as many dollars for each pound as possible when it buys them and the bank wants to give out as few dollars as possible in exchange for every pound when it sells them.

When dealing with exchange rates, **always work from the point of view of the bank.** Hence the rule is:

BUY HIGH: SELL LOW

3.2 Spot rates of exchange and the exchange risk

A spot rate of exchange is a rate of exchange for a foreign currency transaction that is to be settled within two working days of agreeing the rate.

As you will know from your economics studies, spot rates of exchange can fluctuate violently from day to day or from week to week. Hence, for example, UK traders who have receipts or payments denominated in foreign currency that are to be settled in the future, cannot be sure of the ultimate sterling amounts if the currency is simply converted at the spot rate ruling on the date of receipt or payment. This uncertainty as to the exact ultimate sterling receipt or payment is called the **exchange risk**. The exchange risk runs from the moment at which a commercial contract is entered into that involves receipt or payment of foreign currency, and it lasts until the currency receipt or payment has been converted into sterling. The management of exchange rate exposure in its widest sense is analysed in Topics 7 and 8.

3.3 Forward exchange rates and forward contracts

A forward rate is a rate of exchange that is fixed now for a deal which will take place at a fixed date, or between two dates, in the future. Forward contracts can be arranged to cover periods for as long as ten years ahead in some of the major currencies, but periods of between one and 12 months are the most common.

When a forward currency is more valuable than the spot currency, the forward is said to be 'at a premium'. Likewise, when the forward currency is less valuable than the spot, it is said to be 'at a discount'. The term 'par', in connection with forward exchange, means that the spot and forward currencies are of equal value; hence, the spot rate and the forward rates are identical.

A forward exchange contract is a binding contract between a bank and its customer for a purchase or sale of a specified amount of a particular foreign currency at an agreed future date, at a rate of exchange fixed at the time the contract is made.

When the contract is a 'fixed' forward exchange contract, the future date at which the transaction will take place is a fixed date, whereas when the contract is an 'option' contract, the time at which the transaction will take place is any time within a specified future period. The customer has the 'option' to choose which day within the specified future period they will complete the transaction, but apart from this particular aspect the 'option' contract is just as binding as a fixed contract.

While the advantages of forward contracts will be considered later on in more detail, it should be briefly mentioned that the main purpose of a forward contract is to enable exporters to know what the home currency value will be for an amount of foreign currency that will be received at a future date, and likewise to enable UK importers, for example, to calculate the sterling cost of a foreign currency payment that is to be made in the future. When the exact timing of the receipt or payment is uncertain, option forward contracts could apply.

When traders do not take out forward exchange contracts or use some other method to cover known receipts or payments of foreign currency in the future, they are gambling. Nobody can predict with any accuracy what the spot rate will be on any future date, so the amount of home currency received or paid will be an unknown quantity. The trader may, of course, benefit if the spot rate has moved in their favour when the transaction actually takes place, but they may equally well lose if the rate has moved against them.

3.4 How to calculate forward rates for fixed forward contracts

The forward rate is calculated by using the spot rate on the day of calculation and adjusting for the appropriate premium or discount. Let us consider two examples, bearing in mind that this book always works on the UK system of indirect quotes for exchange rates.

Example 3.1

On 1 January a UK bank quotes the following rates for the US dollars:

Spot	One month forward
1.9425–1.9435	0.53c–0.43c pm

The bank's one-month forward rates, quoted on 1 January for deals that will take place on 1 February, will be calculated as follows:

Buying rate

Spot (buy high)	1.9435
Deduct: Premium	0.0043
One-month forward fixed buying rate	1.9392

Note

1.   A premium is always deducted from the spot rate because if a currency is more expensive in terms of the pound, fewer units of it will be needed to be equivalent to a pound.

2.   The bank must deduct when it quotes currency at a premium, but it can deduct either 0.53 cents or 0.43 cents. The bank will always use the premium that is most favourable to it. Because the bank will wish to obtain as much currency as possible for every pound, given that it must deduct either 0.43 cents or 0.53 cents from the spot rate, the bank will deduct 0.43 cents.

Selling rate

Spot (sell low)	1.9425
Deduct: Premium	0.0053
One-month forward fixed selling rate	1.9372

Note: The premium is always deducted from the spot rate. The bank has a choice between deducting 0.43 cents or 0.53 cents. Because the bank wishes to give as little currency as possible in exchange for a pound, it deducts the greater amount, 0.53 cents.

Example 3.2

Note that the relationship of one Danish øre to one Danish krone is the equivalent of the relationship of one penny to one pound (ie one øre equals DKK 0.01).

On 1 January a UK bank quotes the following rates for the Danish Kroner:

Spot   One month forward

9.43-9.44   3 øre–4 øre discount

On 1 January the bank will quote its one month forward fixed rate for Danish Kroner as:

Buying rate

Spot (buy high)   9.44

Add: Discount   <u>0.04</u>

One month forward buying rate   <u>9.48</u>

The bank must add the discount to the spot rate. It has a choice of adding 4 øre or 3 øre. Because the bank always acts in its own best interests, it will add 4 øre to the spot rate, thus buying as high as possible.

Selling rate

Spot (sell low)   9.43

Add: Discount   <u>0.03</u>

One month forward selling rate <u>9.46</u>

The bank must add the discount to the spot rate. It has a choice of adding 4 øre or 3 øre. Because the bank always acts in its own best interests, it will add 3 øre, thus selling as low as possible.

Note: the basic rules can now be seen: spot buy high sell low. Adjustment for premium or discount – deduct premium, add discount. Use the premium or discount that favours the bank.

3.5   The importance of the decimal point

In the US dollar Example 3.1, the relevant forward premium was expressed as 0.43 cents. US\$1 equals 100 cents, hence 1 cent is 0.01 of US\$1. Because 0.43 cents must be less than 1 cent, the expression of this amount in dollar terms must be US\$0.0043.

In the Danish kroner Example 3.2, the relevant forward discount was expressed as 4 øre. One øre is DKK0.01, hence 4 øre must be expressed as DKK0.04.

Table 3.1 should prove useful.

Table 3.1

Country	Name of currency (with standard abbreviation)*	Unit quoted for premium or discount	Relationship of Currency Unit to unit quoted for premium or discount
USA	Dollar ($) (USD)	Cent (c)	100c = 1 USD or 1c = 0.01 USD
Canada	Dollar ($) (CAD)	Cent (c)	100c = 1 CAD or 1c = 0.01 CAD
Norway	Kroner (NOK)	Øre (øre)	100 øre = 1 NOK or l øre = 0.0l NOK
Denmark	Kroner (DKK)	Øre (øre)	100 øre = 1DKK or l øre = 0.01 DKK
Sweden	Kroner (SEK)	Öre (öre)	100 öre = 1 SEK or 1 öre = 0.01 SEK
Japan**	Yen (JPY)	Yen (JPY)	1 JPY = 1JPY = 1 Yen
Switzerland	Franc (CHF)	Centime (c)	100c = 1 CHF or 1c = 0.01 CHF
UK	British £ (GBP)	Pence (p)	100p = £1 or 1p = £0.01
Single European currency	Euro € (euro)	Cent (c)	100c = 1 EUR or 1c = 0.01 EUR
Australia	Dollar (AUD)	Cent	100c = 1 AUD or 1c = 0.01 AUD
New Zealand	Dollar (NZD)	Cent	100c = 1NZD or 1c = 0.01 NZD
Hong Kong	Dollar (HKD)	Cent	100c = 1 HKD or 1c = 0.01 HKD

* These standard abbreviations (eg USD) are used on international money transfers and in dealing transactions to show the name of the currency.

** For the Japanese yen, the unit of currency is also used for quotation of the premium and discount. For all other currencies, premiums and discounts are quoted in smaller units.

3.6 How to calculate rates for option forward contracts

An option forward contract means that the customer can select on which day they will complete the transaction, provided that the choice falls within the option period.

The bank will calculate the forward rates that it would offer for fixed contracts maturing on the first and last days of the option contract and will then choose the rate that is more favourable to itself.

Example 3.3

On 1 January, an importer enters into a contract to buy goods costing a total of US$100,000. Payment has to be made when the goods are shipped and shipment is to take place at some time during March.

The rates ruling on 1 January are:

Spot	Two months forward	Three months forward
1.9425–1.9525	0.90c–0.80c pm	1.40c–1.20c pm

If the importer enters into a forward exchange contract to cover the exchange risk, it will require an option forward contract, with the option period of between two and three months. The bank will calculate the rates as follows:

Spot (sell low)	1.9425	Spot	1.9425
Less: Two-months premium	0.0090	Less: Three-months premium	0.0140
Two-months forward rate	1.9335	Three-months forward rate	1.9285

The bank will choose 1.9285 because this is the most favourable selling rate for the option period. Remember that a bank sells currency to importers, and buys currency from exporters.

Example 3.4

Using the rates quoted in Example 3.3, the bank would calculate its option buying rate for the proceeds of exports invoiced in dollars to be received in March as:

Spot (buy high)	1.9525	Spot	1.9525
Less: Two-months premium	0.0080	Less: Three-months premium	0.0120
Two-months forward buy	1.9445	Three-months forward buy	1.9405

The bank will therefore quote 1.9445 as its option buying rate because this is the higher rate and hence that which is more favourable to the bank.

Note: in practice, bank dealers are involved in a very competitive market. For major customers, the bank may not quote the better of the two rates from its own point of view, but it may compromise by setting the rate somewhere between the two extremes. For exam purposes, however, you must complete the calculations as shown above.

Topic 4

Close- outs and extensions of forward contracts

On completion of this topic the student should be able to:

- understand the contractual position between a bank and a customer in relation to forward contracts;

- appreciate the close-out procedure that a bank must take if a customer fails to fulfil their contractual obligations under forward contracts;

- understand why the forward contract involves a contingent liability on the part of the customer and why a bank 'marks a limit' on the customer's account when it grants a forward contract;

- deal with extensions to forward contracts, as opposed to straight close-outs.

4.1   The contractual position

A forward exchange contract is a binding contract and the customer must ensure that they fulfil their obligations thereunder.

It can happen that a customer, through no fault of their own, cannot complete the agreed transaction. In this case, the bank will have to 'close out' the deal.

If, on the due date, an exporter cannot provide the currency that the bank has agreed to buy from it, the bank will calculate the cost of the sale of the relevant amount of foreign currency at the spot rate ruling on the date of default. The bank will also calculate the amount it would have credited to the customer had the forward contract been fulfilled. The bank will then pass the net debit or credit to the customer's account.

Likewise, if an importer is concerned, the bank will calculate the amount that would have been debited had the forward contract been completed; it will then calculate the value of the currency at the bank's spot buying rate ruling on the date of default. The net debit or credit will again be passed to the customer's account.

4.2   Examples of close- out procedures

Example 4.1

The bank agreed to enter into a forward contract to buy US$100,000 from an exporter. The contract was a fixed forward contract for a transaction due to take place in three months' time.

Unfortunately, the proceeds were not received by the exporter and it had to default. What action would the bank take? The rates on the date that the forward contract was agreed were:

Spot	Three months forward
1.8525–1.8535	0.94c pm 0.89c pm

The spot rates three months later were 1.92-1.93.

Answer

The agreed forward buying rate would be:

Spot	1.8535
Less: Premium	0.0089
Three months forward	1.8446

On the due date the bank would calculate as follows:

(Dr) Cost of sale of $100,000 at 1.92	£52,083.33
(Cr) Proceeds of purchase of $100,000 at 1.8446	£54,212.30
Net credit passed to customer's account	£2,128.97

Example 4.2

Using the rates in Example 4.1, calculate the amount to be passed through the account of an importer if a forward exchange contract was made for the bank to sell US$100,000 for completion in three months and a close-out has to be effected.

Answer

The agreed forward rate would be:

Spot	1.8525
Less: Premium	0.0094
Three months forward	1.8431

On the due date, the bank would calculate as follows:

(Cr) Proceeds of repurchase of US$100,000 at spot rate 1.93	£51,813.487
(Dr) Amount that would have been debited had forward contract been completed (US$100,000 at 1.8431)	£54,256.42
Net debit to customer's account	£2,442.95

Example 4.3 (partial close-outs)

An importer had arranged a fixed forward contract for the bank to sell US$50,000 at 1.55. On the maturity date the importer informed the bank that he required only US$40,000.

The spot rates ruling on the date of the maturity of the forward contract were:

Spot   1.50–1.51

Answer

The bank will sell the US$50,000 at the agreed forward rate, but will buy back any unwanted currency at the spot rate.

(Dr) US$50.000 at 1.55	£32,258.06	
(Cr) US$10,000 at 1.51	£6,622.52	
Net debit	£25,635.54	

Example 4.4 (early close-outs)

If a customer realises that they will be unable to fulfil their obligations well before the expiry date, they can effectively fix the loss or gain under the close-out at maturity by arranging a matching forward contract with the same expiry date.

For example, an exporter may have entered into a three-month fixed forward contract for the bank to buy US$100,000. One month after the commencement of the contract, the underlying commercial deal may fall through. In this instance, the exporter could arrange a two-month fixed forward contract for the bank to sell it US$100,000.

Two months later, at maturity of the two forward contracts, the bank will notionally debit the customer with the sterling equivalent of the two-month forward contract and will notionally credit him with the sterling equivalent of the original three-month forward contract. The net difference between these two amounts will be debited or credited to the account.

The net effect of such a transaction is to fix the loss or gain on the close-out from the time of the creation of the matching forward contract.

Note: banks are developing new variations of the forward contract and, in practice, the customer should check out what the bank's procedures and advice would be for their own particular circumstances, should this situation arise.

4.3   Why is it necessary for the bank to close out?

Many customers believe that the bank is somehow punishing them when they are debited on a close-out. (Their thoughts, if they are credited on a close-out are no doubt different.) There is, however, no element of punishment.

If the bank enters into a forward contract with a customer, the bank will take action to offset any exchange risk to itself. The action could take the form of a temporary 'swap', as described in Topic 2, Example 2.1, or some other way of covering the exchange risk could be undertaken. The point is that, once a bank agrees a forward contract with a customer, the bank itself enters into a contractual obligation with a third party so as to match or offset its own risk. The bank's customer must fulfil their obligations under the forward contract so that the bank can honour its 'matching' commitments to third parties.

If the customer cannot, or will not, fulfil their obligation under the forward contract, the bank must take action to enable it to honour its matching obligation to the third party.

The procedure adopted is the close-out procedure shown in the examples above.

In effect, the bank makes the customer fulfil their obligations under the forward contract by using the spot market. The resultant gain or loss is then credited or debited to the customer's account, as shown in the examples.

4.4 Why the bank 'marks a limit' on the customer's account when it agrees a forward contract

If the customer fulfils their obligation to deliver or to take delivery of the appropriate amount of currency, the bank is not in any danger. If the customer fails to fulfil those obligations, the bank is at risk, because there is a possible loss on the close-out. If the customer has insufficient funds to meet the loss on the close-out, the bank will have incurred a bad debt.

As a consequence, banks usually mark up a limit when they agree a forward contract. The amount of that limit is the bank's estimate of the maximum possible loss on any close-out. This amount will depend on the length of time to the contract's maturity and on the volatility of the currency concerned. The limit marked is usually between 10% and 20% of the sterling value of the forward contract.

The risk involved in a forward contract is called a 'contingent liability' – that is, it is a liability that may or may not occur. The contingent liability must, however, be borne in mind by the bank and that is why a limit is marked on the customer's account. Such a limit will reduce the scope for borrowing in other ways, for example, by overdraft. Indeed, the bank's criteria for deciding whether to agree to a forward contract are very similar to those for granting an overdraft.

4.5 Close-out or extension of forward contracts

If a customer cannot fulfil the transaction when a forward contract has been entered into, the bank will 'close out', as has already been described.

If the customer exports, the bank will buy the currency at the agreed forward rate and sell it to the customer at the spot selling rate ruling on the day the contract should have been completed.

The resultant profit or loss will be the customer's.

Likewise, if the customer imports, the bank will sell at the agreed forward rate and buy it back at the current spot rate.

It sometimes arises that the underlying commercial transaction is merely delayed instead of being totally frustrated. In such a case, the customer would be able to fulfil the contract in due course, but after the date(s) specified in the forward contract.

In these cases, in which the completion of the forward contract will merely be delayed, the bank will extend it. What happens is that the bank 'closes out' in the normal way, but then arranges a new forward contract for completion at the time that the customer expects to have the necessary currency.

In an extension, the new forward rate can be based on the spot rate used in the close-out. Discount or premium is applied to the spot close-out rate in the normal way to calculate the new forward rate.

Example 4.5

The bank arranged a forward contract with its exporter customer to buy US$40,725 at US$1.40 = £1.00. The receipt of proceeds was delayed and the exporter asked for an extension of one month fixed. Show the transactions on the customer's account, if the rates ruling on the maturity date of the forward contract were:

Spot	1.45–1.46
One month forward (ignore commission)	2 c–l c premium

Solution

1. On the date of maturity of the original forward contract, the bank will close out in the usual way:

   (Cr) The bank will buy US$40,725 at the agreed rate of 1.40 =   £29,089.29

   (Dr) The bank will sell US$40,725 at the spot rate of 1.45 =   £28,086.21

   Net amount credited to customer's account =   £1,003.08

2. On the same date as in 1., the bank will agree a new forward contract, one month forward fixed:

Spot close-out rate	1.45
Deduct: Premium	0.01
	1.44

3. One month later, provided that the exporter delivers the currency, he will be credited:

   40,725 at 1.44 = £28,281.25

Notes

a) Those of you who have previously studied for this subject may have learned the 'diagonal rule' as a means of calculating forward rates. If you know this rule, and can apply it correctly to calculate the forward rate on an extension, then continue to use it. Many students are, however, totally confused when applying this rule to extensions. As a result, the diagonal rule is not used in this text.

---

b) The reason that the bank applies the spot close-out rate to extension is that it has already made its 'turn' from the difference between buying and selling rates on the original contract.

c) Recently, there has been a trend by some banks to simply treat any extension of a forward contract as an entirely new transaction. In that case, the close-out would be exactly the same as in 1. above, but the extension rate in 2. above would be:

Spot buy rate	1.46
Deduct premium	0.01
New forward rate	1.45

Thus, the sterling proceeds in 3. above would then be £28,086.21, as opposed to £28,281.25.

d) At least one major bank continues to use the close-out rate (for example 1.45 in 1. above) as the basis of the new forward rate for important customers or for 'large' deals. For less important customers, or for 'small' deals, it would treat the new forward contract as an entirely new transaction with a forward rate of 1.45 as in (c) above. Markets are competitive, and the market/competitive position is similar to that for option forward contracts as shown in the note to Example 3.4 in Topic 3.

Topic 5

Foreign currency options and pure options

On completion of this topic, the student should be able to:

- appreciate the reasons for the development of currency options;
- understand the terminology that applies to currency options;
- appreciate how a currency option differs from a forward contract;
- evaluate the customer benefits of currency options;
- be aware of the competition that exchange-traded options provide;
- understand the customer benefits of currency options provided by banks, as opposed to the customer benefits of exchange traded options;
- appreciate the implications of hybrid products, such as cylinder options, for both banks and customers.

5.1   The reasons for the development of foreign currency options

Foreign currency options give customers far more flexibility than is provided by the conventional, traditional forward contract.

Before defining these options, let us examine the main causes of customer dissatisfaction with the traditional forward exchange contract.

Customers' complaints when currency options were not widely available included the following.

- The customer could have lost money if they failed to comply with the forward contract and the bank had to close out. (Customers conveniently chose to forget that, if rates had moved in their favour, they could be credited with the net profit on a close- out.)
- Customers did not appreciate that the term 'option' in an option forward exchange contract related solely to the period during which the agreed transaction could be carried out. Many customers wrongly thought 'option' in a

forward contract meant that the customer could choose whether or not they wished to complete the transaction; in other words, the customer thought that the word 'option' gave them the right to walk away from the forward exchange commitment if they so wished.

- The following situation was a particularly strong cause of customer dissatisfaction:

  - an option forward exchange contract was arranged;

  - the customer could not fulfil it because of a breakdown in the terms of the underlying commercial contract;

  - the bank had to debit the customer on close- out because the spot rates had moved against the customer.

- Customers felt aggrieved when they took out forward contracts and were then unable to take advantage if spot rates on the date of execution had moved in their favour.

These complaints led to the development of the foreign currency option, which, at a price, overcomes all of the real or perceived customer complaints regarding traditional forward contracts.

The development of the foreign currency option as a widely available foreign exchange risk management tool can indeed be said to be 'market- driven'.

5.2   What is a 'foreign currency option'?

A foreign currency option is an agreement whereby a customer can pay a premium to the bank for the right, but not the obligation, to buy from or sell to the bank a specified amount of a foreign currency at an agreed rate of exchange. Generally speaking, the option can be exercised, at the customer's discretion, at any time up to a specified expiry date, or it can be allowed to lapse by the customer at the expiry date.

As an alternative to exercising the option or allowing it to lapse, it may be possible to sell the option back to the bank.

Watch your terminology, and that of the exam question, when dealing with currency options (the common abbreviation of foreign currency options). In forward contracts the rates are always quoted from the bank's point of view, so that the fixed forward buying rate relates to the rate at which a bank would buy and the fixed forward selling rate relates to the rate at which a bank would sell to a customer. In currency options, however, it is the customer who purchases the right to buy from or sell to the bank the specified amount of foreign currency at the agreed rate of exchange.

5.3   Glossary of terms relating to foreign currency options

5.3.1   'Writer' or 'grantor'

The '**writer**' or '**grantor**' is the bank (or any other organisation) that, in exchange for a fee (known as the 'option premium'), grants the right, but not the obligation, for a purchaser to buy or sell the currency at the agreed rate during a specified period.

5.3.2   'Purchaser'

The '**purchaser**' is the person, usually a customer, who pays an option premium to bank for the right, but not the obligation, to deal under the terms of the option.

5.3.3   'Holder'

The '**holder**' can be the original purchaser of the option, or someone to whom the original purchaser has assigned the rights under the option.

5.3.4   'Call option' and 'put option'

A '**call option**' gives the purchaser the right to buy the currency from the writer and a '**put option**' gives them the right to sell to the writer. Exporters will normally require put options; importers will normally require call options. You are reminded that the terminology differs from that of forward contracts.

5.3.5   'Base', 'counter' and 'underlying currencies'

The '**base currency**' (sometimes called the 'counter currency') is usually US dollars or sterling. The underlying currency is foreign currency, eg euros, which the customer will wish to buy (call option) or sell (put option) to the writer. For example, a sterling- based UK exporter who invoices in euros would take out a put option in which the base currency would be sterling and the underlying currency would be euros. The put option would give the customer the right, but not the obligation, to sell a certain amount of euros to the bank during a specified period at a pre- set rate of exchange.

5.3.6   'Strike price'

The '**strike price**' is the rate of exchange that will be applied if the currency option is exercised. The term 'exercise price' is sometimes used as an alternative to 'strike price'.

5.3.7 'Option premium'

The 'option premium' is the 'up- front' payment made by the purchaser to the writer and it is usually paid at the time the option contract is granted. Once paid, the premium cannot be recovered, irrespective of whether the holder subsequently exercises the option or not.

The option premium is usually denominated in the base currency, ie US dollars or sterling, and is expressed as a percentage of the principal amount. The option premium is determined by the following main factors:

- the strike price and its relationship to the relevant spot and forward rates;
- the period of the option;
- the volatility of the exchange rates of the underlying currencies;
- the relevant rates of interest.

5.3.8 'Boston option'

Occasionally for approved customers the 'up- front' condition concerning the premium can be waived so that the premium, plus interest, is paid at maturity. If the option is exercised, the premium and interest are added to the cost (call option), or deducted from the proceeds (put option). If the option is abandoned, the premium plus interest is claimed from the purchaser at maturity. This is known as the '**Boston option**'.

Obviously, only highly creditworthy customers can be granted Boston- type options and such options are not common.

5.3.9 'Intrinsic value at maturity'

An alternative to exercising the option is to sell it back to the bank at its intrinsic value (if any). The 'intrinsic value at maturity' is the difference between the strike price and the current spot rate of the underlying currency.

For example, a call option may have the following characteristics on the expiry date:

Strike price	3.40
Base currency	Sterling
Underlying currency	Canadian $ (CAD)
Current spot rate	3.10
Amount of base currency	£12,500
Type of option	Call option

The intrinsic value on the expiry day would be:

- CAD, which can be bought by the customer under the terms of the option:

  (12,500 x 3.40) = Can$42,500 at a cost of £12,500;

- Sterling equivalent of Can$42,500 which the customer could sell back at the current spot rate:

  Can$42,500 @ 3.10 = £13,710;

- Intrinsic value:

  £13,710 - £12,500 = **£1,210**.

Thus, on the expiry date, the bank would be prepared to pay £1,210 (ignoring dealing costs) if the holder were to decide that they wished to sell the option back to the bank, rather than exercise it.

Therefore, if the underlying commercial deal had fallen through, the importer could sell the option back to the bank for its intrinsic value.

5.3.10 'Intrinsic value' and 'time value' prior to maturity

Prior to maturity, the amount of the premium consists of two elements: the '**intrinsic value**' and the '**time value**'. For an option prior to maturity, the intrinsic value (if any) in terms of base currency is calculated from the difference between the value of the underlying currency converted at the strike rate (the 'option value') and the value of the underlying currency converted at the forward rate for the unexpired period of the option (the '**forward value**'). The principles are similar to those shown in the intrinsic value calculation immediately above, except that, for intrinsic values on the expiry dates, the spot rate, as opposed to the forward rate, that which is applied.

For a call option, when the option value is below the forward value, the option is said to be 'in the money', because it has intrinsic value. When the option value of the underlying currency at the strike price is more than the value at the appropriate forward rate, the call option is said to be 'out of the money'. Out-of-the-money options (whether puts or calls) can never have a negative intrinsic value, however, because the holder is not obliged to exercise them.

Put options work on the same principles, but they are in the money when the option value is above the forward value and they are out of the money when the option value is below the forward value. When the option value and the forward value are the same, the option is said to be 'at the money'.

The other element of the premium is time value. The greater the time to maturity and the greater the volatility of the exchange rate for the currency pairs, the greater the time value.

When an option is first arranged, the writer will use a computer program to calculate the 'fair value' of an option, but then the premium that is actually quoted is adjusted in the light of the writer's own position in the market and market demand.

5.3.11   'Notification date', 'exercise date' and 'expiry date'

The terms '**notification date**', '**exercise date**' and '**expiry date**' are synonymous. Once the expiry date has passed, the option will automatically lapse unless the holder has notified the writer that they intend to exercise their rights.

5.3.12   'Settlement date'

Once the holder has notified the writer that they intend to exercise the option, they have up to two working days to settle the deal. For example, if a call option, with sterling as the base currency, expires on a Monday, the holder must notify the writer by that day of any intention to exercise the option. If notification takes place on the Monday, the holder has until close of business on Wednesday to provide the necessary sterling to purchase the underlying currency from the bank.

Note: it is too late to notify the writer on Tuesday of the intention to exercise, because the option will have lapsed at close of business on Monday.

5.3.13   'American options' and 'European options'

With an '**American option**', the holder can notify the writer of their intention to exercise the option on any business day between the granting of the option and the expiry date. Notification can be for all, or for part, of the amount of currency covered by the option. The final settlement date for an American option is two working days after the expiry date. Note that some banks may limit the number of drawdowns by placing a minimum drawing amount.

With a '**European option**', there is a single expiry date and a single settlement date. The holder can notify the bank of their intention to exercise only on the one expiry date and must then complete the underlying deal within two working days.

The option premium is higher for American options because of the greater flexibility for the customer and the greater risk to the writer of the option, who must manage the overall options book.

American options are readily available in the UK.

5.3.14   'Over- the- counter (OTC) options'

'**Over- the- counter (OTC) options**' are foreign currency options negotiated as separate, individual contracts between the purchaser customer and the writer bank. Thus the OTC option can be tailor- made to meet a customer's specific needs. Each bank has a minimum amount below which it will not grant currency options.

5.3.15   'Exchange- traded options'

'**Exchange- traded options**' are currency options that are dealt with on organised exchanges. At one time such options were available via the London International Financial Futures and Options Exchange (LIFFE), but LIFFE no longer offers this type of option. Exchanges in the USA and other parts of the world, however, offer currency options.

Exchange traded options are standardised and cannot be tailor-made to meet specific customer needs. Quite often banks themselves take out exchange-traded options to cover their own obligations on OTC options that they have written.

5.4   Comparison of forward exchange contracts and foreign currency options

Table 5.1

Forward contracts	Foreign currency options
These are firm and binding contracts between the customer and the bank, whereby the customer has an obligation to deliver or take delivery of the foreign currency in accordance with the terms of the contract.	This is the right, but not the obligation, for the customer to deliver or take delivery of foreign currency in accordance with the terms of the agreement.
If a customer fails to fulfil the terms of the forward contract, the bank will 'close out'. In this case, the customer will have to stand the loss, or will receive the gain, depending on the spot rate of exchange on the day of close-out.	The currency option gives the holder the right but not the obligation to deal on the terms set out. There is no question of a close-out taking place. The holder has three choices on the expiry date of a currency option: i) exercise it; ii) abandon it; iii) sell it if the currency option has an intrinsic value.
If a bank grants a forward contract, the bank usually marks up a contingent liability facility of between 10% and 20% of the full contract value. This facility is marked to cover the fact that, if the customer defaults, the bank may need to debit the customer with a loss on the close-out. Thus the granting of a forward contract will reduce the available credit facilities for the customer.	A currency option is not classed as a contingent liability, because the customer is under no obligation to deal on the terms set out. Thus, the currency option does not affect the available credit facilities for the customer.
From a customer's point of view, the forward contract eliminates the exchange risk, but the customer cannot gain the benefit if spot rates move in their favour. If the underlying commercial deal falls through, however, the customer will make a gain or loss on the close-out. Thus, forward contracts that are not matched by an underlying currency deal create an exposure.	Under the currency option, the holder can take full advantage if spot rates move in their favour. If the holder has the underlying currency, they can deal spot and abandon the option.
A forward contract is inflexible and affects the credit facilities of the customer. However, the cost of arranging forward contracts is relatively low compared to the cost of a currency option (usually just the bid offer spread).	The currency option gives a holder much greater flexibility. Hence the cost (the option premium) is much more than for a forward contract.

A forward contract is a contract between a customer and the bank. A customer cannot normally sell their rights to a third party.	It may be possible for a holder to sell their rights under a currency option, depending on whether it has an intrinsic value. The right to sell is an alternative to the other two rights: the right to exercise the option or the right to abandon it.

5.5   The customer benefits of currency- related options

The benefits to the customer of currency- related options can be summarised as follows.

- The purchaser can choose the strike price. (One of the factors that influences the option premium is how far the strike price differs from the relevant forward rate.)

- The currency option provides far more flexibility than forward contracts or other methods of covering exchange risks. The option period can be chosen by the purchaser.

- There is no question of marking a limit on the customer's account with currency options, because there is no obligation whatsoever for the customer to deal in accordance with the terms of the option. Hence, currency options do not affect the available borrowing facilities, because they are not a contingent liability. But settlement risk must be considered upon exercise of the option: the bank must be sure that the customer will deliver, or take delivery of, the relevant currency prior to the end of the settlement period.

- The purchaser can take advantage if spot rates move in their favour, simply by abandoning the option.

- If the underlying commercial deal falls through, the purchaser will be able to sell the option back to the bank, provided that the option has an intrinsic value.

- The purchaser's costs are known at the outset and are limited to the amount of the option premium.

- The documentation required to set up the option is simple and straightforward.

5.6   The customer benefits of OTC options as opposed to exchange- traded options

As we saw in Section 5.3, OTC options are provided by banks whereas exchange traded options are obtained on organised exchanges, such as the Philadelphia Exchange in the USA.

The main customer benefits of OTC options as opposed to exchange traded options are that:

- OTC options are tailor- made whereas exchange traded options are standardised and may not match the customer's requirements;

- OTC options involve less administration on the part of the purchaser. With exchange traded options it is necessary to deal via authorized brokers. None of this is required with bank OTC options, which have simple documentation.

5.7 Cylinder options

A '**cylinder option**' is a combination of an option and a forward contract. In exchange for a reduced premium, the holder acquires some, but not all, of the benefits of an option. Let us first of all look at a particular situation in which cylinder options might be used.

5.7.1 Example 5.1

Today:

- X plc expects to have to pay out US$100,000 in three months;
- X plc buys a call option from its bank, strike price US$1.45;
- X plc writes a put option in favour of its bank, strike price US$1.55= £1;
- both options cover an underlying principal of US$100,000;
- both options have an expiry date in three months and are European;
- the premiums net out exactly. (This is not always the case and it depends on the terms of each option. Sometimes the bank's premium as writer will exceed that for the customer as writer, but the opposite could equally apply.)

At maturity in three months, the outcome depends on the spot rate (see Table 5.2).

Table 5.2

	Outcome 1	Outcome 2	Outcome 3
Spot rate at maturity	US$1.30 = £1	US$1.50 = £1	US$1.60 = £1
Sterling value at spot	£76,923	£66,667	£62,500
Sterling value of call	£68,966	£68,966	£68,966
Sterling value of put	£64,516	£64,516	£64,516
Action by call holder	Exercise	Abandon	Abandon
Action by put holder	Abandon	Abandon	Exercise
Result	X plc obtain the US $ at a cost of £68,966 using call rate of 1.45. If the US $ are not required, the call will be sold for its intrinsic value.	Both options are abandoned. X plc acquires the US $ at spot rate, cost £66,667, if the dollars are needed.	The bank sells US $100,000 at 1.55. The cost is £64,516.

From the above example, we can see that the features and benefits of the cylinder option from this customer's point of view are as follows.

- The premium will be lower than for a conventional option, because the customer can offset the premium on the option it has written against the premium on the option written by the bank. In this case the net premium is nil.

- If the spot rate at maturity is in between the two strike prices (ie within the 'cylinder'), both options will be abandoned and the US dollar payment, if made, will be settled at spot. If the US dollar are not required, no action is required on the part of the customer.

- If the rate is outside the cylinder (ie above or below the two strike prices), the call will be exercised if the underlying currency has strengthened and the put will be exercised if the underlying currency has weakened. Likewise, the put will be abandoned if the underlying currency has strengthened and the call will be abandoned if the underlying currency has weakened.

- Provided that the customer still has the underlying currency position at maturity (eg to make a payment of US$100,000), the deal will be transacted as follows:

  - at call strike rate if the currency has strengthened at maturity;

  - at spot rate if this falls within the cylinder;

  - at put strike rate if the underlying currency has weakened at maturity.

- Banks look upon a cylinder option as a credit facility, for the same reason that the forward contract is deemed to carry default risk in the case of a close- out. In this instance, if the underlying currency had weakened at maturity, the bank would need to be sure that X plc would honour its obligations under the put.

- Cylinder options are useful when:

  - the underlying currency position in the cash market at maturity is 'certain',

  - the customer wishes to take advantage (to a limited extent) of the upside potential if the spot rates do move in its favour, but will not pay the full option premium,

  - the customer wishes to cover itself by setting the 'worst rate' that can be applied if rates have moved adversely at maturity.

- Thus, in exchange for a reduced premium, the customer gains a limited maximum upward potential, coupled with the danger of exposure to risk should the underlying currency receipt or payment not come to fruition.

5.7.1 Conclusion on cylinder options

There are infinite variations on the way in which banks can use 'financial engineering' skills to offer a hybrid product that combines the features of options and forwards. The net effect is that, in exchange for a lower premium, the customer forgoes some of the benefits of an option.

Topic 6

Alternatives to forward contracts and currency options, and the benefits of foreign currency invoicing for exporters

On completion of this topic the student should be able to:

- appreciate why it is not always possible for exporters to invoice overseas buyers in their (ie the exporter's) home currency;
- understand the benefits of forward contracts;
- appreciate the alternative techniques for covering the exchange risk;
- understand the benefits and drawbacks of foreign currency invoicing for exporters.

6.1 The drawbacks of home currency invoicing for importers and exporters.

Let us consider UK importers and exporters as an example. Ideally, UK importers would prefer to be invoiced in sterling and UK exporters would prefer to invoice in sterling because this procedure would eliminate foreign currency transaction exposure. But, competitive pressures mean that home currency invoicing is not always possible. Overseas exporters who are in a strong bargaining position may insist that UK importers pay in the seller's currency and may refuse to enter into any deal unless this stipulation is complied with. In addition, overseas buyers may insist on being invoiced in their home currency by UK exporters as a condition of sale.

6.2 The benefits of forward contracts for sterling-based importers and alternative methods of covering the exchange risk

- The sterling cost of the imports is fixed; thus, the importer can set its prices and profit margins more accurately.

- In theory, there is no limit to the amount of sterling that the importer could require on the due date, if it has not covered the exchange risk, because the pound floats freely. The forward contract eliminates this exchange risk.

- Failure to take any action to cover the exchange risk amounts to gambling. The importer will be legally liable to acquire the necessary foreign currency from the date on which it signs a commercial contract.

Some major corporate customers deliberately allow themselves to be exposed to the exchange risk in certain currencies, because they expect spot rates to move in their favour. Such companies are, however, quick to cover the exchange risk if the outlook for the currency in question changes adversely.

Normally, smaller companies should cover the exchange risk, because they probably could not survive a catastrophic change in spot rates.

Alternative forms of hedging include the following.

- Currency call options, which are more expensive than forward contracts and may not be available for the currency and amount required. The currency option enables the importer to deal at the spot rate on the due date, without penalty, if the rates move in its favour (full details of currency options are given in Topic 5).

- The bank could sell the importer the necessary currency immediately at the current spot rate. The currency could then be kept on deposit until required. In determining whether this method is worthwhile, much depends on the post- tax value of the deposit in the two countries.

- The importer might open a foreign currency account, but only if there are receipts and payments in the currency. The importer can then take out a forward contract to cover the anticipated balance, or can delay conversion of the balance until rates move in its favour, or can buy a currency option to cover the anticipated balance. It is possible to have a cheque book for a currency account.

- When a trader has receipts in one foreign currency and payments in another, it can convert the receipts directly into the currency of the payment, using cross rates. Forward contracts may well be available for cross rates.

6.3 Exporters: means of protection against exchange risk

The following methods of protection against exchange risk may be adopted by importers:

- forward contracts;

- borrowing foreign currency now, letting the bank convert it at the current spot rate to sterling and then crediting the current account with the proceeds at once. The currency loan is subsequently repaid from the currency proceeds of the exports. The interest rate is based on the interest rates ruling in the overseas centre;

- opening a foreign currency account, but only if there are receipts and payments in the currency;

- currency put options.

Note: a more detailed analysis of the wider issues regarding exchange rate risks can be found in Topics 7 and 8.

6.4 The advantages of foreign currency Invoicing for exporters

The basic benefit of foreign currency invoicing for exporters is that it gives a product a competitive advantage. The product is more attractive to the buyer because:

- the buyer does not run any exchange risk;

- the buyer can easily understand the price implications if quoted in local currency;

- it is easier for the buyer to compare the price quoted by local competitors.

Note

1. If the exporter has both receipts and payments in currency, it will be more efficient to open a foreign currency account. Forward contracts could be arranged to cover the anticipated net balance.

2. If applicable, a currency option can cover the exchange risk while allowing the customer to 'walk away' if the spot rates move in his favour. Alternatively, a less flexible method, such as the forward contract, could be used.

6.5 Disadvantages of foreign currency invoicing

The following four disadvantages of foreign currency investing should be borne in mind:

1. The exporter runs the exchange risk, which runs from the moment the commercial contract is signed until conversion of the currency.

2. Although the exchange risk can be covered, there is a cost involved (for example, the management time and/or the cost of the premiums for options, or the bid–offer spread for forwards).

3. Currency invoicing creates problems for the accounts staff, unless specialist help such as export factoring is employed (covered in Part IV of this text).

4. Published price lists may need frequent revision.

Topic 7

An overview of the management of foreign currency exposure

On completion of this topic, the student should be able to:

- identify the three main categories of foreign exchange exposure;
- assess the factors that influence the hedging philosophy of companies;
- evaluate the arguments surrounding whether foreign exchange rate risk should be hedged;
- apply appropriate hedging techniques to specific practical situations;
- appreciate the need for accurate forecasting of exposures;
- integrate the preparation of budgets with foreign currency risk management;
- appreciate the difference between the accountancy treatment of derivatives and the economic effect of derivatives;
- appreciate the links between risk management, funding and capital structure in the context of enterprise-wide risk management.

7.1 Introduction

With the increasing trend towards globalisation, foreign currency exposure management is becoming more and more important in the management of major corporates. This topic examines the nature of foreign currency exposure management, and explores the current theoretical and practical considerations in relation to whether such exposure needs to be managed.

This topic defines transaction exposure, translation exposure and economic exposure, and it focuses on the management of foreign currency transaction exposure. Topic 8 will focus on the management of translation and economic exposure.

'Foreign currency exposure' is defined as the vulnerability of a company to changes in its profit and loss and balance sheet positions arising from exchange rate movements. 'Foreign currency' is any currency other than the currency in which the company's published accounts are denominated. Foreign currency exposure is usually classified under the headings of transaction, exposure, translation exposure and economic exposure. Transaction exposure is covered in this topic, and translation and economic exposure will be examined in Topic 8.

There has been considerable academic debate over:

- whether foreign currency exposures should be managed by corporates
- if foreign exchange exposure should be managed by corporates, which principles apply and what techniques should be used.

This topic examines the arguments for and against the management of foreign currency transaction exposure, and it also assesses the techniques, both internal and external, which might be used to manage the various foreign currency exposures.

7.2   Categories of foreign exchange exposure

Foreign exchange exposure is usually classified under three main categories: **transaction**, **translation** and **economic**.

7.2.1   Transaction exposure

'**Transaction exposure**' can arise out of normal overseas trading activities. For exporters who invoice in foreign currency, the transaction exposure exists between the date of the commercial contract and the date of conversion of the receivables into home currency. For importers who are invoiced in foreign currency, the transaction exposure exists between the date of the commercial contract and the date of conversion of home currency into the requisite sum of foreign currency. Transaction exposure also arises in relation to any cash transfer between domestic currency; and overseas currency, thus capital expenditure or capital receipts, such as dividends, when denominated in foreign currency, will give rise to transaction exposures.

7.2.2   Extended transaction exposure

The above is the traditional or legal definition of foreign exchange transaction exposure. But many writers consider that, over and above the legal exposure there is an 'extended transaction exposure', which applies for whatever period a company is committed to selling to certain countries or to buying from certain countries. This exposure will last for the period of time before the corporate is able to switch to other countries. (Some authorities would classify extended transaction exposure as 'economic' exposure.)

7.2.3   Pre- transaction exposure

A third category of transaction exposure, '**pre- transaction exposure**' occurs when a company is committed to receiving payment in a foreign currency if buyers decide to purchase. The two major manifestations of pre transaction exposure are as follows.

- A company might submit a tender for a commercial contract that is to be settled in foreign currency. If the commercial contract is awarded, the company will incur a foreign currency transaction exposure, because the spot rate of exchange at the date the contract is awarded may well be different from that ruling on the day of tender. Taking out a forward contract at the time of the tender could be unwise, however, because if the tender proves unsuccessful, then the forward contract will have created an exposure and the company may gain or lose when the forward is closed out.

- A similar exposure applies when a company issues price lists that are denominated in foreign currency. There is no guarantee of the amount of sales that will actually be made, but the company is committed to fulfilling any sales that may arise at the price set out in the published list. In theory, the exporter could offset any exchange rate movements by altering the price list, but frequent alterations of price lists will be seen by potential buyers as equivalent to invoicing in home currency. As a general point, the cost of entering a national market means that the exporter is committed to maintaining a long-term position there, with prices determined by local inflation and local market conditions.

7.2.4 Translation exposure

'**Translation exposure**' arises from the changes in the value in home currency of overseas assets and liabilities from one balance sheet date to the next. It also relates to the consolidations of the year's profits and the effect on earnings per share when some of the profits relate to an overseas subsidiary.

7.2.5 Economic exposure

'**Economic exposure**', sometimes called 'competitive exposure', assesses the effects of long run changes in exchange rates on the competitiveness of companies from different locations. Both translation and economic exposure are covered in Topic 8.

7.3 The meaning of the term 'hedge'

A '**hedge**' is an action taken by a company to cover itself against risk. The techniques of hedging can usually be categorised as either internal or external.

Internal techniques involve the company in switching its own operations (eg location, sources of supplies, customers) to reduce the impact of foreign exchange exposures.

External techniques, meanwhile, usually involve the use of derivatives such as forward exchange contracts or currency options. These derivatives are available from external providers such as banks. We have already seen in the previous topics how forward exchange contracts and currency options can be used to reduce transaction exposures.

Techniques such as forward contracts and currency options are sometimes known as '**external techniques**'. We have looked at how these techniques operate in the earlier topics of this text. External techniques cannot hedge a business' cash flows against a permanent shift in exchange rates. For example, a company may have a long-term commitment to export to the USA, but it cannot take out a five-year forward contract because of the problem of accurately forecasting currency receipts over such a long period. If the hedge does not match the underlying cash flows, then the hedge itself will have created an exposure.

What external techniques can do when exchange rates are moving in the 'wrong' direction for the company is to provide a breathing space to allow companies time to implement longer term internal techniques, such as the relocation of production to match the cost base of the competitor.

7.4 Internal techniques for hedging transaction exposures

Essentially, internal techniques involve the company in changing its own operations or changing its commercial contractual arrangements.

7.4.1 Invoicing in home currency

Invoicing in home currency would remove any foreign currency transaction risk from the party invoicing, or being invoiced, but such tactics are often not possible due to commercial or competitive pressures, which mean that the invoice must be denominated in foreign currency if the commercial transaction is to take place. In determining which currency is to be used, much depends on the relative bargaining power of the two parties.

7.4.2 Currency variation clauses

Depending on the bargaining power of the two parties, an exporter who invoices in foreign currency may be able to negotiate a currency variation clause in the commercial sales contract. The clause will usually allow for price increases if the foreign currency depreciates and for price reductions if the foreign currency appreciates in value. Detailed rules must be set out in the contract for the calculation of the variations in price.

7.4.3 Switching the currency of the cost base by being invoiced in the currency of revenue

An example of switching the currency of the cost base could be a UK exporter who sells to the USA and who invoices US buyers in US dollars. Such exporters may be able to find local UK based suppliers who are prepared to invoice in US dollars as opposed to in sterling. A typical example would be UK- based subsidiaries of USA multinationals, which may be happy to invoice the UK exporter in US dollars.

7.4.4 Matching

Matching involves the use of foreign currency bank accounts when a company has both receipts and payments in overseas currency. When payments are due before receipts, the company can arrange overdraft facilities, subject to creditworthiness, and when there are receipts due before payments, then interest can be negotiated for the credit balances. Interest rates will be based on those ruling in the overseas centre.

The major benefit of foreign currency accounts is that the company can avoid consistently buying and selling the same currency. In other words, the company avoids the bank's spread between its buying and selling rates. Companies can arrange to hedge the anticipated balances at periodic intervals.

7.4.5 Multilateral netting

The principle involved in multilateral netting is the same as that for matching, but the operation is more complex. This system is useful for large groups of companies with a centralised treasury function. Each operating subsidiary must report the following details to the centre:

- anticipated receipts and payments in every currency other than its own domestic currency;

- an estimate of the subsidiary's exposed position in every currency other than its own domestic currency.

The central treasury will then act as an internal clearing house and will hedge the group's net exposure in any particular currency. This system is only really applicable in large multinational corporations, which have an efficient centralised treasury function.

The requirements for the successful implementation of multinational netting are:

- the budget periods for all operating subsidiaries must be synchronised, otherwise the reported net exposures of the group could be distorted;

- the savings from netting must be sufficient to cover the costs of the information system between the group and its subsidiaries;

- the system must not contravene any local exchange control or tax regulations.

7.4.6   A portfolio approach to foreign exchange rate risk

A portfolio approach to foreign exchange rate risk is a variation on the principles of matching. Some currencies tend to move in the same way against sterling. For example, the Swedish krone (SEK) and the Norwegian krone (NOK) have tended in the past to move in the same way against the pound. Thus a company that has, for example, NOK payables and SEK receivables might offset them and consider the position as being naturally hedged.

If the amounts are large, it may be worthwhile to conduct a value at risk (VAR) exercise to determine the exact nature of the correlation between the £:SEK and the £:NOK exchange rate movements. The exercise should be able to demonstrate that in the past there was a certain confidence level that the two rates would not differ by more than a certain percentage. In cases in which such analysis is available and applicable, companies may decide not to undertake any external hedging – but there is no guarantee that past performance will be mirrored in the future.

7.4.7   Switching location

The company may, as a long-term strategy, switch its manufacturing to other locations, to change the currency of its cost base. For example, in November 2007, Rolls Royce set up a manufacturing plant in Singapore, partly to be located nearer to an important customer segment, but partly to reduce the effect of foreign exchange exposure on its exports to that country. There are obviously major strategic issues involved in such a change, however, over and above the management of foreign currency exposure, which have to be considered before taking this course of action.

7.4.8   Leads and lags

The lead and lag technique applies when a company has not purchased a bank product, such as a forward exchange contract, to hedge a transaction exposure in foreign currency. In other words this is not really a hedging technique at all, but simply an attempt to forecast exchange rates and then to take action based on the forecasts.

If the company has to make a payment in, for example, three months in a foreign currency that is expected to appreciate in value, it will 'lead', ie it will attempt to pay early so as to reduce the home currency cost of the payment. Naturally, the company will attempt to negotiate a discount to compensate for the early payment.

Obviously, the converse would apply if the foreign currency were expected to be about to fall in value. In that case, the company would attempt to 'lag', ie delay payment for as long as possible, subject to contractual obligations.

A similar process applies with exporters who try to lead, ie speed up, receipts if the foreign currency is expected to fall and who try to lag when the currency is expected to rise in value.

When the underlying commercial transactions are between different operating subsidiaries of the same group, there could be tax complications in leading and lagging: expert tax advice is required. In addition, care must be taken to ensure that any overseas exchange control regulations are not contravened. In order to decide whether leading or lagging is a viable proposition, the treasurer needs to know:

- the amount of discount to be paid or received in the leading or lagging;
- the forward rates that are currently available;
- interest rates;
- tax and exchange control implications.

The treasurer can then compare the benefits of leading or lagging with other courses of action.

7.5 Hedging philosophies

The three main philosophies in relation to hedging foreign exchange exposures are:

- hedge nothing;
- hedge everything;
- hedge selectively.

7.5.1 'Hedge nothing'

Small companies that are new to overseas trade often hedge nothing, because they are unaware of the risks of exchange rate exposure and because they do not know about the techniques of hedging. This situation is clearly dangerous, because a small firm is unlikely to have the capacity to absorb any significant exchange rate losses.

In theory, there is a case for larger companies to hedge nothing, because academic economic studies indicate that, *in the long term*, a 'no- hedge' policy should produce the same results as a fully hedged policy. Unfortunately, the famous maxim of Keynes, 'In the long run, we are all dead' can often be applied here: if a company makes a big loss because of an unhedged foreign exchange exposure, it may well go into administration or liquidation, and the fact that the company may, potentially, at some unspecified future date make a compensating fortuitous foreign currency gain will not be of any practical value.

If a company is a 'price maker' in the overseas market, or if demand for its products is inelastic, then it may decide not to hedge extended transaction exposure. The company can simply raise the price of its goods in foreign currency to cover currency depreciation.

7.5.2 'Hedge everything'

Hedging everything can eliminate transaction exposures, but it cannot eliminate economic exposures, and it gives rise to an 'opportunity cost'. For example, if the spot rates were to move in favour of the company between the start of the exposure and the receipt and conversion of the currency, the company will have 'lost out' – ie incurred an opportunity cost – if it has hedged the exchange exposure.

A hedge-everything philosophy is common in heavy engineering companies when currency transactions are large and 'one-off' and within which profit margins are tight. A variation on the policy is to use forward contracts to cover exposures when adverse exchange rate exposures are expected, and to use options when favourable movements seem likely.

In practice, many corporations with a hedge-everything philosophy use forward contracts to cover 'certain' cash flows in foreign currency and use options to cover cash flows that may arise, but which cannot be considered as 'certain'.

7.5.3 Hedge selectively

Selective hedging involves taking a view on the future movements of exchange rates, the object being to hedge only those exposures in relation to which the anticipated risk of loss exceeds the opportunity for gain.

One system of selective hedging is to set a maximum permissible exposure that will be based on the company's capital base, cash flow and profitability and also the degree of the company's risk aversion. Any exposure above the maximum would have to be hedged; any exposure below the stated maximum would either be left uncovered or it would be hedged, depending on the treasurer's decision.

In practice, limits on the size of an individual exposure and on the size of exposure to a particular currency will be set, so that the company does not employ its whole exposure allowance in a single uncovered position.

An open currency position should be monitored on a daily basis and a level set at which cover will be taken. One mechanism for doing this is the use of a 'stop-loss order'. For example, if a UK company is due to receive 10m from its overseas customer in three months' time, it may set the stop loss so as to sell the euro in the forward market if the exchange rate is 5% above the original rate. The stop will be moved downwards, but never upwards. If the exchange rate starts to move up from a low, the stop will be triggered close to, although not at, the lowest rate. (If the rate 'moves up', it means that the euro is depreciating, because there are more euros than previously required to equal £1.)

A policy of selective hedging makes heavy demands on executive time and professional expertise. It requires a treasury system that is integrated into the budgetary control system so that future exchange exposures can be identified in a systematic way.

Many small and medium-sized companies will lack the expertise to hedge selectively and, in practice, such companies will often tend to hedge everything. Some multinational corporations meanwhile, will hedge selectively, unless they are mainly in heavy engineering or similar industries with large, one-off transactions and tight margins.

7.5 The link between hedging philosophy and business risk, operational risk and gearing

Companies that have a high business risk (eg contractors) or high operating risks (when there are high fixed costs that cannot be easily reduced in an economic downturn) should tend towards a hedge everything policy. These companies with a high business and operating risk cannot usually afford a high financial risk from foreign currency exposure. Similar principles apply to gearing and interest rate exposure, so companies with relatively high gearing or relatively low interest cover should tend towards a hedge everything policy.

7.6 A summary of theoretical arguments against hedging transaction exposure

7.6.1 The capital asset pricing model (CAPM)

The capital asset pricing model (CAPM) differentiates between foreign exchange as an unsystematic risk and foreign exchange as a systematic risk. Its conclusion in each case is, however, that hedging is not appropriate.

Unsystematic risks are risks that apply to particular individual companies, rather than to all companies taken as a whole. If exchange rate risk (and interest rate risk, for that matter) can be considered as unsystematic, then investors can eliminate such risks by holding a diversified portfolio of shares. Gains on some shares in the portfolio due to exchange rate movements would be offset by losses on other shares in the portfolio that would be adversely affected by the same exchange rate fluctuations. Thus, CAPM argues that, if foreign exchange exposure is unsystematic, then a no- hedge policy should apply from the point of view of maximising the wealth of a diversified shareholder.

If foreign exchange risk is considered to be a systematic risk – one that is embodied in the market as a whole – then hedging instruments will be priced in a rational way to take account of the volatility of the relevant currencies. When hedging instruments are priced in a rational way, the market can be said to be 'efficient'. If this applies, there will be no added value from hedging, and indeed the cost of hedging, as represented by option premiums, management time and bid – offer spreads, will destroy shareholder value.

7.6.2 The Modigliani and Miller (MM) Propositions (1958)

In 1958, economists Franco Modigliani and Merton Miller argued, in connection with corporate gearing, that shareholders could obtain 'home made leverage' by borrowing on their own account instead of leaving the borrowing to be carried out by the companies in which they owned shares. Taking this proposition a step further, it could be argued that investors should obtain 'home made hedging' by hedging on their own account. Individual shareholders could each make their own personal arrangements to hedge currency exposures from their own portfolio of shares. Hedging by individual corporate entities from the investors' portfolio would be counterproductive, because this corporate hedging would counteract the hedging of the individual investor.

7.7 A summary of arguments that contradict the no hedge recommendations

7.7.1 CAPM

Even if the CAPM is considered valid in relation to foreign exchange exposures, and even if it can be accepted that foreign exchange markets are efficient, there could still be adverse consequences from failure to manage a corporate's currency exposure. If large adverse changes in exchange rates were to coincide with the receipt or payment of a large sum of foreign currency, then the exchange rate movement could give rise to serious liquidity problems.

Although, in the long run, all such gains and losses should cancel out, that would be of little consolation to shareholders, managers and creditors if the liquidity crisis had forced the corporate to go into liquidation. This phenomenon is known as the 'cost of financial distress'.

7.7.2 Modigliani and Miller

Individual investors are unlikely to be able to diversify exchange risk as efficiently as corporates. There are minimum amounts for hedging instruments such as forward exchange contracts, options and futures, so it may not be possible for an individual investor to tailor a hedge to meet their own requirements. Major corporates also might have access to techniques such as accelerating or delaying intercompany payments in accordance with foreign exchange market conditions. In addition, the managers have access to information on their companies' foreign exchange exposures that is simply not available to the private investor. Finally the cost of hedging may be far lower for corporates than it is for individual shareholders.

It may be that the above arguments are less cogent in the case of institutional investors such as pension funds, which should have the same 'bulk power' in hedging deals as major corporates. In addition, the managers of institutions may be capable of hedging the foreign exchange risk from their portfolio of investments in a more cost- effective manner than would be relying on the managers of the various companies to hedge the risk of each corporate entity independently.

In the case of UK pension funds, however, the liabilities of these funds are to pay pensions denominated in sterling, thus UK pension funds would presumably require stability of returns from their shares in terms of sterling. This again would tend to support the hedging of foreign exchange exposures by companies.

7.8 Other arguments supporting the management of transaction exposures by corporates

- Corporate hedging reduces the volatility of earnings and the volatility of future cash flows. This, in turn, reduces the risk of incurring the costs of financial distress.

- In some tax regimes, fortuitous foreign currency gains may be liable to taxation, whereas foreign currency losses may not be tax deductible.

- Where a tax schedule is convex, in that higher rates of tax are levied on the higher amounts of taxable profits in the same way that income tax bands vary with different amounts of taxable income, stable profits over time will mean lower taxes. A volatile range of taxable profits will incur taxes at higher rate bands in years of high profits.

- Lower risk should result in a lower cost of capital. The cost of capital (after some adjustments) is the basis of the discount rate applied to future cash flows when valuing the business; thus the lower the discount rate, the higher the value of the firm.

- A lower risk of financial distress may increase the debt capacity of a hedged company.

- Managers and employees cannot hold a diversified portfolio of jobs. Good managers should be attracted to firms that manage foreign currency exposures, because such firms are likely to be affected to a lesser extent by the costs of financial distress.

- Suppliers and customers will prefer to deal with less risky firms.

7.9 Practical issues relating to the implementation of foreign exchange risk management programmes.

For major companies, it is the corporate treasury division that is charged with the responsibility of managing of foreign currency exposures. A critical success factor is the accurate forecasting of these exposures. The accurate forecasting of foreign currency denominated receipts and payments is essential if the hedging programme is to meet the needs of the organisation. Inaccurate forecasts can result in over-hedging exposures that do not materialise or in under-hedging those that do. In addition, companies would benefit when setting the overall hedging policy (hedge everything/hedge selectively/hedge nothing) from having a clear picture of the financial effects of specific percentage changes in relevant exchange rates and the likelihood of such exchange rate movements occurring.

To implement the day-to-day hedging of transaction exposure management, the corporate treasurer must make meaningful assessments of exposure to uncommitted forecasted transactions, which means that a corporate treasurer needs to understand the commercial reality of the business. Corporate treasurers need to have detailed discussions with the appropriate company managers to ascertain:

- whether it is possible to increase foreign currency denominated sale prices to compensate for adverse exchange rate movements. To the extent that this is possible, then there is already a natural hedge in place;

- whether, and to what extent, increased costs through exchange movements can be passed on to the customer via increased sales prices.

These estimates of price elasticity will help the treasurer to understand to what extent the sales volume decreases due to a sales price increase. These effects need to be modelled to determine the true foreign exchange exposure and hence the hedging policy.

In addition to the understanding of business behaviour, a treasurer needs appropriate treasury systems to help forecast exposures and implement policy, but, the crucial processes of foreign exchange rate exposure forecasting in many organisations still leaves much to be desired. As a result of the requirements of accounting rules, such as International Accounting Standard, for example IAS 39, many non-financial services organisations have developed accounting IT systems that have streamlined the process of confirming, settling and accounting relating to dealing and hedging transactions. These systems only track the resultant process after the dealing and hedging decisions have been made, however, and they are not forecasting tools.

Even now, many multinational companies rely on foreign exchange exposure management forecasting processes that are manually driven, time consuming and prone to error. Many treasury departments neglect the critical pre-trade activities, such as sales, purchasing, credit given and credit taken: key decisions that will determine the extent and timing of the foreign exchange transaction exposure. Many corporate treasurers today rely on manual data entry into complex spreadsheets. This often results in incomplete and unreliable foreign exchange exposure data, due to incorrect data inputting and formula errors. At a more strategic level, techniques such as value at risk, which can be used to provide details of maximum likely changes in exchange rates over a given period at a specific confidence level, are often ignored. This reliance on spreadsheets and specific individual expertise can often mean that companies' hedging programmes are 'not fit for purpose', especially when key individuals move on.

This state of affairs is not inevitable. Sophisticated IT systems are available to enhance the forecasting of specific foreign exchange transaction exposures. Furthermore, multinational companies can look beyond point-in-time foreign exchange exposure forecasts to examine how foreign exchange movements affect cash flows and company value over time. Systems now exist to automate all of these forecasts, making it easier to aggregate the right data, to analyse it over time and to implement decisions to protect cash flows and company value. By installing automated systems, the company is protected when key personnel move on, and information can be produced to facilitate a forward-looking foreign exchange risk management policy that is part of the company's overall strategy.

Pricewaterhousecoopers has produced research (*What's your future FX risk?*, W Koester, 2 October 2007, GT News website) to show that companies that automate risk management processes, as opposed to automating the accounting processes under IAS 39, are 50% more likely to benefit from accurate, timely, consistent and complete risk information. This should result in faster and better risk management decisions. In addition, more timely and efficient information allows the company to execute transactions at the time of day and time of month that affords them the best rate of exchange, rather than rushing to make costly last-minute, end-of-the-month transactions.

Finally, accurate forecasting linked with the accounting (eg IAS 39) systems can be very helpful for compliance with regulations such as Sarbanes-Oxley certification (see Topic 11).

7.10   The role of a 'budget' rate of exchange in planning

Nowadays, even the smallest businesses must plan and one essential basic planning tool is the projected profit and loss account (known as an 'operating budget') and a projected cash budget. For a business with anticipated receipts or purchases denominated in foreign currency, there is an added complication: the projected spot rates at which the receipts or payments will be converted.

Most businesses therefore decide upon a 'budget rate of exchange' and this rate is used to convert all anticipated currency receipts or payments into home currency for the purposes of the operating and cash budgets. The company can select any rate it wishes for this exercise, but, in practice, the three- month or six- month forward rate is usually chosen. The forward rate in no way claims to predict what the spot will be at the end of the relevant period; it simply reflects the current spot rate today and the current interest rate differentials in the two countries. The forward rate is usually selected, simply because it is the one that is available at the time that the budget is prepared.

If all other parts of the budget are totally accurate (which is most unlikely in practice!), then any actual conversions that are made at more favourable rates will result in extra profit and more cash than that projected in the budgets; the converse will apply if the actual rates used for conversion are less favourable. By making regular comparisons between the actual rates of exchange used for conversions and the budget rate, companies should be able to assess the likely effect of exchange rate movements on the company's year- end profits and cash position.

7.11   How internal communication can help to control transaction exposure

Transaction exposure can arise from decisions taken by purchasing and sales personnel who cannot be expected to have a detailed knowledge of the treasury function.

It is essential, however, that sales and purchasing personnel are broadly aware of the impact of their decisions on the company's exposure position and, to this end, they require a broad understanding of:

- hedging techniques and forward rates;
- how to use forward rates in comparison to leading and lagging.

Likewise, the treasurer must be made aware of the likely long- term sales volumes in different currencies and how sensitive such sales are to price changes. This information will be particularly important in monitoring extended transaction exposure.

Treasurers should also liaise on a regular basis with sales and purchasing staff to ensure that these people know the current rates (spot or forward) and can therefore quickly calculate whether a particular deal will be profitable in home currency terms.

7.12   Accountancy and derivatives

The accountancy treatment of derivatives for many corporates will be governed by the US Financial Accounting Standard (FAS) 133 or by the International Accountancy Standard, IAS 39. For our purposes, these regulations can be considered to have the same implications, whichever of them is used by the corporate. Readers will be relieved to learn that this book is not going to attempt to demonstrate how the accounting entries must be made when a position is taken in the derivatives market – but readers need to be aware of the effects of these accounting standards on hedging operations. All companies must have systems that can track derivatives positions from the moment the position in the derivative market is taken to the moment at which that exposure ends, and many companies have sophisticated IT systems to do just that.

There is a potential presentational problem that may arise from the accountancy regulations FAS 133 or IAS 39. This problem can be illustrated in connection with forward exchange contracts. When a company enters into a forward exchange contract, the purpose is to fix the cost or revenue or cash flow in home currency terms. The forward contract will have a value in its own right, so that a forward contract for the bank to sell foreign currency to importers will show a gain if the spot value of that currency rises, or show a loss if the spot value of the currency falls. The opposite will apply to forward exchange contracts for the bank to buy foreign currency from an exporter, because these contracts will show a gain if the spot currency falls in value and they will show a loss if the spot currency rises in value.

Let us consider the position when a forward contract spans company year end, for example when a future foreign currency receipt or payment is hedged by a forward contract entered into in November and maturing in February (assuming that the company's financial year ends on 31 December). Any gain or loss on the forward contract between November and 31 December will have to be shown in the published accounts, but the corresponding change in the value of the underlying hedged item will not appear in the published accounts. Thus the accountancy treatment of the derivative will mean that the company's income statements will show additional volatility from the derivative, whereas the 'economic' effect will be to reduce such volatility by hedging.

The only way in which the above accountancy treatment can be avoided is for the company to obtain the agreement of the auditors that the derivative qualifies for 'hedge accounting' status. The formalities and documentation required to obtain 'hedge accounting' status are, however, time-consuming and complex. Some companies choose not to apply for 'hedge accounting' status for their derivative hedges, and their policy is to explain the income volatility to shareholders and other interested parties. Other companies consider it necessary to obtain 'hedge accounting' status, so as to avoid any artificial volatility appearing in the income statement. Much depends on the assessment of possible shareholder reactions and how willing shareholders, creditors and bankers are likely to be to listen to explanations of how the volatility has arisen. (Readers should note the similarities with translation exposure, covered in Topic 8.)

7.13 An overview of the links between risk management, funding and capital structure in the context of enterprise- wide risk management

Traditionally, risk management in non-financial services companies was dealt with by different departments. The various departments focused on managing what were perceived to be 'their' risks without any consideration of the implications of their actions for the organisation as a whole. This has been described as a 'silo' approach, in which every department jealously guarded its independence as far as risk management was concerned. Thus, for example, an insurance section would deal with insurance, the corporate treasury section would handle foreign exchange and interest rate exposures, and the finance section would manage capital structure (gearing). Each department or section would remain in its own 'silo' and there would be no communication between them.

Nowadays, larger businesses are beginning to practise the concept of enterprise-wide risk management. This discipline recognises that there is a link between risk management (for example, insurance and foreign exchange risk), capital structure (the optimal ratio of debt finance to equity finance for the company) and funding (the mix of long-term committed loan funds and short term borrowed funds), and that, when a change takes place in one of these areas it affects the others.

As time goes by, the concept of Enterprise- wide risk management will become more and more topical in non- financial services corporates, and readers are advised to watch developments.

Topic 8

Foreign currency translation exposure and foreign currency economic exposure

On completion of this topic, you should be able to:

- understand the nature and implications of translation exposure;

- differentiate between profit and loss, and balance sheet translation exposure;

- understand how currency borrowing and swaps can be used to manage translation exposure;

- evaluate the benefits and drawbacks of managing translation exposure;

- understand the nature of foreign currency economic exposure;

- appreciate the difficulties in the management of foreign currency economic exposure.

8.1 Translation exposure

8.1.1 The nature of translation exposure

Translation exposure arises as a result of the changes in the value in home currency of overseas assets and liabilities from one balance sheet date to the next. It also relates to the consolidations of the year's profits and the effect on reported earnings per share when some of the profits relate to an overseas subsidiary.

This topic does not seek to provide a detailed understanding of the accountancy treatment of translation gain or loss, but merely seeks to explain the broad principles.

8.1.2 Translation exposures and balance sheets

The largest translation effect for most international groups is the result of translating the net worth of overseas subsidiaries into the company's reporting currency for the purpose of producing consolidated accounts. The value in the reporting currency of the group is calculated by using the rate of exchange that applied at the balance sheet date. Hence, even if the net worth of the subsidiary were to remain unchanged between balance sheet dates when denominated in the currency of that subsidiary, there would be a translation gain or loss in the reporting currency of the consolidated accounts, depending on the movement of exchange rates between the two balance sheet dates.

8.1.3 Translation exposure and its effect on the profit and loss account

The effect of translation exposure on the profit and loss account is easily explained by an example. A UK- based company may have a subsidiary located in the USA. Naturally, the year's profits, denominated in US dollars, will have to be included in sterling terms in the consolidated accounts. This consolidation will occur even though the profits may be retained in the subsidiary. (Under Standard Statement of Accounting Practice (SSAP) 20, UK companies can use year- end exchange rates or average exchange rates for the year. The US equivalent, FAS B52, allows, in practice a weighted average exchange rate to be applied to the profit and loss statement.)

The sterling figure produced in the consolidated profit- and- loss account will affect the group's annual reported earnings and the reported earnings per share.

8.1.4 Specific examples of translation exposure on profit and loss accounts

---

Example 8.1

In this example, we shall look at a UK company with a Danish subsidiary, which uses the year-end rate to translate its overseas profits for the published accounts.

The profit forecasts by City analysts for the current financial year are £95m, based on forecast UK profits of £45m and forecast profits of the Danish subsidiary of DKK500m at a forecast exchange rate of DKK10 = £1.

The following shows the various outcomes at different year-end exchange rates, assuming that the UK profits are actually £45m and the Danish profits are actually DKK 500m.

Year-end Rate/£	DKK8 = £1	DKK10 = £1	DKK12 = £1
UK profits £m	45	45	45
Danish profits DKK500m	62.5	50	41.7
Group total (£s)	107.5	95	86.7

There are various possible solutions to overcome this potential translation exposure.

1. Arrange a forward contract for the bank to buy DKK500m at the year end. This contract will not be fulfilled, but will be closed out on maturity at the year end.

    If the Danish krone has weakened at the year end, the paper loss on consolidated earnings will be matched by a cash gain on the close- out of the forward contract. If the krone has gained in value at the year end, there will be a paper gain on consolidated earnings matched by a cash loss on close- out.

2. Arrange a currency put option for DKK500m. If the Danish krone has weakened, the currency option can be sold for its intrinsic value to offset the paper loss on consolidated earnings. If the krone has strengthened at the year end, the option will be abandoned, with the cost of the premium having been paid by the company.

3. It may be possible to change accounting policy if the auditors and the accountancy rules allow this, so that, instead of using year- end spot rates to convert the profits in the consolidated accounts, average rates for the year are used. In this case, likely exchange rates to be applied on consolidation of profits should be capable of a reasonably accurate estimate well before year end.

    Most accountancy conventions insist that assets and liabilities are translated at closing rates, but, in some countries – for example the UK – average rates can be used for conversion of the annual profits. Auditors normally allow only occasional changes in the basis of consolidation of profits and companies will certainly not be allowed to chop and change at will, depending on which method proves more favourable each year.

4. The company should undertake a serious public relations exercise to educate analysts to understand the effect of exchange rate movements on the profit stream.

5. For 'strong' companies, treating the investment community with respect and avoiding the use of a 'cash' hedge must be the preferred course, but this may not be possible for a company that is not considered to be a 'blue- chip' company, because of potential adverse reactions from shareholders, bankers and creditors.

8.1.5 Specific examples of translation exposure on balance sheets

---

Example 8.2

A UK company has just acquired a US subsidiary at a cost of US$150m. The payment was funded by a sterling loan of £100m, which was converted to US$150m at the spot rate of 1.5. There was a net worth of £100m immediately before the transaction and no currency assets or liabilities existed until this acquisition. Immediately after the acquisition, the group balance sheet would look like this:

	Assets £m		Liabilities £m
(US $150m) Dollar Assets	100	Debt (£)	100
Sterling Assets	<u>100</u>	Equity	<u>100</u>
	<u>200</u>		<u>200</u>

The gearing is 100% (debt/equity)

The net worth is £100m

In many loan agreements, there are covenants under which banks require companies to meet certain financial conditions. In the documentation, financial targets may have to be met. Two of the most common are the 'gearing test' and the 'maintenance of net worth', or 'consolidated net worth', tests. Let us assume that the bank insisted that this company agree to a loan covenant that requires a minimum net worth of £80m and a maximum gearing ratio (debt/equity) of 125%.

Let us now look at the year-end balance sheet in one year's time, making the unlikely, but necessary, assumption that the only change was the closing spot rate between the pound and the dollar.

There will be various alternative outcomes depending on the year-end spot rate:

Assumption 1:

All sterling debt and dollar rises to US$1 = £1.

	Assets £m		Liabilities £m
(US$150m) Dollar Assets	150	Debt (£)	100
Sterling Assets	100	Equity	150
	250		250

The gearing is 67% (100 ÷ 150 x 100).

The net worth is £150m.

Assumption 2:

Dollar falls to US$2 = £1 and debt is all sterling.

	Assets £m		Liabilities £m
(US$150m) Dollar assets	75	Debt (£)	100
Sterling assets	100	Equity	75
	175		175

The gearing is 133% (100 ÷ 75 x 100).

The net worth is £75m.

What we find from this simple example is that the reported gearing and net worth of the company will be changed each year, depending on the exchange rate prevailing at the year end. Because the company had agreed a 125% gearing covenant and a maintenance of net worth test at £80m, there would be a problem. This is all the worse because the movement in exchange rates may well only be temporary.

8.1.6 The use of foreign currency borrowing to hedge balance sheet translation exposure

In the above example, the solution to the net worth problem is straightforward: all that is required is to match foreign currency assets with foreign currency liabilities. In this case, both sides of the balance sheet will be equally affected, as shown in Example 8.3.

Example 8.3

We repeat, for convenience, the opening balance sheet of the previous example when the spot rate was $1.50 = £1.

	Assets £m		Liabilities £m
(US$150m) Dollar assets	100	(US $150 loans)	100
Sterling assets	100	Equity	100
	200		200

    The gearing is 100%.

    The net worth is £100m.

Let us now examine the outcome had the borrowing been denominated in US dollars (US$150m at 1.50) (**Outcome 1**).

The next year's balance sheet, assuming all conditions are as before (ie the only change is that the year-end spot rate is US$1 = £1) would look as follows.

	Assets £m		Liabilities £m
(US$150m) Dollar assets	150	(US $150 at $1 = £1)	150
Sterling assets	100	Equity	100
	250		250

    The gearing is 150%.

    The net worth is £100m.

Let us now see what happens when the closing rate at the next balance sheet date is US $2 = £1 (**outcome 2**).

	Assets £m		Liabilities £m
(US$150m) Dollar assets	75	(US$150 at US$2 = £1)	75
Sterling assets	100	Equity	100
	175		175

    The gearing is 75% (debt/equity).

    The net worth is £100m.

This currency borrowing achieves the desired effect on maintenance of net worth, but gearing increases as sterling weakens (Outcome 1), and reduces gearing as sterling

---

strengthens (Outcome 2). Thus, matching the net foreign currency assets of the company with foreign currency borrowings will stabilise the reported net worth, but will not stabilise the reported gearing. Treasurers should seek to negotiate loan covenants that will not be affected by translation exposures. If such covenants are not available, they should seek covenants that relate only to net worth, or match the assets by 50% only by currency borrowing if there are gearing covenants (see Section 8.1.7).

8.1.7 Managing translation exposures by matching 50% currency borrowings and 50% sterling finance

Example 8.4

Suppose the US dollar assets of US$150m shown in the previous three balance sheet examples had been originally matched with half sterling and half dollar debt when the spot rate was US$1.50. The balance sheet would have looked like this.

	Assets £m		Liabilities £m
(US $150m) Dollar assets	100	Loans (US$75 at 1.5 = £50 + £50)	100
Sterling assets	<u>100</u>	Equity	<u>100</u>
	<u>200</u>		<u>200</u>

Let us now look at the outcome for the next balance sheet when US$1= £1, ie sterling has weakened.

	Assets £m		Liabilities £m
(US $150m) Dollar assets	150	Loans (US$75 at 1 = £75 + £50)	125
Sterling assets	<u>100</u>	Equity	<u>125</u>
	<u>250</u>		<u>250</u>

The gearing is 100%.

The net worth is £125m.

Now let us see the outcome when sterling has strengthened at the next balance sheet date to US$2 = £1.

	Assets £m		Liabilities £m
(US $150m) Dollar Assets	75	Loans (US$75 at 2 = 37.5 + 50)	87.5
Sterling Assets	<u>100</u>	Equity	<u>87.5</u>
	<u>175</u>		<u>175</u>

The gearing is 100%.

The net worth is £87.5m.

Thus, it is possible to hedge translation exposures in relation to net worth or gearing by currency borrowing. It is not possible to hedge, however, both simultaneously by this method.

8.1.8 Considerations to bear in mind when using currency borrowing to hedge translation exposure

8.1.8.1 Borrowing in the currency of the assets to hedge balance sheet exposures

As we have seen, the company can initially eliminate the translation net worth exposure by financing the overseas asset purchases with borrowings in the same currency. Thus, any increase in the asset value because of exchange rate movements will be matched by an increase in the domestic currency equivalent of the loan, and vice versa.

Although the initial purchase can be hedged in this way, this technique cannot entirely eliminate the exposure in future years. The net worth of the subsidiary in terms of local currency will increase or decrease because of profits or losses, and dividend or interest payments. It is difficult to predict year-end net worth in advance.

Some companies make monthly estimates of translation exposure, so that they will not be 'caught out' by an unexpectedly large translations loss at the year end.

8.1.8.2 Other problems that can arise from foreign currency borrowing to hedge translation exposure

- Foreign currency borrowings will have to be rolled over at maturity and the borrower will have to pay the current market rate of interest at the renewal date.
- The borrowing may contravene local exchange controls.
- If the foreign currency appreciates and the assets are sold, there will be capital gains tax to pay. In some tax jurisdictions, there will be no tax relief against the extra cost of the loan.
- Servicing costs will be denominated in foreign currency and this will create a transaction exposure unless the overseas assets are generating sufficient foreign currency to cover this servicing.
- Foreign currency borrowing facilities are not available in certain soft currencies.
- If the asset does not require borrowings to fund its purchase, then borrowing to hedge translation exposures will artificially inflate the balance sheet and create unnecessary borrowing.
- If the asset is funded by an inter-company loan, there may be withholding tax complications.

8.1.9 Currency swaps

8.1.9.1 The use of currency swaps as an alternative to direct currency borrowing

We have already seen in Topic 2 how banks use short-term currency swaps to cover their own exposures in connection with forward contract commitments. We now examine how, as an alternative to direct currency borrowing, longer dated currency swaps can be used effectively to switch the currency in which a loan is denominated. A typical swap works as follows.

- In a typical currency swap, two different currencies are normally exchanged at the outset.

- During the life of the currency swap, the counterparties agree to exchange interest payments on the principal amounts originally exchanged.

- At maturity, the principal amounts on the currency swap are re- exchanged at a rate agreed at the outset. This pre- set rate is often agreed as the same rate as that which applied to the original exchange.

Note: there may be subsidised rates of interest available (eg export finance from a government- backed export support scheme) and companies might borrow in their own currency from this source and swap into the desired currency.

8.1.9.2   A numerical example of a currency swap

8.1.9.2.1   Example 8.5

A UK company, X plc, wants to borrow US$24m, repayable over ten years, to finance its US subsidiary. The company is not well known in the USA and does not have a credit rating, but it is well known on the UK markets.

Let us assume that the company can issue a sterling debenture at 8%, fixed for ten years, and that the following bank swap quote is available:

Rate US $	1.5 to £1
Interest on US $	5% fixed
Interest on £	8% fixed

The swap will operate as follows.

- **Day one:** X plc borrows £16m in the market and swaps it for US$24m.

- **Annual interest payments:** X plc will receive £1.28m and will pay US$1.2m.

- **At maturity:** X plc will pay the bank US$24m and will receive £16m in exchange.

Figure 8.1   Day one

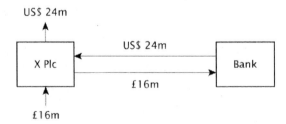

Figure 8.2   Annual interest payments

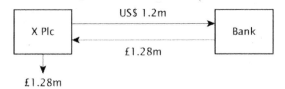

£1.28m

Note: it is assumed that the subsidiary will generate US dollar income to service the swap interest commitment.

Figure 8.3   Maturity

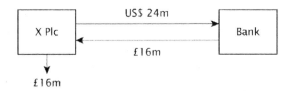

£16m

The company has created a synthetic US dollar loan in this case, but the rate of interest may well be much lower than that which would have been payable on direct US dollar borrowing, if the company has access to subsidised export finance for its sterling borrowing, or if the company is a well-respected borrower on the sterling debenture markets.

At maturity, X plc will be obliged to use £16m sterling towards the purchase of US$24m. If X plc remains creditworthy, however, the bank will almost certainly extend the swap, using the interest rates ruling at the time of maturity as the basis of the subsequent interest rate exchanges.

Note: particular care must be taken to obtain specialist tax advice and accounting advice to ensure that the sterling loan and currency swap are formally linked for tax and audit purposes.

8.1.10   Is it necessary to manage translation exposure?

Translation gains or losses do not result in any cash gain or loss. These changes are recorded in the reserves of the group and represent unrealised gains or losses on conversion of the net worth of overseas subsidiaries, or of other foreign currency denominated assets and liabilities. But such gains or losses affect the reported gearing and net worth of the consolidated position and, as such, they affect the attitudes of lenders, creditors and investors. Thus, translation gains or losses can ultimately result in a cash effect if the behaviour of creditors, bankers and shareholders is changed.

For a strong company with a first-class international reputation, the 'paper' gains or losses from translation exposure are not too important. Such companies can simply explain the true nature of the exposures to analysts and bankers, and there will be no adverse effects. Companies that are not so financially strong, meanwhile, may need to take banker and market perceptions much more seriously.

In addition, truly worldwide multinational companies can afford to ignore translation exposure because paper translation losses in some currencies will be offset by paper translation gains in other currencies.

Some companies do not attempt to manage translation exposure at all for the following reasons.

- There may be no cash inflow or outflow.

- The effect on the balance sheet can be likened to the effect of a revaluation of a factory in the balance sheet of a company with no foreign exchange commitments. If the factory is revalued, the increase in fixed assets in the published accounts is matched by an increase in reserves and a reduced gearing ratio – but there is no change in the actual cash position of the company.

- If hedging techniques are used, companies are paying money to hedge what is purely an accounting exercise. Many writers feel that it is not in the shareholder's interest to hedge paper gains and losses.

- In addition, hedging techniques involve a cash inflow or outflow (eg the gain or loss on a close- out of a forward contract) that is not justified when the translation gain or loss is of a non- cash nature.

- Investing in overseas assets is essentially a strategic decision, and investors may have invested in a particular company to take advantage of its overseas investments. Any form of hedging would nullify that strategic exposure. Indeed, when a company purchases assets in a country with a weak currency, it should ensure that the return on those assets is likely to be sufficient to compensate for the translation exposure.

The main argument for managing translation exposure is that, especially in the case of 'weaker' companies, changes in gearing or net worth, however caused, affect the attitudes of lenders, shareholders and creditors. This must ultimately affect the cash position. In addition, in many countries, translation losses are not allowable for tax purposes. Thus, such losses can affect reserves by more than would the equivalent trading loss.

Whenever any hedging action is taken to cover translation exposure, always:

- take specialist tax advice;

- make sure that the hedge is cost- effective – it is pointless spending precious management time in trying to construct a perfect translation exposure hedge; a hedge that approximately covers the translation exposure will be more cost-effective than a 'perfect hedge'.

In some countries, companies can now denominate their capital in currencies other than home currency if they wish. Hence, a major multinational could have part of its equity capital denominated in overseas currency to match overseas assets. There are, however, major problems in having equity denominated in a cocktail of currencies:

- there will be a need to explain and justify this to the market;

- what happens if the currency base of assets changes?

- the tax position is unclear;

- separate dividend streams would be needed;

- essentially, there would be separate companies for each type of equity.

Hedging profit- and- loss translation exposure is always worthwhile in the following circumstances:

- if the corporate has tight loan covenants covering reported gearing or reported net worth that might be breached because of translation losses;
- if the chief executive has given a profit forecast to the share analysts for earnings that are exposed to translation fluctuations. It may be important to protect this commitment to retain credibility with the capital markets;
- if the company enjoys a high price- earnings ratio because of steady growth of reported accounting profits. This record may be an asset that is worth preserving, even though it means hedging a paper gain or loss with a cash gain or loss.

8.2   Economic exposure

Economic exposure arises from the structure of the business, the currency of competitors, and the way in which costs and prices respond to change. A brief definition might be 'the risk that long- term movements in relative exchange rates will cause structural changes that undermine long- term profitability'.

To illustrate the concept of economic exposure, for a UK company that exported to the USA in competition with Japanese suppliers, the relevant currency exchange rates on the face of it would be:

£:US$ and Japanese yen:US$. The potential implications of long- term changes in these exchange rates for the UK company can be summarised as in Table 8.1.

Table 8.1

Long-term currency movements not matched by changes in relative inflation	Effect on price competitiveness for sales to USA (other things being equal)
US$ appreciates against yen by more than it appreciates against sterling	Prices in dollar terms reduced for both Japan and UK sales Price benefit is greater for Japanese sales than for UK company's sales.
US$ appreciates against yen by less than it appreciates against sterling	Prices in dollar terms reduced for both Japan and UK sales Price benefit is greater for UK company's sales than for Japanese sales
US$ depreciates against yen by more than it depreciates against sterling	Prices in dollar terms increased for both Japan and UK sales Adverse price effect is greater for Japanese sales than for UK company's sales

US$ depreciates against yen by less than it depreciates against sterling	Prices in dollar terms increased for both Japan and UK sales
	Adverse price effect is greater for UK company's sales than for Japanese sales

While Table 8.1 looks quite clear, there is a major problem in trying to quantify economic exposure. In addition to forecasting exchange rate movements, it is necessary to forecast movements in relative inflation rates (or, better still, changes in input costs and output prices). If the move in the exchange rate is caused by relative inflation differences, then the effect of the change of exchange rate should be cancelled out by way of increased or decreased costs or prices. In addition, it is not easy to know exactly what the currency of cost base is for competitors. It is also even more difficult to ascertain whether and to what extent competitors have hedged their currency positions. Such hedging will nullify the effect of exchange rate movements for the amounts so covered.

8.2.1 Theoretical arguments for and against managing foreign exchange economic exposures:

Arguments for not managing foreign currency economic exposure by external techniques	Arguments for managing foreign currency economic exposure by external techniques
Purchasing power parity theory	**Purchasing power parity theory**
Movements in foreign exchange rates will be offset by changes in relative price levels (this is a simplistic summary of the purchasing power parity theory).	There are major problems with purchasing power parity theory.
If the above version of the purchasing power parity theory were to apply in practice, without any time lags, there would be no such thing as foreign exchange exposure, because any loss due to foreign exchange rate movements would be compensated for by a gain in price, and vice versa.	• The theory ignores the existence of international capital flows, as well as the transport and transactions costs associated with trade. • It fails to recognise the fact that many goods or services are not traded internationally.
Even if the purchasing power parity theory were to apply only to long term exchange rate changes, then there would be no pressing need to hedge economic exposures, because these exposures are acknowledged to be long term.	• The role of news is not considered. In the real world major unpredicted events often occur and these unexpected events are often referred to as news. • Exchange rates respond very quickly to new information, so news can often have an immediate impact on spot rates. • But prices of goods normally change much less quickly as a result of news, so the relevant price indices do not adjust as quickly as the spot rates. • In the long term. The general consensus is that there are substantial deviations from the PPP in the short run, but the case is less clear in the long term. • In addition, there is little evidence to support the view that changes in a company's input and out prices adjust in line with the general change in price levels in the countries concerned.

Market efficiency and self insurance	Market efficiency and self insurance
Currency markets do not provide bargains; rather they provide fair gambles based on fair prices.	Managers and employees cannot hold a diversified portfolio of jobs.
In the long run, gains and losses on unhedged foreign exchange exposures will tend to average out. Thus in the long run there will be no benefit from hedging.	Good managers should be attracted to firms that manage foreign currency exposures; as such, firms are likely to be affected to a lesser extent by the costs of financial distress.
The argument concludes that corporates could 'self insure' by simply allowing gains and losses to cancel out, and should aim to maximise the value of the firm without undue concern for the variation of the returns.	
Foreign exchange hedging, so the argument says, will reduce the value of the firm. Unless market imperfections exist, the returns from consistently hedged foreign exchange positions will equal those from consistently unhedged ones, if we ignore the cost of hedging.	

The general position regarding foreign currency economic exposure can be summarised as in Table 8.2.

Table 8.2

Companies that tend not to hedge foreign currency economic exposures:	Companies that are likely to be more inclined to consider hedging foreign currency economic exposures:
These companies:	These companies:
• have competitors with a similar currency of cost;	• compete against companies with a different currency of cost;
• have the flexibility to switch their own currency of cost easily by purchasing from a different source or by manufacturing in another country;	• have high fixed costs;
	• have little flexibility to switch their own currency of cost;
• have a differentiated product that is perceived by the market to have considerable non-price benefits;	• can forecast future uncontracted cash flows with enough certainty to make hedging viable;
• are cash rich (or have unused borrowing capacity) to provide a breathing space for the company to switch its operations should there be a long-term adverse movement in exchange rates;	• can persuade the tax authorities to agree to 'hedge accounting' for any financial instruments used (ie to agree that gains on the instruments can be offset against losses in the cash market, and vice versa, for tax purposes);
• cannot forecast long-term uncontracted cash flows with sufficient accuracy to be confident of the amount of hedging required (to over-hedge would be to speculate).	• can persuade the auditors to agree to 'hedge accounting' so that gains and losses on derivatives and underlying cash flows are netted off for tax and accounting purposes.

In summary, foreign currency economic exposure risks are often not managed because they are:

- not reported in the accounts;
- difficult to quantify.

Although there are sophisticated computer techniques that can provide a logical and quantifiable analysis of the currencies to which a company is economically exposed, many large companies tend not to make full use of these facilities.

8.2.2 Economic exposure and companies that operate only in their home country

A company that is entirely home based and which makes all of its payments and receipts in domestic currency can still have an economic exposure to foreign exchange risk if its market is subject to foreign competition. A typical example might be a UK-based coal- mining operation with all of its costs and revenues denominated in sterling.

In the case of imports from Australia, the foreign currency economic exposure could arise if the Australian dollar were to depreciate against sterling, without a corresponding change in relative price levels. In that situation, assuming the Australian exporter's costs were denominated in Australian dollars and assuming that it did not hedge its sterling receipts, then there would be scope for a price reduction in pound sterling terms for Australian coal.

8.10.2   The minimisation of economic exposure

The best methods for minimising economic exposure are internal techniques such as the following.

- The company must have a high level of efficiency with good profitability. This makes it less vulnerable to adverse economic changes.

- The diversification of suppliers, products, markets and countries of manufacture is essential. Multinational corporations are well placed in this respect.

- There must be active research on new products and new materials to help maintain diversity.

- The company may be able to exert political pressure to reduce competition via imports. (eg to prove that the competitors' products do not meet safety standards).

- The company must not become over- borrowed, otherwise its room for manoeuvre is restricted.

8.10   Brown Construction: a currency management case study

Brown Construction undertakes major construction projects in the USA. Part of the processing of the work is completed in the UK; the remainder is completed in the USA by Brown's wholly- owned US subsidiary.

The US buyers will accept bids only in US dollars, so Brown's prices will have to be US dollar denominated. When setting the price, Brown will be working on a particular budget exchange rate, or a range of rates, for assessing the viability of the deal in sterling terms.

Some of the construction projects are negotiated on a bilateral basis between Brown and the US purchaser, but many of the construction projects in which Brown Construction is involved are put out for competitive tender worldwide. Once again, the contract price will be denominated in US dollars, but there will be a considerable delay (perhaps three months) before Brown will be advised whether its bid for these projects has been successful.

When Brown Construction tenders under the competitive bid system, a tender bond is required as a precondition of tendering. The significance of the tender bond is that it commits Brown to fulfilling a contract should it be awarded. Failure to take up an awarded contract will result in a fine (perhaps 5% of the contract value). Brown's bank will have been a party to the tender bond, so if Brown does not pay any penalty for non- take- up of an awarded contract, then Brown's bank will be committed to making the payment on their behalf. The bank will have recourse to Brown for reimbursement of any such penalty payment. *Thus Brown Construction is committed to accepting US contracts if they are awarded.* (For a more detailed explanation of the problems of tender bonds, please see Topic 22.)

The tenders and all other negotiations are made in the name of the US subsidiary, so it is the subsidiary that receives the dollar payments from the purchasers. The UK parent will have invoiced its subsidiary for costs incurred in the UK. Most tax regimes insist on 'arms length' pricing when sales are made from one member of a group to another. Brown Construction follows this policy. Thus part of the group's profits will be generated in the UK company, representing a 'cost plus' charging policy, and the remainder will be generated in the US subsidiary, representing the added value of the US operation.

Twice a year, the US subsidiary pays a dividend to the UK parent. This represents only part the profit element on the value added in the US operation, because some profits are retained to finance future increases in the subsidiary's work in progress and in its capital expenditure.

The group is in a high- risk, cyclical industry with tight margins. The main competitors are Japanese companies. In addition there will probably be a high ratio of fixed costs to variable ones so that, in a downturn, it is not too easy to reduce costs in line with reduced sales revenue.

Brown Construction sources some of its raw materials from France and these euro-denominated payments constitute about 20% of Brown's cost base.

The sterling bank loan has covenants requiring maintenance of a maximum group gearing ratio (debt to equity). Breach of this covenant could result in the bank having the right to demand immediate repayment of the loan in full. The loan has ten years to go to maturity and interest is at 6% per annum fixed.

Assess the theoretical and practical issues that might determine whether Brown Construction should hedge its foreign currency exposures. If appropriate, suggest how such hedging should be put into effect and consider any precautions that should be taken.

8.3.1 Suggested approach: issues for Brown Construction to consider

8.3.1.1 Practical issues for Brown Construction

8.3.1.1.1 Transaction exposure

The corporate treasurer should check to see whether there are likely to be any changes in capital structure and funding for the organisation. Any changes in these areas would affect the 'risk capacity' of the business and hence would affect the amount of foreign exchange exposure that could be tolerated.

Before an exposure can be managed, it must be measured. Thus the corporate treasurer at Brown must have some information regarding:

- forecasts of the likely amount of US dollar sales from bilateral deals over the next 12 months;

- forecasts of the probability that tenders outstanding plus any other likely major project tenders over the next 12 months will be successful;

- value at risk (VAR) analysis showing a maximum amount by which the £:US$ rate may move adversely over the next 12 months at a given confidence level;

- the monetary effect of different percentage changes in the £:US$ exchange rate on Brown's cash flows and profits over the next 12 months.

Given the recent volatility in the £:US$ rate, it is likely that such forecasts will show that future exchange rate movements will have a significant effect on profit and cash flow, unless they are hedged.

We are told that the company is in a highly risky industry with large one- off payments; in addition, there will probably be a high ratio of fixed costs to variable ones. As Brown Construction is certainly not a price maker, and because dollar receipts will tend to be large 'lumpy' amounts, it cannot afford to take the risk of not hedging.

As a consequence, a hedge- everything policy would seem to be wise in relation to transaction exposure.

Brown should first try internal techniques to hedge the transaction exposure, including the following.

- A larger proportion of the preparatory work might be switched to the USA to switch the cost base. This would be a major, long- term decision, and strategic factors over and above transaction exposure will be involved in such decisions.

- Brown should ascertain whether any UK suppliers will be prepared to invoice in US$. Some suppliers – for example subsidiaries of US multinationals – may be willing to co- operate. Brown should, however, check that the dollar prices are still competitive in sterling terms.

- Brown should obtain quotes for cross rates to convert some US dollar receipts to euros, crediting the proceeds to a euro bank account. The benefit here is that euros credited to this account can cover the euro payments to French suppliers. In addition the impact of the bank's bid-offer spread will be reduced, because, by using a euro- denominated bank account, Brown avoids converting dollars to sterling, and then converting sterling to euros to pay French suppliers. Foreign currency bank accounts can be opened with the UK bank if required.

After netting as far as possible by means of internal techniques, external techniques can be considered for managing the remaining transaction exposures. Because the current (2007) trend seems to be for the US dollar to weaken against the pound, forward contracts should be used to cover amounts that can be considered certain. If the US$ continues to weaken against the £, forwards will hedge the downside at no cost, except for the bid–offer spread. Options could be used to hedge potential but uncertain receipts.

The dividend paid by the subsidiary to Brown should be hedged with a forward exchange contract, because both the amount and the timing of the payment are under Brown's control.

8.3.1.1.2   Pre- transaction exposures

The tenders are effectively pre- transaction exposures. Here, Brown is committed to accepting a commercial contract denominated in US dollars if the tender is successful, but if the tender is unsuccessful, there will be no US dollar receipts.

The problem with hedging pre- transaction exposures with a forward contract is that Brown Construction will not know for three months whether the commercial contract has been awarded. If a forward contract is taken out to cover this 'contingent' cash flow, the forward exchange contract itself could create an exposure. For example, if the commercial contract is not awarded, then there will not be any dollar receipts, so the bank will close out the forward contract. The result could be a gain or a loss for Brown, depending on the spot rate at the close out date.

Brown could hedge the pre- transaction exposure by way of options, but this will involve a large premium, bearing in mind that the underlying amount of dollars will be large.

Brown should consult its bankers to see if they can offer any solution to the problem. Sometimes, in cases in which a large international bank knows the industry and the companies that are tendering, it can enter into an arrangement with some of the bidders about the option. For example, there will be one currency option set up by the bank with an agreement that only the company whose bid is successful will take up the option and pay the premium. If none of the bank's clients are successful, the arrangement could be that the premium cost is split between the clients. In any event, every arrangement will depend on the particular circumstances that apply.

Alternatively, Brown may follow a policy as follows:

- if the company thinks there is an 85% or better chance of obtaining the contract, it may take out a forward exchange contract;
- if the company thinks there is a 35–85% chance of obtaining the contract, it may take out an option;
- if the company thinks there is less than a 35% chance of obtaining the contract, it will not take out any derivative cover.

8.3.1.1.3   Implementation issues for hedging transaction exposures

Given the gearing covenants in the loan documentation, the company should ensure that it obtains 'hedge accounting' status for its derivative hedges. Otherwise, there could be a breach of covenant caused by the 'mark to market' effect of derivatives.

In addition to the understanding of business behaviour, a treasurer needs appropriate treasury systems to help forecast exposures and implement policy. These systems will help with auditing and compliance with Sarbanes–Oxley regulations (see Topic 11)

8.3.1.1.4   Translation exposures

Given the nature of the business and the gearing covenants, any substantial loss shown in the published accounts could adversely alter the perceptions of bankers, shareholders and creditors. Thus, although translation exposure does not involve any cash gain or loss, it is probably wise for a company of this type to hedge it.

One method of hedging could be to borrowing US dollars and convert the proceeds to sterling to pay off the sterling loan. This would create a dollar liability (the dollar borrowing) to match the US dollar denominated assets. A currency swap would be a more appropriate technique, however, because this leaves the existing sterling borrowing undisturbed and thus avoids any penalties for early repayment of the sterling loan.

Because there are gearing covenants in the sterling loan agreements, it may be wise for Brown to match around half of the US dollar assets with a currency swap. This will hedge translation gearing, as opposed to hedging translation net worth. Brown should take specialist tax and accountancy advice to ensure that the swap and the assets are matched for tax and accounting purposes. The US dollar interest cost will help to hedge some of the US dollar transaction exposure.

If any profit forecasts have been made to market analysts, the company should take out a currency option to ensure that credibility is not lost by adverse exchange rate movements. This will be less necessary if the average rate is used for consolidation of profits.

8.3.1.1.5 Economic exposure

On the face of it, the relevant rates are £:US$ and Japanese yen:US$, but in practice, this economic exposure probably cannot be quantified. Brown may not know the currency cost base of its competitor nor whether the competitor hedges. Thus this exposure may not be hedged, because it will not be reported in the published accounts and it will be difficult to quantify.

Brown should try to be as competitive as possible in non- pricing areas to help offset any competitive disadvantage from any long term adverse movements in exchange rates. In addition, it will help if Brown has some committed unused bank facilities available, or some 'disaster recovery' plans, whereby emergency cash can be generated by selling assets or reducing costs if this becomes necessary.

8.3.1.1.6 Other arguments to support the hedging of exchange rate risks by Brown Construction

1. Corporate hedging reduces the volatility of earnings and the volatility of future cash flows. This in turn reduces the risk of incurring the costs of financial distress.

2. Lower risk should result in a lower cost of capital. The cost of capital (after some adjustments) is the basis of the discount rate applied to future cash flows when valuing the business, thus the lower the discount rate, the higher the value of the firm.

3. A lower risk of financial distress may increase debt capacity for a hedged company.

4. Managers and employees cannot hold a diversified portfolio of jobs. Good managers should be attracted to firms that manage foreign currency exposures, because such firms are likely to be affected to a lesser extent by foreign exchange fluctuations.

5. The theoretical arguments against hedging (CAPM, PPP, Market Efficiency and self- insurance), even if valid in general terms, are all applicable over long

periods – but a single large loss on foreign currency could be enough to put Brown Construction into liquidation.

For more detailed explanation of point (5.), please refer back to Topic 7 and the earlier sections of this topic.

Please refer to Topic 11 for details of internal controls that should help to reduce the danger of fraud and human error in connection with foreign exchange and derivative transactions. These aspects have not been covered in Topics 7 and 8.

Topic 9

Interest rate risk

At the end of this topic, you should be able to:

- explain and assess the factors that influence the short and long term rates of interest and changes in these rates of interest;
- differentiate between real and nominal rates of interest;
- understand the principles that determine forward rates of interest;
- assess the factors that determine how companies manage interest rate risk;
- understand how derivatives such as FRAs, caps, collars and interest rate swaps can be used to manage interest rate risk.

9.1   Introduction

In economic theory, interest is the price paid to persuade those with money to invest it rather than spend it. Interest rates should reflect the interaction between the demand for, and the supply of, money.

Rates of interest are normally expressed as a percentage payable (in the case of fixed rate bonds, this is known as a 'coupon') and the percentage is calculated on a per annum basis, unless there is anything specifically stated to the contrary. Thus, for example, if a saver puts £100,000 into a fixed-term, one-year deposit at a stated interest rate of 10% per annum, they will receive £10,000 interest at the end of the one-year term. If a saver puts £100,000 into a fixed-term six-month deposit at a stated interest rate of 10% per annum, however, they will receive approximately £5,000 interest at the end of the six-month term. The reason for expressing interest rates on a per annum basis is to make comparison easier.

There is an inverse relationship between the prevailing rate of interest at any one time and the market value at that time of fixed coupon loans or bonds: ie fixed-interest or fixed-coupon bond prices fall when interest rates increase and these bond prices rise when interest rates fall. For instance, imagine a 10% coupon bond with exactly two years to maturity and a nominal value of £100. If an investor were to purchase this bond on the market and hold it to maturity, the cash flows for the investor would be £10 (the coupon) in one year's time and £110 (the coupon and the nominal value at maturity) in two year's time. If the prevailing rate of interest for such a bond on the date of purchase were 5%, then its market price would be the present value of the future cash flows discounted at 5% per annum. Conversely, if the prevailing rate of interest for this bond on the date of purchase were 7%, then its market price would be the present value of the future cash flows discounted at 7% per annum.

For those readers who are familiar with discounted cash flow techniques, the market prices of the bond at the two prevailing rates of interest would be as shown in Table 9.1. Readers who are not familiar with discounted cash flow techniques will note that future monetary cash flows are converted to present values by dividing by the required rate of interest adjusted by the number of years to maturity. Obviously, the bigger the divisor, the lower the present value. Finally, please note that terms such as 'yield to maturity', 'gross redemption yield' and 'required rate of return' are synonymous with 'required rate of interest' for the purposes of these calculations.

Table 9.1

	Cash flow in money terms (£)	Present value calculation if Required rate of interest is 5%	Present value at 5% (£)	Present value calculation if required rate of interest is 7%	Present value at 7% (£)
Year one cash flow	10	$10 \div 1.05$	9.52	$10 \div 1.07$	9.35
Year two cash flow	110	$110 \div (1.05)^2$	99.77	$110 \div (1.07)^2$	96.08
Market value today			109.29		105.43

There is an important distinction between 'nominal' and 'real' interest rates. A real rate of interest is the nominal or 'coupon' rate, *less* the rate at which money is losing its purchasing power. Calculating real interest rates can involve controversy, because there are significantly different ways of calculating rates of inflation. For example, in the UK there are the Retail Price Index (RPI) and Consumer Price Index (CPI) indices, each of which gives different figures for inflation because the items on which their calculations are based are different. In November 2007, the RPI showed an annual inflation rate of 4.2%, whereas the CPI showed a rate of 2.1%.

It is generally agreed that savers demand a real return from their investments. Academic studies disagree on what this real required return is and, in any case, other factors, such as the creditworthiness of the borrower, influence investors' requirements. Let us assume, however, that, for a particular bond with a long maturity, the required real return is 2%. If inflationary expectations over the life of the bond are expected to be 3%, then the required return on that bond will be 5% per annum. If there is a change in the expected rate of inflation over the life of the bond to, say, 4%, for example, then the required rate of return on the bond will rise to 6% per annum.

This requirement for a real rate of return arises because inflation reduces the purchasing power of money. For example, let us consider an extreme hypothetical scenario in which a bond has a nominal return of 5% and inflationary expectations are 8% over the life of the bond. In this case, the interest received on the bond would be more than offset by the loss of purchasing power via inflation on future interest and capital repayment. Thus inflationary expectations are a key determinant of interest rates, especially of longer term rates. Changes in the forecasts of future inflation are therefore likely to be reflected in changes in the longer term interest rates.

In addition to inflation and inflationary expectations, rates of interest also reflect investor perceptions of varying degrees of risk. For example, the rates of interest on German government bonds and on Italian government bonds of the same maturity are different despite the fact that both sets of bonds are denominated in euros. This reflects differing risk perceptions on the part of investors.

Thus, within any economy, there will be a multiplicity of interest rates, reflecting varying expectations of inflation and risk.

9.2 Short- term interest rates

'Short- term' is normally taken to cover deposits for periods of up to a year. Short- term interest rates are heavily influenced by the rates set by central banks or similar bodies. In the UK short- term interest rates are heavily influenced by the Monetary Policy Committee (MPC), while in the euro area it is the European Central Bank (ECB) that performs this function. Central banks, or their equivalents, usually consider price stability to be their primary role, so they set short- term rates with the objective of keeping future inflation within a predetermined band. When there seems to be a danger that inflation may rise above the top band limit, short- term interest rates are raised to encourage people to save rather than spend and to encourage businesses to defer capital spending. Thus, higher short- term rates are applied with the objective of reducing demand (after a time lag) and hence reducing inflation (after a time lag). Conversely, when inflation seems likely to fall below the bottom of the target band, rates of interest are reduced with the objective of increasing borrowing, increasing demand, raising economic growth and reducing unemployment (again, all after a time lag). Thus, it is fair to say that, other than in emergencies or as a result of political pressure (see below), central banks are likely to aim for 'neutral' short- term interest rates – that is, rates that are just high enough to prevent economic overheating and to prevent unacceptable future inflation, but not so high as to kill economic growth and raise unemployment.

Despite the Central Bank consensus, it needs to be borne in mind that political support for the price- stability objective is not guaranteed. An alternative objective might be the maintenance of full employment, with interest rates being kept low to boost investment. In Autumn 2007, for example, there were reports that the French president, Nicolas Sarkozy, wanted the ECB to reduce short- term interest rates to boost employment and make French exports more competitive by lowering the value of the euro. This contrasted with reports that a German- led group of ECB governors was pressing for an interest rate rise to stave off inflation.

There are also times when actual short- term rates in the wholesale markets differ widely from those that the central banks or MPC would wish to set. In Summer/Autumn 2007, events in the sub- prime markets caused a 'credit crunch', meaning that banks and others became reluctant to lend and, when they did lend, the rates of interest could be up to 60 basis points (ie 0.60%) above the recommended MPC rate. (A basis point is 1% of 1%, so 60 basis points are 60% of 1 %.)

9.3 Long- term rates

Nominal long- term interest rates tend to reflect inflationary expectations, risk perceptions and exchange rate expectations. Long- term rates are influenced by short- term interest rate changes, but the link is not straightforward. For example, a rise in short- term rates can lead to a rise in long- term rates, but, a rise in short- term rates may alternatively lead to a *fall* in long- term interest rates if the markets become convinced that the rise in short- term rates will curb future inflation.

National fiscal policies have also played a major part in determining long-term interest rates. Countries with high budget deficits and/or a high total level of government debt can find that this has forced up long-term interest rates.

Finally, the integration of the world's financial markets and the broad agreement between central banks on the use of short-term rates in the pursuit of price stability is tending to make real long-term interest rates likely to converge on an international norm.

9.4   The term structure of interest rates

The 'term structure' of interest rates considers the relationship between the required interest rate, (also known as 'yield' or 'cost of borrowing') and the time to maturity on the debt of a given borrower in a given currency. For example, in the UK it is common to construct a graph from UK government gilt yields for different maturities. The time to maturity is plotted on the horizontal axis and the required yield is plotted on the vertical axis. The resultant graph is called the yield curve, as seen in Figure 9.1.

Figure 9.1   A normal yield curve

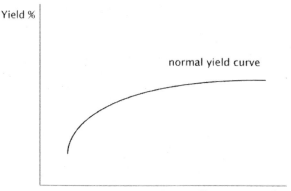

When expectations are equally balanced between forecasts of rising and falling interest rates, then the term 'normal' is usually applied to a yield curve. The normal yield curve slopes upwards to the right as shown in Figure 9.1. This is to be expected because, other things being equal, the longer the time to maturity, the greater the risk and the greater compensation lenders require for giving up liquidity.

There are times (for example, in the UK at Autumn 2007), however, when short-term yields are above long-term yields. In this case, the yield curve slopes downwards to the right and this is sometimes called an 'inverted' yield curve. Inverted yield curves can imply that the market believes inflation will remain low. Thus the market expectation is that even if there is a recession, a low long dated bond yield will still be sufficient to offset the expected low future inflation.

There are various theories relating to the factors that affect different yields on different maturities of the same credit quality:

- the expectations theory.

- the preferred market or preferred habitat theory.

- the market segmentation theory.

9.5 Forward rates of interest

Banks and other financial services providers are willing to quote forward rates for deposits and borrowing periods that are due to commence at a known future date. For example, on 1 February 2008, banks could quote a rate of interest for a one year borrowing period that is due to start on 1 February 2009 and end on 31 January 2010. Forward rates can be quoted for periods of less than one year: for example, a forward rate quoted on 1 February 2008 for a two- month deposit that would commence on 1 May 2008 would be known as a '3 x 5' rate. The borrowing starts in three months and ends in five months.

The easiest way to illustrate the use of the forward market is to study an example of how a London- based bank might deal and quote in that market.

For ease of reference, it should be noted that the London Inter Bank Offered Rate (LIBOR) can be considered as the rate of interest that a participant would have to pay if it borrowed on the wholesale money markets and the London Inter Bank Bid Rate (LIBID) is the rate that a participant would receive on a deposit on the wholesale money markets. The operations shown in the following two examples are not derivative transactions. The operations are sometimes known as 'forward–forward deals'.

Example 9.1

A bank dealer has been asked to quote a rate of interest today for a three- month £10m deposit rate starting in two months' time (in other words, to specify the interest rate that the will pay on such a sum deposited with the bank in two months' time). In order to set a suitable rate for a forward three- month deposit, the dealer has to know the break- even rate. To determine this, they require the following information:

	LIBID	LIBOR
Two- month rates (consists of 60 days)	5.25%	5.35%
Five- month rates (consists of 150 days)	4.93%	5.06%

The dealer first borrows an amount that will equal £10m in two months' time. Given that two- month spot LIBOR is 5.35%, the amount that the dealer needs today is:

$$\frac{£10,000,000}{1 \div (0.0535 \times \frac{60}{365})} = £9,912,821.48$$

The repayment of this loan with interest will be exactly offset by the proceeds of the incoming £10m deposit in two months' time on which the dealer has to quote.

The dealer deposits the £9,912,821 for five months (150 days) at the spot LIBID rate of 4.93%, which will produce £10,113,658 on maturity.

They can therefore pay £113,658 interest on the three- month (90- day) deposit and break even on the transaction. From this interest amount, the dealer can derive a forward deposit rate, as an equivalent annual rate (EAR):

$$\frac{113,658}{10,000,000} \times 365/90 = 4.609\%$$

This is the break- even rate. If the dealer wishes to make a profit on the transaction, they would reduce the deposit rate quoted (known as 'deduct a spread') reflecting the required profit margin.

9.5.1 Calculation of forward–forward rate for future deposits

In practice, the dealer would use the following formula to determine a break- even rate for a forward three- month deposit. Because the dealer is a depositor for five months at LIBID and a borrower for two months at LIBOR, they will use these two rates to arrive at a so- called 'forward–forward' bid rate.

$$\text{Forward–forward bid rate} = \left\{\left(\frac{1+(R_l \times D_l/365)}{1+(R_s \times D_s/365)}\right)-1\right\} \times \frac{365}{Df}$$

where:

R_l = LIBID for the long period
R_s = LIBOR for the short period
D_l = actual number of days in the long period
D_s = actual number of days in the short period
D_f = actual number of days in the forward period

Thus, in Example 9.1, the forward–forward bid rate would have been:

$$\left\{\left(\frac{1+\left(0.0493 \times \frac{150}{365}\right)}{1+\left(0.0535 \times \frac{60}{365}\right)}\right)-1\right\} \times \frac{365}{90} = 4.609\% \text{ as above}$$

9.5.2 Calculation of the forward–forward rate for a future borrowing

If the bank dealer in Example 9.1 had been asked to quote an interest rate for a three-month borrowing of £10m starting in two months' time, they would have used the following formula, given the LIBOR/LIBID data as above:

$$\left\{\left(\frac{1+(R_l \times D_l/365)}{1+(R_s \times D_s/365)}\right)-1\right\} \times \frac{365}{Df}$$

where:

R_s = LIBID for the short period
R_l = LIBOR for the long period
D_l = actual number of days in the long period
D_s = actual number of days in the short period
D_f = actual number of days in the forward period

Note: the number of days would be 360, as opposed to 365, for many non- sterling currencies.

On the basis of the LIBOR and LIBID rates quoted in the example, the dealer's break-even forward–forward offer rate would be:

$$\left\{\left(\frac{1+\left(0.0506 \times \frac{150}{365}\right)}{1+\left(0.0525 \times \frac{60}{365}\right)}\right)-1\right\} \times \frac{365}{90} = 4.891\% \text{ per annum.}$$

9.6 The broad nature of interest rate risk as a speculative risk for non- bank corporates

Interest rate risk can be defined as the 'risk that movements in market rates of interest will result in a change in cash flow, profit or valuation for a company'. For example, a change in interest rates can affect a business in some or all of the following ways:

- it may change the cost of borrowing or the interest income from surplus funds.
- It may influence the level of sales by changing the customers' disposable income.
- It may affect the cost of purchases because, when interest rates rise, suppliers may try to increase their own prices to compensate for their own higher borrowing costs.

When a company borrows at 'floating' rates of interest, it means that the borrowing cost is adjusted at frequent intervals to take account of changes in market rates. Thus, for example:

- on 1 January, a company negotiates a 12- month loan at a margin of 1% over six- month LIBOR;
- six- month LIBOR is 6% on 1 January;
- The company will pay interest at 7% from 1 January until 30 June, irrespective of any changes in six- month LIBOR over this period;
- If six- month LIBOR is 7% on 1 July, then the company will pay interest at 8% for the period from 1 July to 31 December.

If a company has borrowed for a ten- year period at a fixed rate of 6%, then the company will pay 6% interest throughout the life of the loan, irrespective of whether market rates rise or fall.

Obviously, depositors or investors can lend money at fixed or floating rates in the same way as borrowers can borrow at fixed or floating rates.

'Pure risks' are those such as fire damage, in relation to which there is only downside potential. But interest rate risk is a 'speculative risk', because the ultimate effect of interest rate movements on profits, cash flows and company valuation can be beneficial or detrimental depending on whether the company is a borrower or an investor of cash and on whether the interest rate change is upwards or downwards.

Thus, with hindsight, a borrower who has borrowed at fixed rates could either have gained or lost by that decision, depending on whether market rates have risen or fallen over the borrowing period. What fixed- rate borrowing does achieve, however, is certainty in terms of interest cost and this facilitates budgeting.

9.7 The economic case for floating rate borrowing as opposed to fixed rate borrowing

As we have already seen (see Section 9.4), a yield curve is simply a graph that plots the return on securities of equal credit quality, such as gilts, against the time to maturity. When expectations are equally balanced between forecasts of rising and falling interest rates, then the term 'normal' is usually applied. The normal yield curve slopes upwards to the right as shown above.

The long-term difference between fixed and floating rates is that floating rates are priced from the short end of the yield curve (three-month LIBOR/six-month LIBOR), whereas fixed rate borrowing is priced from the longer end.

Given that the 'normal' yield curve slopes upwards to the right, it can be seen that for most of the time, short-term interest rates will be lower than long-term ones. While at any given time, either long-term rates may be lower than short-term rates or vice versa, on average over a long period – for example, five to ten years – short-term rates (ie floating rates) should prove to be lower than long term (ie fixed) interest rates.

In the long run, therefore, it could be argued that interest rate risk management is unnecessary and that companies should borrow at floating rates, because floating-rate borrowing should prove cheaper in the long run. Some companies, however, have a business risk profile that is very high. Such companies cannot afford to take any risks with interest rate costs, because the extra cost burden if floating rates rise could cause severe liquidity problems. Such companies will aim for mainly fixed-rate borrowing, so that known costs are budgeted in advance. Indeed, for two identical companies, one of which borrows at fixed rates and the other at floating rates, a rating agency will always give a higher credit rating to the fixed-rate borrower.

Each business may have its own unique circumstances that will affect the relationship between its interest rate risk and business risk. The following examples will illustrate various ways in which the link applies.

9.8 The link between interest-rate risk and business risk

In each case, the assumption is that the company has interest bearing borrowings.

9.8.1 Car manufacturers

When interest rates rise, car manufacturers usually face problems because:

- they are usually heavily borrowed, due to the capital-intensive nature of the industry. Thus, interest forms a significant portion of the cost base and therefore rising interest rates on an unhedged floating rate position will have a detrimental impact on costs;

- when interest rates rise, reductions in disposable income tend to result in reduced sales of items such as new cars, after a time lag;

- suppliers may try to increase their prices to offset their own added interest costs.

Thus, car manufacturers face a double exposure when interest rates rise: a squeeze on revenue and pressure for increased costs. They can be said to have 'high operational gearing', with a relatively high ratio of fixed costs to variable costs.

9.8.2 Manufacturers of spare car parts for the retail market

The sales of spare car parts may benefit from higher interest rates, because car owners will tend to keep their cars longer if higher interest rates reduce disposable income. Thus additional borrowing costs due to higher interest rates could be offset against greater sales and operational profits from the underlying economic situation.

9.8.3 Supermarkets

Supermarkets may not be as badly hit by interest rate rises, because they generally have very little working capital (sales are for cash whereas purchases are on credit) and because sales of essential goods will not be as badly affected by reduced disposable income caused by interest rates rises. In addition, the larger supermarkets may have the buying power to resist any attempt by suppliers to raise prices to compensate for higher interest rates.

Clearly, it can be seen that each company must assess the impact of changes in interest rate risks on its own operations and that different types of business will be affected in different ways by interest rate changes.

9.9 Formulating an interest rate management policy that is consistent with the general business risk of the company

There should be a formally documented interest- rate management policy for every company. This policy should be based on the analysis of the impact of changes in interest rates on borrowing costs (or interest income) on sales and on input costs. The policy should lay down clear guidelines as to the fixed – floating rate mix of borrowings or deposits, and should also specify what external techniques (derivatives) can be used to change the interest rate profile of the underlying borrowings or deposits.

As a generalisation, the more risky the underlying business and the higher the gearing (the ratio of borrowed funds to equity), the more a company should move towards fixed- rate funding.

9.9.1 A portfolio approach to managing interest- rate risk

If the optimal policy is not to have all borrowings at fixed rates or all borrowings at floating rates, then a 'portfolio' policy can be introduced. This might involve, for example, a policy to keep the overall borrowings within the following parameters:

- maximum at floating rates 75%, minimum 25%;
- maximum at fixed rates 75%, minimum 25%.

When the overall outlook for interest rates is for falling rates, the portfolio will tend towards 75% floating: 25% fixed. When the likelihood is that market rates will rise, however, the trend will be towards 25% floating: 75% fixed.

Alternatively, some borrowing companies adopt a portfolio approach of:

- 40% borrowing at floating rates;
- 20% covered by an interest rate option (which gives effectively the right, but not the obligation, to borrow at a pre- set rate at a given future date);
- 40% at fixed rates.

Such companies are 60% protected when market rates rise, because the fixed rate stays unchanged and the interest rate option will be exercised to ensure that the 20% so covered is not affected. Thus, only the 40% at floating rates will be affected by an upward change in interest rates. When market rates fall, however, 60% will benefit, because the option will be allowed to lapse and the floating rate borrowing will automatically benefit. The obvious drawback to this strategy is the cost of the premium for the option. (Interest rate options are dealt with in more detail under the external techniques later in this topic.)

9.10 An overview of the external techniques of managing short- term interest rate exposures

External techniques (derivatives) are available from banks and from Exchanges such as Euronext.liffe.

This section will focus on the derivatives that banks provide, as opposed to the exchange- traded derivatives from Euronext.liffe and other exchanges. In addition, this section will focus on the use of derivatives by companies that are borrowing, although similar principles apply to derivatives that are used to fix the rates on deposits.

For short- term interest rate management, the main derivatives are outlined below.

- **Forward Rate Agreements (FRAs):** these are derivatives that banks can supply to borrowers effectively to fix the interest rate for a future known borrowing period. FRAs apply to interest rates on similar principles to the way forward exchange contracts apply to foreign exchange rates.

- **Interest rate options:** these effectively give the right, but not the obligation, to borrow at a pre- set rate of interest over a stated future borrowing period. If the market rate at the start of the set borrowing period is below the strike rate of the option, the holder will abandon the right to borrow at the strike rate and will borrow at spot rates. If the market rate at the start of the set borrowing period is above the strike rate of the option, the holder will exercise the option and borrow at the strike rate.

- **Collars:** the collar has two strike rates and works on the basis of similar principles to those that cylinder options apply to foreign exchange. In a similar way to cylinder options, a collar has two strike rates, one higher than the other, because it consists of two separate option contracts. As with cylinder options, the premium on a collar is lower than that of a pure option with the same strike rate. When the borrowing period commences, the decisions made by the borrower are as follows:
  - if market rates are above the 'higher' strike rate, it can exercise the option and borrow at the upper strike rate;
  - if market rates are in between the two strike rates, the collar is abandoned, and the borrower can borrow at market rates;
  - if market rates are below the 'lower' strike rate, the borrower effectively has to borrow at the lower strike rate and cannot take advantage of any reductions in interest rates below this figure.

FRAs, caps and collars are generally short- term techniques that usually cover periods of two years or less, although longer periods could, in principle and in practice, be covered by FRAs if desired. Interest rate swaps normally cover periods in excess of two years.

9.11 Further details on FRAs

The FRA agreement is totally separate from any underlying lending or deposit. Indeed, there may be occasions when there is no actual underlying borrowing or lending associated with the FRA at all. In such circumstances, any FRA transaction is speculation, rather than hedging.

A 'buyer' of a FRA is the person wishing to be compensated if interest rates rise and a 'seller' is a person wishing to be compensated if interest rates fall. The calculations are made by reference to an agreed market 'reference' rate, such as the British Bankers' Association Interest Settlement Rate (BBAISR) for three or six- month LIBOR.

Note:

1. No premium is payable for a FRA and the bank's profit comes from the spread. A typical margin would be 0.125%, split 0.0625% off bid and on offer.

2. For FRAs, the word 'buyer' is simply a term to denote that this person will gain from the FRA if market rates rise above the FRA strike rate. The buyer does not pay any money up front, unless the bank insists on an upfront payment as security against counterparty risk. Likewise, the word 'seller' is simply a term to denote that this person will benefit if market rates fall below the FRA strike rate. The 'seller' of an FRA does not receive any money up front.

3. FRAs can be tailor- made to meet client requirements.

4. FRAs cover notional borrowing for periods from three months up to a normal maximum of two years. A FRA with a notional deposit or borrowing of three months commencing in two months would be called a '2 x 5' FRA, and so on.

5. A bank's client may take out a FRA that is not matched by any underlying future deposit or borrowing. In such cases, the client is effectively speculating on interest rate movements in the future. A buyer of an FRA that is not matched by underlying borrowing will benefit if interest rates rise and a seller of a FRA not matched by a deposit will benefit if interest rates fall.

6. Banks mark a contingent liability facility against any counterparty to an FRA. This is to allow for any default on the compensation payment if market rates should move against the counterparty.

9.12   Further details on interest rate options, guarantees, caps and floors

Interest rate options, guarantees, caps and floors are all instruments based on the principles of options. A '**guarantee**' is effectively a short- term cap for one- off transactions.

A '**cap**' protects the borrower against a rise in interest rates above a specified level. A cap is normally purchased to cover ongoing requirements, with a minimum period of 12 months. A treasurer may buy a cap when they think that interest rates will rise. If the interest rate prevailing at an agreed fixing time exceeds the cap's strike rate, the writer pays the buyer the difference. If interest rates fall, the option can be abandoned and benefit accrues from the fall in interest rate costs.

A '**floor**' protects a depositor against a fall in interest rates below a specified level. The treasurer may buy a floor (effectively a series of options) when they think that interest rates are going to fall and want to protect their investment income. If the prevailing rate falls below the strike price, the writer pays the buyer the differential.

An '**interest rate option**' provides a right, but not an obligation, to purchase a FRA with pre- set terms 'with hindsight' – that is at the time the relevant BBAISR is known. Thus, for an up- front premium, the holder of an interest rate option has the right to fix a rate of interest on a prearranged sum for an agreed period, which will commence on a set future date. If the holder wishes to fix the maximum rate on a future borrowing, the instrument is usually called a cap. If the borrowing takes place, the holder of the cap will exercise the right to purchase the FRA if the relevant BBAISR LIBOR is above the FRA rate at the start of the notional period. This will fix the maximum rate on the borrowing, because the FRA compensation paid by the bank will offset the rise of the LIBOR. If LIBOR has fallen, however, the holder of the cap will let it lapse and will simply take advantage of the lower market rate for the borrowing.

If the purpose is to fix the minimum number rate of interest on a future deposit, a floor will be purchased.

The up- front option premium varies with:

- the strike rate of interest (or reference rate of the option);
- the period of the option;
- the volatility of the underlying rates of interest.

Simple example of an interest rate option in action

Rollover rate = 6% = strike rate.

The treasurer of a company with variable rate borrowings determined by reference to six months LIBOR may be concerned about a possible rise in rates before the next fixing ('rollover') date in two months' time. The treasurer does not wish to pay more than 6% at the next rollover date.

In response to the requirement, the company's bank could arrange an interest rate option with, for example, a strike rate of 6%, with a premium of 0.33%. The premium is non-refundable and is paid up-front.

Three possible outcomes at the next rollover date are as follows.

1. Rollover rate = 6%
   In this case, the treasurer's cost of borrowing is 6% plus the premium of 0.33%. The treasurer will abandon the option.

2. Rollover rate = 8%.
   Here the treasurer will exercise the option and borrow at an effective rate of 6.33%, saves 1.67%

3. Rollover rate = 5%.
   The option will be abandoned and the net cost of borrowing will be 5.33%.

A detailed numerical example will be given later in the topic.

Note

1. If interest rates rise, the cost of borrowing is capped.
2. If interest rates fall, the option can be abandoned and benefit accrues from the fall.
3. When the holder is a borrower, the interest rate option can be described as:
   - 'out of the money' – the strike rate is above the current rate of interest and the option is currently worthless.
   - 'at the money' – the strike rate is the same as the current rate of interest.
   - 'in the money' – the strike rate is below the current rate of interest.

4. Interest rate options are available to depositors and the three terms are then reversed:

   - 'out of the money' – the strike rate is below the current rate;
   - 'at the money' – the strike rate is identical;
   - 'in the money' – the strike rate is above the current rates.

9.13   Collars

A '**collar**' is a combination of a floor and a cap. A borrower may require protection against interest rates rising, but is prepared to forgo some of the upside in exchange for a reduction in the premium. The objective of the collar is to reduce premiums. In a volatile market, premiums can become very expensive and collars can reduce the premium.

9.14   Comparing the short- term bank products that can be used to hedge short- term interest rate risk

The calculations relating to FRAs, caps, collars and floors can be complex at first glance, so the following examples will illustrate how these derivatives work.

9.14.1   FRAs, collars and interest rate options: example

Let us consider a company, LMN, that has a known six- month borrowing requirement, which is expected to commence at a known future date. LMN can borrow from the bank at 1% over BBAISR six- month LIBOR for the relevant amount and period, and borrowing facilities are available from the bank if required.

The corporate treasurer could take a chance and borrow at 1% over whatever the six- month LIBOR rate happened to be at the start of the period. Because interest rate risk is a speculative risk, LMN may gain or lose by this, depending on whatever the spot six- month LIBOR turns out to be at the start of the borrowing period.

Alternatively, the treasurer could consider fixing the rate now, or obtaining some more flexible arrangement whereby the maximum rate was set, but where there was some scope to take advantage of any subsequent fall in six- month LIBOR. The three main bank products for this situation are the FRA, the collar and the cap.

We shall now consider a specific scenario in which these products could be compared.

On 1 February, LMN plc has the following 'one- off' cash items in its cash forecast.

1. A payment of £10m to be made upon delivery of capital equipment which is expected on 1 July.
2. A receipt of £11m due on 31 December at the maturity of a fixed term money market deposit with a major UK bank.

The treasurer, therefore, expected to have a borrowing requirement of £10m for a six- month period, commencing in five months (1 July) and ending in 11 months (31 December). The number of days in the six- month period from 1 July to 31 December is 184.

The following information is available on 1 February.

FRA	Interest rate option	Collar*
Current quoted strike rate for 5 x11 FRA (ie commencing 1 July and ending 31 December) with a notional principal of £10m is: 6.80%.	Current rates quoted for an option to cover the same notional principal and period: 6.8% with a premium of £10,000 payable up front.	Current quotes for a collar relating to the same notional principal and period: • cap written by bank at a strike rate of 6.80%, premium £10,000; • floor to be written by LMN plc at a strike rate of 6.00%, premium £10,000. As can be seen from this example, the respective premiums would net out.

* If LMN plc has written a floor, then it will take on the obligations of option writers. The bank will be the purchaser of the floor and the bank will have the right, but not the obligation, to sell a 6% FRA to LMN on 1 July in the full knowledge of what the BBAISR LIBOR settlement rate is. Thus if the relevant six- month LIBOR on 1 July were to be below 6%, the bank would enter into the FRA arrangement as a seller.

The outcome of FRA if the borrowing were to commence on 1 July and end on 31 December as forecast and if the BBAISR six- month LIBOR on 1 July were to be 8% is as follows.

FRA Compensation	Discounting process	Effective interest rate
The FRA rate is below the BBAISR six-month LIBOR rate ruling on 1 July, so the bank must pay compensation to LMN. The amount is the difference between the FRA Rate and the LIBOR rate on the notional principal for 184 days. $(0.080-0.068) \times {}^{184}/_{365} \times 10m$ $= £60,493$	The compensation is paid at the start of the FRA notional borrowing period. Thus it is discounted: $60,493 \times \dfrac{1}{1+(0.08 \times {}^{184}/_{365})}$ $= £58,148$ This sum is paid by the bank to LMN at the start of the notional FRA borrowing period, ie 1 July. Thus LMN needs to borrow only £10m – £58,148 $= £9,941,852$ The rate of discount is always the relevant BBAISR	LMN pays interest at 9% per annum for 184 days on the sum actually borrowed. Thus the amount to repay including interest is: $£9,941,852 \times [1 +(09 \times {}^{184}/_{365})]$ $= £10,392,912$ So interest cost on an annual basis = $\dfrac{392,912 \times 365}{10m \times 184} = 0.078$ ie 7.8% Thus the net interest cost is 7.8%% which is the FRA rate of 6.8%, plus the 1% margin

Note: for the calculation of the FRA compensation payable at the start of the notional borrowing period, the following formula can be used:

Settlement amount at start of contract period =

$$\frac{(S-F)P \dfrac{n}{365}}{1+\left[S \dfrac{n}{365}\right]}$$

where:

S = settlement rate (or BBAISR)
F = contract rate (or FRA rate)
P = contract amount
n = number of days in contract period

Thus in the above example, the settlement amount (or FRA compensation) could be calculated as:

$$\frac{(0.080-0.068) \times 10m \times \dfrac{184}{365}}{1+\left(0.08 \times \dfrac{184}{365}\right)} = £58,148$$

The outcome of the 6.8% option if the borrowing were to commence on 1 July and ends on 31 December as forecast, and if the BBAISR six- month LIBOR on 1 July were to be 8% is as follows.

Option compensation	Discounting process	Effective Interest rate
The cap gives LMN the right, but not the obligation to buy an FRA on 1 July at a strike rate of 6.8%. Because the relevant BBAISR LIBOR is 8% on 1 July, LMN will exercise its right. The compensation paid by the bank will be £60,493 as for the FRA above.	£60,493 is discounted to £58,148, as in the FRA above. This is paid by the bank to LMN on 1 July. Thus LMN needs to borrow only £10m − £58,148 = £9,941,852.	£9,941,852 grows to £10,392,912 at 9% pa for 184 days. So the interest cost on an annual basis is: $\dfrac{£392,912 \times 365}{£10m \times 184} = 0.078$ Thus the borrowing cost is effectively at 7.8%, but we should add the cost of the cap, which is 0.1% (£10,000/£10m), so the total cost is 7.9%. In common with many writers, we ignore the fact that the premium will have been paid on 1 February, when calculating the effective cost of borrowing with a cap.

The outcome of a collar if the borrowing were to commence on 1 July and end on 31 December as forecast, and if the BBAISR six- month LIBOR.on 1 July were to be 8% is as follows.

Collar compensation	Discounting process	Effective Interest rate
The floor rate is below the BBAISR six-month LIBOR rate ruling on 1 July, so the bank will abandon its floor, but LMN will exercise its cap, because the relevant LIBOR is above the cap rate. The compensation paid by the bank is now £60,493, as calculated previously for the 6.8% FRA.	£60,493 discounts back to £58,148 (see 6.8% FRA). Thus LMN needs to borrow only £9,941,852.	£9,941,852 grows to £10,392,912 at 9% pa for 184 days. So interest cost on an annual basis is: $\dfrac{£392,912 \times 365}{£10m \times 184} = 0.078$ Thus the borrowing is effectively at 7.8% which is the cap rate of 6.8% + the 1% margin. NB If there had been a net premium payable, this would have had to have been taken into account in calculating the effective cost of interest.

The outcome if the LIBOR had been 5.5% on 1 July is as follows.

Cap compensation	Discounting process	Effective Interest rate
LMN abandons the cap and borrows at the spot LIBOR on 1 July + margin.	Not applicable, cap abandoned.	Spot LIBOR + the 1% margin = 5.5% + 1% = 6.5%. The cost of the cap premium must be added as in the previous example to give a net rate of 6.6%.

Position with 6.8% FRA on	Discounting process	Effective interest rate
LMN pays compensation as follows to the bank: £10m x (0.068–0.055) x $^{184}/_{365}$ = £65,534	This is discounted in the usual way. $£65,534 \times \dfrac{1}{1+\left(0.055\times^{184}/_{365}\right)}$ = £63,766. Net actual borrowing £10,063,766	£10,063,766 @ 6.5% for 184 days becomes: £10,063,766 x $[1+(0.065\times^{184}/_{365})]$ =£10,393.526. ·Effective borrowing rate is: $\dfrac{£393.526 \times 365}{£10m \times 184} = 0.078$ The effective rate is 7.8%

Collar at rates 6.0% – 6.8 %	Collar discounting	Effective interest rate
Cap is abandoned by LMN, but floor is exercised by bank. LMN pays bank: £10m x (0.060–.0550) x $^{184}/_{365}$ = £ 25,205	$£25,205 \times \dfrac{1}{1+\left(0.055\times^{184}/_{365}\right)}$ = £24,525. LMN borrows a total of £10,024,525	£10,024,525 @ 6.5% for 184 days becomes £10,353,000 The effective rate of interest is $\dfrac{£353,000 \times 365}{£10m \times 184} = 0.070$ This 7% rate is the lower collar rate of 6.0% + a margin of 1%.

9.14.2 The features, benefits and drawbacks of FRAs and collars

The following comparison uses the details of the example in 9.14.1 for clarity.

	FRA	Collar
Effect on borrowing capacity	Borrowing capacity reduced to cover the contingent liability. There would have been a bank claim for compensation if spot six-month LIBOR had been below the 6.8% FRA rate on 1 July.	Borrowing capacity reduced to cover the contingent liability that there would be a bank claim for compensation if the spot six-month LIBOR had fallen below the 6.0% floor rate on 1 July.
Effective rate of interest if the borrowing is actually required for the six-month period commencing 1 July	FRA rate + any credit margin, whatever the spot rate for six-month LIBOR is on 1 July. Thus LMN will borrow at an effective rate of 7.8%.	If spot six-month LIBOR on 1 July is above the 6.8% 'top rate' of the collar, LMN will borrow at that effective rate + the margin of 1%. (See calculation of the 7.8% rate above.) If the spot six-month LIBOR is below the floor rate of 6.0%, LMN will borrow at 7.0% (ie the floor rate + the 1% margin). If spot LIBOR is between the collar rates, LMN will borrow at that spot rate + the margin of 1%. Both the cap and the floor will be abandoned in this situation.
Effect if borrowing is not required on 1 July.	Compensation payment made, which depends on the market rates. Company could gain or lose. In the example where the BBAISR was 8% on 1 July, LMN would gain a compensation payment of £58,148 from the bank, but if six-month LIBOR were to be below 6.8% on 1 July, LMN would have to pay compensation to the bank.	Compensation payment made if market rates are outside the collar. Company could gain or lose in this case. If BBAISR six-month LIBOR is above 6.8% on 1 July, the company will receive compensation; if the BBAISR LIBOR is below 6.0%, LMN will have to pay compensation to the bank. If BBAISR LIBOR on 1 July is within collar rates, no compensation will be payable either way, and the floor and the cap will each be abandoned.
Scope for gain if market rates fall and borrowing is required	None	Yes, but only down to the floor level of the collar

	FRA	Collar
Fee payable	None (FRAs have bid–offer spread)	Premium payable, but less than for a pure option. The bank will pay a premium for the floor that LMN has written and LMN will pay a premium for the cap that the bank has written. Only a single net payment need actually be made.
Characteristics	A forward-type derivative, which fixes the rate if the borrowing is undertaken as forecast. If the borrowing is not undertaken, LMN will either pay or receive compensation, depending on the relevant BBAISR on 1 July.	A hybrid derivative, with some benefits of pure options, but not all. The reduced premium means fewer benefits than would apply to a pure option.

9.15 The management of longer term interest rate risk using interest rate swaps

An interest rate swap is the exchange by two organisations (counterparties) of one stream of future interest payments for another. The main features are that:

- only interest payments are swapped – there is no exchange of the principal;
- interest payments are swapped at rates and for a term agreed at the outset, based on an agreed notional principal;
- transactions are usually governed by a standardised swap contract (but the amount and terms are not standardised);
- the rights and obligations under a swap are entirely separate from the rights or obligations of any underlying borrowing;
- interest swaps normally cover initial periods of anything from two years to ten years or more.

Note: banks used to act mainly as brokers or clearing houses, but banks now take on one side of a swap only, with a view to obtaining a matching swap later. The term 'warehousing' is used to describe this process. Banks quote bid and offer swap prices representing the fixed rate payable or receivable against LIBOR.

9.19.1 Uses of interest rate swaps

Interest rate swaps do not involve any exchange of principal. What they do involve is an agreement between two parties to exchange annually or semi- annually, interest payments on an agreed amount, known as the notional principal, for an agreed period of time.

Suppose X plc has recently agreed a five- year bank loan of £100m at six- month LIBOR, which is currently 6.6% per annum. Suppose that the company's over- all profile is high risk and it cannot therefore support floating rate borrowing.

Let us suppose that a swap dealer offers X plc the following deal:

- swap dealer to pay to X plc half yearly, for the next five years, a sum of money calculated on the interest that would have been paid on £100m at six- month LIBOR over the period;

- X plc to pay swap dealer each half year, for the next five years, a sum of money calculated on the interest that would have been paid on £100m at 6.6% fixed over the period.

Note: the amount on which the swap interest payments are based (£100m here) is known as the 'notional principal'. Only interest payments are exchanged, there is no exchange of the £100 notional principal under the swap.

Overall Rate of LIBOR for year	Net interest from borrowing and the swap	
LIBOR 6.6%	To bank loan	(£6.6m)
	To swap dealer	(£6.6m)
	From swap dealer	£6.6m
	Net interest	(£6.6m)
LIBOR 8%	To bank loan	(£8.0m)
	To swap dealer	(£6.6m)
	From swap dealer	£8.0m
	Net Interest	(£6.6m)
LIBOR 4%	To bank loan	(£4.0m)
	To swap dealer	(£6.6m)
	From swap dealer	£4.0m
	Net interest	(£6.6m)

Thus X plc's interest will be £6.6m per annum whatever happens to LIBOR.

In practice, the swap is usually shown by way of a swap diagram, rather than by way of absolute amounts of interest paid.

Thus, the swap diagram for this particular swap would be as shown in Figure 9.2.

Figure 9.2 Swap diagram

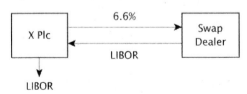

Note: the swap contract is independent of the borrowing contract. Thus if the borrowing is repaid early (ie within five years), the swap will still continue to be a valid contract.

Methods of international settlement through banks

On completion of this topic, the student should be able to:

- differentiate between nostro and vostro accounts;

- understand the bookkeeping involved in funds transfer;

- appreciate the different methods of international settlement, ie SWIFT, telegraphic transfer, mail transfer and bank draft;

- understand the benefits of using a bank with an international branch network for overseas payments;

- consider the implications of continuous linked settlement (CLS);

- appreciate the importance of linking SWIFT to national domestic clearing systems;

- appreciate the problems involved in the use of personal cheques for international settlement;

- appreciate the issues set out in the EU Directive on cross-border payments.

10.1   Introduction

With the increased globalisation of the world economies and the vast increases in international trade, the pressure has been on financial organisations to deliver ever speedier and more efficient means of payment between countries for international trade. The disappearance of exchange control regulations restricting transfers of funds in and out of countries has removed official barriers and delays to international money transmission in most countries, although it is important that full and accurate records of all transactions are maintained for statistical purposes, and also to aid detection of money laundering and other economic crimes. Most banks now offer a full range of choices for international financial transactions, with prices reflecting the speed with which the transaction is completed: the rule is generally that the quicker the beneficiary receives cleared funds in their account, the will be higher the charge for the transaction. In today's IT-enabled environment, funds can be transferred instantaneously around the world by interlinked computers at very little cost to banks.

10.2   Interbank transfers

The main requirement to enable banks to make transfers between themselves is the transmission and receipt of an authenticated instruction from one bank to another authorising the recipient bank to credit the account of the beneficiary. Once upon a time, such instructions were transmitted by sea or air mail in signed documents to correspondent banks overseas and took a correspondingly long time to be acted upon, Each correspondent bank was sent specimen books of authorised signatures so that messages could be confirmed as authentic by the recipients and such signature books had to be regularly updated when staff changed. Later, instructions were transferred to correspondent banks by telex or cable and, lacking authenticatable signatures, the messages were encoded and carried test keys, for which banks at either end held books of code tables.

Transfers made under such systems were called 'mail transfers' (MTs) or 'cable/telegraphic transfers' (TTs) and, for a long time, both systems ran side by side, with both being used depending upon the urgency of the transfers in question.

Nowadays, funds transfer instructions are moved between banks almost instantaneously through the interlinking of computers, using systems such as 'SWIFT' or 'TARGET' (see details later in Sections 10.4 and 10.7), and such transfers tend to be called 'international payments', 'priority payments', 'express payments', or 'ordinary' or 'urgent' payments, depending on the bank and type of payment required. Authentication is by encryption built into the systems.

10.2.1   'Nostro' and 'vostro' accounts

Of course, as well as actually transmitting instructions to one another authorising transfers, banks need to have systems for settling up with each other financially in respect of such payments and, when different currencies are involved, **nostro** and **vostro** accounts are used.

The word 'nostro' means our and 'vostro' means your.

From the point of view of a UK bank, a nostro account is its account in the books of an overseas correspondent bank, denominated in foreign currency. An example would be an account in the name of HSBC Bank, in the books of Citibank New York, denominated in US dollars. HSBC is a customer of Citibank.

From the point of view of a UK bank, a vostro account is an overseas bank's account with the UK bank, denominated in sterling. An example of a vostro account would be an account in the name of Citibank maintained in the books of HSBC Bank. The account would be denominated in sterling and Citibank would be a customer of HSBC.

When funds are remitted from the UK, nostro accounts are used if the payment is denominated in foreign currency and vostro accounts are used if payment is denominated in sterling.

Banks treat their nostro accounts in the same way as any other customer would treat their bank account. The bank will maintain its own record of the nostro account, known as a 'mirror account', and will reconcile the bank statements against these mirror accounts.

In order to maintain accurate records, the bank tries to value date all transactions. The bank estimates the date on which authorised transactions will actually be debited or credited to the nostro account and it uses these dates in its mirror account.

10.2.2   Bookkeeping for transfers of funds

When a UK bank customer wishes to transfer funds denominated in sterling to the bank account of a beneficiary abroad, the bookkeeping is as follows, assuming that an account relationship exists between the respective banks:

- the UK customer is debited with the sterling amount, plus charges, and this amount is credited to the sterling account of the overseas bank (this is a vostro account from the UK bank's point of view);

- on receipt of the advice, the overseas bank withdraws the sterling from the vostro account, converts it to currency, and then credits the beneficiary with the currency equivalent, less its charges.

If the transfer is denominated in foreign currency, the bookkeeping is:

- the customer is debited with the sterling equivalent, plus charges, of the required currency amount and the nostro account is credited with the currency (if the UK customer maintains a foreign currency account, the appropriate currency amount can be debited to that account, and there will be no need to arrange for conversion into sterling);

- the overseas bank is advised that it can debit the nostro account with the requisite amount of currency and credit the funds to the account of the beneficiary.

The various methods of settlement all involve the same bookkeeping. The only difference is the method by which the overseas bank is advised about the transfer.

10.3   International funds transfers

There are many different names for the process of transferring funds abroad under bank- to- bank transfers. Traditionally, the two methods were called 'mail transfer' and 'telegraphic transfer'. Under each method, a remitter instructed their own bank to transfer funds to a beneficiary at a bank abroad. The difference was that the payment details were sent abroad by mail in the one instance and by telex or similar means in the other.

From the point of view of a UK remitter, the UK bank will need to know whether to credit the account beneficiary with a named bank (in which case, it will request the bank account number) or whether it is instructed to request the overseas bank to advise and pay the beneficiary, if the beneficiary bank is elsewhere. In the case of transfers of funds to a private individual, the overseas bank can be asked to pay the beneficiary on application and identification.

Figures 10.1 and 10.2 show typical customer order forms.

Figure 10.1

| VPRPMT |
| To HSBC Bank plc |

HSBC

PRIORITY PAYMENT

Only Forms bearing an original issuing till stamp are acceptable

PLEASE READ THE TERMS OVERLEAF

Date
PLEASE PRINT OR TYPE IN BLOCK CAPITALS
AS PAYMENT IS TO BE SCANNED

Method of Payment – *Please tick the appropriate box*

Pyt. No.

BANK USE ONLY

BANK USE ONLY

☐ 1. Advise & credit account of beneficiary (Bank req'd)

Date Received

RC

☐ 2. Advise & pay beneficiary (Bene Address req'd)

☐ 3. Pay beneficiary on personal identification & application (Bank req'd)

Time Received

CX

Amount in words

Amount in figures

CH

CC

Name of currency · Value Date · Customer Ref. (SD)

TC

Exchange Rate (XER) · Sterling Equiv. in Figures £ · Forward Contract/Deal No. (FD)

PA

CU

Remitter's Name and Address (OC)

PB

Covering Agent – Bank Use Only

PT

PZ

Overseas Bank Code

CB

Beneficiary's Bankers

CT

Full Name and Address of Beneficiary (BC)

CO

INPUT

Beneficiary Account No.

Message to Beneficiary – Max. 140 characters (DE)

CHECKED

Bank Message (BI) – (Bank Use Only)

VA

CHARGES – PLEASE TICK APPROPRIATE BOX

HSBC Bank charges to be paid by (1) ☐ Remitter (2) ☐ Beneficiary

Foreign bank charges to be paid by (3) ☐ Remitter (4) ☐ Beneficiary

Name

BANK USE ONLY

WATCHWORD – MPD PAYMENTS ONLY

Please debit my Account Number

Branch Contact
Midnet No.

Seq. No

Orig S/C

Currency of Account

Payment instruction authenticated and authorised for payment

Area Code

Account to be debited for charges if different from above

Payment Amount

Date

Curr. Amt.

Commission

Ben. A/C No.

Sort Code 40

Total

Curr. Code

Signatures

Authorised Signature

Ben. Name

To be signed in accordance with the Bank Mandate

Codeword

MAC

1796 4 12/98 · UOI – Dept 96

Figure 10.2

Terms & Conditions

Branch Issuing Stamp

Please note that whilst forms will not be accepted without the original stamp of the issuing branch, this stamp is for bank purposes and does not constitute confirmation that the payment has been made.

The Bank's responsibility

Reasonable care in the processing of payment will be exercised by the staff of the Bank and of its correspondents. Should such care not be exercised, the Bank will be responsible for any loss of a kind which would be ordinarily expected to occur. This includes interest but not loss of contracts or profits or other consequential loss.

In some jurisdictions (e.g. New York), payments may be made to a designated account number, whether or not this account number correctly identifies the intended beneficiary. The customer is, therefore strongly urged to ensure that both the account number and the name of the beneficiary are correctly stated in the customer's instructions to the Bank. THE BANK DOES NOT ACCEPT LIABILITY FOR ANY KIND OF LOSS OCCASIONED BY THE CUSTOMER'S MISDESCRIPTION OF THE BENEFICIARY'S NAME OR ACCOUNT NUMBER IN ANY SUCH INSTRUCTIONS TO THE BANK.

Effecting Payment

Bankers can achieve same day value in few financial centres, otherwise customers can expect payments to been received by the beneficiary's bankers within 3 to 4 business days, (a business day being a day when banks are open for business both in London and in the financial centre where a payment is to be made). Value may, however, be delayed if there are complications in the routeing of payments or in overseas banking systems. In addition all banks apply cut-off times for the processing of payments to different parts of the world.

AS A RESULT, WE CAN GIVE NO GENERAL ASSURANCES ON THE ACHIEVEMENT OF VALUE DATES. CUSTOMERS ARE URGED TO DISCUSS THEIR NEEDS IN ADVANCE WITH THE BANK'S STAFF.

Cancellation of Payment

The customer is not entitled to cancel the payment. The Bank may, however, be willing to agree to the customer's request for cancellation and endeavour to retrieve funds on their behalf. Any refund of the amount retrieved will be made net of incidental expenses.

Expenses of Correspondents

Any expense incurred by the Bank in employing the payment services of correspondents may be debited to the customer's account, but only net of any prepayment the customer has made on account of this expense.

Other charges and expenses

A charge will be made for enquiries receive in respect of both inward and outward payment where HSBC Bank has not made an error, e.g. refunds, cancellations, amendments, duplicate advices, fate of funds, copies of cleared payments etc. (A charge will be made per payment instruction).

On receipt of the customer's instructions, the bookkeeping shown above will be applied. With a mail transfer, the UK bank will advise the overseas bank of the transaction by airmail and the instruction must be signed by authorised signatories. In practice, paper-based mail transfers are becoming much less common with the advance of IT.

If a telegraphic transfer is used, the same procedure as for mail transfers is adopted, except that the instructions to the overseas bank are sent by cable or telex and the overseas bank will require a special authenticating code word before it will act.

10.4   The Society for Worldwide Interbank Financial Telecommunications (SWIFT)

SWIFT is a computerised method by which banks are able to remit messages using interlinked bank computers administered by the Belgian head office of the Society for Worldwide Interbank Financial Telecommunications (SWIFT). SWIFT is similar to cable or telex, except that it is a computerised link and is totally secure. Almost all banks are now linked into the SWIFT system.

Urgent SWIFT is an alternative to a telegraphic transfer. The accounting entries and procedures are identical for telegraphic transfer or for urgent SWIFT. The only difference is the method whereby the message is remitted to the overseas bank. These SWIFT transfers are sometimes known as 'express international money transfers'.

Ordinary SWIFT is used as an alternative to mail transfers. These transfers are sometimes known as 'international money transfers'.

The distinction between 'priority' and 'non priority' SWIFT occurs in the speed of action undertaken by the overseas bank, not in the time it takes to deliver the message. For ordinary SWIFT, the UK bank will ask the overseas bank to value date the transaction forward to the date when an airmail instruction, sent at the same time, would be expected to arrive.

10.4.1   Application of charges to SWIFT and other international payments

The UK customer can instruct the bank as to who is responsible for charges.

This is best shown by an example. Suppose a transfer is for sterling £10,000 and the UK bank's charge is £20. The customer's authority will state who is responsible for the charges.

There are three combinations.

UK bank's charges	Australian bank's charges
a) Remitter	Beneficiary
b) Remitter	Remitter
c) Beneficiary	Beneficiary

a)   The account entries for the remitter–beneficiary charges would be as follows:

Debit UK customer	£10,020
Credit commission	£20
Credit vostro account	£10,000

The Australian bank will deduct its charges from the amount credited to the beneficiary.

b) The account entries for the remitter–remitter charges would be as follows:

Debit UK customer	£10,020
Credit vostro account	£10,000
Credit commission	£20

The Australian bank will credit its customer with the full £10,000 and will claim its charges from the UK bank, which will debit the UK customer's account in reimbursement.

c) The account entries for all beneficiary–beneficiary charges would be as follows:

Debit UK customer	£10,000
Credit vostro account	£9,980
Credit commission	£20

The Australian bank will deduct its own charges from the £9,980 before crediting the beneficiary.

10.4.2   The advantages and disadvantages of international transfers and SWIFT

International transfer systems and SWIFT systems are secure, in that the payments cannot be stolen in the same way as a cheque or bank draft could be – but, with mail transfer, there is always the danger that the instruction itself could be lost in the post.

The main disadvantage of express international payments or urgent SWIFT is that banks make an extra charge for remitting an urgent message. The beneficiary can receive the funds much sooner, however, and this reduction in float time can save interest for both remitter and beneficiary. For large sums, TT or its equivalent will save far more in interest than will be lost by the extra charge.

10.5   Special problems with the value dating of TTs

From the conditions shown on the reverse of the Priority Payment form shown in Figure 10.2, the reader can see that same-day value from a priority SWIFT transfer (ie the beneficiary receives cleared funds on the same day as the remitter is debited) is possible in some financial centres. This will generally apply when both remitting and receiving banks are in a nostro-vostro account relationship, or where the remitting bank has links with the overseas clearing system, or when the remitting bank has a branch in the overseas country. In many countries, the SWIFT link may only be with the head offices of the banks concerned, with local clearing systems being used for the remaining legs of the journey. These may not be nearly as efficient as the UK Bankers Automated Clearing (Bacs) or Clearing House CHAPS systems.

Such situations are by no means the norm, and however, delays can arise due to complexities, such as early 'cut-off times' and having to use more than one bank when there is not a direct nostro/vostro relationship between the remitting and receiving banks. In addition, banks in a particular country may be closed on certain saints days or other special holidays and this will inevitably delay the receipt of funds by the beneficiary.

The problem with value dating express payments is best illustrated by the following example.

Example

It is 9.30am. Your customer instructs you to transfer 50,000 to a beneficiary in Rouen, France, and US$50,000 to a beneficiary in Lookout Mountain in Tennessee, both payments to be made by telegraphic transfer. The customer says that they e- mailed both beneficiaries the previous day and received replies from them. The customer therefore assumes that the funds will be received by the beneficiaries by close of business today.

1. Advise the customer whether it is likely that the beneficiaries will receive the funds today.

2. Are there any particular points that could help to speed up the transfer of funds?

Answer: Example part 1.

- Many overseas banks have cut- off times, sometimes as early as 8.00am. Any instructions received after this time are processed on the next working day.

- It is most unlikely that the UK bank will have a nostro–vostro account relationship with the bank in Tennessee; likewise, the French transfer will most likely have to be routed through a bank in Paris. The funds will therefore have to be transmitted through intermediary banks.

- The messages between intermediary banks have to be authenticated, causing further delay.

- On the Continent there are often local holidays, when banks may be closed. Hence there is no guarantee that funds will be received by the beneficiaries today.

Note: When transferring money eastwards, do not forget the time difference: banks in the east may have closed before a bank in the UK even transmits the transfer instructions.

Answer: Example part 2.

- Ask if there are any particulars that can be quoted, eg bank-branch and account number of the beneficiary.

- The intermediary banks must be advised to remit all instructions by telex or telephone, or teletransmission.

10.6 How major international banks can reduce the delays in receipt of funds by the beneficiary

In the previous example, there was no account relationship between the banks involved, but there are instances in which many of the delays seen in that example can be reduced.

A few global banks do have a major competitive advantage in funds transfer. These banks are members of clearing systems in many different countries, so when acting as remitting banks they can convert their customers' payment instruction into a form that will enable them to pass automatically into the clearing system of the country of the beneficiary.

This obviously saves time and there is even greater benefit if the remitting bank has a branch in the overseas country in which the beneficiary bank is located.

In other instances, banks in different countries have formed 'payment clubs', whereby bilateral systems are developed to speed up receipt of cleared funds by the beneficiary.

The development of continuous linked settlement (CLS) will be a major factor in speeding up interbank settlement.

10.7   European Clearing Systems

UK readers will be aware of the two main money transmission systems used by UK banks for sterling transactions.

The Bankers Automated Clearing System (Bacs) is the day- to- day workhorse of the system, being used to clear cheques, standing orders, direct debits and other direct payments in great quantities every working day at minimal cost. Clearing through BACS normally takes three working days.

For high- value urgent payments, requiring value to be in the recipient's account the same day, the Clearing House Automated Payments System (CHAPS) can be used. Charges can be as high as £20 per transaction, but substantial discounts are available for bulk users.

Both the above system can, with prior arrangements, be accessed direct, for inputting such payments and receiving direct advice of receipts, by approved bank clients. Strict terms and conditions regarding security will apply, but much lower charges per transaction will be available.

There are various European clearing systems, but most cross- border Euro clearing is now done under the auspices of the Trans- European Automated Real- Time Gross Settlement Express Transfer (TARGET), founded in 1999 with the help of SWIFT, comprising 15 national real- time gross settlement (RTGS) systems and a European Central Bank payment mechanism. These are interconnected by common procedures, known as the 'interlinking system', giving the 30,000 institutions throughout the European Union (EU) connected to the system a uniform platform for the processing of payments. CHAPS Euro is the UK euro RTGS system, linked through target to all of the other EU RTGS systems for payments in Euros. More than 2trn of transactions passed through TARGET on average each working day during 2006 at a cost of between 0.80 and 1.75 per transaction. It is anticipated that TARGET2, an improved version due shortly will reduce these costs to 0.12 – 0.60 per transaction.

10.7.1   The Single European Payments Area (SEPA)

Article 3 of the EC Regulation on cross- border payments in euro was adopted in December 2001 and should be fully operational in all countries of the EU member

States by 1 January 2008. The rules are that all small value (ie up to 50,000), cross-border, non- cash payments in euros should cost no more in bank commission than a corresponding domestic payment. Because most countries' banks currently make no charge for domestic transfers, then qualifying eurocurrency transfers will also attract no charges. Cash and paper cheque transactions are excluded from the rules and will probably continue to be charged for. The savings on transfer charges will give an added competitive advantage to those businesses trading in euros throughout the EU. For customers to benefit from this, banks are insisting that all transfers must include full and clear beneficiary bank and account details. These are known as Bank Identifier Code (BIC) and International Bank Account Number (IBAN) details, and are usually quoted at the head of bank statements of current account holders in the EU.

10.7.2   BICs and IBANs

A typical BIC would appear as follows, and identifies the bank and branch:

MIDLGB22123

consisting of a bank code (MIDL), a country code (GB), followed by a branch identifier number (22123).

A typical IBAN can be up to 34 characters long and would look as follows:

GB15MIDL40051512345678

consisting of the country code (GB), a check number (15), the bank code (MIDL), followed by a sort code (400515) and an account number (12345678).

Inclusion of both of these codes in funds transfer instructions enables banks using SWIFT to send messages to each other using Straight Through Processing (STP), eliminating delays and queries.

An IBAN- checking tool and more information on some of the above systems is available online at The Association for Payment Clearing Services (APACS) website (www.apacs.org.uk) and the European Committee for Banking Standards website (http://www.ecbs.org).

Since 1 January 2007, any euro payment not quoting the correct BIC and IBAN codes can be returned or rejected, after deduction of a fee, so it is vital to ensure that the correct codes are used when making payments outwards and that people making payments to you are given the correct information clearly.

10.8 Continuous Linked Settlement (CLS)

10.8.1 What is 'CLS'?

CLS Bank is a purpose- built bank in New York that links more than 65 global banks, all of which CLS members and shareholders, in a centralised clearing system for interbank currency settlements between members. Each member maintains a multi- currency account with CLS Bank, which must be kept in credit.

The processing of nostro–vostro account entries between individual CLS member banks to settle individual foreign exchange transactions will be replaced by a single funds transfer between the individual bank and CLS Bank. CLS Bank records details of all transactions between members and, by midnight central European time (CET), gives member banks an orderly schedule of when each bank must make payments during the following day to honour these obligations. A single payment of a relatively small amount is then enough to settle a bank's multiple transactions for that day, even though their gross value may be many times the CLS settlement figure. An example of the figures involved was given in the 16 November 2002 edition of *The Economist*, which quoted CLS Bank as settling on one day, 15,200 transactions, totalling US$395bn with only $17bn of payments between member banks.

10.8.2 The benefits of CLS

- **It eliminates counterparty settlement risk.** In interbank foreign exchange transactions, there is a risk that one party to the transaction will settle its obligations by transferring cleared funds, but the other party will not. This risk is often called 'Herstatt risk', after a German bank that was closed halfway through a trading day in 1974, leaving a large part of its foreign exchange obligations unpaid. The failure of the bank caused panic in the foreign exchange market. Since the Herstatt debacle, bank regulators and senior bank managements have been trying to formulate plans to combat Herstatt risk and the CLS Bank operates on simultaneous settlement of obligations each way.

- **It simplifies cash movements.** The reduced number of settlement transactions (see above example) provides the member banks with cost and operational savings.

- **It offers real- time information to members and reduced settlement periods.** This should encourage more efficient cash management for members.

- **It promises competitive advantage over non- CLS members.** Settlement of interbank obligations will be speeded up by CLS, so member banks will be able to speed up the value dating of transactions for customers. For example, under the traditional nostro–vostro system, if a company had been due to pay Japanese yen and receive US dollars in return, the yen transaction would have had to be settled one day before the US dollar one, due to time zone differences. Under CLS, this will not apply and the two payments will be made simultaneously across the accounts of CLS bank.

10.8.3 Possible future CLS developments

CLS Bank began operations in October 2002 and it is too early to predict what its ultimate effect will be on the interbank settlement of foreign exchange obligations. The nature of nostro–vostro accounts could change, however: non- CLS members could tend to have a nostro–vostro account relationship with only one CLS settlement member, rather than with many, for administrative reasons. This single relationship will become more important than the multiple relationships that existed previously.

10.9 The settlement of inward payments to UK beneficiaries

One possible cause of delay in the crediting of cleared funds into the account of a UK beneficiary could be the time taken between receipt of the funds from overseas by a London office of a UK bank and the transferring of those funds from that London bank to the branch bank of the beneficiary. The methods used depend on whether the payment is denominated in sterling or in foreign currency.

10.9.1 Inward sterling payments

In relation to inward sterling payments, sterling will have been credited to the vostro account of the UK bank by the remitting overseas bank. Usually, this vostro account will be maintained at the London office of the UK bank or at one of the major international division branches in the provinces. Provided that the beneficiary's bank account details, as quoted on the incoming transfer show the account as being held at one of the branches of the bank holding the vostro account, there should be no problem regarding delays. The payment would normally be credited as cleared funds through the bank's internal systems on the date of receipt, or on the value date advised by the remitting bank.

When the beneficiary's bank account details show a branch of a different bank, the CHAPS system could be used to transfer the funds on receipt of payment or on the value date quoted by the remitting bank. In theory, CHAPS involves a same- day transfer of sterling funds between bank accounts in the UK, but there are cut- off times after which the transfer cannot be effected until the next working day. Some banks have built an interface between SWIFT and their CHAPS gateways to facilitate the rapid processing of international sterling payment instructions.

Usually payments of under £1,000 are made by banker's payment, which is, for all practical purposes, a cheque drawn on the head office of the bank holding the vostro account. For transfers by this method, delay is inevitable both on account of postal time and on account of the time required to clear the banker's payment. Although such banker's payments are certain to be honoured if drawn on a reputable bank, there will be a delay before the payment is treated as cleared for interest purposes.

As an alternative to a banker's payment, the bank holding the vostro account may use the bank giro system to transfer the funds to the beneficiary's bank account. This method is superior to a banker's payment, because the beneficiary will receive cleared funds on the second working day after the transaction has been initiated. Bank giro transfers can be for any amount.

When the overseas remitting bank's advice merely quotes a name and address of the beneficiary, without bank details, the bank holding the vostro account will usually send a bank draft to the address shown. Once again, postal and clearing delays could apply.

10.9.2 Inward currency payments

Initially, inward currency payments will be made into the nostro account in the name of the UK bank. When the beneficiary banks at a branch of the same bank as that holding the nostro account, the relevant branch must be contacted for confirmation that the beneficiary requires the funds to be converted to sterling. Once that confirmation has been received, the currency will be converted to sterling and the beneficiary will receive the funds in the same way as has already been detailed for the inward sterling funds.

When the beneficiary banks at another bank, the bank holding the original nostro account will simply transfer the funds to the nostro account of the beneficiary's bank. That bank will then be responsible for transferring the funds into the relevant account of the beneficiary.

10.9.3 How a UK beneficiary can reduce delays within the UK in relation to funds received from abroad

- Always specify bank account details on the contracts and invoices sent to the buyer.

- Whenever possible, insist that the buyer quotes the beneficiary's bank as the correspondent bank through which settlement is to be made by the remitting bank.

- If currency payments are to be received, the beneficiary should ensure that their bank is given clear instructions as to the disposal of funds. The bank should have been instructed in good time as to whether to convert the currency into sterling or whether the monies should be credited to a currency account in the customer's name.

- The beneficiary should, whenever possible, insist that the buyer telexes the remitting bank's remittance reference. In the event of any delay in receipt of funds, the UK bank can be advised of this detail to help it to trace the payment.

- Whenever cash flow and interest considerations justify the expense, arrangements should be made to have all transactions advised by quickest possible means. This will ensure that internal UK transfers are made by CHAPS. For smaller amounts in relation to which the CHAPS fee is not justified, however, arrangements should be made for internal transfers to be made by bank giro, rather than by banker's payment.

10.9.4   The disadvantages of the buyer using their own cheques in settlement of overseas debt

- In some countries (but not in the UK), sending a cheque abroad may contravene the exchange control regulations of the buyer's government.

- The buyer's bank and the beneficiary's bank usually impose heavy charges for handling such cheques.

- There is an inevitable delay between the time at which the cheque is collected and the time funds are actually remitted by the buyer's bank. One method of speeding up the process of clearing cheques is to use a 'lockbox' facility, which is particularly useful for UK exporters who sell to the USA and who are paid by the buyer's cheque. The buyer is instructed to post the cheque to a post office (PO) box address in the USA. A local bank opens the 'lockbox' at least once a day and initiates the clearing of the cheques. This process dramatically reduces the clearing time, because the cheque itself does not have to go from the USA to the UK and back again. UK banks can organise 'lockbox' facilities by making arrangements with correspondent banks abroad.

  Lockbox facilities are also widely available within the EU. Arrangements can be made for the proceeds of the cheques collected via the 'lockbox' system to be held in a collection account with the overseas bank. The funds can then be drawn down as and when required to meet the local currency needs of the UK seller.

- From the beneficiary's point of view, there is no guarantee that the cheque will be paid.

10.10   Bank drafts

A bank draft is, in effect, a cheque drawn by one bank on another. If sterling payment is required, the draft will be drawn on the vostro account; if currency payment is required, then the draft is drawn on the nostro account.

The UK bank will place sterling in the vostro account, or currency in the nostro account, to meet the drafts. The customer's account will be debited in reimbursement and charges will be passed.

The UK customer will forward the draft to the beneficiary who will pay it into their bank for credit to their account. Ultimately, the draft will be debited to the appropriate nostro or vostro account.

There are major disadvantages to the use of drafts for large transfers:

- the remitter is debited at the time that the draft is issued, but there is a delay before the beneficiary can pay the draft into their bank account and obtain cleared funds;

- if the beneficiary does not bank at the bank on whom the draft is drawn, the funds will be treated as uncleared;

- the draft could be lost or stolen and banks are reluctant to 'stop' a bank draft because it amounts to dishonouring the bank's own paper. In any case the bank will require an indemnity from the customer authorising the bank to debit the customer's account if it should suffer any loss by stopping the draft and issuing a duplicate.

10.11 Developments within the EU regarding payments

- For some time now, corporate treasurers have been able to initiate CHAPS transfers from their own desktop terminals. This facility is now available for international transfers by way of SWIFT or telegraphic transfer. In addition, the payment details of regular suppliers can be retained on computer so that the corporate treasurer merely needs to input the amount and value date to initiate a payment. Naturally, appropriate security procedures are laid down to cover direct payments.

- The direct debit system has existed for many years in the UK. This has now been extended to international payments in parts of the EU. Thus a UK importer could authorise its bank to accept claims from its suppliers, subject possibly to maximum amounts and frequencies, at the debit of its account.

- Suppliers, purchasers and bankers are becoming linked in electronic data interchange. This enables simultaneous real- time transfers to be made with automatic advice and reconciliation against invoice for the supplier (see also Appendix 2).

- Lockbox systems can be used to speed up the collection of cheques.

- Different giro systems are being linked in different countries to speed up international bank giro transfers.

- Credit cards are being developed to facilitate person- to- person and person- to- company transfers.

- Banks are increasingly seeking to develop new networks and links throughout the EU.

- There are currency clearing systems in London whereby cheques drawn on foreign currency accounts by UK drawers may be cleared.

Topic 11

Money laundering, terrorist financing and fraud

At the end of this topic the reader should be able to:

- Recognise in what areas financial crime may intrude upon international trade;
- appreciate the need to be vigilant and how to deal with suspicions of financial crime;
- realise the extent of penalties imposed upon those found guilty of financial crimes;
- understand the links between money laundering and terrorist financing.

11.1   Money laundering

With the globalisation of all types of business, leading to more and more cross-border activity all around the world, it is not surprising that the criminal fraternity has been in the forefront of this trend.

For many years, criminals have been aware that international (and in some countries, state) boundaries have enabled them to escape the clutches of the guardians of the law.

They now find that it is also important for the cash proceeds of their crimes to be similarly mobile. Crimes are perpetrated to make money and many crimes result in large cash proceeds. It has always been very difficult to escape the notice of the authorities when spending large amounts of cash and, in the past, many criminals have been apprehended by being careless in the disposal of their ill-gotten gains. The authorities around the world have realised this and the Financial Action Task Force (FATF) set up by the G7 Group of countries in the late 1990s has concentrated on encouraging all countries throughout the world to bring in legislation against money laundering.

11.1.1   What is money laundering?

Money laundering is the process of converting the proceeds of illegal activities, the disclosure of which would trigger financial losses or criminal prosecution, into real or financial assets, the origins of which are hidden from the law enforcement officials and from society in general. It is estimated that there is a global financial money laundering industry handling up to US$1,000bn (GBP500bn) each year, or around 5% of gross world product (GWP). Around one third of this is thought to originate from drug smuggling and the remainder from other serious crimes, such as people trafficking.

Because the originating criminal activity is often international in nature, the laundering of the proceeds regularly involves international financial transactions, converting and transferring currencies around the world on a regular basis. If these transactions can be identified and the criminals behind them brought to justice, the thinking is that the underlying crimes may eventually become less worthwhile for criminals and that criminal activity will fall.

11.1.2 How does money laundering work?

There are many ways of carrying out money laundering activities, but most of them involve three main stages.

1. Introducing 'dirty' money into the financial system by some means can involve such methods as front businesses or 'Trojan horse businesses' pretending to be genuine businesses, opening bank accounts, and paying in regular 'takings' from the businesses. In some cases, criminals will recruit several small players to open individual accounts through each of which relatively small amounts of funds are regularly laundered. This is known as 'smurfing' and it is believed that the small amounts involved in each account will not attract unwelcome attention. Indeed, 'smurfers' are often recruited online by seemingly innocuous emails inviting people to apply for jobs collecting funds and transferring them overseas. Money transfers based on non- existent or overvalued trading transactions (ie 'padded invoices') are often used when transferring funds overseas. Sometimes, 'dirty' cash is used to purchase items of value, which are then sold on in return for 'clean' proceeds, such as dealer's cheques or money transfers.

2. 'Layering' is the next stage, at which the ostensibly clean funds produced above are moved through several accounts to avoid attempts to track the money. In cases in the past, banks in offshore tax havens or banks with questionable ownership in some eastern European countries have been used for this process.

3. Once the funds have been 'layered', they are then 'integrated' back into the legal economy through the use of legitimate bank transfers or drafts, the history of which cannot be traced, which are paid into the bank accounts of the beneficiaries.

The people involved in money laundering are often people you do not know, but sometimes they can be people you have known well for a long time, who have been tempted by the rich rewards offered by criminals to those who will help them to launder their criminal funds. Eminently respectable customers as well as bank employees, have been tempted by the very large sums on offer.

In international trade, businesses around the world have been persuaded to 'pad' invoices or to allow their systems to be used for money transfers with no underlying genuine commercial transactions.

In some countries, whole banks have been purchased by criminals and used mainly for criminal activity and, in a few countries, it has been alleged that governments and politicians' relatives have been involved in such activities, with the local police turning a blind eye to blatant money laundering. In such cases, honest banks have to take great care when entering into correspondent banking relationships with banks they have not dealt with before and must be extra vigilant when an existing correspondent bank changes ownership, or they may find themselves inadvertently handling laundered money fed into the system by their correspondents.

11.1.3 The penalties for money laundering

The G7 Financial Action Task Force has worked hard over the past ten years to persuade all countries in the world to introduce legislation against financial crime, particularly money laundering. Countries that did not comply were placed on a 'black list', and other countries were supposed to avoid dealing with them. The FATF black list, first published in 2000, named more than a dozen countries, but, over the last two years, the last three named countries – Myanmar, Nigeria and Nauru – were dropped from the list, so that no countries are currently blacklisted. Bankers are, however, aware that just because countries have put in place legislation against money laundering, the application of such laws varies around the world.

The latest legislation in England and Wales (there is similar legislation in Scotland, which has a different legal system) covering money laundering was the Proceeds of Crime Act 2002 and the Money Laundering Regulations 2003, but other legislation dating back to the Prevention of Terrorism and Drug Trafficking Acts of the 1980s has applied over the past two decades. UK banks are consequently now familiar with what they are required to do in respect of money laundering. In addition, the Third European Union Money Laundering Directive came into place at the end of 2007. Most of the above legislation emphasises the need for banks and other involved parties to identify their clients fully, to keep full and accurate records of clients and transactions and to report suspicious transactions. The Proceeds of Crime Act 2002 additionally enables the UK government to confiscate proceeds of crime under certain circumstances.

The main requirements in the UK are to ensure that all staff are fully trained to recognise unusual transactions and that such transactions are reported, initially to the bank's own internal Compliance Officer, who will collate reports and pass them on to the authorities in the form of suspicious transaction reports (STRs). Over 200,000 STRs were made to the UK's National Criminal Intelligence Service (NCIS) in 2006, up from 18,000 in the year 2000. Unusual transactions may be of any amount - there is no minimum or maximum figure - and reports of a series of relatively small transactions has resulted in criminals being arrested in the past. In the USA, on the other hand, all transactions over US$10,000 must be reported to the Federal Bureau of Investigation (FBI), and it is are said to be overwhelmed by the sheer volume of reports received every day.

The criminal penalties for contraventions of money laundering regulations range from up to two years in jail (or a fine, or both and possible revocation of licence to trade) for failing to train staff adequately, to jail sentences of up to 14 years for assisting others to retain the benefits of crime. (Indeed, it often seems that those assisting criminals to launder money could receive longer sentences than those customary for the crimes that generated the funds.) The laws apply to all residents of the UK, not only to banks, and solicitors, insurers, casinos, bureaux de change, building societies, investment advisers and others handling funds for clients must comply or risk criminal prosecution. There has been a fourfold increase in prosecutions for money laundering in the UK between 2002 and 2007.

As well as criminal prosecution, of course, organisations that do not comply with money laundering regulations run further risks, such as loss of reputation, investigations by police and regulatory bodies, loss of licence to trade and closure. Needless to say, UK banks, in particular, ensure that they have very robust systems and training in place to combat money laundering.

Bankers dealing with international trade need to be watchful and must bear in mind that they must report any suspicious transactions going through their books without warning the customer. They should only deal with known clients and with known correspondent banks, and should keep their knowledge of their counterparties up to date. They should watch out for unusual transactions with areas of the world known to be less fussy about money laundering than the UK and those dealing with trade documents should be mindful of the need to report possibilities of invoice 'padding' or unusual cargoes to or from areas of high criminal activity. Regular transfers for round amounts may attract suspicion if the underlying trade transactions do not justify them. Any approaches from clients, old or new, to bend the rules or deal with unusual transactions should arouse suspicion.

There are four main things that banks and international traders need to do to ensure that they do not fall foul of the Money Laundering Regulations in the UK and similar precautions will stand them in good stead in other jurisdictions too:

1. **Know your customer.** This means knowing your client, and, if the client is acting as an agent, knowing for whom they are acting. Banks are protected under s 4 of the Cheques Acts of 1957 and 1992 when collecting clients' cheques, but those Acts insist that the banks have fully identified their customers before commencing business with them, and this applies even more so when dealing with foreign trade transactions, because the protection provided by the above Acts does not apply.

2. **Keep good records of all transactions**. This is particularly the case in terms of audit trails for money transfer procedures. Banks might reasonably be expected to follow good practice, so you can be assured that the courts would take a very dim view of any bank that failed to do this conscientiously.

3. **Recruit good quality staff and train them fully in the requirements of the Money Laundering Regulations.** This is an area in which banks have been found to be lax in the past, and fines for such laxity are very heavy.

4. **Report all unusual transactions.** Banks will do this through their in-house compliance departments, which collate internal information before passing it along to the authorities, if appropriate. Banks must not make their clients aware that they have been reported!

Remember that, as bankers, you must report such activities to protect yourselves and your banks from criminal prosecution and very severe penalties.

A short case study in money laundering

The following is a brief summary of a real case in which the writer was involved some years ago. Some of the details have been changed to protect the innocent.

At a small town branch of a UK bank, the account was held of a Mrs S. Mrs S had banked with the branch for many years, had strong family connections locally, was highly respected and her bank account was well run. She lived in a large house locally with her husband and a daughter who was studying at a private school.

Mrs S was heavily involved in all of the usual small town activities such as the church and the Mothers Union. She was a very intelligent, cultured and sociable lady, on good terms with all of the branch staff, from the manager downwards, and well connected with those who mattered in the town. She did not have a full time job, but worked for local charities in fundraising. She drove a top of the range small sports car, but occasionally came to town in her husband's luxury Bentley saloon. The branch records showed that her husband, a wealthy self-employed businessman, maintained his own accounts with a competitor bank in a town some 20 miles away.

It was noticed by the branch counter staff that Mrs S. had started paying into her account sums of between £10,000 and £20,000 cash, mainly consisting of £5, £10 and £20 notes, every two weeks or so, telling the cashiers that her husband, Mr S was working with some of his staff on a contract in the Middle East. He was being paid for the contract in cash stage payments and, for safety, his workers were bringing the cash back to Mrs S in the UK when they returned home on leave, and she was paying it into her account until Mr S returned home on completion of the contract.

This continued for some months and, eventually, the branch reported the transactions to the bank's money laundering officer at head office in London under the money laundering legislation in force at the time. A brief acknowledgment of the report was received and nothing more. No mention of this report was made to Mrs S, who continued making regular cash payments into her account. The branch received no instructions regarding the operation of the account, which was permitted to continue as normal.

Nothing more happened until the branch manager was shocked to read in the paper that the local police had raided the family house early one morning armed with a search warrant. No arrests were made at the house. It was later reported that Mr S had been arrested on his private yacht in a south coast marina. On board, the police found 4 tons of the drug marijuana.

Mr S was subsequently found guilty of several offences, including drug smuggling, and was sentenced to eight years in prison. No charges were made against Mrs S or her daughter, who were able to convince the police that they knew nothing of Mr S's illegal activities. The crimes took place before the Proceeds of Crime Act applied, so the family retained all of their assets.

This true case illustrates the fact that even highly respectable clients whom you know well can be involved in money laundering or other financial crime if they have been persuaded to act on behalf of others.

11.2   Terrorist financing

If money laundering can be described as converting 'dirty' money into clean, then, in some ways, terrorist financing could be described as converting clean money into dirty.

Well- meaning people contribute funds to bodies that may use them to buy arms and explosives to wage guerrilla warfare using guns or bombs.

Current examples of some of the organisations branded as terrorists are the Tamil Tigers in Sri Lanka, the PKK Kurdish Workers Party in Turkey and, of course, Osama bin Laden's al Qaeda.

Indeed, for many years, an organisation called Noraid openly collected funds in North America, particularly the USA, to support the Irish Republican Army (IRA), parts of which were active in the UK in shooting and bombing in support of the independence for Northern Ireland. Contributors were extremely generous, having been told that the funds were to be used for welfare work in Northern Ireland. Of course, the IRA is no longer deemed a terrorist organisation, having now been accepted into government in the province.

Banks do not wish to be involved in holding accounts or transferring money for any organisations, often described as charities, which are collecting and transferring funds for 'terrorists'. Such activity is not good for the reputation of a bank and, indeed, banks are often ordered (by court order in the UK) to reveal details of such activity to the police.

Such activity now tends to avoid the formal banking system, but police suspicion has fallen upon some of the operations of informal money transmission systems such as 'Chop', 'Fei- Ch'ien', 'Hundi' and 'Hawallah' common in various ethnic minority communities. Such systems operate on personal contact and usually leave no audit trails for police to investigate. They rely on closely knit family or business connections receiving funds for transfer in one country and arranging for similar amounts to be paid out to beneficiaries in other countries, usually against delivery of some identifying token by the beneficiary, with few other records being maintained.

11.3   Fraud in international trade

It was estimated recently in research carried out in March 2007 for the Association of Chief Police Officers (ACPO) in the UK that reported fraud alone costs the UK economy and society at least £13.9bn a year, and that much other fraud goes unreported. The financial services industry in the UK generates 8.5% of the UK economy and is a prime target for financial crime, as are those who use it to assist their international trading activities.

International trade brings many opportunities for fraudulent activity by one party at the expense of another. Many businesses are keen to export their goods and services, and will take orders and ship goods or deliver services without first checking out the good faith and financial strength of the buyer. Once delivery is made, there is little an exporter can do to obtain payment if the buyer has no intention of paying. To this end export documentary credits and outward documentary collections are provided by banks to try to reduce cases of non- payment. Exporters can help themselves more, however, by being more careful about who their buyers are and by making suitable enquiries on potential buyers through their banks, the Chamber of Commerce or trade attaches based in British embassies, consulates or High Commissions in the country of the buyer.

In some cases, however, exporters have been persuaded to ship goods overseas on receipt of documentary credits that turn out to be forged. It is therefore important that such exporters should bring such documentary credits to their bankers, so that they can be thoroughly checked and authenticated before shipping goods. If in doubt, the exporter could insist on a confirmed irrevocable documentary letter of credit, which would carry the guarantee of a UK bank. Documentary credits are covered in Topics 18, 24 and 25.

At the other end of the scale, exporters who have been ultra-cautious in how they receive payment and have asked for advance payment in cash before shipment have found themselves in possession of forged notes, or under suspicion of money laundering when paying the funds into their bank accounts.

Importers too can be on the receiving end of fraudulent activity: whichever way they choose to pay for their imports, they may find that the goods, on arrival, are of poorer quality than expected, or not not even the goods they ordered. They have accepted the word of the seller, or the description of the goods on a bill of lading, and have been deceived.

The only way to avoid such problems is to arrange for the goods to be inspected prior to shipment by a trusted international firm such as Société Générale de Surveillance (SGS), which can certify the quantity and quality of the goods. This is a very expensive exercise, however, and the exporter and importer will have to agree who will bear the cost.

In some parts of the world, and for certain types of transaction, importers are asked to make an advanced payment before orders will be prepared or shipped. There have been many cases of such advanced payments being made and the shipment never taking place. Importers asked to make advanced payments should ask the exporter to provide them with a bank advanced payment guarantee (see Topic 22), so that a claim can be made on the exporter's bank if the order is not fulfilled.

In all such cases above, exporters or importers must be mindful that, if money is lost, it is extremely difficult and expensive to take legal action in a foreign jurisdiction to recover lost funds, assuming that the person who has deprived them of the funds can be traced and has any funds worth claiming. It is therefore best to take extra precautions as described to avoid getting into that position in the first place.

Business people often receive convoluted letters asking for help in transferring funds from a deceased's estate out of a foreign country. These letters, usually known as 'advanced payment scams', or '419 letters' after the section of the Nigerian Criminal Code covering them, ask for details of your business bank account and a deposit of funds in advance to cover costs. They often originate from Africa and offer a large proportion of a multimillion US dollar estate overseas in exchange for use of your account into which to transfer it. These are invariably fraudulent and are used to obtain funds from you by way of the advance payment, and details of your bank account for future fraudulent activity. They should be reported to your local police, who usually have a department dealing with such frauds.

There are many other types of fraud that might be perpetrated on the unwary international trader, against which protection may be difficult. Even today, piracy and the theft of cargoes on the high seas is still taking place, particularly around the Horn of Africa, the coasts of Indonesia and other areas of South East Asia, and the deliberate scuttling of ships, after first removing their cargoes, to claim insurance money is not uncommon. Indeed the International Chamber of Commerce (ICC) has specialist committees working flat out on these and other frauds.

In the UK, the following legal structures have come into effect over the past decade to address financial crime and support the law enforcement agencies:

- Part I of the Criminal Justice Act 1993 (brought into force 1 June 1999);
- The Financial Services and Markets Act (FSMA) 2000.
- The Anti- Terrorism, Crime and Security Act 2001.
- The Proceeds of Crime Act 2002.
- The Extradition Act 2003.
- The Crime (International Co- operation) Act 2003.
- The Serious Organised Crime and Police Act 2005.
- The Fraud Act 2006.

A new Serious Crimes Bill is currently passing through Parliament.

11.4   Internal controls in major companies to minimise the impact of fraud and human error

So far in this topic, we have considered the implications of external fraud whereby criminals from outside the company try to defraud it, or try to use the company as a vehicle for money laundering. We shall now look at the implications of internal fraud whereby employees of the company try to defraud it, or whereby human errors by employees can cause loss.

In major non- financial services companies, one key department relating to finance and derivative transactions is the corporate treasury division. We shall identify and assess the issues that are relevant to the internal control of corporate treasury divisions.

Every organisation is different and the critical success factor in the management of internal fraud and reduction of losses through human errors is to identify the key areas in which the company is at risk, and to decide how much control is required in each area.

Nowadays, there is increasing awareness of the dangers, which can arise from unsupervised treasury operations. Well- publicised losses in companies such as Enron and Worldcom have made boards of directors very sensitive to the need for strict treasury controls. It is the board of directors that has the ultimate responsibility of establishing an internal control policy.

11.4.1   The US Sarbanes- Oxley Act (SOX) of 2002

In order to help reduce the dangers of internal fraud and human error, the Sarbanes- Oxley Act of 2002 was introduced in the USA. This legislation affects US registered companies, but it also affects companies that have their shares listed in the USA. The purpose of the Act was to improve the internal control of financial reporting, which includes:

- the maintenance of records that, in reasonable detail, accurately and fairly reflect the transactions and dispositions of the assets of the company;
- the provision of reasonable assurance that transactions are recorded as necessary to permit preparation of financial statements in accordance with generally accepted accounting principles (GAAP);

- the provision of reasonable assurance that the receipts and expenditure of the company are being made only in accordance with authorisations of management and directors;

- the provision of reasonable assurance regarding prevention or detection of unauthorised acquisition, use or disposition of the company's assets that could have a material effect on the financial statements.

The Sarbanes-Oxley Act has proved unpopular due to its rigorous rules and due to the penalties that can apply to senior executives who sign off published financial statements that prove inaccurate. Indeed, some companies have switched their share listing from New York to London to avoid having to comply. Others, however, consider that good internal financial controls are basic to all properly run businesses and that well-run companies should be doing what SOX requires as a matter of course.

11.4.2   Policies for the control of dealing in foreign exchange and derivatives transactions

Senior managers, with the approval of the directors, should set out clear written procedures for dealing and hedging. These procedures should cover, among other matters:

- dealing authority, stating who can authorise deals with external counterparties such as banks and stipulating any maximum amounts to which they can commit;

- a schedule, prepared for each derivative, setting out a brief description of the derivative, detailed circumstances in which the instrument can be used and the counterparties with whom such deals can be transacted;

- maximum counterparty limits should be stipulated so that the corporate does not become too exposed to one particular bank;

- reporting procedures, to show the exposure on derivatives (this procedure is now required, in any event, under many of the accounting conventions, such as International Accounting Standard 39);

- procedures for documentation, with stipulation as to any standard documentation required;

- rules for a clear separation of procedures for dealing, confirmation and settlement of derivative positions (failure to keep the functions separate can play a large part in facilitating internal fraud).

The treasury policy manual must be readily accessible to everyone at all levels within the treasury and finance functions. This will facilitate compliance with these policies, especially regarding:

- hedging policy;
- liquidity guidelines;
- loan covenants;
- bank mandates.

11.4.3   Implementation of internal dealing room controls to reduce errors or fraud in relation to derivatives and international transfers of money

Simple basic internal procedures can be applied to help prevent unauthorised position taking or even outright fraud.

- Ensure that the dealer sits in a room where others can hear their conversations.

- Rotate dealing duties so that dealers can never be sure that they will be dealing on any particular day and to ensure that they have to explain their positions to others at frequent, but irregular, intervals.

- The treasury manager must make frequent, but irregular, visits to the dealing room and should ask apparently silly questions.

- The treasury operations manager should not have any dealing authority, so that they are free to sign confirmations.

- All conversations by dealers with counterparties should be recorded and control of the recordings should be vested in independent administrators.

- There should be a computer based audit trail recording all deals.

- Mandates to counterparties such as banks should be authorised by the board and must be issued by someone who is independent of the treasury, such as the company secretary.

- Mandates should stipulate who within the company has authority to deal, in what instrument and at what a maximum amount.

The precise procedures will vary from company to company and all procedures are costly. The consequences of not following such procedures could, of course, be even worse for the company.

Readers may remember the collapse of Barings Bank in 1994 following unsupervised dealings by Nick Leeson, its 'rogue trader' in Singapore, whose escapades were later described in a book and a film.

11.4.4   Credit risk

There must be a list of approved counterparties (including banks), together with maximum exposure limits for each counterparty, to help control credit risk. Procedures should be developed for monitoring and reporting any credit excesses. Specific action should be taken to ensure the netting of positions on derivatives so that potential losses against individual counterparties can safely be set off against potential gains to establish the net value at risk in connection with all individual counterparties. This will require expert legal advice on documentation and other procedures.

11.4.5   Internal reporting to help reduce the losses from fraud and human error

The treasurer should receive daily reports as follows:

- any breach of counterparty credit limit;

- a list of all deals done in the day (foreign exchange, derivatives, financial instruments, such as commercial paper);

- any changes to standing data, such as changes to formulae in special sheets.

11.4.6 Physical controls

There should be backup IT systems to enable the treasury to continue if the systems cease to function. If the company has a separate dealing room, the door should be kept locked at all times, so that only authorised personnel can enter. All computers should be password protected, especially any computers that interface with electronic banking systems. These computers should have 'screensaver passwords' to prevent access other than by password if the computer is left unattended. Cells on some spreadsheets should be 'read only' if they contain formulae that are vital.

11.4.7 Treasury personnel

'Soft factors', such as recruitment, selection and training, can help to ensure that the people employed have the right skills and outlook. There should be an up-to-date and comprehensive procedures manual to help new staff understand what is expected of them. It should also be a rule that treasury staff must have at least one period of ten continuous working days' leave per year. This will ensure that a different person must carry out the duties on a day-to-day basis for two working weeks. This will help to detect any fraudulent practices.

Corporate treasury departments are relatively small and some writers argue that, where there is a high degree of teamwork and high staff morale, there is less risk of fraud or human error, because since everyone wants to contribute to success and will help other team members achieve that aim.

Part III

Introduction

You will recall that, at the very outset, it was claimed that students would find *International Financial Services* a stimulating and enjoyable challenge. In Part II, you applied sensible logical principles to practical aspects of foreign exchange and money transmission. No doubt you can now see that the claim made at the beginning of the book was perfectly valid.

In Part III of this book, we examine the documents used in international trade. The selection of documents is inexorably and logically linked with the shipping and payment terms agreed between exporter and importer, and this link is carefully analysed. Students should be aware that there continue to be developments towards replacing many of these paper- based documents with electronic equivalents.

In Part IV, we consider the main methods of payment for exports, together with their attendant risks and methods of containing that risk. These methods of payment are analysed in detail purely from the point of view of the exporter and its bank. A detailed analysis of the considerations of importers and their banks is given in Part V.

Topic 12

Transport documents used in international trade

On completion of this topic, the student should be able to:

- understand the basic meaning of open account payment terms;

- appreciate the role of the bill of lading in international trade;

- differentiate between transport documents that are documents of title and those that are not.

12.1 The meaning of 'open account' payment terms

When a buyer and seller agree to deal on 'open account' terms, it means that the seller will ship their goods to the buyer and will also send an invoice, together with any other supporting documentation such as transport and insurance documents, requesting payment. The seller loses control of the goods as soon as they are shipped, placing trust in the buyer that they will pay in accordance with the invoice. If the buyer does not pay, however, the seller is in a difficult position, because the goods are now in the buyer's possession.

Despite these problems, open account terms are very common, especially for trade within the EU. It is estimated that open account transactions represent around 80% of world trade today. The role of documents as discussed in this topic will relate solely to their use under open account payment terms. Their application under a documentary collection or a documentary credit is described in Topics 17 and 18.

12.2 The bill of lading

A 'bill of lading' normally embodies the following details, the numbers of which correspond to those on the specimen bill of lading (see Figure 12.1).

1. The name of the shipping company (sometimes known as the 'carrier').

2. The name of the shipper, who is usually the exporter, or the exporter's agent.

3. The name of the consignee. If the word 'order' appears here, then the shipper (exporter) must indorse the bills of lading either in blank or to a named party.

When the bills of lading have been indorsed in this way, it is transferable by delivery. The bills of lading may also be issued 'to order' of a named party, ie 'to order of [name of importer]'. Once the goods arrive at their destination, they will be released to the holder of one original bill of lading (see also item 11 below).

As an alternative to 'order', the name and address of the importer can appear as consignee. In this case, the document is known as a 'straight consigned' bill of lading. In such cases, the importer can obtain the goods, once they have arrived at their destination, by presenting an original bill of lading, together with identification. It should be noted that some shipping companies will allow release of goods to the named consignee, under a straight consigned bill of lading, without production of an original bill of lading.

Normally, bills of lading are made out to order and indorsed by the exporter.

4. The 'notify' party is the person whom the shipping company or its agent will notify upon arrival of the goods. This is usually the importer or its agent.

5. This is the name of the carrying vessel.

6. These are the ports of loading and discharge of the goods. In the example shown in the specimen, the goods are to be transported from the port of discharge (Hong Kong) to the premises of Woldal Ltd in Kowloon, and thus a place of delivery is mentioned in addition to the two ports.

7. The marks and numbers will appear on the cases in which the goods are contained, so that it is quite clear which cases are covered by this bill of lading. If goods are packed in containers, only the container number and, possibly, the seal number of the container will appear.

8. This gives a brief description of the goods.

9. This shows how many cases. In this particular shipment, the goods are packed into five cases.

10. This shows whether the freight costs have already been paid, as they have in this case, or whether payment of freight is due on arrival at the overseas destination. This is often shown by wording or stamp on the bill of lading stating 'Freight Paid' or 'Freight Payable at Destination'.

11. This shows how many original bills of lading have been issued. An original bill of lading is one that is signed by the shipping company, the ship's master or by an agent of the shipping company.

12. This bill of lading is an original, having been signed on behalf of the shipping company.

13. For the specimen shown, this is the date on which the shipping company received the goods for shipment. (see preprinted wording 'Received by the carrier ...'). In these circumstances, the shipping company or its agent will normally place an on- board notation on the bill of lading, which will indicate the date of shipment. The preprinted wording could also indicate 'Shipped on board ...', in which event the date of issuance of the bill of lading is taken as the date of shipment.

Figure 12.1 A specimen bill of lading

Shipper (Complete name, address and phone number)			Bill of Lading For Combined Transport or Port to Port Shipment		
SPEIRS AND WADLEY LTD [2] ADDERLEY ROAD LONDON E8 1XY ENGLAND			B/L No : 45969648 Booking Ref: 1234587 Shipper's Ref Job 5678		
Consignee (Not negotiable unless consigned to order) TO ORDER [3]			**Seaway Line** [1]		
Notify party (Carrier not to be responsible for failure to notify) WOLDAL LTD NEW ROAD KOWLOON HONG KONG [4]					
Pre-carriage by*		Place of receipt*			
Vessel CARDIGAN BAY [5]	Voy No.	Port of loading TILBURY [6]			
Port of discharge HONG KONG [6]		Place of delivery* KOWLOON	*Applicable only when this document is used as a Combined Transport Bill of Lading		

Marks and Nos Container Nos. /Seals	No. of packages	Description of packages and goods	Gross weight (kg)	Measurement (cbm)
WL 124 HONG KONG [7] 1/5	5 [9]	5 WOODEN CASES CONTAINING 400 ELECTRIC POWER DRILLS MODEL LM 425 2 SPEED (900RPM/2400RPM) 425 WATT HIGH TORQUE MOTOR 2 CHUCKS 12.5MM AND 8MM SUPPLIED WITH EACH DRILL [8]	950	2.376
		ABOVE PARTICULARS DECLARED BY SHIPPER: CARRIER NOT RESPONSIBLE		

Freight and charges (indicate whether prepaid or collect)			RECEIVED by the Carrier from the shipper in apparent good order and condition (unless otherwise noted herein) the total numbers or quantity of Containers or other packages or units indicated above stated by the shipper to comprise the cargo specified above, for transportation subject to all the terms hereof (including the terms on the reverse hereof) from the place of receipt or the port of loading, whichever applicable, to the port of discharge or the place of delivery whichever applicable.
Origin Inland Haulage charge... PREPAID.... Origin terminal Handling/ LCL Service charges PREPAID.... Ocean Freight PREPAID Destination Terminal Handling/ LCL Service charges... PREPAID.... Destination Inland haulage charges... PREPAID.... [10]			Delivery of the Goods will only be made on payment of all freight and charges. On presentation of this document (duly endorsed) to the Carrier, by or on behalf of the holder, the rights and liabilities arising in accordance with the terms hereof shall (without prejudice to any rule of common law or statute rendering them binding upon the shipper, holder and Carrier) become binding in all respects between the carrier and holder as though the contract contained herein or evidenced hereby had been made between them. In witness whereof three (3) original Bills of Lading unless otherwise stated below have been issued, one of which being accomplished, the others to be void. Freight, charges and primage whether prepayable or not and whether paid or not shall be considered as fully earned upon shipment and shall be paid vessel and/or cargo lost or not lost. (CONTINUED ON REVERSE SIDE)
			Place and date of issue TILBURY 1 AUGUST XXXX [13]
Declared value by shipper (see clause 5 C.A and tariff)		Movement	Signed for the Carrier By [12] *John Robinson*
Releasing Agent		Freight payable at	
		Number of original B/L [11] TWO (02)	For and on behalf of the Carrier Seaway Line

12.2.1 How the bill of lading would be used in an open account transaction

12.2.1.1 Example

A UK exporter, Speirs and Wadley Ltd, has agreed to sell electric drills to Woldal Ltd, with Speirs and Wadley Ltd being responsible for all costs and risks until the goods are delivered to Woldal's premises in Kowloon.

The transaction will proceed as follows, assuming open account terms have been agreed.

1. Speirs and Wadley will pack the drills into cases and will arrange a contract with its forwarding agent or the shipping company to deliver the goods.

2. Speirs and Wadley will deliver the cases to Seaway Line or its agent, who will issue two signed original bills of lading in exchange for the goods. The bills of lading will be given to Speirs and Wadley.

3. Speirs and Wadley will airmail or courier one of the original bills of lading to Woldal Ltd, along with any other necessary documents. The other original will probably be sent by a later mail in case the first happens to go astray, although this is generally unnecessary if a courier is used.

4. When the goods arrive at Hong Kong port, Seaway Line or its agent will notify Woldal and will make arrangements to move the goods from the port, overland, to the Kowloon premises of the importer.

5. Seaway Line or its agent will release the goods to Woldal only against surrender of one of the original bills of lading.

6. If not done so already, Woldal will then pay Speirs and Wadley in accordance with the arrangements they have made between themselves.

12.2.2 The functions of a bill of lading

There are four main functions of a bill of lading.

1. A bill of lading acts as a receipt for the goods from the shipping company to the exporter. Note the words 'Received by the carrier from the shipper in apparent good order and condition' at the bottom right- hand corner of the front of the specimen bill of lading in Figure 12.1.

   When there is no indication of damage to the goods, a bill of lading is said to be 'clean'. The specimen bill is a clean bill of lading, because the words 'Received in apparent good order and condition' are not qualified in any way by reference to a defective nature of the goods or their packaging.

2. The bill of lading is evidence of the contract of carriage between Speirs and Wadley and the shipping company. In the specimen we can see the basic details of the journey (by the ship *Cardigan Bay* from Tilbury to Hong Kong and thence overland to Kowloon).

   The full terms and conditions of the contract of carriage generally appear on the reverse of a bill of lading. A detailed knowledge of these conditions is not required for the purpose of this syllabus.

3. A bill of lading is a quasi- negotiable document. Any transferee for value who takes possession of an indorsed bill of lading obtains good title to it, provided that the transferor had good title in the first place.

4. If a bill of lading is issued 'to order' and indorsed in blank, or indorsed to a named party, or is issued 'to order of [named party]', it acts as a document of title for the goods being shipped. The goods will be released by the shipping company or its agent only against surrender of one of the original bills of lading.

   Original bills of lading are usually issued in sets (the number of originals will be indicated on the bill of lading), with two or three being the usual number of originals issued.

   Because any one original bill of lading will enable the holder to obtain the goods, possession of a complete set is required before control of the goods is assured. Shipping companies or their agents often issue unsigned non-negotiable copies of the bill of lading for record purposes. These non-negotiable copies are not documents of title.

12.2.3 The different types of bill of lading

There are many different types of bill of lading, but the main ones we need to consider are outlined below.

12.2.3.1 Combined transport or multimodal bills of lading and similar documents

A combined transport or multimodal bill of lading is generally used if the goods have, for example, been collected from a named inland place (in the country of export) for shipment to a port, inland container depot or factory or warehouse of the importer (in the country of import).

Depending on the shipment terms that are determined in the sales contract (known as 'Incoterms' and explained in Topic 14), the importer may have to make separate arrangements to have the goods collected from the port or inland container depot in its country and delivered to its factory or warehouse.

A 'through' bill of lading is a similar document that may evidence shipment of goods to a named destination, for example, the importer's warehouse. Strictly speaking, if the two parties agree that goods will be sent at the expense of the seller to the buyer's own premises, a through bill of lading should be used if any part of the journey is covered by a sea voyage.

In practice, combined or multimodal transport documents are often used in place of a through bill of lading, as can be seen from the Speirs and Wadley combined transport bill of lading (Figure 12.1). In this document, it appears that the delivery point is the warehouse of Woldal Ltd in Kowloon.

12.2.3.2 Transhipment bills of lading

Transhipment bills of lading are basically a normal port-to-port bill of lading, but evidencing transhipment when the goods have to be transferred from one ship to another during the course of carriage. Transhipment usually occurs on long sea journeys or if shipping companies only operate certain routes and one or more ports is designated as a hub port for transhipment to occur. Once again, the carrier takes full responsibility for the whole journey and these documents are usually considered to be documents of title if the appropriate **negotiable** wording appears.

12.2.3.3 Container bills of lading

When goods are packed in containers, shipping companies or their agents issue bills of lading that simply act as a receipt for a container. 'Container' bills of lading can be issued to cover goods being transported on a traditional port-to-port basis, or they can cover transport, for example, from an inland container depot in the exporter's country to an inland container depot in the importer's country.

Once again, the shipping company is responsible for the whole journey and these bills of lading are considered to be documents of title, provided that they contain the appropriate **negotiable** wording.

12.2.3.4 Marine bills of lading or conventional ocean bills of lading

'Marine' or 'conventional ocean' bills of lading are issued when the goods are being transported from one port to another by ship.

12.2.3.5 Short form bill of lading

The 'short form' bill of lading does not contain the full details of the contract of carriage on the reverse, but will make reference to a document or source from which the terms of carriage may be determined. It fulfils all of the other functions of bills of lading and, in particular, may be issued as a document of title provided that it contains the appropriate **negotiable** wording.

12.2.3.6 Liner bills of lading

The 'liner' bill of lading fulfils all of the normal functions of a bill of lading, including that of document of title, where applicable. The liner bill of lading indicates that goods are being transported on a ship that travels on a scheduled route and has a reserved berth at the destination; thus the exporter can reasonably assume that its goods will reach the buyer's country by a set date.

12.2.3.7 Charter party bill of lading

A 'charter party' bill of lading is issued to the exporter by the owner of a ship, the master, the charterer or their respective agent. The terms of the bill of lading are subject to the contract of hire between the ship's owner and the charterer. Such bills are usually marked 'subject to charter party'. Charter party bills of lading are usually issued if bulk cargoes such as oil, wheat, sugar, etc, are shipped.

Because of the legal complexity involved, while charter party bills of lading are often issued to order of a named party, they are not always considered to be documents of title.

12.3   Sea waybills

A 'sea waybill' (sometimes known as a 'ship's waybill') is a transport document that can be issued by the shipping company or its agent as an alternative to bills of lading, especially if short sea journeys are involved.

The functions of a waybill are similar to those of a bill of lading, except that a waybill is not negotiable and it is not a document of title. On arrival at their destination, the goods will be released by the shipping company or its agent to the named consignee against identification.

When exporters agree to sell on open account terms, it follows that the exporter should ask for sea waybills rather than bills of lading.

The objective with open account is for the goods to reach the importer with the minimum formality and waybills can meet that objective. As soon as the goods reach their destination, the shipping company or its agent will notify the consignee, who, in most cases, will be the importer. The importer can then collect the goods, without the need to produce the waybill.

If bills of lading go astray, there are problems for the importer in collecting the goods, whereas it is immaterial to the importer whether or not it has possession of a waybill.

In the example shown in Figure 12.2, it can be seen that the layout and structure of a sea waybill is very similar to that of a bill of lading (as shown in Figure 12.1).

Sea waybills are very similar in scope to air waybills, a specimen of which we will examine next.

12.4   Air waybills

'Air waybills' (also known as 'air consignment notes' are issued by airlines or their agents when goods are dispatched by air. There is no equivalent of a negotiable bill of lading with air transport.

Figure 12.2 Specimen sea waybill

APL NON-NEGOTIABLE SEA WAYBILL

SHIPPER (Principal or Seller licensee and full address)	BOOKING NUMBER / WAYBILL NUMBER
	EXPORT REFERENCES
CONSIGNEE (Name and Full address)	FORWARDING AGENT (References, F.M.C. No.)
	POINT AND COUNTRY OF ORIGIN OF GOODS
NOTIFY PARTY (Name and Full address)	ALSO NOTIFY (Name and Full Address)/DOMESTIC ROUTING/ EXPORT INSTRUCTION/PIER – TERMINAL/ONWARD ROUTING FROM POINT OF DESTINATION
INITIAL CARRIAGE (MODE)* / PLACE OF RECEIPT*	
EXPORT CARRIER (Vessel, voyage & flag)* / PORT OF LOADING	
PORT OF DISCHARGE / PLACE OF DELIVERY*	

PARTICULARS FURNISHED BY SHIPPER Payment by Cheque must be made to the order of APL Co. Plc. Ltd

MKS & NOS/CONTAINER NOS	NO. OF PKGS	DESCRIPTION OF PACKAGES AND GOODS	GROSS WEIGHT	MEASUREMENT
		SPECIMEN		

AWB TO BE RELEASED AT	OCEAN FREIGHT PAYABLE AT		
FREIGHT RATES, CHARGES, WEIGHTS AND/OR MEASUREMENTS (SUBJECT TO CORRECTION)	PREPAID US$	COLLECT US$	Local Currency
TOTAL PREPAID			
Vessel / Voyage / Office / TOTAL COLLECT			

The undersigned Carrier hereby acknowledges receipt of the sealed container or packages or other shipping units said to contain the Goods described above in apparent external good order and condition unless otherwise stated. The Shipper agrees, and the Consignee and every person having an interest in the Goods is advised that the receipt, custody, carriage and delivery of the Goods are subject to all the terms and conditions set forth and incorporated by reference on this side and the reverse hereof, whether written, stamped or printed. This sea waybill is a non-negotiable document, which need not be surrendered in exchange for delivery of the Goods, and the carrier shall be justified in delivering the Goods to
(a) a person who is lawfully entitled to the possession of the Goods or
(b) the consignee named in the waybill

THE CARRIER

By:
Authorised Signature
Date and
Place issued

FCC	FORWARDER	SHIPPER	CONSIGNEE	LD PORT	DIS PORT	DEST	NOTIFY	CSC	SEA WAYBILL NUMBER

*APPLICABLE ONLY WHEN USED AS THROUGH WAYBILL

TERMS AND CONDITIONS

CLAUSE 1. Received by the Carrier from the Shipper in apparent good order and condition (unless otherwise noted herein) the total number of Containers or other packages or units enumerated on the front of this Sea Waybill, for Carriage from the Place of Receipt or Port of Loading, whichever is applicable, to the Place of Delivery or Port of Discharge, whichever is applicable, accorrding to the terms of the contract evidenced by this Sea Waybill.

CLAUSE 2. Unless instructed otherwise in writing by the Shipper delivery of the Goods will be made only to the Consignee or his authorised representative. Delivery to be made upon proper proof of identity and authorisation without the need of producing or surrendering a copy of this Sea Waybill.

CLAUSE 3. The contract evidenced by this Sea Waybill is subject to the terms, conditions, exceptions, limitations and liberties (including those relating to pre-carriage and on-carriage) set out in and incorporated by the Carrier's Bill of Lading. The terms of the Carrier's Applicable Tariff are incorporated herein. Particular attention is drawn to the terms therein relating to Container and vehicle demurrage.

Unless the context otherwise requires the term or any reference to "Bill of Lading" and "Applicable Tariff" wherever appearing in the Carrier's Bill of Lading shall be deemed to include and refer to this Sea Waybill.

The Shipper accepts the said terms, conditions, exceptions, limitations and liberties on it's own behalf and on behalf of the Consignee and the Owner of the Goods and warrants that it has authority to do so.

CLAUSE 4. The Consignee by presenting this Sea Waybill and/or by requesting delivery of the Goods undertaked all liabilities of the Shipper hereunder, such undertaking being additional and without prejudice to the Shipper's own liability. The benefit of the contract evidenced by this Sea Waybill shall thereby be transferred to the Consignee.

CLAUSE 5. A copy of the Carrier's Bill of Lading and the Carrier's Applicable Tariff may be inspected and will be supplied on request by any of the offices of the Carrier or its agents.

CLAUSE 6. Subject to Clause 6 of the Carrier's Bill of Lading, the Hague or Hague-Visby Rules, whichever would have been applicable if this Sea Waybill were a Bill of Lading, shall apply to the contract evidenced by this Sea Waybill. The contract evidenced by this Sea Waybill is deemed to be a contract of Carriage as defined in Article 1(b) of the Hague Rules and the Hague-Visby Rules.

CLAUSE 7. The term "Consignee" shall include any Person to whom the Goods are delivered pursuant to the written instructions of the Shipper.

CLAUSE 8. The contrace evidenced hereby or contained herein shall be governed by Singapore Law. Any contract or other disputes thereunder shall be solely determined by Singapore Courts unless the Carrier otherwise agrees in writing.

Figure 12.3   Specimen air waybill

| 125 | | | | 125-67891234 |

Shipper's Name and Address	Shipper's Account Number
SPEIRS AND WADLEY LTD ADDERLEY ROAD HACKNEY LONDON E8 1XY ENGLAND [1]	A9127653B

Not negotiable

Air Waybill

Issued by   [1]

Member of IATA

ORIENT Air Cargo

Copies 1, 2 and 3 of this Air Waybill are originals and have the same validity.

Consignee's Name and Address	Consignee's Account Number
PHILMEN INT LONGTOWN CALIFORNIA [1]	C8376542D

It is agreed that the goods described herein are accepted in apparent good order and condition (except as noted) for carriage SUBJECT TO THE CONDITIONS OF CONTRACT ON THE REVERSE HEREOF. ALL GOODS MAY BE CARRIED BY ANY OTHER MEANS INCLUDING ROAD OR ANY OTHER CARRIER UNLESS SPECIFIC CONTRARY INSTRUCTIONS ARE GIVEN HEREON BY THE SHIPPER. THE SHIPPER'S ATTENTION IS DRAWN TO THE NOTICE CONCERNING CARRIERS' LIMITATION OF LIABILITY. Shipper may increase such limitation of liability by declaring a higher value for carriage and paying a supplemental charge if required.

ISSUING CARRIER MAINTAINS CARGO ACCIDENT LIABILITY INSURANCE

Issuing Carrier's Agent Name and City	Accounting Information
BRUNSWICK AIR LONDON GATWICK	

Agent's IATA Code	Account No.
93-5-2221	SW 123456

Airport of Departure (Addr. of First Carrier) and Requested Routing)

GATWICK   [2]

| To
LTN | By First Carrier
XY100 | Routing and Destination | to | by | to | by | Currency
1.98 | CHGS
Code | WT/VAL
PPD COLL | Other
PPD COLL | Declared Value for Carriage | Declared Value for Customs
[3] |

Airport of Destination	Flight/Date	For Carrier's Use only	Flight/Date
LONGTOWN [2]			

Handling Information   5 CASES   [4]
WL
124
LONGTOWN

No. of Pieces RCP	Gross Weight	kg lb	Rate Class Commodity Item No.	Chargeable Weight	Rate Charge	Total	Nature and Quantity of Goods (incl. Dimensions or Volume)
5	950	K	4401	1000KG	0.80c [5]	800.00	5 WOODEN CASES CONTAINING 400 ELECTRIC POWER DRILLS [6] MODEL LM 425 2 SPEED (900RPM/2400RPM) 425 WATT HIGH TORQUE MOTOR 2 CHUCKS 12.5MM AND 8MM SUPPLIED WITH EACH DRILL
5	950						

Prepaid	Weight Charge	Collect	Other Charges
800.00 [7]			
	Valuation Charge		
	Tax		
25.00	Total Other Charges Due Agent		
60.00	Total Other Charges Due Carrier		

Shipper certifies that the particulars on the face hereof are correct and that insofar as any part of the consignment contains dangerous goods, such part is properly described by name and is in proper condition for carriage by air according to the applicable Dangerous Goods Regulations.

[8]

Signature of Shipper or his Agent

Total Prepaid	Total Collect
885.00	[9]

Currency Conversion Rates	CC Charges in Dest. Currency

| For Carrier's Use only
At Destination | Charges at Destination | Total Collect Charges |

FOR BRUNSWICK AIR   [10]

James Jameson   Executed

Signature of Issuing Carrier or its Agent

1 AUGUST XXXX   LGW
on (date)   at (place)

125-67891234

ORIGINAL 3 (FOR SHIPPER)

An air waybill normally features the following details, the numbers of which correspond to those on the specimen air waybill (Figure 12.3).

1. This shows the names and addresses of the exporter (shipper), importer (consignee) and the carrier, Orient Air Cargo. The words 'not negotiable' indicate that this is not a document of title.

In this particular example, the airline or its agent will notify the consignee, Philmen Int, when the goods arrive. Philmen Int will then be able to collect the goods without the need to produce this waybill.

2. This shows the names of the airports of departure and destination, together with details of any special route.

3. This shows the declared value for customs purposes (when stated). A detailed knowledge of customs procedures is not required for this syllabus.

4. These marks fulfil the same function as the shipping marks on a bill of lading. The marks will appear on all the cases.

5. This shows details of the freight charge or rate.

6. This gives a brief description of the goods.

7. This shows whether freight is prepaid or whether it is payable at destination.

8. This space is for the exporter or its agent to sign to confirm the certification shown above. In practice, however, this segment is rarely signed.

9. This shows the date on which the airline or its agent accepted the goods for carriage.

10. This is the space for signature by the carrier or an agent on behalf of the carrier.

12.5   Other transport documents

When goods are sent by rail or road haulage, the transport documents will be 'rail or road consignment notes', or 'truck/carrier receipts'. In Europe, these are known as the 'CMR note' (truck) and the 'CIM note' (rail). These are not documents of title and goods are released to the consignee (importer) on application and identification. An example of a CMR note is shown in Figure 12.4.

Figure 12.4   A CMR note

LETTRE DE VOITURE INTERNATIONALE	(CMR)	INTERNATIONAL CONSIGNMENT NOTE

Sender (Name, Address, Country) Expéditeur (Nom, Adresse, Pays)	1	Customs Reference/Status Référence/désignation pour mise en douane UKG7805678	2
Speirs and Wadley Ltd Adderley Road London E8 1XY		Sender's/Agent's reference Référence de l'expéditeur/de l'agent W2345AX07	3
Consignee (Name, Address, Country) Destinaire (Nom, Adresse, Pays)	4	Carrier (Name, Address, Country) Transporteur (Nom, Adresse, Pays)	5
Woldal Ltd Bahnstrasse 15 Frankfurt		Roadway Carriers Ltd, London, UK	
Place & date of taking over the goods (place, country, date) Lieu et date de la prise en charge des marchandises (Lieu, pays, date)	6	Successive Carriers Transporteurs Successifs	7
Hackney, London – 4 October xxxx			
Place designated for delivery of goods (place, country) Lieu prévu pour la livraison des marchandises (lieu, pays)	8	This carriage is subject, notwithstanding any clause to the contrary, to the Convention on the Contract for the International Carriage of Goods by Road (CMR) Ce transport est soumis nonobstant toute clause contraire à la Convention Relative au Contrat de Transport International de Marchandises par Route (CMR)	
Frankfurt, Germany			

Marks & Nos; No & Kind of Packages; Description of Goods* Marques et Nos; No et nature des colis, Désignation des Marchandises* 9	Gross weight (kg) 10 Poids Brut (kg)	Volume (m³) 11 Cubage (m³)
WL 5 Wooden Cases containing: 124 400 Electric Power Drills Model LM 425 Frankfurt 2 Speed (900rpm/2400rpm) 425 watt high torque motor 1/5 2 chucks 12.5mm and 8mm supplied with each drill	950	2.376

Carriage Charges Prix de Transport	12	Sender's instructions for Customs, etc... Instructions de l'Expéditeur (optional)	13
Prepaid			
Reservations Réserves	14	Documents Attached Documents Annexés (optional) Invoice, certificate of origin, warranty certificate	15
		Special agreements Conventions particulières (optional)	16
Goods Received/Marchandises Reçues	17	Signature and stamp of Carrier/Signature et timbre du Transporteur 18	Company completing this note Société émettrice 19
		For Roadway Carriers Ltd *Simon Bristown* 4 October xxxx	Speirs and Wadley Ltd Place and Date; Signature Lieu et Date; Signature 20 Hackney – 4 October xxxx *David Johnson*

When goods are sent by post, the document evidencing postage is a parcel post receipt or courier receipt.

All forms of waybill, consignment note, parcel post receipt, or courier receipt fulfil two of the functions of a bill of lading: they act as a receipt for the goods by the carrier and they give some evidence of the contract of carriage. These documents are not negotiable, however, and are not documents of title. Usually, the words 'not negotiable' will appear on these documents to indicate that they are not documents of title and that goods will be released or delivered to the named consignee.

Topic 13

Documents other than transport documents

On completion of this topic, the student should be able to:

- appreciate the important features of invoices;

- describe the various types of invoice that can be required in international trade;

- appreciate the open cover method of insurance of goods and understand the significance of the insurance certificate in this respect;

- understand the significance of the standard clauses of the Institute of London Underwriters;

- appreciate the importance of certificates of origin;

- be aware of other documents that may be encountered in international trade.

13.1 The commercial invoice

A 'commercial invoice' provides details of the goods and delivery terms, a detailed breakdown of the monetary amount due and details of how payment is to be made. Invoices are prepared by the seller or exporter.

If we study the specimen document (Figure 13.1), we can see the main details that appear on invoices (the numbers correspond to those on the document).

1. Name and address of the exporter.

2. Name and address of the importer.

3. Invoice number date of issue (tax point).

4. Terms of delivery (sometimes called 'Incoterms', sometimes called 'shipment terms', which are discussed fully in Topic 14).

5. Shipping marks (note how these tie up with the marks on the specimen bill of lading and on the specimen air waybill).

6 & 7. Quantity of packages and description of goods.

Figure 13.1 Specimen commercial invoice

	INVOICE	FACTURE FACTURA	RECHNUNG FACTUUR	

Seller (name, address, VAT reg. No.) SPEERS AND WADLEY LTD ADDERLEY ROAD HACKNEY LONDON E8 1XY ENGLAND [1]	Invoice number 247546 [3]		Sheet no. 1
	Invoice date (tax point) 11 AUG xxxx [3]	Seller's reference JOB NO. 6678	
	Buyer's reference 124	Other reference	
Consignee WOLDAL LTD NEW ROAD KOWLOON HONG KONG [2]	Buyer (if not consignee) VAT no		
	Country of origin of goods EEC UNITED KINGDOM	Country of destination HONG KONG	
	Terms of delivery and payment CIP KOWLOON HONG KONG [4]		
Vessel/flight no. and date CARDIGAN BAY	Port/airport of loading TILBURY		
Port/airport of discharge HONG KONG	Place of delivery KOWLOON		

Shipping marks; container number WL 124 HONG KONG 1/5 [5]	No. and kind of packages, description of goods 5 WOODEN CASES – ELECTRIC POWER DRILLS [6]	Commodity code	Total gross wt (kg) 950	Total cube 2.376
			Total net weight (kg)	

Item/packages 5	Gross/net/cube Description 5 WOODEN CASES CONTAINING 400 ELECTRIC POWER DRILLS MODEL LM 425 2 SPEED (900RPM/2400RPM) 425 WATT HIGH TORQUE MOTOR 2 CHUCKS – 12.5MM AND 8MM SUPPLIED WITH EACH DRILL [7]	Quantity 400 [9]	Unit price £10.27	Amount £4108
	[10]	Invoice total £4108.00 STG		
FREIGHT £96.00 INSURANCE £12.00 [8]				
		Name of signatory J McDONALD – SHIPPING MANAGER		
VAT REG NO. 241 8235 77		Place and date of issue LONDON 11 AUGUST XXXX [3]		
		Signature		

8. Breakdown of the cost of freight and insurance (it is not always necessary for the exporter to supply this information).

9. Quantity of goods (in this case, 400 electric power drills).

10. Total amount payable by the importer.

11. Signature of the exporter (although a signature is not always necessary).

Note: for exports to other EU countries, the invoice must show the VAT number of the buyer to enable the exporter's goods to qualify for zero rating in relation to VAT. This formality is unnecessary for exports outside the EU.

13.2   Other types of invoice

13.2.1   The pro forma invoice

A 'pro forma invoice' is very similar to a commercial invoice, except that it will not include any shipping marks, and it will be clearly stamped 'pro forma'.

A commercial invoice is a claim for payment in connection with goods already shipped, whereas a pro forma invoice is an invitation to buy, which is sent to a potential buyer. Once a definite order has been placed and once the goods have been shipped, the commercial invoice will be issued.

In some overseas countries there are exchange controls that restrict the remittance of funds abroad unless the central bank has given approval. Often, a pro forma invoice is required by the central bank before approval can be given to pay for imports.

13.2.2   The consular invoice

A 'consular invoice' is required by some importing countries for customs purposes. The forms can be obtained from the embassy or the consulate of the importer's country. The exporter completes the details on the form and the document is then authenticated by the consulate of the country of the importer. This consulate is usually located in the exporter's country.

The purpose of consular invoices is to certify that the exporter is not dumping goods at artificially low prices. Their other function is to provide information that forms the basis of the import duty to be paid on the goods.

Not all importing countries require production of consular invoices, but those that do almost always charge a fee for certification. When a consular invoice is not available, the consulate will authenticate the exporter's own invoice. This is known as a 'legalised invoice'.

13.3   The insurance of goods

It is a matter for negotiation between the exporter and the importer as to who is responsible for insuring the goods during their journey from the exporter's premises to the importer's premises. In some transactions, it may be agreed that the exporter will insure the whole journey, while in others the onus may be on the importer. It is also possible for the agreement to say that the exporter must cover part of the journey and the importer cover for the rest. (The precise details of who does what are set out in Incoterms, which are covered in Topic 14.)

For the moment, let us consider the position of an exporter who is responsible for the insurance of goods.

When an exporter sells goods on a regular basis, it will normally arrange an open policy of insurance to cover all of its exports during a specific period. This provides insurance cover at all times within agreed terms and conditions. Each time a shipment is made, the exporter declares the details and pays a premium to the insurer. A certificate of insurance is then issued by the exporter, who sends one copy to the insurance company for its records.

The benefit of the open cover system is that it avoids the need to negotiate insurance terms each time a shipment is made and it avoids the necessity of issuing a separate policy for each individual shipment.

If an exporter sells goods on a one-off basis, it will negotiate terms with an insurer and an insurance policy or certificate will be issued.

In the UK and in many other countries, an insured person must have a policy before they can take legal action against an insurer. A certificate alone is insufficient evidence on which to base a legal action. This legal problem is important only if the importer needs to go to court because the insurance company has challenged a claim.

13.3.1   The risks covered by an insurance policy

The insurance cover is often based on the standard clauses of the Institute of London Underwriters. A detailed knowledge of these standard clauses is not required for this syllabus, but exam questions sometimes mention the standard clauses in connection with risks.

There are three main standard clauses of the Institute of London Underwriters that refer to risk. Institute Cargo Clause A begins:

> This clause covers all risk of loss or damage to the subject matter below except as provided in clauses 4, 5, 6 and 7 below.

Clause A provides the fullest available cover against risks and students should not be misled into believing that the 'except' clause is detrimental: importers and exporters are generally satisfied that Institute Cargo Clause A is perfectly acceptable cover against all risks.

Institute Cargo Clauses B and C also cover risks, but the extent of cover they provide is less than that provided by Clause A.

13.3.2 The insurance certificate

Figure 13.2 Specimen insurance certificate

Copy

Exporters Reference

AMLIN TRANSIT [1]
St. Helen's, 1 Undershaft, London EC3A 8ND
Telephone 020 7746 1666   Facsimile 020 7746 1221

CERTIFICATE OF MARINE INSURANCE NO.   17579

This is to Certify that the Underwriters have insured
the goods specified below under Open Policy No.
subject to the Policy Terms, Conditions and other details shown hereon.

in favour of

[2]

Conveyance	From (Commencement of transit)	
Via/to	To (final destination)	Insured Value and Currency [4]

Marks and Numbers	Interest

SPECIMEN

[5]

SHIPPED UNDER DECK BUT CONTAINER SHIPMENTS ON OR UNDER DECK.

SURVEYS

In the event of loss or damage for which the Underwriters may be liable, immediate application must be made by the ASSURED or his agents or the consignee to the UNDERWRITERS or the following agents to arrange for a Surveyor to be appointed:-

[6]

CLAIMS payable at [6]
by

Please refer to instructions printed overleaf.

Failure to comply with these instructions may prejudice any claim.
If the Assured shall make any claim knowing the same to be false or fraudulent, as regards amount or otherwise, this Insurance shall become void and all claims hereunder shall be forfeited.

CONDITIONS OF INSURANCE:
Subject to the conditions printed overleaf, as applicable to the type of interest shown above.

Signed for the Underwriters by

[1]

Amlin Underwriting Services Limited

(The Institute Clauses referred to are those current at the time of commencement of transit or risk)

THIS CERTIFICATE REQUIRES ENDORSEMENT BY THE INSURED.

This certificate is not valid unless countersigned by an authorised person   [7]

[8]

Place and Date of Issue

Authorised Signatory

Amlin Transit is a trading name of Amlin Underwriting Services Limited.
Registered in England No. 423615 Registered Office: St. Helen's, 1 Undershaft, London EC3A 8ND
Authorised and regulated by the Financial Services Authority

Institute Cargo Clauses (A)
Institute Cargo Clauses (Air) (excluding sending by post)
Institute War Clauses (Cargo)
Institute War Clauses (Air Cargo) (excluding sending by post)
Institute War Clauses (Post)
Institute Strikes Clauses
Institute Strikes Clauses (Air Cargo)
Institute Classification Clauses
Institute Radioactive Contamination, Chemical, Biological,
Bio-Chemical and Electromagnetic Weapons Exclusion Clause
Institute Cyber Attack Exclusion Clause
Institute Replacement Clause
Cargo ISM Endorsement (JC 98/019 1/5/98)

[3]

appropriate to the mode of transit to which this certificate applies and these clauses shall be deemed to be incorporated herein as if set out in full. If the full text of the appropriate clauses are not already known to the rightful holder of this certificate copies may be obtained from the Underwriters, Survey Agent or Claims Settling Agent.

Also subject to other conditions as may be shown hereon but in no case shall they afford wider cover than the Institute Cargo Clauses as above. All other Terms & Conditions of the open cover are to apply.

SECURITY: This insurance is underwritten 100% by Syndicate 2001 at Lloyd's.

IMPORTANT

PROCEDURE IN THE EVENT OF LOSS OR DAMAGE FOR WHICH UNDERWRITERS MAY BE LIABLE

LIABILITY OF CARRIERS, BAILEES OR OTHER THIRD PARTIES

It is the duty of the Assured and their Agents, in all cases, to take such measures as may be reasonable for the purpose of averting or minimising a loss and to ensure that all rights against Carriers, Bailees or other third parties are properly preserved and exercised. In particular, the Assured or their Agents are required:-

1. To claim immediately on the Carriers, Port Authorities or other Bailees for any missing packages.

2. In no circumstances, except under written protest, to give clean receipts where goods are in doubtful condition.

3. When delivery is made by Container, to ensure that the Container and its seals are examined immediately by their responsible official. If the Container is delivered damaged or with seals broken or missing or with seals other than as stated in the shipping documents, to clause the delivery receipt accordingly and retain all defective or irregular seals for subsequent identification.

4. To apply immediately for survey by Carriers or other Bailees Representatives if any loss or damage be apparent and claim on the Carriers or other Bailees for any actual loss or damage found at such survey.

5. To give notice in writing to the Carriers or other Bailees within 5 days of delivery if the loss or damage was not apparent at the time of taking delivery.

NOTE:

The Consignees or their Agents are recommended to make themselves familiar with the Regulations of the Port Authorities at the port of discharge.

DOCUMENTATION OF CLAIMS

To enable claims to be dealt with promptly, the Assured or their Agents are advised to submit all available supporting documents without delay, including when applicable:-

1. Original certificate of insurance.

2. Original or copy shipping invoices, together with shipping specification and/or weight notes.

3. Original Bill of Lading and/or other contract or carriage.

4. Survey report or other documentary evidence to show the extent of the loss or damage.

5. Landing account and weight notes at final destination.

6. Correspondence exchanged with the Carriers and other Parties regarding their liability for the loss or damage.

NOTE: It is necessary for the Assured when they become award of an event which is "held covered" under this Insurance to give prompt notice to the Underwriters and the right to such cover is dependent upon compliance with this obligation.

This Certificate represents and takes the place of the Policy which has been deposited with the Underwriters on behalf of all parties interested and conveys all the rights of the original policy-holder for the purpose of collecting any loss or claim as fully as if the property was covered by a Special Policy direct to the holder of this Certificate and is free of any liability for unpaid premiums.

THIS INSURANCE IS SUBJECT TO ENGLISH JURISDICTION

Insurance documents usually show the following details, the numbers of which correspond to those on the document.

1. The name and signature of the insurer.

2. The name of the exporter.

3. The risks covered (as you can see, this information consists merely of a list of standard clauses that apply).

4. The sum insured (normally this is expressed in the same currency as that of the invoice and is normally for the invoice value plus 10%, which is to cover an element of profit that the importer would have made and any associated costs).

5. The description of the goods that are the subject of the insurance.

6. The place at which claims are payable, together with any details of the agent to whom claims are to be directed.

7. The signature of the exporter, which is required to validate the certificate. (The certificate forms are usually pre- signed by the insurer. The exporter must complete the details and then sign.)

8. The date of issue. (This date should be the same as, or earlier than, the date on the transport document. If the date on the insurance document is later, indications are that the goods have been uninsured for a time.)

13.4 The certificate of origin

Some countries insist on the issuance of a 'certificate of origin' before they will allow goods into the country. The exporter inserts the relevant details and, depending on the requirements of the importing country, the form may then require authenticating by an independent body, such as a Chamber of Commerce. The details shown on the certificate of origin, in relation to the shipment, should tie up with those on other documents such as the invoice or bill of lading. The regulations of the importing country may require that the certificate of origin be issued on the letterhead of a Chamber of Commerce (as shown in Figure 13.3). Otherwise, the document may be issued on the letterhead of the exporter.

13.5 Other documents that are used in international trade

13.5.1 The black list certificate

A 'black list certificate' will certify that the goods have no connection with certain countries, such as Israel. Many countries in the Middle East will insist upon such a document before allowing goods to be imported. Recent political developments could reduce the need for such black list certificates.

Figure 13.3   Specimen certificate of origin

CERTIFICATE OF ORIGIN

	No. AE12345YZ	ORIGINAL
1 Consignor SPEIRS AND WADLEY LTD ADDERLEY ROAD HACKNEY, LONDON E8 1XY		
2 Consignee WOLDAL LTD NEW ROAD KOWLOON HONG KONG	**EUROPEAN COMMUNITY** **CERTIFICATE OF ORIGIN**	
	3 Country of origin UNITED KINGDOM	
4 Transport details (Optional) BY SEA – CARDIGAN BAY FROM TILBURY TO HONG KONG THEN TO KOWLOON	5 Remarks	

6 Item number; marks; numbers and kind of packages; description of goods	7 Quality
WL 5 WOODEN CASES: 124 ELECTRIC POWER DRILLS HONG KONG MODEL LM 425 2 SPEED (900RPM/2400RPM) 1/5 425 WATT HIGH-TORQUE MOTOR 2 CHUCKS – 12.5MM AND 8MM SUPPLIED WITH EACH DRILL	

9   THE UNDERSIGNED AUTHORITY CERTIFIES THAT THE GOODS DESCRIBED ABOVE ORIGINATE IN THE COUNTRY SHOWN IN BOX 3

LONDON CHAMBER OF COMMERCE

Place and date of issue, name, signature and stamp of competent authority

W. Smith

London .... W. Smith .... 12 August xxxx

London Chamber of Commerce

13.5.2   The third- party inspection certificate

A 'third- party inspection certificate' is issued by an independent third party attesting to the standard or quality of the goods that have been shipped. Sometimes, the term 'clean report of findings' may be used.

Occasionally, the importer will insist that such a document is issued and this stipulation can form part of the terms of the sale contract. In certain countries, particularly in Africa, it is common for a clean report of findings to be a standard requirement for any import or import of certain types of goods.

13.5.3   The packing list, or weight list

A 'packing list' or 'weight list' gives packing details of the goods that have been shipped and/or a list of the weights of individual items, together with a total weight.

13.5.4   Transport international routier (TIR) carnets

When goods travel overland across different frontiers outside the EU, a 'transport international routier' (TIR) carnet may be necessary. This document certifies that the vehicle or container has been sealed by the customs authorities in the exporter's country and ensures that no duty is payable in intermediate countries. When goods travel solely within the EU, the TIR carnet is unnecessary. TIR carnets usually accompany the goods on their journey. Bankers will not often see these documents, and a detailed knowledge of their issue and procedures is unnecessary.

13.6   The automated preparation of shipping documents

Efforts are constantly being made on a national and international basis to introduce methods of standardising and simplifying export documentation procedures. In the UK, the Simpler Trade Procedures Board (SITPRO) is charged with carrying out this task.

The basic methods of simplification all have one common factor: all documents in a set will be prepared on the basis of one single input of information.

SITPRO has produced an aligned series of export documents whereby the whole set of documents (from invoice, through bill of lading, to insurance document) are produced by the single input of relevant data onto a master document. The relevant information from the master document is then transferred onto the individual documents, using overlays and masks. For example, if the SITPRO master were to have been used in connection with the invoice (Figure 13.1) and certificate of insurance (Figure 13.2) shown on the preceding pages, then the details of the quantity, unit price and amount would have been transferred from the master to the commercial invoice, but these details would not have been transferred onto the insurance certificate. Other details, such as the shipping marks and goods description, would have been transferred from the master onto both of the other documents.

With the onset of technology, a single input of data into a computer can be used to provide the basic information for every document in a set. This technology will form the basis of e- commerce initiatives in the future.

Finally, SITPRO can provide a computerised system for preparing both the shipping documents and the relevant bank forms. For example, the SITPRO Aligned Series of Export Documents and, more recently, its UNeDocsUK system can be used by exporters to prepare both shipping documents and documentary collection orders. (Documentary collections are covered in Topic 17.)

Topic 14

Incoterms

On completion of this topic, the student should be able to:

- understand the purpose of Incoterms;

- describe the obligations that the various Incoterms impose;

- understand how Incoterms affect the documents that an exporter must produce;

- assess the cost implication of Incoterms.

14.1   The purpose of Incoterms

In international trade there are likely to be three separate contracts of transport for the goods:

- from the exporter's premises to a transport operator within the exporter's country;

- from the transport operator's premises in the exporter's country to a named point in the importer's country (eg a port, airport or container depot);

- from the port, etc, in the importer's country to the importer's own premises.

It is vital to establish a clearly defined cut-off point to show where the exporter's responsibility ends and where the importer's responsibility begins. This cut-off point refers, in the main, to payment of freight and to insurance of the goods while in transit. Unless the demarcation of responsibility is clearly understood, it will be difficult for an exporter to price its goods accurately and for an importer to calculate accurately the full cost of the importation.

The problem in international trade is that different countries have different interpretations of the same contract wording, and this problem can be solved only by creating a set of internationally agreed terms.

The purpose of the International Commercial Terms (Incoterms) is to provide such a set of standardised terms that mean exactly the same to both parties and which will be interpreted in exactly the same way by courts in every country. They were drafted by the International Chamber of Commerce (ICC) and full details can be found in its Publication No. 560, which is entitled *Incoterms 2000*.

Incoterms are not incorporated into national or international law, but they can be made binding on both importer and exporter, provided that the sales contract specifies that a particular Incoterm will apply.

Note: In the context of the examination, the words 'shipment terms' or 'terms of delivery' might be substituted for the word 'Incoterms'. For examination purposes, all of these words and phrases are synonymous.

14.2   The 13 Incoterms

There are 13 different Incoterms and each term sets out the obligations of the seller or exporter. It is not necessary to memorise the 13 terms, but it is necessary to be able to work out their implications, should such a term appear in an examination question. An easy way of recalling the various Incoterms is that they are grouped according to the first letter of the term: ie 'E' terms, 'F' terms, 'C' terms and 'D' terms.

Generally speaking, if Incoterms set out the obligations of the exporter, by a process of elimination, any obligation that does not appear in a particular Incoterm must be the responsibility of the importer.

In Topics 12 and 13, we examined various documents relating to a sale by Speirs and Wadley Ltd of Adderley Road, Hackney, to Woldal Ltd of New Road, Kowloon. Table 14.1 explains the implications, where appropriate, to both parties for the different Incoterms that could be applied to such a sale. The various Incoterms are set out in a logical order, starting with that which imposes least obligation on Speirs and Wadley and ending with that which imposes the most obligation.

Table 14.1   Implications of specific Incoterms for exporters and importers

Incoterm	Standard ICC Abbreviations	Obligations of Speirs and Wadley Ltd (Exporter)	Responsibilities of Woldal Ltd (Importer)
Ex works [named place, eg Adderley Road, Hackney]	EXW	Make the goods available for collection from Adderley Road, Hackney by Woldal Ltd. Once collected by Woldal, all responsibility of Spiers and Wadley is ended. A commercial invoice or electronic equivalent electronic message will be provided for Woldal. Goods will be suitably packaged unless it is the norm for the goods involved to be delivered unpacked.	Take delivery from Adderley Road. Make all arrangements at own cost to take goods to own premises. It is in Woldal's interests to arrange appropriate insurance to cover this journey. The obtaining of relevant export and/or import licences and also the completion of any customs formalities and payments for the export of the goods is the responsibility of Woldal.

Incoterm	Standard ICC Abbreviations	Obligations of Speirs and Wadley Ltd (Exporter)	Responsibilities of Woldal Ltd (Importer)
Free carrier [named place, eg Hackney Container Depot]	FCA	Make the goods available to Hackney Containers at the inland container depot on the exporter's means of transport not unloaded. **Note**: If the goods were to have been made available at the premises of Speirs and Wadley, delivery would be incomplete until the goods had been loaded onto the carrier's own transport. Advise delivery of the goods at Hackney container depot to Woldal. Complete export and customs requirements, including obtaining any export licence and paying any costs, duties and taxes. Supply Woldal with commercial invoice or its equivalent electronic message, together with proof of delivery to Hackney container depot, eg a multimodal transport document. Goods will be suitably packaged unless it is the norm for the goods involved to be delivered unpacked.	Make all arrangements at own cost and risk to cover transport of goods to own premises from Hackney container depot. It is in Woldal's interests to arrange appropriate insurance to cover this journey. Woldal should obtain any import licence and perform any customs requirements necessary for the import of the goods, including paying all costs, duties and taxes.
Free alongside ship [named port of shipment, eg Tilbury]	FAS	Complete export and customs requirements, including obtaining any export licence and paying any costs, duties and taxes. Supply Woldal with commercial invoice or its equivalent electronic message, together with proof of delivery, eg a transport document. Deliver goods to the quayside alongside the nominated vessel at the port of Tilbury, after which the liability of Speirs and Wadley basically ends. Goods will be suitably packaged unless it is the norm for the goods involved to be delivered unpacked.	Make arrangements with a shipping company for transport of goods by sea to Hong Kong. Notify Speirs and Wadley of the day and time that delivery is required at the port of Tilbury and the name of the nominated vessel. Woldal is responsible for all risks from the quayside in Tilbury to the delivery of the goods to their final destination. It is in Woldal's interests to arrange appropriate insurance to cover this journey. Woldal should obtain any import licence and perform any customs requirements necessary for the import of the goods, including meeting all costs involved, duties and taxes.

Incoterm	Standard ICC Abbreviations	Obligations of Speirs and Wadley Ltd (Exporter)	Responsibilities of Woldal Ltd (Importer)
Free on board [named port of shipment, eg Tilbury]	FOB	As for FAS, but Speirs and Wadley's delivery liability does not end until the goods have crossed the ship's rail and have been loaded on board a named ship at Tilbury.	As for FAS, but with the exception of not being responsible for the goods until they have crossed the ship's rail in the port of Tilbury.
Cost and freight [named port of destination, eg Hong Kong]	CFR	Arrange and pay for transport of goods to Hong Kong port. Loading and unloading costs should be met if they form part of the charge for carriage. Complete export and customs requirements, including obtaining any export licence and paying any costs, duties and taxes. Advise Woldal of delivery of the goods on board the carrying vessel and also details of the voyage. Supply Woldal with a commercial invoice or its electronic equivalent, together with the relevant transport document, eg a bill of lading. Goods will be suitably packaged unless it is the norm for the goods involved to be delivered unpacked. Speirs and Wadley are free of liability (for insurance purposes) once the goods have crossed the ship's rail in Tilbury port.	Woldal should obtain any import licence and perform any customs requirements necessary for the import of the goods, including meeting all costs involved, duties and taxes. It is in Woldal's interests to arrange and pay for insurance of the goods from when they cross the ship's rail in Tilbury. If unloading costs are not covered by the charge for carriage, Woldal must also pay these.
Cost, insurance and freight [named port of destination, eg Hong Kong]	CIF	As for CFR, but, in addition, Speirs and Wadley must insure the goods as far as the port of Hong Kong and supply Woldal with evidence of this, eg an insurance policy or certificate.	As for CFR, but insurance risk falls on Woldal only when the goods have crossed the ship's rail at Hong Kong.

Incoterm	Standard ICC Abbreviations	Obligations of Speirs and Wadley Ltd (Exporter)	Responsibilities of Woldal Ltd (Importer)
Carriage paid to [named destination]	CPT	Similar to CFR, except that Speirs and Wadley must arrange and pay for transport to the named place of destination, which could be an inland container depot in Hong Kong as opposed to Hong Kong port. Speirs and Wadley must advise Woldal of details of the shipment and the name and address of the shipping company into whose custody the goods have been given, so that Woldal can arrange insurance. Complete export and customs requirements, including obtaining any export licence and paying any costs, duties and taxes. Supply Woldal with commercial invoice or its equivalent electronic message, together with the relevant transport document. Goods will be suitably packaged unless it is the norm for the goods involved to be delivered unpacked.	Woldal should obtain any import licence and perform any customs requirements necessary for the import of the goods, including meeting all costs involved, duties and taxes. It is in Woldal's interests to arrange and pay insurance for the goods from when they are delivered into the custody of the shipping company at Tilbury. If unloading costs at place of destination are not covered by the charge for carriage, Woldal must pay them. Also it must pay all costs of transport from Kowloon Freight Yard to its own premises.
Carriage and insurance paid to [named destination]	CIP	Similar to CPT, except that Speirs and Wadley must pay insurance charges during the carriage. The relevant insurance policy or certificate must be supplied to Woldal.	Similar to CPT, except that Woldal does not have to arrange and pay insurance charges, which are met by Speirs and Wadley.
Delivered at frontier [named place]	DAF	This term is normally used when goods are in transit overland across a continent and would therefore not be an appropriate term for the example upon which we are basing this review. Where this term is applicable, Speirs and Wadley would arrange and pay for transport of goods to a named point on the frontier of a country, which may be Hong Kong, but not necessarily so. It is in the interests of Speirs and Wadley to insure the goods for the journey to the named place. Sufficient notice should be given to Woldal of dispatch of the goods, so that the latter can make arrangements to take delivery of them. Speirs and Wadley must supply a commercial invoice or its electronic equivalent together with the relevant transport document or delivery order to Woldal. Arrange issue of any export licence and complete customs formalities (including payment of all costs, duties and taxes). Goods will be suitably packaged unless it is the norm for the goods involved to be delivered unpacked.	Woldal should obtain any import licence and perform any customs requirements necessary for the import of the goods, including meeting all costs involved, duties and taxes. All costs and risks from the frontier point are the responsibility of Woldal, including the costs of unloading the goods from the arrival means of transport at the frontier in order to take delivery. It is in the interests of Woldal to arrange for insurance of the goods from the named place of delivery.

Incoterm	Standard ICC Abbreviations	Obligations of Speirs and Wadley Ltd (Exporter)	Responsibilities of Woldal Ltd (Importer)
Delivered ex ship [named port of destination]	DES	Similar to CIF, except that the liability of Speirs and Wadley does not cease until the goods have been placed at the disposal of Woldal on board a vessel at the named port of destination. Theoretically, Speirs and Wadley need not insure the goods but, in practice it would be wise to do so.	Similar to CIF. The liability of Woldal exists from the time when goods are placed at its disposal in the named port of destination.
Delivered ex quay [named port of destination]	DEQ	Deliver the goods on the quay or wharf at the named port of destination and pay unloading costs. Supply Woldal with a commercial invoice or its electronic equivalent together with the relevant transport document or delivery order. Arrange any export licence and complete export customs requirements, including payment of costs, duties and taxes. Arrange and pay for contract of carriage to the named port of destination. Advise Woldal of the expected time of arrival of the vessel carrying the goods so that arrangements can be made to take delivery. Theoretically, Speirs and Wadley need not insure the goods on their voyage. However, in view of their liability for the goods, such action would be unwise. Goods will be suitably packaged unless it is the norm for the goods involved to be delivered unpacked.	Woldal should obtain any import licence and perform any customs requirements necessary for the import of the goods, including meeting all costs involved, duties and taxes. Accept delivery of goods at the named port of destination. Woldal is liable for goods and costs from the time the goods are placed at its disposal on the quay or wharf.
Delivered duty unpaid [named destination]	DDU	Deliver the goods not unloaded to the named place in the importing country and bear costs and risks involved in carrying the goods to the named place of destination. Advise Woldal of dispatch in sufficient time for the company to make arrangements to take delivery of the goods. Arrange any export licence and complete export customs requirements including payment of costs, duties and taxes. Supply a commercial invoice or its electronic equivalent, together with the relevant transport document or delivery order to Woldal. Theoretically, Speirs and Wadley need not insure the goods on their voyage, but in view of its liability for the goods, such action would be unwise. Goods will be suitably packaged unless it is the norm for the goods involved to be delivered unpacked.	Woldal should obtain any import licence and perform any customs requirements necessary for the import of the goods, including meeting all costs involved, duties and taxes. Woldal must take delivery of goods at named place of destination and is liable for all risks from then on.
Delivered duty paid [named destination]	DDP	Similar to DDU, except that Speirs and Wadley is responsible for all import requirements and payments in addition.	Similar to DDU, except that Woldal is not responsible for all import requirements and payments.

14.3 How Incoterms affect the documents that exporters must produce

One function of all documents in international trade is to act as proof that an exporter has fulfilled its obligations under a commercial sales contract. Because the Incoterm in the sales contract will determine where the exporter's obligations end, proof of fulfilment of the commercial obligations of the exporter will depend on whether the documents conform to the relevant Incoterm.

Examples of the documents that meet the requirements of the major Incoterms are set out in Table 14.2, using specific examples from the Speirs and Wadley–Woldal sale.

Table 14.2 Documentation to be produced by exporter

Incoterm	Relevant transport document to be produced by Speirs and Wadley Ltd	Relevant insurance document to be produced by Speirs and Wadley Ltd
Ex works [named place]	None. All that is required is a receipt from Woldal or its agents for the goods.	None
Free carrier [named place, eg FCA Hackney Container Depot]	Receipt from Hackney container depot for the goods. Normally, this would be a container bill of lading or a through bill of lading marked 'freight payable at destination'.	None
Free carrier [named place, eg FCA Gatwick Airport]	Air waybill showing Woldal as consignee, marked 'freight payable at destination'. The details of the flight must conform to those specified by Woldal. (If goods are sent by rail or road, a rail consignment note (ie CIM) or a road consignment note (ie CMR) will be used showing the goods consigned to Woldal, marked 'freight payable at destination'.)	None
Free alongside ship [named port of shipment, eg FAS Tilbury]	Bill of lading marked 'received for shipment' and 'freight payable at destination'. Details of the shipping line to conform to those stipulated by Woldal and the port to be shown as Tilbury.	None
Free on board [named port of shipment, eg FOB Tilbury]	Bill of lading marked 'shipped on board' and 'freight payable at destination'. Details of the ship or shipping line to conform to the details stipulated by Woldal (eg the port must be shown as Tilbury).	None
Cost and freight [named port of destination, eg CFR Hong Kong]	Bill of lading marked 'shipped on board' and 'freight paid'. The destination of the ship must be Hong Kong.	None

Incoterm	Relevant transport document to be produced by Speirs and Wadley Ltd.	Relevant insurance document to be produced by Speirs and Wadley Ltd.
Cost, insurance and freight [named port of destination, eg CIF Hong Kong]	Same as for CFR.	Insurance policy or certificate covering journey from Tilbury to Hong Kong port. The date of the insurance document must be on or before the date of the bill of lading.
Carriage paid to [named destination, eg CPT Kowloon Freight Yard]	Combined transport or multimodal transport document marked 'freight paid', covering the journey to Kowloon Freight Yard.	None
Carriage and insurance paid to [named destination, eg CIP Kowloon Freight Yard]	Same as for CPT.	Insurance policy or certificate covering the journey from Tilbury to Kowloon freight yard. The date of the insurance document must be on or before the date of the combined transport or multimodal transport document.
Delivered ex ship [named port of destination, eg DES Hong Kong]	Bill of lading marked 'shipped on board' and 'freight paid'. The destination of the ship must be Hong Kong.	None, but Speirs and Wadley will normally arrange insurance. Speirs and Wadley is responsible for the goods up until the time they have been placed at the disposal of Woldal on board the vessel at the named port of destination.
Delivered ex quay (duty paid) [named port of destination, eg DEQ Hong Kong]	Bill of lading marked 'freight paid'. The destination of the ship must be Hong Kong.	None, but Speirs and Wadley will normally arrange insurance for the voyage. It is responsible for the goods until they have been placed at the disposal of Woldal on the quay or wharf of the named port of destination.
Delivered duty unpaid [named destination, eg DDU, New Road, Kowloon, Hong Kong]	Combined transport or multimodal transport document marked 'freight paid' and showing the destination as New Road, Kowloon, Hong Kong.	None, but Speirs and Wadley will normally arrange insurance of the goods for the whole journey to the named place of destination. It is responsible for the goods up to that point.
Delivery duty paid [named destination, eg DDU, New Road, Kowloon, Hong Kong]	[Spiers & Wadley] Combined transport document marked 'freight paid' and showing the destination as New Road, Kowloon, Hong Kong.	[Wodal] None. However, Spiers & Wadley will normally arrange insurance of the goods for the whole journey to the named place of destination. They are responsible for the goods up to that point.

Notes

- Incoterms enable documents to be transmitted electronically using electronic data interchange (EDI). Both exporter and importer must agree to such a method being used.

- Usually, it is assumed that transport of goods from the exporter's factory to its local port or airport, or container depot, is covered by its general insurance. Hence, it would be unusual for an exporter to be asked for proof of insurance for the domestic part of the journey. For example, in a CIF Hong Kong contract, Speirs and Wadley would not normally be expected to produce documentary evidence of insurance of the goods from Adderley Road to the port of Tilbury. It would, however, be expected to produce documentary evidence of insurance for the journey from the time the goods were received by the shipping company (ie the date of the bill of lading) and this insurance should cover the goods on their journey from Tilbury to Hong Kong.

- CIF and CIP are the only Incoterms that stipulate responsibility for insurance. Under these, the exporter must arrange insurance for the importer's benefit. Minimum cover (usually 110% of the gross invoice value) is often arranged and if the importer requires greater cover it must agree this with the exporter. The latter will often be the case if manufactured goods are involved. If other Incoterms are used, it is up to the importer and exporter to agree who will meet the cost of insurance cover.

- Obviously, the transport documents and the insurance document must describe the goods in a similar manner as they are described in the sales contract. Generally speaking, a brief general description, which is not conflicting with the sales contract, will suffice.

- When bills of lading are used, the exporter must indorse them in blank if the consignee box shows 'order'.

- When waybills are used, the consignee must be the importer or an agent of the importer who is specified in the sales contract. When bills of lading are used, the exporter must provide a full set of bills of lading. The bills of lading are usually made out to 'order' and blank indorsed.

- When an insurance policy or certificate is required, it must be indorsed in blank by the exporter unless the importer or other agreed party is shown as the insured.

14.4 Why is insurance for the goods necessary?

If goods are damaged in transit, the normal reaction would be to claim from the shipping company. Most transport contracts, however, contain widely drawn clauses, which, to a great extent, exclude liability on the part of the shipping company unless damage is caused by their gross negligence. It is therefore necessary for either the importer or the exporter to take out insurance to cover the relevant parts of the journey.

One special form of insurance that an exporter can take out is transit insurance, or seller's interest insurance. While the importer is responsible for arranging insurance for the sea voyage under an FOB or CFR contract, the exporter can, for a much reduced fee, take out its own seller's interest cover. This insures the exporter against loss or damage to the goods on the sea voyage when the importer has failed to fulfil its insurance responsibility. Naturally, the existence of such insurance is not generally disclosed to the importer.

14.5   The cost implications of Incoterms for exporters

Both exporters and importers need to know the precise financial implications of Incoterms in order to be able to set sensible prices and calculate costs.

It is unnecessary to set out the full implications of all 13 Incoterms, because the application of logic will provide the required information. A few examples from the most commonly used Incoterms will suffice. The examples below refer to sales by UK-based exporters.

14.5.1   FAS Southampton

The exporter must take account of the following extra costs when setting its prices:

- the insurance of the goods from the UK factory to Southampton;
- the cost of transport to Southampton.

14.5.2   FOB Southampton

In addition to the costs referred to in the FAS example above, the exporter must bear in mind the cost of loading the goods on board the ship.

14.5.3   FOB UK port

The pricing implications of this term can be difficult to assess. The importer could specify any UK port as the port of loading. If the specified port were situated in a remote part of the country, the cost of transport and insurance could be very high.

14.6   The cost implications of Incoterms for importers

The implications for importers are the mirror image of those for exporters and can be deduced by logical thought. The examples below refer to sales by UK- based importers.

14.6.1   FOB Antwerp

In addition to the sales contract price, the importer will have to bear all transport costs from Antwerp to its premises in the UK. The importer must pay the insurance for this journey, because any damage to the goods while in transit would be the importer's responsibility.

14.6.2 CIF Tilbury

In addition to the sales contract price, the importer will have to bear the cost of unloading the goods from the ship at Tilbury and all freight costs from the port of Tilbury to its premises. The importer must also pay for insurance of the goods from the time they cross the ship's rail in Tilbury to the time they arrive at its own premises, because any damage on this part of the journey would be the importer's responsibility.

Topic 15

An overview of terms of payment

On completion of this topic, the student should be able to:

- understand what is meant by terms of payment;
- distinguish between the four basic terms of payment;
- appreciate which terms of payment are more secure for the exporter and which terms are more favourable to the importer;
- understand the significance of the words 'terms of payment' in an examination context.

15.1   The meaning of 'terms of payment'

'Terms of payment' reflect the extent to which the exporter requires a guarantee of payment before it loses control of the goods. The more trustworthy and creditworthy the importer, the less will the exporter need to have payment guaranteed before losing control of the goods.

There are four different terms of payment, as follows:

- open account;
- documentary collection;
- documentary credit;
- payment in advance.

15.2   An overview of the four terms of payment

It is necessary for the exporter and importer to agree the terms of payment and incorporate the details in the contract of sale.

A detailed analysis of open account, documentary collection and documentary credit transactions appear in the remaining topics of this part of the text. This topic contains a brief overview of these three terms, with full coverage of payment in advance.

15.2.1   Open account

A brief description of the term 'open account' has already been given at the beginning of this part of the book (see section 12.1). To recap, then, open account terms mean that the exporter effects shipment of its goods to the importer and invoices it for payment. If there are any documents of title to the goods, these documents must also be sent directly to the importer. It is usual for the exporter to send at least an invoice, a packing list and a transport document.

The exporter loses all control of the goods at the time that it ships them, trusting the importer to effect payment.

Terms such as 'net cash on receipt of goods' are sometimes used and they are synonymous with open account.

15.2.2   Documentary collection

In a 'documentary collection', the exporter effects shipment of its goods, but instead of sending the documents directly to the importer, it uses the banking system.

The sequence of events when a documentary collection is used can be briefly summarised as follows.

1. The exporter ships goods and obtains the required documents, including any document of title.

2. The exporter sends the documents to its bank with appropriate instructions.

3. The exporter's bank sends the documents to the importer's bank, with the instruction that they can only be released:

   – on payment; or

   – on acceptance of a bill of exchange (which, for the moment, we shall simply consider as being a legally binding undertaking to pay the exporter on a set or determinable future date).

4. On payment or acceptance of the bill of exchange, the importer's bank releases the documents so that the importer can obtain the goods on their arrival in its country.

It can be seen that the exporter retains control over the goods under this method, when there are documents of title, until either payment is made or a legally binding undertaking to pay is given.

A full explanation of this method, including the procedures adopted when the transport documents are not documents of title, is given in Topic 17.

15.2.3   Documentary credit

Briefly, a 'documentary credit' is an undertaking to pay given to an exporter by the importer's bank, subject to the exporter presenting specified documents within a stipulated period that comply to the terms and conditions of the letter of credit.

If a documentary credit has been arranged, the exporter can arrange shipment of its goods in the knowledge that it is relying not on the importer's integrity and creditworthiness, but rather on the reputation and creditworthiness of the importer's bank. Obviously, the exporter must fulfil the terms and conditions of the credit if the undertaking is to be relied upon.

The procedure in brief is as follows.

1. The exporter and importer agree on payment by documentary credit and incorporate the details in their sale contract.

2. The importer requests that its bank issue a documentary credit.

3. The importer's bank, if it is in agreement, issues its documentary credit and advises it to the beneficiary through a bank in the exporter's country, which then advises the exporter of the existence of the credit.

4. The exporter ships the goods, obtains the documents required under the credit, presents these documents to the bank nominated to honour or negotiate and, if the documents comply, is paid.

15.2.4   Payment in advance

'Payment in advance' means exactly what it says: the importer pays the exporter at some agreed stage prior to shipment of the goods.

Although full payment in advance is obviously most desirable for the exporter, it will only be able to obtain such terms when there is a 'seller's' market, or when such terms are customary in that particular trade.

It is quite common for a sales contract to require partial payments in advance: for example, the contract might stipulate 20% payable on the signing of the contract, with the remaining 80% payable after shipment of the goods under one of the other terms of payment.

15.3   The order in which the terms of payment are attractive to the parties to a sale contract

A moment's thought will show that from the exporter's point of view the order in which the terms of payment are attractive (from most secure to least secure) is as follows.

1. Payment in advance

2. Documentary credit

3. Documentary collection

4. Open account

The reverse order applies in relation to their attractiveness (from most favourable to least favourable) to importers, as follows.

1. Open account

2. Documentary collection

3. Documentary credit

4. Payment in advance

15.4 Illustrative examples

Because this brief topic serves only as an overview, we shall look at two illustrative example questions that explain the significance of terms of payment in an examination context. An explanatory comment follows each question.

Example 15.1

Your exporter customer has completed a sales contract with an overseas buyer and it contains the following details:

CIF Charleston. Payment in US $ by TT on terms: net cash one month after receipt of goods.

Explain the possible risks to your customer in accepting the terms of payment that appear in this contract.

Comment

In this question, you should describe the risks to an exporter under open account terms. You should **not** comment on TT settlement, because this is a method of transfer of funds, and you should **not** comment on the exchange risk if the question simply refers to the terms of payment. The exchange risk would also apply if a documentary collection or documentary credit had been selected as the term of payment.

Example 15.2

John Brown's Body Ltd is a funeral directors. It has developed a business providing complete funeral services, including coffins, to British and American expatriates based in continental Europe, who wish to ensure that their deceased loved ones are returned to the UK or the USA for burial or cremation.

The company, which is sterling-based, has recently received orders for coffins from army units based in Germany. The terms of shipment will be either on a CIF Hamburg basis for shipments by sea, or on a CFR Frankfurt basis for air consignments. The cost of repatriation to the UK or the USA will be borne by the army groups outside the terms of the new orders.

Because the customer has usually sold on an ex-works basis, a director asks you for an explanation of these terms of shipment and how they would affect the company.

You are informed that payments will be received in euros, and that the company has no other foreign currency receipts or outgoings.

Explain:

1. the terms of shipment mentioned, including the responsibilities of the contracting parties under these terms;

2. any risks, other than the credit risks, that the company will incur by agreeing to accept the payments as indicated in the question.

Comment

1. An explanation of the Incoterms CIF Hamburg and CFR Frankfurt is required, including the responsibilities of the parties.

2. An explanation of the exchange risk is required.

Note: 'Terms of payment' refers to the credit risk, which is specifically excluded from this question, whereas the word 'payment' refers to the fact that the sale is denominated in euros. In addition, the danger of damage to the goods on the journey to Germany could be mentioned, along with the need to insure. Finally, under CFR or CIF terms, the customer will need to ascertain the cost of transport to Germany.

Topic 16

Open account terms

On completion of this topic, the student should be able to:

- appreciate the major risks that apply to exporters who sell on open account terms;

- appreciate how an exporter can reduce the risks inherent in open account terms;

- acquire an overview of the role of the Export Credits Guarantee Department (ECGD) and Atradius as insurers against bad debts on export sales.

16.1 Introduction

So far, this text has covered matters from the point of view of both the exporter and the importer. Up to and including Topic 22, we shall now concentrate on the subject matter from the point of view of a UK exporter and of its bank. Other providers of services to exporters will also be introduced where appropriate.

The position of importers and their banks as regards terms of payment will be covered from Topic 23 onwards. Remember, then, that for the remaining three topics in this part ,we are looking at matters from a UK exporter's point of view.

16.2 The major risks that apply to exports on open account terms

The major risks that apply to exports on open account terms can be classified under three main headings:

- buyer risk;

- country/political risk;

- transit risk.

16.2.1   Buyer risk

'Buyer risk' is also known as 'credit risk' and it covers the danger that the buyer may not pay for the goods because of insolvency or wilful default.

Remember that when shipping goods are sold on open account terms, the exporter loses control of the goods at the moment it despatches them.

16.2.2   Country or political risk

The importer may be perfectly willing and able to pay, but the importer's government may introduce laws, often called 'exchange controls', that prevent payment from being made.

The reason for the imposition of exchange controls can be political. Alternatively, exchange controls can simply result from financial pressures, such as the debt problem in the developing world, which means that the importer's country cannot afford to pay for imports.

16.2.3   Transit risk

Goods travel much farther in international trade than they do in a domestic deal and therefore there is more danger of loss or damage to goods on their journey from seller to buyer.

Note: Exchange risk also applies if the exporter invoices in foreign currency, but exchange risk will always apply in these cases, irrespective of the terms of payment between the two parties.

16.3   How an exporter can reduce the risks under open account terms

16.3.1   Buyer risk

In order to reduce buyer risk, the exporter can obtain a credit report on the buyer and such reports should be updated at regular intervals. Alternatively, organisations such as the Department for Business Enterprise & Regulatory Reform (formerly the Department of Trade and Industry) can supply more detailed reports on potential buyers. A favourable status report does not guarantee that the importer will pay its debts, but it does serve as a useful indication of its creditworthiness and integrity.

In addition, the exporter can insure against non- payment by the importer (see section 16.4.).

16.3.2   Country or political risk

Most UK banks provide political and economic reports that comment on the situation in various overseas countries. These reports can give full details of current exchange control regulations in the overseas country and can help the exporter to assess whether any additional restrictions are likely, which enables it to reduce country or political risk.

In addition, insurance can be taken out to cover loss because of newly imposed exchange controls.

16.3.3   Transit risk

In relation to transit risk, the obvious remedy is for appropriate insurance cover to be taken. If an Incoterm has been specified in the sale contract, it will be quite clear where the exporter's obligation ends and where the importer's obligation begins. In addition, the exporter can take out seller's interest insurance to cover itself against damage to goods if the importer has failed to insure under terms such as CFR.

Freight forwarders are firms that specialise in organising overseas transport. Most freight forwarders are capable of arranging appropriate transport, insurance and documentation, if they are given a copy of the sale contract.

The exporter's bank may be able to provide a list of suitable freight forwarders and the forwarder can arrange appropriate insurance of the goods, if required.

16.4   Credit insurance

At one time, credit insurance was provided by the Export Credits Guarantee Department (ECGD), a government department. Since 1991, however, when the short-term credit insurance business arm (ie credit insurance for up to two years) was sold off to the Netherlands- based NCM Group, the market has opened up to private credit insurers.

Since then, the credit insurance market has become increasingly competitive. The main players in private sector credit insurance are Atradius, which grew out of NCM and German insurer GKS (the credit insurance arm of the Gerling Group), Euler Hermes and Coface.

Other insurers, such as Creditshield, Amlin, CIFS, ACE, AIG, QBE and Zurich, are also making a name for themselves, although often with niche products designed for particular sectors of the market.

16.4.1   Atradius' credit insurance

Atradius provides a range of credit insurance products for all sizes of company in all sectors, from small, one- man firms, to multinational corporations. Atradius will tailor an insurance policy to suit the requirements of a particular company's business profile and objectives. While the cover provided is predominantly for short- term credit transactions – normally with a credit period of up to 180 days – cover can extend to credit periods of two years and pre- credit periods (see below) of five years.

As a prudent insurer and to offer competitive premiums, Atradius will usually look to insure a wide spread of risk. Cover is, however, also available for a more selective range of risks, including single buyer and single contract cover.

16.4.2   The risks covered

The contract of insurance usually lasts a year, although two- or three- year plans are not unusual. The risks that can be covered are:

- buyer insolvency;
- the buyer's failure to pay within six months of the due date for goods accepted;

A buyer's failure may be due to their own credit condition or to country events, including:

- a moratorium on debt repayment decreed by the government of the buyer's country;
- transfer delay – ie delay in the transfer of foreign exchange from the buyer's country;
- a statute passed in the buyer's country that discharges the debt if it is paid in other than the currency of the contract;
- war, civil unrest or similar action outside the UK that prevents completion of the contract (war between the five major powers is specifically excluded);
- natural disaster – ie cyclone, flood, earthquake, volcanic eruption or tidal wave – or other forms of natural disaster in a buyer's country that disrupt payment;
- contract frustration – ie a foreign government action that delays or prevents completion of the contract;
- export restrictions imposed by the seller's government after the date of the contract;
- the non- renewal or cancellation of a supplier's export licence.

If a buyer is recognised by Atradius as a 'public buyer' by a credit limit condition, eg local or regional government, the exporter will be covered if the buyer fails to complete the contract.

16.4.3   Additional available cover

The additional cover available includes the following.

- The policy normally covers the exporter from the date on which the goods are sent to the buyer. By payment of an additional premium, cover can be provided from the date of the contract. This is known as 'covering pre- credit risk' and includes pre- shipment contract repudiation and contract frustration. It is of particular benefit to exporters that manufacture specialist, one- off items that would have no other market if the underlying contract were to fail.
- Payment of royalties or licensing agreements.

- Third- country risk (ie shipment to a country other than that in which the buyer is located).
- Sales through overseas subsidiaries.
- Services provided for foreign customers, eg maintenance contracts or professional services.
- Sale of goods held overseas, including those exhibited at trade markets or exhibitions.
- Insurance against unfair calling of bonds and demand guarantees may be available.
- Protection against adverse exchange rate movement between the time a bid is tendered and the contract is awarded.

16.4.4 Costs of cover

In terms of the costs of cover, premiums are negotiable, but primarily depend upon the spread of risks, the width of markets, the policy structure, the trade sector and the amount of cover involved. Obviously, if an exporter is negotiating business deals in a high- risk area of the world, premiums are likely to be higher than in other, more stable areas.

Costs normally include the following:

- a payment of annual policy set- up and maintenance charges;
- a payment of a monthly fee based on the amount of business that is transacted each month;
- a payment for formal credit limit charges approved by Atradius;
- market rate additions to cater for riskier markets.

16.4.5 The amount of cover available

The amount of cover available can be summarised as follows:

Risk covered	Maximum % covered by Atradius
Buyer insolvency	90
Buyer default	90
Political/country risk	95

16.4.6 Pay- out of claims

In relation to the payment of claims submitted to Atradius, in the case of buyer insolvency, pay- out will be immediate, provided that evidence of insolvency is furnished.

In the case of payment default by the buyer on goods accepted or services provided, payment will be made six months after the payment due date and, for the remainder of losses, payment will be made six months after the payment due date.

As part of the Atradius credit insurance policy, collection is provided and Atradius collections will endeavour to collect any debts. For insured debt, Atradius will normally be prepared to defray costs incurred for the recovery action.

16.4.7   ECGD export insurance policy (EXIP)

In 1998 ECGD launched its export insurance policy (EXIP) as a replacement for its supplier insurance policy. It mainly supplies non- payment cover against commercial or political risks related to large- scale projects, and the provision of capital goods and services. The EXIP is, however, flexible and, unlike its predecessor, can be a stand-alone policy specifically designed for an individual exporter's needs in addition to being used in conjunction with an ECGD buyer credit or supplier credit financing facility.

The EXIP covers the following risks, in relation to occurrences outside the UK:

- buyer insolvency;
- the buyer's failure to pay within six months of the due date;
- default by the buyer or guarantor to meet a final judgment or award within six months of its date;
- default in payment or default in performance of the contract by the buyer that prevents the supplier from carrying out its part of the contract;
- statutes introduced in the buyer's country that discharge the debt if it is paid in other than the currency of the contract;
- political or economic moves that prevent the transfer of contractual payments. (this would include a general moratorium on debt repayment enforced by the buyer's government);
- any action by a foreign government that prevents the performance of the contract;
- any natural disasters, wars or civil strife that prevent the performance of the contract.

In relation to events within the UK, the EXIP covers:

- the non- renewal or cancellation of a supplier's export licence;
- measures introduced after the contract date that hamper the performance of the contract;
- a withdrawal of finance by ECGD if it has withdrawn cover on the buyer's country.

Additional cover is available for bonds risk (see Topic 22).

The EXIP provides cover for 95% of the insured risk, with the exporter bearing the remaining 5%.

16.4.8   Additional ECGD insurance facilities

16.4.8.1   Tender to contract scheme

The tender to contract scheme is available to exporters who tender for contracts in foreign currency. These contracts must have a UK content of £5m or more.

The risks covered include losses incurred due to adverse exchange rate movements between the date of tender and the date of contract.

The amount of cover is normally limited to between 1% and 25% of the contract price.

Should exchange rates move in the exporter's favour during the period covered, any gain must be paid to ECGD.

Cover can be arranged for tendering periods of up to nine months.

An additional facility to the normal tender to contract scheme is the forward exchange supplement. It is designed for exporters who believe that they may have problems in arranging forward contracts for large sums over long time periods. If these forward contracts provide less sterling than expected, ECGD will make up the balance within the limits mentioned previously. This forward exchange supplement can also be set up as a free- standing facility.

16.4.8.2   The overseas investment insurance scheme

The aim of the overseas investment insurance scheme is to encourage UK investment overseas.

It covers political risks for up to 15 years, including:

- expropriation, eg nationalisation or other overseas government action to the detriment of the investor;
- war or revolution;
- restrictions on remittance (to help investors to overcome the potential problems that may arise if the transfer or return of funds to the UK were to be restrained or delayed).

The scheme is aimed at companies carrying on business in the UK and their overseas subsidiaries. Insurance is available for new investments of equity capital in the form of cash, plant or knowledge, for loans to overseas entities in relation to which the repayment period is at least three years from the date of payment and for some guarantees of loans that have been arranged outside the UK. The investor must apply for cover before committing itself to any investment. Cover may be arranged in some cases in which there are some existing investments, but this will be based on each individual case.

The amounts available under the scheme are as follows:

- **equity investments** – the amount of investment plus retained profits up to a maximum of double the amount of the original investment;
- **loan investments** – the principal loan amount plus any accrued interest.

In relation to expropriation, the claim will be paid one year following the commencement of the relevant action.

In relation to war, it will be paid on evidence of damage to physical assets, or if the overseas entity has been unable to operate for one year, or in cases in which the overseas entity has been operating, when it has been unable to make profits for three consecutive years.

In cases of a restriction on remittance, the claim will be paid subsequent to an inability for six successive months to repatriate currency. In relation to loan investment, six months must have passed since the due date for an unpaid amount of capital or interest.

Any recoveries or compensation will be divided between the ECGD and the investor on the same basis as the loss was suffered.

16.4.9 The ECGD fixed- rate finance (FRF) scheme

In order to attract business, exporters sometimes have to be able to offer favourable interest rates to overseas buyers. ECGD supports this through its fixed- rate finance (FRF) scheme, which provides reimbursement to banks that are supplying funds at fixed rates in relation to which the actual cost of funds is greater than the fixed rate.

Commercial interest reference rates (CIRRs) form the basis of this system of minimum fixed- interest rates. They are reviewed monthly. The advantage of the FRF scheme to exporters is that it can quote a firm fixed- interest rate to a potential buyer that can be maintained for up to four months pending the satisfactory completion of preliminary talks culminating in a signed agreement or contract.

Topic 17

Documentary collections

On completion of this topic, the student should be able to:

- understand what is meant by bills of exchange;
- appreciate the difference between sight drafts and term drafts;
- describe the detailed operation of documentary collections;
- appreciate the difference when an air waybill is the chosen transport document;
- appreciate the significance of the various clauses on a collection instruction;
- understand the meaning and purpose of the ICC Uniform Rules for Collections (URC);
- describe the checks that a remitting bank makes before it sends the documents overseas;
- appreciate the difference between theory and practice as regards the timing of payments;
- understand the risks to an exporter with documentary collections and how these risks can be reduced;
- appreciate the difference in security between D/P (documents against payment) and D/A (documents against acceptance).

17.1   Introduction

This introduction is a reminder of the point made at the beginning of Topic 16: this topic will consider documentary collections only from the point of view of the exporter and its bank.

17.2   A definition of 'bills of exchange'

The definition of a 'bill of exchange' can be found in the Bills of Exchange Act 1882. There are nine major aspects, which are as follows:

1. a bill of exchange is an unconditional order in writing;

2. addressed by one person (the drawer);

3. to another (the drawee);

4. signed by the drawer;

5. requiring the person to whom it is addressed (the drawee);

6. to pay;

7. on demand or at a fixed or determinable future date;

8. a certain sum in money;

9. to, or to the order of, a specified person (the payee) or to bearer. (In the case of the specimen bills of exchange in Figures 17.1 and 17.2, the drawer and payee are identical. The words 'our order' indicate the order of Speirs and Wadley.)

For convenience, the above phrases are numbered to correspond to the reference numbers that appear on the specimen bills of exchange shown in Figures 17.1 and 17.2.

These specimen bills of exchange relate to an export sale by Speirs and Wadley to Woldal. Because the exporter is the person who requires payment from the importer, we can see that, in documentary collections, the exporter is the drawer and the importer is the drawee.

Note: The word 'draft' is often substituted for 'bill of exchange'. The words are synonymous for our purposes.

17.3   Sight drafts and term drafts

As you will have noted, the two specimen bills of exchange are identical, apart from item (7), which relates to the due time for payment.

The bill that requires payment **at sight** (Figure 17.2) is a 'sight draft' or an 'on- demand draft'. The drawee, Woldal, should pay the bill as soon as it is presented, if the bill is to be honoured. Woldal will not need to sign the bill in any way. All that is required is for it to authorise payment via its bank.

On the other draft (Figure 17.1), payment is due 90 days **after sight**. When the bill of exchange is presented to the drawee, the drawee should accept it if it wishes the bill to be honoured. Thus, Woldal would sign the bill of exchange on the front and insert the date of acceptance. Woldal would be legally bound to pay 90 days after the date of acceptance shown on the bill of exchange.

Such drafts that are payable at a future date are called 'term drafts'. Other descriptions that are synonymous are 'tenor draft' and 'usance draft'. When a term draft specifies a future date (eg if Figure 17.1 were to say 'on 1 January ... pay') the drawee would accept the draft and there is no requirement to indicate the date of acceptance or the date when payment is due. When the words specify payment on a fixed period after sight, however, the drawee must accept the bill *and* insert the date of acceptance, otherwise it will be impossible to calculate the due date for payment.

Figure 17.1   Specimen bill of exchange 1

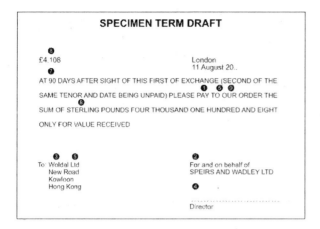

Figure 17.2   Specimen bill of exchange 2

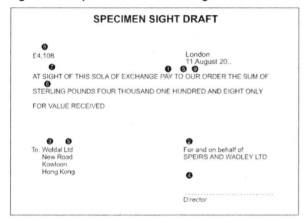

17.4   The operation of a documentary collection

Note: The following uses as an example goods that are being transported by sea.

1. The exporter ships the goods and obtains a negotiable bill of lading from the shipping company or its agent.

2. The exporter, who is known as the 'principal', hands the following documents to its bank (which will act as the remitting bank):

    - a bill of exchange drawn on the importer;

    - documents of title (ie a complete set of clean shipped on board bills of lading) and other relevant documents (eg an invoice, a packing list and an insurance policy or certificate, if shipment terms are CIF). It should be noted that it is advisable for the exporter to present the full set of negotiable bills of lading to the remitting bank in order to maintain control over delivery of the goods;

- a collection instruction, which contains the exporter's instructions to the remitting bank.

3. The remitting bank completes its own collection instruction addressed to the importer's bank as may be indicated by the exporter on its collection instruction. In the absence of a name of the importer's bank, the remitting bank will use one of its correspondent banks in the country of the importer for the purpose of handling the collection. This collection instruction contains the same instructions as the exporter's original collection order. This collection order is then sent to the importer's bank or correspondent bank, along with the shipping documents. This bank is then known as the 'collecting bank' (or 'presenting bank').

4. If the instructions are D/P (documents against payment), the collecting bank will release the documents to the importer only against payment.

    If the instructions are D/A (documents against acceptance), the collecting bank will release the documents only against acceptance of the bill of exchange by the importer.

5. If and when the bill of exchange is paid, the collecting bank remits the proceeds to the remitting bank for credit to the principal's account.

    The importer will require a bill of lading in order to obtain the goods from the port. The bill of lading can only be obtained by payment (D/P) or by acceptance (D/A) of the bill of exchange. Therefore, the importer cannot obtain the goods without paying or accepting the bill of exchange and, conversely, an exporter retains control of the goods until payment or acceptance of the bill of exchange.

    When goods are sent by air freight, the air waybill could show the importer's bank as consignee. Once again, the importer must pay or accept a bill of exchange to be able to obtain the goods. Once the importer has paid or accepted the bill of exchange, the importer's bank will issue a delivery order. The delivery order is an authority, signed on behalf of the bank, authorising the airline or its agent to release the goods to the named importer. An exporter should obtain the prior agreement of the importer and the importer's bank before it consigns goods to that bank. In practice, the importer's bank will not often agree to be named as consignee, unless its own customer is of major importance.

Notes

1. When D/P terms are used, it is unnecessary to include a bill of exchange because the collecting bank can release documents on payment of the invoice amount. Sight drafts are, however, usually included.

2. In some overseas countries, stamp duty is levied on bills of exchange. In such situations, it may be possible to use a banker's receipt instead of a bill of exchange to avoid these duties. The banker's receipt is used extensively in Italy and is known as a *ricevuta bancaria*.

3. There are variations on traditional remittance methods for documentary collections.

4. Some companies use online computerised collection instruction forms.

17.4.1   The accelerated bills service provided by some remitting banks

A UK exporter completes a collection instruction, quoting from a prearranged series of reference numbers, but instead of submitting the collection to the UK remitting bank, the collection is sent by the exporter directly to the collecting bank abroad. A copy of the collection instruction is sent to the exporter's UK bank or, alternatively, the UK bank has access to this data through its electronic banking solution.

All subsequent correspondence is dealt with by the UK bank and the UK bank maintains records of the position of all bills collected in this way. If the exporter is linked to its bank via a computer terminal network, the bank can advise the exporter of the position via this network.

The benefits to the exporter are:

- reduced bank charges;

- reduced processing time, which should mean quicker payment.

This method is useful when the exporter submits many collections to the same buyers over a period of time, because the UK bank can then preselect an appropriate collecting bank(s).

17.4.2   Direct collections

In some cases, exporters may simply send their collections directly to the overseas collecting bank, without involving their own UK bank in any way. The overseas bank would act as agent of the UK exporter in obtaining the proceeds. The benefits from the exporter's point of view are a saving in time and a saving of UK bank charges.

The drawbacks from the exporter's point of view are that:

- all correspondence, including that for any follow- up action in the event of default, is directly with the overseas bank;

- the exporter may find it difficult to trace payment of the bill proceeds without the benefit of a UK bank's reference number;

- the documents are not reviewed by the UK bank before being sent abroad.

17.5   The collection instruction

The specimen collection instruction in Figure 17.3 is a standard form of authority that enables the exporter to include specific instructions to its bank regarding the documentary collection.

Figure 17.3   Specimen collection instruction

HSBC

EXPORT TRADE COLLECTION/NEGOTIATION

To: HSBC Bank plc, ...International Branch

Please collect on our account the attached bill/documents as detailed below and *either*:

☐ do not advance funds (Collection)   ☐ advance funds to our account (Negotiation)
(see points 7–12 on reverse)

Our reference	Bank reference (Bank use)	Export account number (if known)

Currency of bill	Amount (in figures)	Tenor/Due Date	Drawee's bank	
Drawee's name and address				
			(Leave blank for bank use unless a specific bank must be used)	

Documents	Bills of Exchange/ Drafts	INVOICES			Certificate of Origin	GSP Form A	Insurance Policy/ Certificate	Bills of Lading	PCR/ CMR/ AWB	Parcel Post Receipt	Packing Weight List	Other	Other
		Commercial	Certified	Consular									
No. of originals/ copies													
Bank Use	First Mail												
	Second Mail												

Please follow the instructions marked below

Send documents by   ☐ Airmail   ☐ Courier

Release documents against   ☐ Payment   ☐ Acceptance

If unaccepted or unpaid   ☐ Protest   ☐ Do not Protest (do not tick this box if Advance of Funds)

Acceptance or payment   ☐ May   ☐ May Not   be deferred pending arrival of goods

☐ Collect all charges from the drawee. These   ☐ May   ☐ May Not   be waived if refused

☐ or Collect foreign bank charges from the drawee (HSBC Banks' charges for our account)   ☐ May   ☐ May Not   be waived if refused

Advise non-acceptance/payment by   ☐ Airmail   ☐ Cable

Advise acceptance and due date by   ☐ Airmail   ☐ Cable

Chase non-acceptance/payment by   ☐ Airmail   ☐ Cable

Request remittance of proceeds by   ☐ Airmail   ☐ Cable

In case of need refer to [_____] for assistance only

Other instructions [_____]

Please complete these details:-

Advance funds/credit proceeds to our	Account number	Branch sort code	Branch name	Currency of account

UTILISING   ☐ SPOT RATE   OR   ☐ FORWARD CONTRACT NUMBER [_____]

It is understood that this collection/negotiation is only undertaken by you subject to the terms and conditions set out overleaf.

Drawer	Authorised signature/s
Date	Contact Name

TERMS AND CONDITIONS OF EXPORT TRADE COLLECTION

1. This Collection is subject to the current Uniform Rules for Collections as published by the International Chamber of Commerce from time to time.

2. The Bank reserves the right to send documents by the method that it considers most suitable.

3. I/We undertake to reimburse you for all charges whether or not this collection is paid.

4. Where the drawee's bank is not specified, the Bank will endeavour to use the HSBC Group's office or associated bank.

5. Protest is not always available in all jurisdictions.

6. Charges if refused by the drawee are the drawers responsibility and will be deducted from the proceeds of the bill in accordance with Article 11a and 21c or URC 522.

ADDITIONAL TERMS AND CONDITIONS WHERE AN ADVANCE OF FUNDS IS REQUESTED (NEGOTIATION)

7. I/We confirm that a banking facility has been established with you for this purpose and that any advance requested is subject to the terms and conditions of this facility.

8. In no case does the Bank advance funds without recourse. Advance of funds is made at sight.

9. Should any bill of exchange/draft be dishonoured by non-acceptance or non-payment, the Bank or the collecting bank are authorised to note/protest the bill of exchange/draft and to dispose of the goods to which such bill of exchange/draft relates, at my/our risk.

10. I/We undertake to reimburse you for all interest whether or not this collection is paid.

11. Interest will be charged from date of advance until receipt of funds by the Bank.

12. The Bank will request that all advices are sent by telex/cable/SWIFT.

GENERAL INSTRUCTIONS FOR COMPLETION OF EXPORT TRADE COLLECTION FORM

13. Please detail any extra powers of the Case of Need in the "Other Instructions" box.

14. Please ensure that the "Currency of the account" quoted matched that of the "Account number" quoted.

15. Please ensure that any Bills of Exchange are correctly drawn and endorsed.

16. Where applicable, please ensure that any Bills of Lading are correctly endorsed.

17. Insurance Certificates, where applicable, must be endorsed on the reverse.

The top third of the form is largely self-explanatory, but you will see that specific instructions are required on the following points.

- Release documents to the importer against payment (D/P) or against acceptance (D/A) – normally, D/P will apply with sight drafts and D/A will apply with term drafts.

- If documents are not taken up on arrival of goods, instructions are required on whether to warehouse and insure the goods. This clause is known as a 'store and insure' clause.

If the importer does not pay or accept the bill of exchange, it cannot obtain the goods, but the goods will be at the docks or airport, or container depot, in the overseas country. If this clause is adopted, the collecting bank will be instructed to warehouse and insure the goods if documents are not taken up. The cost of this operation will be claimed from the remitting bank, which will debit its customer, the principal. If the goods are warehoused and insured, they are protected, giving the exporter time to find an alternative buyer or to ship the goods back to the UK. It should be noted that the collecting bank is under no obligation to store and insure the goods.

If waybills showing the importer as consignee are used, the store and insure clause will be superfluous.

- The collection instruction will state whether bank and other charges have to be collected in addition to the face value of the bill of exchange. The exporter should complete the clause in accordance with the details agreed in the sales contract.

- Specific instructions are required on whether or not to protest in the event of dishonour by either non- payment or non- acceptance.

If a bill of exchange is protested, a lawyer or notary public in the overseas country will undertake formal procedures whereby they will ask the drawee the reason for dishonour and make appropriate notes on the bill of exchange.

Again, it will be the collecting bank that instructs the lawyer or notary public to protest. The collecting bank will have to be reimbursed by the remitting bank, which will then debit its customer.

It should be noted that, in some countries, the law requires a dishonoured bill of exchange to be protested within one working day or similarly short time frame, otherwise the drawer cannot sue on the bill.

- Advice of dishonour, with reasons, should be given by SWIFT or airmail. SWIFT (see Topic 10) is most desirable, but again the cost will ultimately be borne by the exporter.

- When goods are transported by sea and documents go by air, it is quite common for the collection to be presented to the drawee before the arrival of the goods. If this clause is adopted, the collecting bank will often be authorised to await the arrival of the goods before pressing the drawee for payment or acceptance.

- The 'case of need' referred to on the collection instruction is an agent of the exporter who is resident in the importer's country. The case of need can act in an advisory capacity or have full powers. The latter will allow the case of need to overrule the instructions contained in the collection schedule. If a case of need is named, the collecting bank will refer to that party in the event of dishonour for guidance or instruction.

- Finally, instructions as to the method of settlement are required. Obviously, SWIFT will be best from the exporter's point of view, but this is a more costly method than mail transfer.

17.6   The ICC Uniform Rules for Collections (URC)

The ICC Uniform Rules for Collections (URC) are an internationally accepted code of practice covering documentary collections. The URC are not incorporated in national or international law, but become binding on all parties when the collection instruction states that the collection is subject to the URC. The URC will apply unless the collection instruction states otherwise or the laws in one of the countries concerned specifically contradict them. The current Rules do not extend to transactions that use EDI. The working party that drew up the URC felt that there were too many legal problems for international rules on electronic collections to be drafted at that time.

You must have a good knowledge of the URC. Matters solely affecting the collecting bank and drawee are covered later.

17.6.1   Summary of the provisions of the URC

- **Article 1** states that banks do not have to deal with collections, but must advise the party, from whom they receive the collection, of their decision as soon as possible.
- **Article 2** defines and differentiates between various terms:
  - financial documents are the instruments used for the purpose of obtaining payment, eg cheques;
  - commercial documents relate to the goods themselves, eg invoices and waybills;
  - clean collections consist of financial documents that are not accompanied by commercial documents;
  - documentary collections are commercial documents that may or may not be accompanied by financial documents.
- **Article 3** identifies the main parties to a collection:
  - the principal, ie the exporter;
  - the remitting bank (the bank to which the principal entrusts the collection, normally the exporter's own bank);
  - the collecting bank (any bank, other than the remitting bank, that is involved with the collection, which will usually be the banker of the importer or another bank in the importer's country);
  - the presenting bank (the collecting bank that notifies the drawee of the arrival of the collection and which requests payment or acceptance);
  - the drawee (normally the importer to whom presentation will be made in accordance with the collection instruction).

  Example 17.1 will clarify the relevant positions of these parties in respect of a documentary collection.

Example 17.1

An exporter (the principal) hands in a documentary collection to its bank (HSBC – the remitting bank), drawn on an importer (drawee) in New York, USA. If the principal does not specify which collecting bank to use, HSBC will choose its New York office (the collecting and presenting bank). If the importer banks at Citigroup, HSBC New York may request Citigroup to handle the actual presentation. In this latter case, Citigroup will be the presenting bank and HSBC the collecting bank.

- **Article 4** mainly covers the constituent parts of a collection instruction. Additionally, it states that banks need not examine documents to ascertain instructions and can ignore any instructions from a party other than that from whom the collection was received, unless the collection instruction states otherwise.

- **Articles 5**, **6**, **7** and **8** discuss procedures relating to the presentation, release and creation of documents.

- **Article 9** states that banks will act in good faith and exercise reasonable care.

- **Article 10** excludes banks from responsibility or liability when goods are despatched directly to the address of a bank or consigned to a bank for which prior permission has not been granted. Banks, in such circumstances, need not accept delivery of the goods.

- **Article 12** obliges bank recipients of a collection instruction to advise, without delay, the sender of this instruction of any documents that are not as listed or are not received.

- **Articles 16–19** cover payment procedures. An important point to note here concerns partial payments: in respect of clean collections, such payments can be accepted, provided that such an action is considered lawful in the place at which payment is made; in relation to documentary collections, partial payments are permissible only if the collection instruction expressly allows them.

- **Articles 20** and **21** relate to action to be taken by banks in cases in which payment of interest, charges and expenses is refused by the drawee.

- **Article 24** states that a bank need not protest in the event of non- payment or non- acceptance unless expressly authorised to do so in the collection instruction.

- **Article 25** indicates that a case of need (ie an agent of the exporter who is resident in the importer's country) must have their powers expressly stated in the collection instruction. In the absence of this, banks will not accept any instructions from the case of need.

- **Article 26** imposes upon the collecting bank the duty of advising the fate of a collection, without delay, to the bank from which the collection instruction was received.

Note: this section of the topic is merely a summary of the contents of the URC.

17.7 The legal and practical positions regarding the duties of the remitting bank

Example 17.2

An exporter customer hands you a documentary collection. What is your bank's liability regarding examination of the documents and what other points would the bank check, in practice?

Suggested answer

The bank's legal liability is set out in the URC. Banks must check that they appear to have received the documents specified in the collection instruction, but they have no liability to examine the documents in more detail.

In practice, however, a remitting bank will usually make the following additional checks before it sends the documents to the collecting bank.

- It will ensure that the bill of exchange is correctly drawn, signed and indorsed.
- It will ensure that the amount of the bill of exchange agrees with the invoice (and collection order, if applicable).
- If the bill of lading is made out to order, it will ensure that it is indorsed in blank by the shipper (who is usually the exporter).
- If bills of lading are used, a full set will normally be required. If any are missing, an explanation will be sought and the collecting bank must be advised accordingly (see Figure 17.3, other documents and the whereabouts of any missing bills of lading).
- If the invoice shows which Incoterms apply, the bank will check that the documents conform to it: for example, in relation to CIF, the bill of lading must be marked 'freight paid' and an insurance document should be presented.
- It will make sure that the instructions on the collection order are logical, eg release documents on payment if a sight draft is presented.
- It will check the bank's reference book to see if there are any special documentary requirements in the importer's country.
- It will ensure that the customer has signed the collection instruction.

Note: If the remitting bank does not make a review of the documents, disaster can quickly result. For example, there may be some special requirement in the importer's country. Failure to fulfil the documentary requirements could mean that the goods are physically present in the importer's country, but that the importer cannot obtain possession. In this case, the exporter has lost physical possession of the goods, but will not be paid for them.

If a remitting bank fails to exercise reasonable care, the exporter will more than likely entrust its future collections to another bank.

17.8 Payment under the documentary collection system: in theory

The exporter should be able to make an accurate assessment of when payment can be expected. With sight drafts, the payment should be made as soon as (or shortly after) the documents reach the presenting bank. The only additional delay will be if a 'payment may be deferred pending arrival of goods' clause applies. There may be some delay while the importer is contacted by the presenting bank, but usually the importer will be eager to obtain the documents, and hence the goods, as quickly as possible.

The same timing considerations apply with term bills, except that the period allowed after sight must be added.

17.8.1 The timing of payments: in practice

Some banks publish a list of countries and the average length of time that can be expected to elapse in each in terms of:

- remittance of the collection from the UK when it is a sight draft;
- number of days after due date when it is a term draft.

Obviously, the time taken will depend on the method of remittance of proceeds (MT or SWIFT).

An industry expert has stated:

> Most experienced exporting companies appreciate that when they sell goods in a foreign country, a sight bill means, in effect, giving 20–30 days' credit, and similarly 20-30 days can be 'added on' to the due date of any usance bill. This is simply due to the delay in receiving funds.

17.9 Acceptance pour aval

Acceptance 'pour aval' is an alternative to straightforward D/A. If the collection order states 'release documents against acceptance pour aval', it means that the bill of exchange must be accepted by the drawee and then guaranteed for payment at maturity by the drawee's bankers. Only then may the documents be released. The benefit to the exporter is that:

- the drawee's bank is liable on the bill, thus eliminating the risk of non- payment provided that the bank is sound;
- funds will be remitted on the due date, thus reducing the delay of up to 20- 30 days that is normally encountered.

The prior permission of the importer and its bank should be obtained before submitting such a collection.

17.10 Risks to exporters who sell on documentary collection terms

The risks for exporters who sell on documentary collection terms are the same as the risks for those who sell on open account, ie importer risk, country risk and transit risk. As with all of the terms of payment, the exchange risk applies if the exporter invoices in a currency other than its own.

17.10.1 Ways to minimise the risks

Country risk, exchange risk and transit risk are reduced by the same methods as those applying to open account (see section 16.3).

The importer risk can also be reduced by taking status enquiries and by insurance against bad debts.

17.10.2 How to further reduce the importer risk in relation to D/P collections

Provided that documents of title are used, the importer cannot obtain the goods without paying the bill of exchange (or, if a bill of exchange is not included, paying the amount specified on the invoice or collection instruction).

In cases in which an importer refuses to pay, however, the physical goods are at the overseas port, in danger of being damaged or stolen and possibly incurring demurrage ('demurrage' means the charges that are levied by port authorities for goods that are not collected).

To overcome this problem, a store and insure clause should be incorporated on the collection schedule. The exporter knows that the goods will then be protected until an alternative buyer can be found.

If the exporter has a reliable agent, it can insert details of a case of need on the collection instruction. If the agent is reliable, the collection instruction will give them full authority to sell the goods on behalf of the exporter.

With air freight, the air waybill could show that the goods are consigned to the collecting bank. The bank's prior permission is required, however, and this will not often be forthcoming.

17.10.3 How to reduce the risk in relation to D/A collections

The additional risk in relation to a D/A collection is that the documents, and therefore the goods, are released on acceptance, with no guarantee that the payment will be forthcoming at maturity.

Once the bill of exchange has been accepted, the exporter is in no better position than under open account terms, except that there is an accepted bill of exchange on which it can sue the importer if it is dishonoured at maturity.

If the exporter, importer and collecting bank agree beforehand, however, the collection order can stipulate 'release documents against acceptance pour aval'. This means that the collecting bank will also accept the bill of exchange and hence guarantee payment.

17.11   A set of shipping documents being sent for collection

Figures 17.4–17.9 constitute a set of shipping documents presented by the drawer (exporter) to its bank for collection. An examination of the documents will establish that they appear to be in order.

Points to note are that:

- the drawee will be able to obtain delivery of the goods;
- it may claim from the insurers in the case of loss;
- the invoice and bill of exchange amount agree;
- the bill of exchange is properly drawn;
- bills of lading are marked 'freight paid' (CIF invoices);
- the insurance cover is at least the amount of the invoice;
- according to the reference books, no additional documentary requirements are necessary to satisfy the importing authorities;
- the instructions on the collection instruction form have been completed and are not contradictory.

Figure 17.4

FOREIGN BILL AND/OR DOCUMENTS FOR COLLECTION

Drawer/Exporter Power Woollen Company Limited PO Box 799 Bradford West Yorkshire BD1 1AA	Drawer/Exporter's Reference(s) (to be quoted by Bank in all correspondence) 34/1 18-5- 34/1
Consignees Tulla AS HC Andersens Boulevard 18 Copenhagen Denmark	Drawee (if not Consignee)
To (Bank)	For Bank use only

FORWARD DOCUMENTS ENUMERATED BELOW BY AIRMAIL. FOLLOE SPECIAL INSTRUCTIONS AND THISE MARKED X

Bill of Exchange	Comm'l Invoice	Cert'd./Cons. Inv.	Cert. of Origin	Ins'ce Pol./Cert	Bill of Lading	Parcel Post Rec'pt	Air Waybill
1	3			1	2/2		

Combined Transport Doc.	Other Documents and whereabouts of any missing Original Bill of Lading

	ACCEPTANCE	PAYMENT		Protest	Do Not Protest
RELEASE DOCUMENTS ON		X	if unaccepted ————►		
If documents are not taken up on arrival of goods	Warehouse Goods	Do Not Warehouse	and advise reason by	Cable	Airmail
	Insure against fire	Do Not Insure	if unpaid ————►	Protest	Do Not Protest X
Collect ALL Charges		X	and advise reason by	Cable X	Airmail
Collect Correspondent's Charges ONLY			Advise acceptance and due date by	Cable	Airmail
Return Accepted Bill by Airmail			Remit Proceeds by	Cable	Airmail X
In case of need refer to				*For Guidance	Accept their instruction

SPECIAL INSTRUCTIONS: 1. Represant on arrival of goods if not honoured on first presentation.

Date of Bill of Exchange 18 May	Bill of Exchange Value/Amount of Collection GBP 683.75
Tenor of Bill of Exhange SIGHT	
Bill of Exchange Claused:-	Please collect the above mentioned Bill and/or Documents subject to the Uniform Rules for Collection 1978 Revision ICC publication No 322 I/We agree that you shall not be liable for any loss, damage, or delay however caused which is not directly due to the negliegence of your own officers or servants.
	Date and Signature Bradford 18 May *Richard King*

Figure 17.5

INCORPORATING BILL OF EXCHANGE				**ADDITIONAL COPY** FOREIGN BILL AND/OR DOCUMENTS FOR COLLECTION			

Drawer/Exporter	Drawer/Exporter's Reference(s) (to be quoted by Bank in all correspondence)
Power Woollen Company Limited PO Box 799 Bradford West Yorkshire BD1 1AA	34/1 18-5- 34/1

Consignees	Drawee (if not Consignee)
Tulla AS HC Andersens Boulevard 18 Copenhagen Denmark	

To (Bank)	For Bank use only
English Banking Ltd Mill Street Bradford BD1 1AA	

FORWARD DOCUMENTS ENUMERATED BELOW BY AIRMAIL. FOLLOE SPECIAL INSTRUCTIONS AND THISE MARKED X

Bill of Exchange	Comm'l Invoice	Cert d./Cons. Inv	Cert. of Origin	Ins'ce Pol./Cert.	Bill of Lading	Parcel Post Rec'pt	Air Waybill
1	3			1	2/2		

Combined Transport Doc.	Other Documents and whereabouts of any missing Original Bill of Lading

	ACCEPTANCE	PAYMENT			Protest	Do Not Protest
RELEASE DOCUMENTS ON		X	if unaccepted ⟶			
If documents are not taken up on arrival of goods	Warehouse Goods	Do Not Warehouse	and advise reason by		Cable	Airmail
	Insure against fire	Do Not Insure	if unpaid ⟶		Protest	Do Not Protest X
Collect ALL Charges		X	and advise reason by		Cable X	Airmail
Collect Correspondent's Charges ONLY			Advise acceptance and due date by		Cable	Airmail
Return Accepted Bill by Airmail			Remit Proceeds by		Cable	Airmail X
In case of need refer to					For Guidance	Accept their instruction

SPECIAL INSTRUCTIONS: 1. Represent on arrival of goods if not honoured on first presentation.

SITPRO OVERLAYS 1979

447/496-
Pear

Date of Bill of Exhange

BILL of EXCHANGE for   GBP 683.75

At   **Sight**   Pay against the sole of exchange to our order the sum of   Six hundred and eighty three pounds 75.

Tulla AS
HC Andersens Boulevard 18
Copenhagen
Denmark

DRAWEE

Power Woollen Co Ltd
    0274 4330

Richard King

FOR VALUE RECEIVED
Bradford 18 May

Signature

Figure 17.6

Exhibit 3: Invoice (three copies required for collection)

INVOICE	FACTURE FACTURA	RECHNUNG FACTUUR

Seller (name, address, VAT reg. No.)	Invoice number 34	0003	Sheet no.
POWER WOOLLEN COMPANY LIMITED P.O BOX 799 BRADFORD WEST YORKSHIRE BD1 1AA	Invoice date (tax point) 18 May xxxx	Seller's reference 34/AE34567	
	Buyer's reference 345	Other reference	

Consignee	Buyer (if not consignee)	VAT no
TULLA AS MAIN STREET COPENHAGEN DENMARK		

	Country of origin of goods UNITED KINGDOM	Country of destination

Terms of delivery and payment
FOB UK PORT PLUS FREIGHT AND INSURANCE. CASH AGAINST DOCUMENTS THROUGH ENGLISH BANKING LTD, MILL STREET, BRADFORD

Vessel/flight no. and date CHARLOTTE	Port/airport of loading TILBURY
Port/airport of discharge COPENHAGEN	Place of delivery

Shipping marks; container number	No. and kind of packages, description of goods	Commodity code	Total gross wt (kg)	Total cube (m3)
TUL 345 COPENHAGEN 1/1	1 CARTON – 1000 PAIRS WOOLLEN KNEE LENGTH STOCKINGS ASSORTED COLOURS TYPE 92		60KG	1.25m3
			Total net weight (kg)	

Item/packages	Gross/net/cube	Description	Quantity	Unit price	Amount
TUL 345 COPENHAG-EN 1/1		1 CARTON – 1000 PAIRS WOOLLEN KNEE LENGTH STOCKINGS ASSORTED COLOURS TYPE 92	1000	£0.65 EACH	£650.00
		FREIGHT		£30.00	£30.00
		INSURANCE		£3.75	£3.75
			Invoice total	GBP £683.75	

Name of signatory	RICHARD KING
Place and date of issue	BRADFORD 18 MAY XXXX
Signature	

Figure 17.7

Shipper (Complete name, address and phone number) POWER WOOLLEN COMPANY LIMITED		**Bill of Lading** **For Combined Transport or** **Port to Port Shipment**	
Consignee (Not negotiable unless consigned to order) TULLA A/S		B/L No. 87 Booking Ref. 6063 Shipper's Ref 34890123	
Notify party (Carrier not to be responsible for failure to notify) TULLA A/S MAIN STREET, COPENHAGEN		**Seaway Line** +	
Pre-carriage by*	Place of receipt* BRADFORD		
Vessel Voy No. CHARLOTTE	Port of loading TILBURY		
Port of discharge COPENHAGEN	Place of delivery* COPENHAGEN	*Applicable only when this document is used as a Combined Transport Bill of Lading	

Marks and Nos. Container Nos. /Seals	No. of packages	Description of packages and goods	Gross weight (kg)	Measurement (cbm)
TUL 345 COPENHAGEN 1/1	1	1 CARTON STOCKINGS	60KGS	1.25M3
		ABOVE PARTICULARS DECLARED BY SHIPPER. CARRIER NOT RESPONSIBLE		

Ocean Freight PREPAID		**RECEIVED** by the Carrier from the shipper in apparent good order and condition (unless otherwise noted herein) the total numbers or quantity of Containers or other packages or units indicated above stated by the shipper to comprise the cargo specified above, for transportation subject to all the terms hereof (including the terms on the reverse hereof) from the place of receipt or the port of loading, whichever applicable, to the port of discharge or the place of delivery, whichever applicable. Delivery of the Goods will only be made on payment of all freight and charges. On presentation of this document (duly endorsed) to the Carrier, by or on behalf of the holder, the rights and liabilities arising in accordance with the terms hereof shall (without prejudice to any rule of common law or statute rendering them binding upon the shipper, holder and Carrier) become binding in all respects between the carrier and holder as though the contract contained herein or evidenced hereby had been made between them. In witness whereof three (3) original Bills of Lading unless otherwise stated below have been issued, one of which being accomplished, the others to be void. Freight, charges and prileuges whether prepayable or not and whether paid or not shall be considered as fully earned upon shipment and shall be paid vessel and/or cargo lost or not lost. (CONTINUED ON REVERSE SIDE)	
		Place and date of issue TILBURY 18 MAY XXXX	
Declared value by shipper (see clause 5 C 4 and tariff)	Movement	Signed for the Carrier By	
Releasing Agent	Freight payable at PREPAID	*Grant Powers*	
	Number of original B/L THREE (3)	For and on behalf of the Carrier Seaway Line	

Figure 17.8

Exporter's Reference 34/

Norwich Union Fire Insurance Society Ltd.
Maritime Insurance Company Ltd.

NORWICH HOUSE, WATER STREET, LIVERPOOL L2 8UP.

INSURANCE CERTIFICATE No. A.R./   CODE No. 66/KK/

This is to Certify that
have been issued with an Open Policy and this certificate all rights of the policy for the purpose of collecting any loss or claim) as fully as if the property were covered by a special policy direct to the holder of this certificate but if the destination of the goods is outside of the United Kingdom this certificate may require to be stamped within a given period in order to comply with the Laws of the country of destination. Not withstanding the description of the voyage stated herein, provided the goods are at the risk of the Assured this insurance shall attach from the time of leaving the warehouse, premises or place of storage in the interior.

Conveyance Charlotte	From London	
Via/To Copenhagen	To	Insured Value/Currency GBP 750 so valued

Marks and Numbers	Interest
TUL 345 COPENHAGEN 1/1	1 Carton – 1000 pairs woollen knee length stockings assorted colours Type 92

SPECIMEN

CONDITIONAL:– ALL RISKS as per current Institute Cargo Clauses (All Risks)
    Subject to Institute Replacement Clause. (as applicable).
    Including War, Strikes, Riots and Civil Commotions as per current Institute Clauses
    Refer to Clauses as over.

SURVEY CLAUSE:– In the event of loss or damage which may give rise to a claim under this certificate, notice must be given immediately to to the undernoted agent/s so that he/they may appoint a Surveyor if he/they so desire

Agents at .... are ....

CLAIMS:– In the event of a claim arising under this Certificate it is agreed that it shall be settled in accordance with English Law and Custom

and shall be so settled in Liverpool or at ....

by ....

G. W. Unmson

Liverpool Marine Underwriter

This Certificate Requires Endorsement

Dated
Bradford 18 May
Signed
Richard King

The original Certificate must be produced when claim is made and must be surrendered on payment.

Figure 17.9

IMPORTANT
PROCEDURE IN THE EVENT OF LOSS OR DAMAGE FOR WHICH UNDERWRITERS MAY BE LIABLE
LIABILITY OF CARRIERS, BAILEES OR OTHER THIRD PARTIES

It is the duty of the Assured and their Agents, in all cases, to take such measures as may be reasonable for the purpose of averting or minimising a loss and to ensure that all rights against Carriers, Bailees or other third partied are properly preserved and exercised. In particular, the Assured or their Agents are required:–

1. To claim immediately on the Carriers, Port Authorities or other Bailees for any missing packages.

2. In no circumstances, except under written protest, to give clean receipts where goods are in doubtful condition.

3. When delivery is made by Container, to ensure that the Container and its seals are examined immediately by their responsible official.

   If the Container is delivered damaged or with seals broken or missing or with seals other than as stated in the shipping documents, to clause the delivery receipt accordingly and retain all defective or irregular seals for subsequent identification.

4. To apply immediately for survey by Carriers' or other Bailees' Representatives if any loss or damage be apparent and claim on the Carriers or other Bailees for any actual loss or damage found at such survey.

5. To give notice in writing to the Carriers or other Bailees within three days of delivery if the loss or damage was not apparent at the time of taking delivery.

NOTE:– The Consignees or their Agents are recommended to make themselves familiar with the Regulations of the port Authorities at the port of discharge.

SURVEY AND CLAIM SETTLEMENT

In the event of loss or damage which may involve a claim under this insurance, immediate notice of such loss or damage should be given to and a Survey Report obtained from the Office or Agent nominated herein.

In the event of any claim arising under this insurance, request for settlement should be made to the Office or Agent nominated herein.

DOCUMENTATION OF CLAIMS

To enable claims to be dealt with promptly, the Assured or their Agents are advised to submit all available supporting documents without delay, including when applicable:–

1. Original policy or certificate of insurance.

2. Original or copy shipping invoices, together with shipping specification and/or weight notes.

3. Original Bill of Lading and/or other contract of carriage.

4. Survey report or other documentary evidence to show the extent of the loss or damage.

5. Landing account and weight notes at final destination.

6. Correspondence exchanged with the Carriers and other Parties regarding their liability for the loss or damage.

The Institute clauses stated herein are those current at the date of printing of this certificate but where such clauses are revised the Institute clauses current at the time of commencement of the risk hereunder are deemed to apply.

Topic 18

Documentary credits

On completion of this topic, the student should be able to:

- give a clear and accurate definition of a 'documentary credit';
- explain briefly who are the parties to a credit and describe their main responsibilities;
- understand the meaning of revocable and irrevocable and unconfirmed and confirmed;
- understand how a documentary credit operates;
- understand the meaning of honour (ie 'payment', 'acceptance', and 'deferred payment') and negotiation;
- understand the meaning and purpose of the ICC Uniform Customs and Practice for Documentary Credits (UCP);
- understand the meaning and purpose of the ICC Uniform Rules for Bank-to-Bank Reimbursements under Documentary Credits (URR);
- understand the benefits and drawbacks of documentary credits for exporters;
- appreciate the reasons behind the creation of the ICC Rules for Documentary Instrument Dispute Resolution Expertise(DOCDEX).

18.1   The definition of and parties to a documentary credit

A 'documentary credit' can be simply defined as a conditional guarantee of payment made by a bank to a named beneficiary, undertaking that payment will be made, provided that the terms and conditions of the credit are complied with. These terms and conditions will state that the beneficiary must submit specified documents, usually to a stated (nominated) bank and by a certain date.

Before considering how documentary credits operate and the responsibilities of the various parties involved, however, it is important that students become familiar with the more detailed definition taken from the ICC Uniform Customs and Practice for Documentary Credits (UCP).

18.1.1   The 'applicant'

The 'applicant' is the buyer or importer who requests its bank, the issuing bank (see below), to issue the credit. The applicant is also referred to as the 'opener' or the 'accreditor'.

18.1.2   The 'issuing bank'

The applicant is a customer of the 'issuing bank' and it is the issuing bank that issues a credit at the request of the applicant. An issuing bank can also, in certain circumstances, be the applicant. The credit, when issued, constitutes a conditional undertaking in favour of the beneficiary.

18.1.3   The 'advising' bank

The 'advising bank' is usually domiciled in the beneficiary's country and is requested by the issuing bank to advise the beneficiary of the terms and conditions of the credit. By advising the credit, the advising bank signifies that it has satisfied itself as to the apparent authenticity of the credit, and that the advice accurately reflects the terms and conditions of the credit received. If the advising bank elects not to advise the credit, it must inform the issuing bank without delay. If the advising bank is not able to satisfy itself as to the apparent authenticity of the credit, it must so inform, without delay, the bank from which the instructions appear to have been received. In addition, the advising bank may, if it wishes, advise the unauthenticated credit, but, at the same time, it must inform the beneficiary that it has not been able to satisfy itself as to the apparent authenticity of that credit.

There is no liability on the part of the advising bank to honour or negotiate under a credit.

18.1.4   The 'beneficiary'

The 'beneficiary' is the seller or exporter in whose favour the credit is issued. Note that, in most countries, banks can issue letters of credit on behalf of clients in favour of beneficiaries in the same country, who may themselves be importing the goods.

18.1.5   The 'confirming bank'

The 'confirming bank' is a bank that, at the request or authorisation of the issuing bank, adds its own irrevocable undertaking to honour or negotiate under the credit. Banks will only confirm irrevocable credits.

This undertaking is in addition to, and not in substitution for, that already given by the issuing bank. Naturally, there is no liability on the part of the confirming bank if the beneficiary fails to comply with the terms and conditions of the credit.

In most cases, the advising and confirming bank are one and the same.

Obviously, a confirmed irrevocable documentary credit is the safest form of credit from the exporter's point of view, but it will be more costly than an unconfirmed credit due to the cost of the confirmation (ie in the form of a risk premium) that is being added. It is common for the beneficiary to bear the cost of any confirmation.

Under the UCP (see Section 18.4), branches of the same bank in different countries are considered to be separate banks. Hence, for example, HSBC in London could be requested to confirm a credit issued by one of its own overseas branches. Branches of banks in the same country are deemed to be the same bank.

18.1.6 'Revocable' and 'irrevocable'

All credits should state whether they are 'revocable' or 'irrevocable' and, in the absence of any such indication, the credit will be deemed to be irrevocable. An irrevocable credit cannot be amended or cancelled without the consent of the issuing bank, the beneficiary and the confirming bank (if any). A revocable credit, however, can be amended or cancelled without the consent of the beneficiary. For obvious reasons, most credits are irrevocable and a bank requested to add its confirmation would not do so if the credit was designated as being revocable.

18.2 How a documentary credit operates

Let us return to our old friends, Speirs and Wadley and Woldal Ltd, and assume that these two companies have agreed that payment terms will be by way of an irrevocable, confirmed documentary credit.

The following items are detailed on the specimen letter of credit (Figure 18.1). The numbers correspond with those shown on the letter.

1. The type of credit (irrevocable).
2. The name and address of the exporter (beneficiary).
3. The name and address of the importer (applicant).
4. The amount and currency of the credit.
5. The name of the party on whom the bills of exchange are to be drawn and whether they are to be at sight or of a particular tenor.
6. The Incoterm in the underlying sales contract.
7. Precise instructions regarding the documents against which payment is to be made.
8. A brief description of the goods covered by the credit (too much detail should be avoided because it may give rise to errors, which can cause delay).
9. Shipping details, including whether transhipment and partial shipment is allowed. Also recorded should be the latest date for shipment and the names of the ports of shipment and discharge. (It may be in the best interests of the exporter for shipment to be allowed from a range of ports, ie *from any UK port* so that the exporter has a choice if, for example, some ports are affected by strikes. The same applies for the port of discharge.)
10. The expiry date and place for presentation of documents.
11. The credit is confirmed, as evidenced by a request to HSBC in the text.

Figure 18.1   The letter of credit

INCOMING SWIFT MSG – 700

{1: A34DTBANKHK2XXX342908}
S: 904739273347720HSBCBANKXXX453}

FROM:
DOWNTOWN BANK AND TRUST COMPANY
HONG KONG

27:	Sequence of Total 1/1	
40A:	Form of Documentary Credit IRREVOCABLE	[1]
20:	Documentary Credit Number UTDC65432	
31C:	Date of Issue XX0720	
40E:	Applicable Rules UCP LATEST VERSION	
31D:	Date and Place of Expiry XX0831 LONDON	[10]
50:	Applicant WOLDAL LTD NEW ROAD KOWLOON, HONG KONG	[3]
59:	Beneficiary SPEIRS AND WADLEY LTD ADDERLEY ROAD Hackney, LONDON E8 1XY	[2]
32B:	Currency Code, Amount GBP4108.00	[4]
39B:	Maximum Credit Amount NOT EXCEEDING	
41D:	Available with ..By ..Name/Address HSBC LONDON BY PAYMENT	[10]
42C:	Drafts at SIGHT	[5]
42A:	Drawee HSBC LONDON	[5]
43P:	Partial Shipment NOT ALLOWED	[9]
43T:	Transhipment ALLOWED	[9]
44E:	Port of Loading/Airport of Departure TILBURY	[9]
44F:	Port of Discharge/Airport of Destination HONG KONG	[9]
44C:	Latest Date of Shipment XX0810	[9]
45A:	Description of Goods and/or Services 400 ELECTRIC POWER DRILLS [8] CIF HONG KONG [6]	

46A: Documents Required   [7]
+ SIGNED COMMERCIAL INVOICE IN TRIPLICATE
+ FULL SET OF CLEAN ON BOARD BILL(S) OF LADING MADE OUT TO ORDER AND BLANK
ENDORSED MARKED 'FREIGHT PAID' AND 'NOTIFY WOLDAL LTD, NEW ROAD, KOWLOON, HONG KONG'
+ INSURANCE POLICY OR CERTIFICATE IN DUPLICATE FOR 110% OF THE INVOICE VALUE COVERING INSTITUTE CARGO
CLAUSES (A), WAR RISKS AND STRIKES RISKS

47A: Additional Conditions

71B: Charges
ALL CHARGES OUTSIDE COUNTRY OF ISSUANCE FOR ACCOUNT OF BENEFICIARY. CONFIRMATION CHARGES ARE FOR
ACCOUNT OF BENEFICIARY.

48:   Period for Presentation
WITHIN 21 DAYS AFTER SHIPMENT

49:   Confirmation Instructions
CONFIRM   [11]

78:   Instructions to Paying/Accepting/Negotiating Bank
IF DOCUMENTS STRICTLY COMPLY WITH THE TERMS OF THIS DOCUMENTARY CREDIT, WE UNDERTAKE TO REIMBURSE
YOU IN THE CURRENCY OF THIS DC IN ACCORDANCE WITH YOUR INSTRUCTIONS

{5: {AMB:9A3RY45O} {CHK:67B57D8H4923}}

The procedures that now occur are as follows.

1. Woldal requests its bankers, Downtown Bank and Trust Co, to issue an irrevocable credit and to request confirmation by HSBC. Let us assume that Downtown Bank agrees.

2. Downtown Bank, the issuing bank, request HSBC to advise the beneficiary, Speirs and Wadley Ltd, of the details. HSBC is asked to confirm the credit and we shall assume that it agrees to this.

3. HSBC, as advising bank, now writes to Speirs and Wadley, enclosing a copy of the irrevocable credit issued by Downtown Bank and Trust Company (Figure 18.1). In its letter enclosing a copy of the credit, HSBC will indicate to Speirs and Wadley that it has added its confirmation to the credit and that it will pay, provided that the documents presented by Speirs and Wadley comply with the terms and conditions of the letter of credit.

4. Speirs and Wadley should immediately check that it will be able to produce the required documents by the appropriate time.

5. Speirs and Wadley ships the goods and obtains the necessary documents, which are presented to HSBC along with the bill of exchange.

   Because sight drafts are called for and because HSBC is the drawee, Speirs and Wadley will receive immediate payment, provided that it has complied strictly with the terms and conditions of the credit.

6. HSBC sends the documents to Downtown Bank and Trust Co, and claims reimbursement of the sterling funds paid to Speirs and Wadley from the vostro account in the name of Downtown.

7. Provided that Woldal has the funds, Downtown debits its account with the Hong Kong dollar equivalent of £4,108 and releases the documents. (Even if Woldal does not have funds, Downtown is bound by the terms of the credit to honour the presentation.)

8. The goods are delivered by the transport operator to Woldal upon surrender of an original bill of lading.

18.3   Types of credit

Unless the credit states that it is available only with the issuing bank, all credits must nominate the bank that is authorised to honour (ie to pay, to incur a deferred payment undertaking or to accept) or to negotiate. In a credit that is designated as 'freely available' or 'available with any bank', any bank is a nominated bank.

If you examine the specimen letter of credit text advised by HSBC to Speirs and Wadley (Figure 18.1), you can see that, while the drafts under this particular credit were to be presented to HSBC for payment, the alternatives of negotiation, acceptance or deferred payment could also have been applicable.

The four terms apply as follows.

18.3.1 Payment

The meaning of the term 'payment' is self- evident: the nominated bank will pay the beneficiary on receipt of the specified documents, and upon the nominated bank's determination that the terms and conditions of the credit have been complied with.

Sometimes, the issuing bank nominates itself as paying bank, in which case payment will be made on receipt of the correct documents at its counters. On other occasions and particularly in relation to confirmed credits, the issuing bank will nominate the advising or confirming bank to pay. This is the position in relation to the specimen letter of credit (Figure 18.1).

The term applies only to sight drafts that are drawn on the nominated bank or those that are drawn on the issuing bank and the credit nominates the issuing bank as the paying bank.

18.3.2 Negotiation

Sometimes, the issuing bank will nominate the advising bank to 'negotiate' under a credit.

If a bank negotiates, it will either advance funds to the beneficiary on presentation of the required documents and will charge interest on the advance from the date of the advance until such time as it receives reimbursement from the issuing bank or it will agree to advance, ie it will agree to advance the funds on a due date or on a date that falls after the date on which it determines that the documents comply.

Such advances are said to be 'with recourse', so that, if reimbursement is not ultimately forthcoming from the issuing bank, the negotiating bank will be able to claim repayment from the beneficiary of the advance.

If the negotiating bank has confirmed the credit and the terms and conditions of the credit have been complied with, however, the advance will be on a 'without recourse' basis.

18.3.3 Acceptance

The term 'acceptance' can apply only when the credit calls for usance bills (term bills), ie bills of exchange payable at a specified time after acceptance by the drawee.

The acceptance credit is also referred to as a 'term credit' or 'usance credit', which means that the exporter draws a draft on the nominated bank demanding payment at a determinable future date, eg 'at 30 days' sight' instead of 'at sight', as shown in the specimen letter of credit (Figure 18.1).

In practice, this means that, instead of receiving immediate payment on presentation of the documents (at sight), the exporter's draft is returned to them indorsed on the face with the nominated bank's acceptance. This acceptance represents an undertaking by the bank to honour payment of the draft on the due date. It is quite common for the exporter to request the nominated bank to 'discount' the bill of exchange and to effect immediate settlement less interest from the date of payment until the due date (maturity) of the bill of exchange. Alternatively, the exporter may request the accepting bank to hold the accepted draft until maturity and then pay.

18.3.4   Deferred payment credits

Normally, the terms of a documentary credit will include an instruction to the beneficiary to draw bills of exchange and the issuing bank undertakes that such bills will be honoured, provided that all of the terms and conditions of the credit are complied with.

In 'deferred payment credits', however, there is no need for the exporter to draw a bill of exchange. The issuing bank or confirming bank simply undertakes that payment will be made on a fixed or determinable future date, provided that the terms and conditions of the credit have been complied with.

Although the exporter does not draw a bill of exchange, in all other respects these credits are identical to other documentary credits. Although bills of exchange are not drawn, in practice some banks will prepay or purchase the documents provided that they are entirely satisfied with the standing of the issuing bank and the beneficiary.

One benefit of a deferred payment credit is that it avoids the need for payment of stamp duty on bills of exchange. In some countries, stamp duty is set at a low rate, or there may not be any stamp duty at all, whereas in other countries stamp duties can be calculated as a percentage of the amount of the bill of exchange.

18.3.5   The wording of the credit in relation to payment, deferred payment, acceptance or negotiation

All credits must clearly indicate whether they are available by sight payment, by deferred payment, by acceptance or by negotiation. All credits must nominate a bank (the 'nominated bank'), which is authorised to pay, to incur a deferred payment undertaking, to accept drafts or to negotiate. When the nominated bank is a bank other than the issuing bank, then, unless it is the confirming bank, nomination by the issuing bank does not constitute any undertaking by the nominated bank to honour or negotiate under the credit. If the nominated bank does honour or negotiate, then, provided that the credit terms and conditions have been complied with, the nominated bank is entitled to claim reimbursement from the issuing bank.

Thus, in cases in which the nominated bank is neither the issuing bank nor the confirming bank, the beneficiary must bear in mind that the nominated bank is not obliged to honour or negotiate under the credit unless that nominated bank has expressly agreed with the beneficiary that it will be obligated (and has communicated that fact to the beneficiary).

18.4   The ICC Uniform Customs and Practice for Documentary Credits (UCP 600)

The ICC's Uniform Customs and Practice for Documentary Credits (UCP) is a set of internationally accepted rules and definitions that cover the liabilities and duties of all parties to a documentary credit. All bank authorities and advices of documentary credits will state that the credit is 'subject to UCP 600'. If the terms and conditions of the credit exclude or modify a rule in the UCP 600, the terms and conditions of the credit will prevail, and if national laws conflict with UCP, national laws will prevail.

The main provisions of UCP 600, which came into effect on 1 July 2007, as they affect exporters and their banks, are as follows and would apply unless the letter of credit stated otherwise.

- **Article 3** – a credit is deemed irrevocable even if there is no indication to that effect.

- **Article 4** – banks are concerned only with the documents presented under the credit. Even when the underlying sales contract is mentioned in the credit (eg as part of the goods description), the bank's decision to honour or negotiate depends solely on whether the documents represent a complying presentation.

  Note: The issuing bank should ensure that a credit is workable when it is established (eg if the sales contract is FOB, do not call for an insurance document) and beneficiaries should ensure that the credit meets their requirements as soon as it is advised to them.

  Once the credit has been issued, however, the bank's decision to honour or not depends solely upon whether the documents presented comply with the credit. The only way in which payment can be made against discrepant documents is if the applicant agrees to accept them (ie to provide a waiver) despite the discrepancies and authorises the issuing bank to debit its account, and if the issuing bank agrees to accept such a waiver.

- **Article 5** – banks deal with documents and not with the goods, services or performance to which the documents may relate.

- **Article 6** – in summary, all credits must stipulate an expiry date and a place for presentation of documents for honour or negotiation. If a credit is freely available, the documents may be presented to any bank.

- **Article 9** – in summary, if the advising bank elects to advise the credit, it must satisfy itself as to the apparent authenticity of the credit. If the advising bank cannot satisfy itself as to the apparent authenticity, it must inform the bank from which the instructions appear to have been received without delay. The advising bank may advise an unauthenticated credit but, if it does so, it must inform the beneficiary that it is unable to satisfy itself as to the apparent authenticity of the credit. In all cases, there is no obligation on the part of the advising bank to advise a credit, but if it elects not to do so, it must inform the issuing bank without delay.

  Note: If a credit is received by the beneficiary directly from the issuing bank, the beneficiary should ask its own bank to attempt to satisfy itself as to its apparent authenticity before acting thereunder.

- **Sub- article 14 (a)** – a nominated bank acting on its nomination, a confirming bank, if any, and the issuing bank must examine a presentation to determine, on the basis of the documents alone, whether or not the documents appear on their face to constitute a complying presentation.

  A complying presentation is defined in article 2 as '*a presentation that is in accordance with the terms and conditions of the credit, the applicable provisions of [UCP 600] and international standard banking practice*'.

- **Sub- article 14 (b)** – banks shall have a maximum of five banking days following the day of presentation of the documents in which to determine whether the presentation is complying. This period is not curtailed or otherwise affected by the occurrence on or after the date of presentation of any expiry date or last day for presentation.

- **Sub- article 14 (c)** – banks will refuse documents if they are presented more than 21 calendar days after the date of shipment as evidenced on an original transport document or later than any other period that may be specified in the credit.

- **Sub- article 14 (d)** – data in a document, when read in context with the credit, the document itself and international standard banking practice, need not be identical to, but must not conflict with, data in that document, any other stipulated document or the credit.

- **Sub- article 14 (f)** – if a credit requires presentation of a document other than a transport document, insurance document or commercial invoice, without stipulating by whom the document is to be issued or its data content, banks will accept the document as presented if its content appears to fulfil the function of the required document and otherwise complies with sub- article 14 (d).

- **Sub- article 14 (g)** – a document presented but not required by the credit will be disregarded and may be returned to the presenter.

- **Sub- article 14 (h)** – if a credit contains a condition without stipulating the document to indicate compliance with the condition, banks will deem such condition as not stated and will disregard it.

- **Sub- article 14 (i)** – a document may be dated prior to the issuance date of the credit, but must not be dated later than its date of presentation.

- **Sub- article 14 (l)** – transport documents issued by freight forwarders – a transport document may be issued by any party other than the carrier, owner, master or charterer provided that the transport document meets the requirements of articles 19, 20, 21, 22, 23 or 24 [of the UCP 600].

- **Article 17 (b)** – a bank shall treat as an original document any document bearing an apparently original signature, mark, stamp, or label of the issuer of the document, unless the document itself indicates that it is not an original.

Any mark or stamp executed or adopted by a party with the intention to authenticate should be accepted as a signature. One example of such a signature is the traditional chop mark used in Asia, which is a legal and valid form of signature.

- **Article 18** – article 18 (a) (iv) states that invoices *'need not be signed'*. Article 18 (c), meanwhile, states that the description of the goods, services or performance in a commercial invoice must correspond with the description in the credit.

In all other documents, the goods may be described in general terms that do not conflict with the description stated in the credit.

The invoice must appear to have been issued by the beneficiary and must be made out in the name of the applicant (except in the case of transferable credits, which come under article 38 and are covered in Part V of this book).

- **Article 19** – multimodal or combined transport- type transport documents – in summary article 19 states the following:

  - A transport document covering at least two different modes of transport must appear to indicate the name of the carrier and must be signed by the carrier or master or their respective agent. When an agent signs on behalf of the carrier or master, they must indicate the capacity in which they are signing, ie ABC Co as agents for XYZ Co, the carrier.

- The document must indicate the date on which the goods have been despatched, taken in charge or shipped on board at the place stated in the credit. If this indication is preprinted, then the date of issuance is deemed to be the date of despatch, taking in charge or shipped on board.

- If this indication is by means of a stamp or some other additional notation, the date of despatch, taking in charge or shipped on board appearing therein is deemed to be the date of shipment.

- Transport documents that are subject to a charter party – for example, charter party bills of lading – will be refused.

- Because this article covers shipment using at least two different modes of transport, transhipment will occur. Therefore, the article makes provision that, should the credit specify (inadvertently) that transhipment is prohibited, transhipment will nevertheless be allowed.

- Transport documents covering at least two different modes of transport need not be titled 'combined' or 'multimodal transport' documents to be acceptable under this rule. The concept is of a document 'however named' that complies with the terms and conditions of the credit and the applicable provisions of UCP 600, including article 19.

- **Article 20 – Bill of lading** – in summary, a bill of lading must appear to indicate the name of the carrier and must be signed by the carrier or master or their respective agent. When an agent signs on behalf of the carrier or master, they must indicate the capacity in which they are signing, ie ABC Co as agents for XYZ Co, the carrier.

  The bill of lading must indicate that the goods have been shipped on board a named vessel at the port of loading stated in the credit. Shipped on board may be indicated by preprinted wording, in which case the date of issuance of the bill of lading will be deemed to be the date of shipment. If shipped on board is evidenced by a notation on the bill of lading, the shipped on board date within the notation will be deemed to be the date of shipment.

  A full set of bills of lading is required unless the credit stipulates otherwise. The bill of lading will indicate the number that have been issued and signed. If a carrier issues only one original bill of lading, that sole bill of lading will constitute a 'full set'.

  Transport documents that are subject to a charter party – for example, charter party bills of lading – will be refused.

  When a bill of lading indicates that transhipment (ie the unloading and reloading from one vessel to another during the course of ocean carriage) will or may take place, such a bill of lading will be accepted, provided that the entire carriage is covered by one and the same bill of lading.

  Even if transhipment is prohibited by the credit, as long as the bill of lading indicates that the cargo is shipped in containers, trailers and/or lighter aboard ship (LASH) barges, transhipment is acceptable.

  If the credit prohibits transhipment, a bill of lading that indicates the carrier reserves the right to tranship is still acceptable.

- **Article 21 – Non- negotiable sea waybill** – this article contains similar provisions to those in article 20 covering bills of lading. The stipulations concerning transhipment and charter party sea waybills are identical. A non-negotiable sea waybill differs from a bill of lading, in that it is not a document of title. Non- negotiable sea waybills are generally used on short sea shipments.

- **Article 23 – Air transport documents** – an air transport document must appear to indicate the name of the carrier and must be signed by the carrier or its agent. When an agent signs on behalf of the carrier, they must indicate the capacity in which they are signing, ie ABC Co as agents for XYZ Co, the carrier.

- **Article 27 – Clean transport documents** – a clean transport document is one bearing no clause or notation expressly declaring a defective condition of the goods or their packaging. Banks will only accept clean transport documents. If the goods being imported are of a type in relation to which a statement as to the condition of the goods is necessary – ie for steel shipments, 'rusty' or 'atmospheric rust' – then the credit must make an allowance for this and permit such clauses.

- **Article 28** – in summary, insurance documents must be expressed in the same currency as the credit, they must cover the CIF or CIP value plus a minimum of 10%, must show cover effective from the date of shipment (eg shipped on board date on the bill of lading), they must be issued by an insurance company, underwriters or their agents, and any certificates must be signed or authenticated by the shipper (where applicable). Insurance certificates or declarations under an open cover policy, presigned by the insurers, are acceptable.

  Cover notes are not acceptable.

  Note: If the CIF or CIP value cannot be determined, the bank will accept, as a minimum amount, 110% of the gross amount of the goods or 110% of the amount for which honour or negotiation is requested, whichever is the greater.

  Where the credit calls for an all- risks insurance document, any form of words on the insurance document covering all risks is acceptable, including the standard London Underwriters Cargo Insurance, 'Institute Cargo Clauses (A)'.

- **Article 29** – when the expiry date of a credit falls on a non- banking day (for reasons other than force majeure), banks will accept presentation on the following banking day, but any last date for shipment is not similarly extended.

- **Articles 30 and 31** – the words 'about' or 'approximately' indicate that a tolerance of 10% plus or minus is allowed.

  Where the goods are described by volume or weight, a 5% tolerance in the amounts actually shipped is allowed, provided that the monetary amount claimed does not exceed the amount of the credit. Partial shipments or drawings are allowed.

- **Article 34** – banks assume no liability for the form, accuracy, genuineness, falsification or legal effect of any document.

18.5 The Supplement to the Uniform Customs and Practice for Documentary Credits for Electronic Presentation (eUCP)

The Supplement to the Uniform Customs and Practice for Documentary Credits for Electronic Presentation (eUCP) was first published in January 2002. It was introduced in order to reflect the movement towards the greater use of non- paper- based trade transactions. In particular, it was designed to provide a link between the then- current UCP 500, covering paper- based credits, and rules covering the growing usage of the electronic- based equivalent (eUCP). Following the revision of UCP 500 and the implementation of UCP 600 in July 2007, an updated version (Version 1.1) of the eUCP supplement is now in operation.

It must be emphasised at the outset that eUCP is not a replacement for the UCP but is to be read in conjunction with the UCP. To a great extent, eUCP helps to clarify the situation when the electronic equivalents of paper- based credits are used, rather than individual parties trying to interpret and apply UCP 600 to such equivalents, which would no doubt have inconsistent and chaotic results.

In an interview in 2002, Dan Taylor, co- author of the guide to the eUCP, stated:

> 'In my view, the use of the eUCP will develop slowly over time ... I believe we will begin to see banks utilising the eUCP next year [2003] and we are likely to see a steady growth in electronic presentations over the next several years.'

Unfortunately, and for many reasons, including the acceptability to all parties of a consistent and often solitary electronic platform or system, the reality of moving to electronic presentations is still awaited for the vast majority of transactions.

The supplement comprises 12 articles (e1–e12). A summary of the main provisions of these articles is as follows.

- **Article e1** – covers the limits of eUCP and specifically states that it not only covers the presentation of electronic records on their own, but also their presentation in conjunction with paper documents.

- **Article e2** – is important in that it explains the relationship between eUCP and UCP. This prevents any misunderstanding for concerned parties as to which applies.

  The article specifies that any credit subject to eUCP is automatically subject to UCP, even if this is not mentioned in the relevant documentation. When eUCP applies and when its provisions would have a different effect upon the outcome from the provisions of UCP, however, the former will be prevalent. Conversely, if an eUCP credit gives a beneficiary the choice of using electronic records or paper documents and the latter is chosen, only UCP will apply.

- **Article e3** – provides definitions of terms. Two major terms mentioned here are 'electronic record' and 'electronic signature'.

  An electronic record is electronic data that can be authenticated and also can be analysed as to its ability to comply with the provisions and terms of an eUCP credit.

  An electronic signature is a method of authenticating the identity and authority of a person who provides an electronic record.

- Article e4 – relates to the format in which electronic records can be provided. Acceptable formats must be stipulated in the eUCP credit, but, in cases where this information is lacking, any format is acceptable.

- Article e5 – concerns the presentation of electronic records (and paper documents).

  A place for presentation must be identified for both electronic records and paper documents. It is the responsibility of the beneficiary of the credit to advise the bank to which presentation is made when the presentation has been completed, because it is not necessary for electronic records to be presented at the same time. This notice from the beneficiary can be in an electronic or paper format. Presentation is considered to be incomplete until this notice has been received by the relevant bank.

An immediate problem that could arise would be if a bank were to be open but its system unable to receive an electronic record that was sent to it. This would have particular impact if such a transmission were to occur on the credit's expiry date or on the final day for presentation of the period of time after the date of shipment. This article covers that situation by stipulating that in such circumstances a bank would be considered to be closed and therefore the date of presentation would be extended to the next banking day, when the bank was able to receive an electronic record.

A proviso to this is given in respect of the notice of completeness by the beneficiary being the only electronic record outstanding. The article states that such a notice, whether provided by telecommunication or in paper form, will be considered 'timely' if it has been sent prior to the bank being able to receive an electronic record.

This article also contains two further important points. Firstly, in cases in which an electronic record or paper documents are presented under an eUCP credit, the relevant eUCP credit to which they belong must be clearly identified, otherwise the presentation may be deemed to have not been received.

Secondly, an electronic record that is incapable of being authenticated will be considered not to have been presented.

- Article e6 – looks at the examination of electronic records. When examination of an electronic record entails reference to an external system or contains a hyperlink to such a system and that system cannot be accessed, such an occurrence constitutes a discrepancy.

When a nominated bank forwards an electronic record, it is, in fact, indicating that it has satisfied itself as to the apparent authenticity of the electronic record.

If the issuing or confirming bank fails to examine an electronic record, this will not be grounds for refusing a presentation.

- Article e7 – relates to the notice of refusal of a presentation. Initially, it confirms that the period for examination of documents begins on the banking day following the banking day on which the notice of completeness is received. In relation to circumstances under which a bank has been given a time extension for the presentation of documents or a notice of completeness, the examination time starts on the first banking day after that on which the bank is able to receive the notice of completeness.

If an issuing or confirming bank (or a nominated bank acting on behalf of either of these) provides a notice of refusal of a presentation to a given party and receives no instructions from the latter within 30 calendar days of the date of the refusal notice, the bank concerned can deal with the electronic records as it wishes, without responsibility on its part. Any relative paper documentation should be returned to the presenter.

- Article e8 – stipulates that any electronic record will meet the criteria for an original or copy of a document called for under a UCP or eUCP credit.

- Article e9 – states that the date of issuance of an electronic record will be the date on which the issuer sent it unless this is at variance with a particular issuance date included in the electronic record itself, which would take prevalence. If no date is mentioned concerning the date of receipt, this will be held to be the date on which the electronic record is sent.

- Article e10 – confirms that, if a transport electronic record does not contain the date of shipment or despatch, this will be regarded as the date on which the electronic record was issued.

- Article e11 – provides that, if a corrupted electronic record has been received by an issuing bank, confirming or nominated bank, the relevant bank can ask for the electronic record to be re- presented.

  In such instances, the examination time is postponed until the electronic record is re- presented. If re- presentation does not take place within 30 calendar days, the relevant bank can consider the electronic record as not having been presented and that any deadlines have not therefore been extended. When a nominated bank is not the confirming bank, the former must advise the issuing bank (and any confirming bank) of the re- presentation request and the subsequent postponement of the examination time.

- Article e12 – is merely a disclaimer of liability for banks regarding the presentation of electronic records.

Full details of the eUCP are available from the International Chamber of Commerce (ICC), Paris, France.

18.6   The ICC Uniform Rules for Bank- to- Bank Reimbursements under Documentary Credits (URR)

Documentary credit operations have increased and become more refined over the years. As already seen in section 18.4, the UCP are the main set of rules to which parties to documentary credits adhere and these have been regularly updated. The current version is UCP 600 (2007 revision), which came into effect on 1 July 2007.

Article 19 of UCP 500, which came into effect on 1 January 1994 (and its predecessor articles in previous revisions), was seen as not covering the procedures in bank- to- bank reimbursements in sufficient depth and it was thought that bank- to- bank reimbursement required its own set of rules to complement this article. Therefore, following the implementation of UCP 500, a working group was put together to create a separate set of rules.

Interbank reimbursement procedures have, to a great extent, materialised out of practices that are considered acceptable at a local level in the major financial centres. The one exception to this has been in the USA, where rules were in existence long before the ICC created an international set of rules. From the work of the working group evolved ICC Publication No 525, *Uniform Rules for Bank-to-bank Reimbursements under Documentary Credits* (URR). It became operational in July 1996 and consists of 17 articles. Practitioners should ensure that they read these rules in order to appreciate their full implications.

Article 13 of UCP 600, which covers bank- to- bank reimbursements, makes specific reference to the URR, in relation to credits in which these rules are stated to apply and to standard rules of reimbursement to which the rules are not applicable.

18.7   The importance of documents in documentary credits

As can be seen from article 5 of UCP 600, banks are concerned only with the documents that have been presented under the credit. If the documents do not comply, the issuing bank is freed from liability under its undertaking. If the documents do comply, the issuing bank must honour.

A common occurrence, which causes a problem for the beneficiary, arises when its customer makes contact directly and requests a change in transport arrangements. If the transport document that is subsequently presented does not comply with the credit, the presentation will be refused by the banks. The fact that the applicant and the beneficiary have agreed to the change is immaterial, unless the applicant agrees to request the issuing bank to amend the credit and the issuing bank agrees to that request.

18.8   Documentary credits: the advantages and the problems

With a documentary collection, exporters retain a measure of control over the goods, either until they are paid or until the importer accepts a bill of exchange. When D/P collections are used, importers can refuse to have anything to do with the collection, thus leaving the exporter with the problem of arranging an alternative sale while needing to pay the costs of storing and insuring the goods. With D/A collections, importers may not pay the accepted bill of exchange on the due date, thus leaving the exporter unpaid and without any control of the goods.

With a documentary credit, however, exporters know that they have a bank undertaking to honour or negotiate provided that they comply with the terms and conditions of the credit. Thus, on receipt of an advice of a documentary credit, exporters can confidently begin to assemble and ship the goods knowing that they hold a bank undertaking.

The buyer risk is virtually eliminated, because an unknown buyer's agreement to pay is replaced by a conditional bank undertaking.

Neither does the transit risk really apply, provided that the exporter produces the insurance document, if any, specified in the credit. Banks are concerned only with the documents, not the goods, and payment will be forthcoming against a complying presentation, irrespective of any damage that may have arisen to the goods themselves during the course of carriage.

Country risk, however, can still occur because the importer's government may prevent the issuing bank from making payment. In addition, there are certain areas of the world in which banks are not as sound as they might be and the issuing bank could possibly fail.

Finally, two problems that exporters often overlook are:

- if the credit advice is received direct from an unknown bank, there is a danger that it may be a forgery;

- the exporter may not be able to fulfil the terms and conditions of the credit, because it calls for documents that it cannot provide.

18.8.1 How the exporter can minimise the problems

The actions that the exporter can take to minimise such problems are as follows.

- If the credit is received directly from an unknown bank, the exporter should ask its own bank to try and ascertain the apparent authenticity of the credit.

- If there is any doubt about the standing of the issuing bank, the credit should be confirmed by a bank in the exporter's own country. Confirmation will also overcome country risk.

- Immediately on receipt of the advice, the exporter should check that it will be able to produce the required documents. If not, it should ask the importer to arrange for the issuing bank to amend the credit suitably.

18.8.2 An alternative course of action if an exporter has presented documents that do not conform to the credit

By far the best course of action if an exporter produces non- conforming documents is to have the documents corrected or amended locally, but it is not always possible to do this before the expiry date of the credit. When these corrections are not possible, the alternatives are as follows.

- The exporter could present the documents to the nominated bank and ask that they be forwarded to the issuing bank as a presentation under the issuing bank's credit. It can request the issuing bank to seek waiver from the applicant for the discrepancies in the documents.

  If the exporter is sure of the creditworthiness and integrity of the importer, this is a reasonable step to take, but it must bear in mind that the issuing bank (and the confirming bank, if any) is freed from its undertaking.

- The exporter could request the nominated bank to honour or negotiate despite any discrepancies. In these circumstances, the bank would not be prepared to negotiate if there were discrepancies, but may be willing to take up the documents under reserve for its own customer or against a bank indemnity from the beneficiary's bankers.

  The nominated bank would require the exporter to join in a suitable indemnity whereby the exporter undertook to reimburse the bank if payment were later refused by the issuing bank on account of the discrepancies.

  When the exporter is a customer of the nominated bank, the bank will consider creditworthiness before agreeing to pay under reserve against an indemnity. When the exporter is a non- customer, the exporter's bankers will be required to join in the indemnity.

- The bank could send a SWIFT message to the issuing bank, seeking permission to honour or negotiate despite the discrepancies. The issuing bank will require the authority (waiver) of the applicant before such permission can be granted and the issuing bank will not be bound by a decision of the importer to approve the discrepancies. The cost of the SWIFT message will be charged to the beneficiary.

18.9 The ICC Rules for Documentary Instrument Dispute Resolution Expertise (DOCDEX)

Most presentations under documentary credits are found to have discrepancies on their first presentation, many of which can be easily corrected. There have, however, been a growing number of disputes between parties to documentary credits that have been difficult to resolve within the operative time period of the credits concerned.

Consequently, the ICC has established the Rules for Documentary Instrument Dispute Resolution Expertise (DOCDEX), which are designed to expedite the resolution of disputes by providing impartial and expert-recommended solutions. The ICC's International Centre for Expertise oversees the operation of DOCDEX. Use of the DOCDEX process is normally considered only when both parties have exhausted all other avenues of communication in an attempt to resolve differing viewpoints on the status of the documents.

For use of the DOCDEX process, one or both parties must agree to bear the costs involved.

Full details and the rules themselves can be found online at www.iccwbo.org under the link to 'Banking Technique & Practice'.

It should be noted that this is not an immediate service and that, generally, decisions are given 30-60 days after submission of the paperwork for review by the nominated experts.

Part IV

Introduction

In the earlier part of the book, we examined foreign exchange, methods of settlement between banks, documents, Incoterms and methods of payment.

Now that we have a sound understanding of the mechanics of foreign trade, we can proceed to study the remaining bank services for exporters. These services can be divided into financial and non- financial categories, and we shall see that in many cases there is a link between the terms of payment and the relevant service.

The syllabus for the examination requires an understanding of the services that are offered by non- bank competitors and it is in this part of the book that this aspect is of most relevance.

Finally, please remember that this part of the book is in no way connected with importers. The services that banks and others provide for importers are covered in Part V.

Topic 19

Short- term finance for exports

At the end of this topic, the student should be able to:

- understand what is meant by short-term finance;
- distinguish between pre-shipment and post-shipment finance for exporters;
- appreciate the significance of with recourse and without recourse finance; and
- describe the various forms of short-term finance that clearing banks and their group affiliates can provide.

19.1   The definition of 'short- term finance'

No legal definition of 'short- term finance' exists, but, for our purposes, we shall consider any facility that would normally be repaid within two years to be of a 'short-term' nature.

Facilities that cover a period of between two and five years are usually classed as 'medium- term' facilities and those that cover any period in excess of five years are normally classed as 'long- term'.

Usually, exporters of consumer goods require short- term finance because importers do not expect long periods of credit. Exports of capital goods are often sold on medium- or long- term credit.

19.2   The difference between post- shipment and pre- shipment finance

'Post- shipment' finance is money that is required to finance the exporter between despatch of goods and receipt of payment. Usually, this period is longer for exporters than it is for businesses that sell purely in the domestic market and special schemes have been developed to meet the needs of exporters.

'Pre-shipment' finance is the money required to finance the business between the commencement of the manufacturing process and the despatch of goods. This period will be identical for the exporter and the non-exporter.

19.3 With recourse and without recourse finance

If finance is provided 'with recourse', then the exporter is legally responsible for repayment of that money.

If finance is provided 'without recourse', it means that the lender has agreed to look to someone other than the exporter for repayment.

With recourse finance must be shown on the customer's balance sheet as a liability, whereas, subject to the agreement of the company auditors, without recourse finance will not appear there.

19.4 An overview of the short-term facilities available to exporters from banks and their group affiliates

Table 19.1   Credit periods and recourse arrangements

Name of facility	Exporter/importer facilities that are appropriate	Credit period	With or without recourse	Special payment terms
Loan or overdraft	Open account of documentary collection	Up to two years	With recourse	–
Loan or overdraft secured by an assignment of the exporter's credit policy	Open account or documentary collection	Up to two years	With recourse	–
Banks' special export finance schemes	Open account or documentary collection	Up to two years	With recourse	–
Negotiation of collections	Documentary collection	Usually short term, for example, maximum six months	With recourse	–

Name of facility	Exporter/importer facilities that are appropriate	Credit period	With or without recourse	Special payment terms
Bill advance	Documentary collection	Usually short term, for example, maximum six months	With recourse	–
Acceptance credit	Usually documentary collection	Six months is the usual maximum	With recourse	Minimum transaction, usually £100,000
Negotiation of bills drawn under documentary credits	Documentary credit	Usually short term, for example, maximum six months, but longer periods can apply	With recourse if the credit is unconfirmed Without recourse if it is confirmed	–
Assignment of proceeds of documentary credit	Documentary credit	Provides pre-shipment credit	See detail in Section 19.7	–
Red clause documentary credit	Documentary credit	Provides pre-shipment finance	With recourse to the issuing bank only	–
Export factoring invoice discounting	Open account (or documentary collection)	Usually six months maximum	Usually without recourse	–

Note: Hire purchase, leasing, forfaiting and export house-type facilities may be for both short and medium-term credit periods. For convenience, these facilities are covered in Topic 20.

19.5 Loans, overdrafts, the use of credit insurance policies as security and specialised bank exporter schemes

19.5.1 A loan or overdraft to be repaid from the export sale proceeds

Loans or overdrafts to be repaid from the export sale proceeds can be secured or unsecured, and the bank's considerations are those that apply to any lending proposition. (Lending criteria are examined in one of the specialised option papers and a detailed knowledge of credit assessment is not required for this examination.)

The customer benefits of an overdraft facility are its simplicity and flexibility. Interest is charged only on the debit balances actually outstanding on a day- to- day basis.

Loan accounts and overdrafts for export or import finance are completely exempt from the Consumer Credit Act 1974.

19.5.2   A loan or overdraft secured by assignment of a credit insurance policy

A loan or overdraft secured by assignment of a credit insurance policy is a traditional type of facility that has formed the basis of many of the specialist schemes covered in the next section.

The exporter signs a standard assignment form, which instructs the insurance company to allow the lending bank to take over the exporter's rights to:

- any claim against the policy; or
- any claim against a particular buyer; or
- any claim against any buyer from a particular country.

This assignment is useful backing to the bank if an exporter cannot repay because a particular buyer has defaulted. The bank will be able to 'stand in the shoes' of the exporter and, eventually, will be able to receive the proceeds (if any) of the claim from the insurance company.

Some students mistakenly believe that this form of security is absolutely safe, but this is not the case: the bank's rights are no better than the exporter's. Thus, if the exporter's claim is refused by the insurance company, the bank's assignment will be worthless.

An exporter's claim under credit insurance could fail because:

- the exporter did not fulfil the commercial contract;
- the exporter did not declare the shipment and pay the premium;
- the amount outstanding from the buyer who defaulted exceeded the credit insurance limit for that buyer.

In addition, the maximum percentage of risk covered by the policy is 95%.

Nevertheless, for a commercially reliable exporter, such assignment is a very useful security for a lending bank and some banks will charge a slightly lower rate of interest than would apply to an ordinary unsecured overdraft.

19.5.3   Individual banks' short- term export finance schemes

Over the years, major banks have provided off- the- shelf schemes for exporters under which the latter have acceptable credit insurance (either their own policy or under the umbrella of the banks' policy). It has been the case, however, that banks have suffered losses in respect of these schemes.

Such losses have arisen for a number of reasons. The first has been the inability of exporters to meet the conditions laid down in the relevant insurance policies, either deliberately or by accident. Another has been the provision of funds for one- off export situations, which naturally have a higher risk factor. There has also been a growth in fraudulent activity in respect of the presentation of documentation.

Consequently, the banks are nervous about the provision of short- term export finance schemes. Students should therefore ascertain what schemes are currently being offered by their banks and make a note of their salient points.

In general, banks have had two main schemes on offer:

- the 'smaller exports scheme' is aimed at businesses with annual export turnover of under £1m;
- the 'finance for exports scheme' has a target market of businesses with an annual export turnover of more than £1m.

Both of these schemes are marketed as 'without recourse' facilities, which is not technically true. If the exporter has failed to fulfil the terms of the credit insurance policy, or the terms of the underlying commercial contract, or has reneged on the payment of the credit insurance premiums, the schemes are considered to be 'with recourse' to the exporter. In relation to non- payment of premiums and contravention of credit insurance conditions, however, some banks have agreed with the credit insurers that the latter will cover such risk.

19.5.3.1 The smaller exports scheme

The smaller exports scheme provides post- shipment finance for up to 100% of the invoice value for up to 180 days' credit.

The customer's exports are covered under a bank's own credit insurance policy. This will normally cover up to 95% of the invoice amount with the remaining 5% of risk being stood by the bank itself. Facilities are only offered subject to status.

The scheme is appropriate for exporters who trade on open account or who use promissory notes or bills of exchange.

The scheme operates as follows.

1. The exporter will furnish the bank with a copy of the buyer's order, relevant invoice and evidence of despatch or shipment, eg a bill of lading, together with the appropriate lodgment form.
2. In relation to open account trade, details of the payment terms must be given to the bank, together with confirmation that such payments will be forwarded direct to the bank. In regard to bills and notes, the relevant bill and note will be given to the bank.
3. The exporter's bank then sends the relevant documents to the buyer's bank on a collection basis via its bills department.
4. Payment will then be forwarded by the buyer's bank on the due date through the banking system to the exporter's bank.
5. As stated above, in the event of buyer payment default, the bank will seek restitution under its credit insurance policy for up to 95% of the invoice amount, with the remaining 5% of risk being stood by the bank itself.

19.5.3.2 The finance for exports scheme

The main differences in the finance for exports scheme, when compared with the smaller exports scheme (other than the difference in annual export turnover), are as follows:

- credit periods can be for up to two years;

- finance is normally only available for up to 90% of the invoice amount;

- exporters participating in this scheme can hold their own credit insurance, although if they do not do so, the exporter and the bank can become joint policyholders on an appropriation policy, subject to the credit insurer accepting the exporter (and bank) as such.

19.6 Negotiations of documentary collections, bill advances and acceptance credits

19.6.1 The negotiation of documentary collections

When a customer sells on documentary collection terms, it may be able to arrange a negotiation facility with its bank. A negotiation facility is a lending facility, and normal lending criteria apply.

The facility works as follows.

1. The exporter submits the normal documentary collection items to its bank, but, instead of signing a collection instruction, it signs a 'negotiation request', which is very similar to the collection instruction. This form requests a negotiation facility and gives the exporter's bank the right to deal with the documents in any way it thinks fit, to ensure repayment. By negotiating, the bank is, in fact, buying the bill of exchange and documents from the exporter and therefore collects the proceeds in its own name. The advance is therefore for 100% of the bill amount.

2. If the bank agrees to the facility the procedure is as follows.

   - If the bill of exchange is drawn in sterling, the bank immediately credits the customer's current account with the full face value. If the bill is drawn in foreign currency, the bank credits the current account with the sterling equivalent at the bank's spot buying rate, assuming that the customer does not maintain an account with the bank denominated in that currency.

   - The bank debits a negotiation account with the face value of the bill of exchange. If the bill is drawn in sterling, there is a sterling amount debited to the negotiation account, and if the bill is drawn in foreign currency, then a foreign currency account is debited.

3. The exporter's bank then sends the collection to the collecting or presenting bank in the usual way. The standard customer authority gives the exporter's bank the right to vary the customer's instructions on the collection order, should it so wish. The exporter's bank is known as the 'remitting bank'. Generally speaking, the remitting bank will wish to include 'protest instructions', even if the customer prefers not to do so. As far as the collecting or presenting bank is concerned, the collection is received and dealt with in the same way as

any other documentary collection. The exporter's bank completes its own standard collection order, so the collecting or presenting bank will not know of the negotiation facility.

4. On receipt of the proceeds, the negotiation account is cleared. Interest is calculated and then debited to the current account.

   If the negotiation account is denominated in foreign currency, then the interest is calculated in that currency and the customer's current account is debited with the sterling equivalent at the bank's spot selling rate. Naturally, the rate of interest will be based on the interbank rates for the relevant currency.

5. If the bill of exchange is dishonoured, the exporter's bank has rights against:

   - the exporter, because this finance is with recourse;
   - the drawee, provided that it has accepted the bill of exchange;
   - the goods, provided that they have not been released to the importer. Under a D/P collection (see Topic 17), goods will not have been released, but under D/A terms, the goods will have been released to the importer on acceptance.

6. The bank's basic considerations when asked to grant a negotiation facility are:

   - the creditworthiness of the exporter:
   - the creditworthiness of the importer;
   - the existence of exchange control regulations in the importer's country;
   - the saleability of the goods if on D/P terms;
   - whether the terms are D/P or D/A (D/P being much more secure);
   - whether credit insurance is held and, if so, whether it is assigned to the bank;
   - whether there is an agreement for acceptance pour aval (see Topic 17) on D/A terms;
   - whether the documents give full control of the goods.

19.6.2   Bill advance

'Bill advance' works in exactly the same way as the negotiation facility, except that the bank advances only a percentage of the amount of the bill, instead of lending the full face value. The bank then collects the proceeds on behalf of the exporter.

Bill advances will apply:

- when the exporter does not need to borrow the full face value;
- when the bank does not feel justified in lending the full face value;
- when the bank is not entirely satisfied with the status of the importer or its country.

Note: with a negotiation, the bank has recourse only in the event of dishonour, whereas with a bill advance the bank can recall the advance at any time.

19.6.3   Acceptance credit

Acceptance credit facilities are generally only available for transactions of £100,000 minimum and thus only large, established customers can use them.

The exporter's bank allows the exporter to draw a bill of exchange on the bank itself, and the bank accepts that bill of exchange. Because this bill is a bank bill, the exporter can discount it in the discount market at a fine rate, which may be below the LIBOR rate (see Topic 9).

As security, the exporter's bank usually obtains authority to take over all rights to a documentary collection, which it submits on the exporter's behalf. For undoubted customers, the bank may agree to grant an acceptance credit facility when the exporter sells on open account terms.

Traditionally, acceptance credits have been made available only by merchant banks, but clearing banks are now active in this market.

19.7   The special facilities available in connection with documentary credits

19.7.1   The negotiation of bills of exchange drawn under documentary credits

The negotiation of bills of exchange drawn under documentary credits operates in the same way as the negotiation facility described at section 19.6 except that the bill of exchange is always drawn on the issuing bank. Provided that the issuing bank is sound and that the credit terms and conditions have been complied with, the bill will be accepted by the issuing bank and honoured at maturity. Thus the exporter's bank will look upon such facilities as being risk-free.

Such finance is with recourse, unless the lending bank has confirmed the credit.

19.7.2   The discounting of bills of exchange drawn under documentary credits

Bills of exchange that have been drawn on and accepted by banks and are drawn for a period of 180 days' sight or less are called 'eligible bills'. The rates of discount are much lower on eligible bills. The term 'fine rate of interest' is used to indicate that a bill is an eligible one that qualifies for lower rates.

For example, when the credit calls for sterling bills at a tenor of below 180 days, the UK bank may be nominated as the accepting bank. Hence, such bills will automatically become eligible bills once the UK bank has accepted them.

Finally, exporters should remember that it may be possible to persuade the importer to pay the costs of negotiating or discounting bills of exchange drawn under documentary credits. If such an agreement is made, the details should be incorporated in the credit at the time of issuance.

19.7.3   The assignment of the proceeds of a documentary credit

The assignment of the proceeds of a documentary credit is a means of obtaining pre- shipment credit with the co- operation of the exporter's bank. The exporter's bank, acting on its customer's authority, issues an assignment notice to the exporter's local suppliers indicating:

- that the exporter is the beneficiary of a documentary credit;
- that the bank is authorised to pay over, direct to the supplier, a certain sum from the proceeds (if any) of the credit if documents are presented through that bank;
- that the documents comply with the terms and conditions of the credit;
- that settlement is made under the credit.

This assignment notice may persuade the exporter's local suppliers to grant pre- shipment and post- shipment credit to the exporter.

19.7.4   Red clause documentary credits as a form of pre- shipment finance

A 'red clause documentary credit' contains an instruction from the issuing bank for the advising bank to make an advance to the beneficiary prior to shipment. When the exporter subsequently presents the documents, the amount of the advance, and interest will be deducted from the full amount of the credit.

The advance can be in two forms:

- 'conditional', whereby the beneficiary must sign an undertaking to use the money to help it to assemble the goods referred to in the credit. In some cases, the beneficiary may have to produce receipts for specified goods or raw materials before the advance can be made;
- 'unconditional', whereby the beneficiary merely signs a receipt for the money.

In either case, the issuing bank will be responsible for reimbursing the advising bank if the exporter should subsequently fail to present the documents called for under the credit. (The issuing bank will then seek reimbursement from its customer, the applicant.)

It is known as a 'red clause' credit due to the fact that when documentary credits were issued in paper form (as opposed to via SWIFT or telex), the clause regarding the advance was always typed in red ink.

19.8   Export factoring and invoice discounting

19.8.1   Export factoring and invoice discounting compared

Table 19.2

Export factoring	Invoice discounting
The bank's customer sends its invoices to the factor (most factoring companies offer invoice discounting services).	The bank's customer sends its copy invoices to the factor.
For approved debts, the factor will advance up to 80% of the invoice at once. The factor then collects the debt itself.	The factor will advance up to 80% of the invoice value. The customer collects the debt itself.
The debtor receives an invoice from the factor and sends its remittance to the factor.	The client's debtor pays the client in the usual way.
The factor then pays over the balance to the exporter, less interest and charges.	The client settles with the factor when the debtor's remittance is received.
The factor takes over the sales ledger administration of the exporter.	The exporter is responsible for sales ledger administration.
Factoring is disclosed to the debtor.	Invoice discounting is not disclosed to the importer.
Charges are usually between 1% and 3% of turnover, plus interest on any advances.	Interest is charged on the amounts advanced. The administration fee is relatively small, because the factor is not involved in any sales ledger administration.
The factor will deal with every invoice of the exporter. In other words, the factor takes over the sales ledger administration.	The factor deals only with invoices against which an advance is required.
Factoring is applicable if the exporter does not have the personnel to handle sales ledger administration.	Invoice discounting is applicable when the customer wishes to continue to handle sales ledger administration itself.
Usually, bad debt insurance is included as part of the package and the facility is without recourse.	Usually, bad debt insurance is included as part of the package and the facility is without recourse.

19.8.2   The conditions that apply to factoring and invoice discounting

- Both facilities are applicable to fast- growing companies with good- quality debtors. The minimum annual turnover varies between factoring companies.

- The terms of trade must be simple, with no complex documentary requirements. With factoring, normally only open account terms will apply, although documentary collection will be appropriate for invoice discounting.

- The factor must approve the debtors. Debtors should be well spread and the factor may be more keen to cover the export business if the UK exporter has a good spread of domestic business that is offered as well.

19.8.3   The customer benefits of factoring and invoice discounting

The benefits to the customer of factoring can be summarised as:

- sales ledger administration (with overseas debtors, the factor can handle correspondence in the language and even in the dialect of the overseas debtor);

- protection against bad debts, which is available for an extra fee;

- the client has the benefit of the factor's computerised credit reference system;

- cash flow is more predictable, because the client knows that it can claim up to 80% as an immediate advance against his invoices;

- debtors settle more quickly, because the factor is more efficient at collecting the debt (some clients use the factor purely for this reason and do not use the right to advances against the invoice);

- saving in management time (all overdue debts are 'chased' by the factor);

- advice on trading terms in export markets;

- local collections and assistance with the resolution of disputes;

- protection against exchange risk when invoicing in foreign currency;

- swifter transfer of funds to the UK;

- expert local knowledge of overseas buyers' creditworthiness;

- financial facilities available in sterling or major currencies.

Note: UK factors will provide factoring facilities to overseas exporters who sell to UK buyers. The overseas exporter sends its invoices to the UK factor.

The customer benefits of invoice discounting, meanwhile, can be summarised as follows.

- They are similar to those of factoring, except that the client must run its own sales ledger administration.

- Invoice discounting is not disclosed to the debtors of the factor's client.

- It is useful if the client has an efficient sales ledger team of its own.

- It is a very fast- growing service for exporters.

19.8.3 Conclusions regarding export factoring and invoice discounting

Using these export services means that the exporter can spend more time developing a positive sales relationship with export customers. It can adopt a more aggressive approach to its marketing, in the knowledge that collection problems and bad debts will be taken care of.

Export factoring and invoice discounting are particularly suitable for exports to the USA or to the EU. These facilities are not always appropriate for exports to developing countries.

Medium and long- term finance for exports

On completion of this topic, the student should be able to:

- distinguish between supplier and buyer credit;
- understand the role of Export Credits Guarantee Department (ECGD) guarantees in the provision of medium and long-term finance;
- know how forfaiting operates and appreciate its customer benefits;
- understand the various ways in which hire purchase and leasing can provide finance for exports;
- appreciate the services offered by members of the British Exporters' Association.

20.1   Introduction

There are several specialist forms of longer term export finance available. It is vital that the student can distinguish between these different facilities, because the examiner often sets practical problems to which only one of the various types of finance is applicable. If the student chooses an inappropriate facility, they will receive no marks because, in the real world, this would be of no help whatsoever to the customer.

20.2   Supplier credit and buyer credit

In Topic 19, we considered the terms 'pre- shipment' and 'post- shipment' finance; in this topic, our two major definitions are 'supplier' and 'buyer' credit.

- 'Supplier credit' involves the exporter's bank in the lending of money to the exporter, to provide post- shipment finance. The onus is on the exporter to repay the bank.

- 'Buyer credit' facilities involve a loan from a UK bank to enable the buyer to pay the full cash price of the export on shipment. (The loan can be made directly to the overseas buyer, or via an intermediary organisation in the importer's country.) There is no recourse to the exporter if the buyer defaults, because it is the buyer who has borrowed the money, not the exporter. Buyer credit facilities turn the export sale into a cash on shipment sale from the exporter's point of view.

20.3 The ECGD supplier credit financing (SCF) facility

The Export Credits Guarantee Department (ECGD) supplier credit financing (SCF) facility enables exporters to obtain credit usually for between two and five years, although this upper time limit can be extended if the surrounding circumstances warrant it. The SCF is principally used by those exporters dealing in semi-capital or capital goods. The minimum value of contracts under this scheme is £25,000. There is no obligation on the exporter to cover all of its export business, because cover under the facility can be provided on a contract-by-contract basis. It also has the added benefit to the exporter of being on a 'without recourse' basis, for the most part. It is only in a relatively few cases that ECGD will insist upon the exporter having a recourse responsibility, such as those in which there are complicated or substantial contract obligations. Such a recourse responsibility would normally be limited in value to a maximum of 15% of ECGD's total liability under the contract.

Finance under the facility is not purely limited to sterling and is available in a range of currencies for up to 85% of the contract price.

20.3.1 The operation of the SCF facility

Banks offering finance under the SCF facility will have joined in a master guarantee agreement (MGA) with ECGD. This details the terms and conditions under which the banks can provide the finance and the SCF facility. The exporter can approach any bank in the scheme and must obtain approval for the transaction to be covered by ECGD. Initially, however, the exporter will require to know the likely premium for the facility and the interest rate. It is possible to obtain a commitment from ECGD on the credit terms and interest factor for up to four months prior to the signing of the commercial contract. This is of great help to the exporter when concluding negotiations with the overseas buyer.

Interest rates will normally be at commercial interest reference rates (see Topic 16).

If the exporter wishes to go ahead under the scheme, an application must be made via the bank. It is at this time that the exporter must apply for pre-finance insurance cover under the ECGD export insurance policy, if required (see Topic 16 for details).

ECGD will then make an offer of finance and an export insurance policy (if requested). This will be accepted by the exporter and the bank, which will complete declaration and acceptance forms and forward the required premium.

The exporter will then receive an ECGD 'acknowledgment', a copy of which will be forwarded to the bank. (The exporter will also receive an ECGD export insurance policy document, if it has been requested.)

Once the exporter has carried out its obligations under the commercial contract, the 'certificate of approval' should be presented to the bank, together with the following:

- bills of exchange or promissory notes, which have been guaranteed or avalised, normally by financial institutions;
- documentary evidence of the delivery of the underlying goods or of the performance of the services contracted for;
- a confirmation warranting that the terms agreed between the relevant parties have been met;
- any other documents that may have been stipulated by the bank in its facility letter.

The bank will ensure that the documents are in order and will then purchase the bills or notes from the exporter for their full value. If the buyer were to default, the bank is not at risk. It would initially seek restitution from the avaliser or guarantor and, if payment were not forthcoming, the bank would then look to ECGD for repayment.

Under the SCF, bond insurance is an additional facility that is available (see Topic 22).

Note: it is necessary to arrange for a third party (a bank or a government) to avalise or guarantee payment of the bills of exchange before the UK bank can advance the funds.

20.4   The ECGD buyer credit facility

20.4.1   Its operation and availability

The ECGD buyer credit facility is usually available if the contract value is for a minimum of £5m. The exporter and its bank should contact the ECGD before commercial negotiations begin, to see if the facility will be available. Certainly, the exporter should be aware of the ECGD's attitude and likely conditions before it submits any tender or quotation to the overseas buyer. The credit, or repayment period, must be at least two years.

Normally, the overseas purchaser makes a down payment of about 15% of the contract value and the UK bank lends the buyer the remaining 85% so that it can pay cash for the exports.

20.4.2   The position if the buyer defaults

The loan from the UK bank to the buyer is guaranteed in full by the ECGD. There is no right of recourse by the ECGD if the buyer defaults on the loan, unless the exporter is in default on the commercial contract. Hence, two particular advantages of buyer credit facilities for the exporter are that there:

- are no contingent liabilities that need to appear in the exporter's balance sheet, because there is no right of recourse;
- is no need to take out any form of ECGD insurance because, from the exporter's point of view, the sale is on cash terms.

20.4.3   Other advantages to the exporter of buyer credit facilities

- The exporter does not have to pay interest on the loan, because the loan is made to the buyer.
- The interest rate, payable by the buyer, is fixed. Commercial interest reference rates apply in exactly the same way as for the ECGD SCF facility.
- The ECGD may be prepared to grant bond support (this aspect is covered in Topic 22).

20.4.4   The disadvantages of buyer credit facilities

- There is usually a minimum contract value of £5m.
- The documentation is complex and takes a long time to finalise.
- The buyer may object to having a loan from a UK bank and to paying interest and charges to a UK bank. (This is usually for political reasons.)

20.4.5   The procedure for buyer credit facilities

1. The exporter, importer, UK bank and ECGD agree, in principle, that buyer credit guarantees are suitable.
2. Four agreements are made simultaneously:
    - the supply contract – the commercial contract of sale;
    - the loan agreement – from the UK bank to the overseas buyer;
    - the support agreement – the UK bank;
    - the premium agreement – exporter – ECGD.
3. The money covered by the ECGD buyer credit facility is paid directly to the exporter by the lending bank, against presentation of documents specified in the loan agreement and in the supply contract. Legally, this transaction amounts to a transfer of loaned funds on the buyer's instructions and the buyer becomes liable to repay.

20.5   ECGD lines of credit

20.5.1   Common principles that apply to all types of lines of credit

From the UK exporter's point of view, lines of credit operate in a similar way to buyer credit. The lines of credit cover loans to buyers to enable them to pay on cash terms for UK exports of capital, semi- capital goods and associated services.

Common factors that apply to both buyer credits and to lines of credit include:

- commercial interest reference rates apply in exactly the same way as for the other two facilities already described;

- the buyer must pay a percentage of the contract value from its own resources;

- as a buyer credit facility, there are no contingent liability problems;

- because there is no recourse to the exporter, the exporter does not require any ECGD insurance of the debt, but must contribute towards the overall cost of the ECGD cover given to the lending bank.

Details of all lines of credit are available from the specialist export finance departments of the banks, or from the ECGD.

How then does a line of credit differ from buyer credit? The basic difference is as follows: from the individual exporter's point of view, the minimum amount (although varying with different lines of credit) can be as low as US$25,000, as opposed to the usual £5m minimum contract value of a buyer credit.

20.5.2 Project lines of credit

Project lines of credit are useful for major projects in which a number of UK suppliers are nominated by the overseas buyer to provide goods and services.

The ECGD will guarantee a loan from the UK bank to the overseas buyer or procurement agent. The buyer can split up the loan, using it to pay various UK suppliers on individual contracts that may be worth as little as US$25,000 each. The total amount lent to the overseas buyer will normally exceed £3m, but, as already shown, this sum can be divided to cover individual contracts of US$25,000 minimum, with credit periods of two to five years.

20.5.3 General- purpose lines of credit

In the case of general- purpose lines of credit, the UK bank lends a sum normally in excess of £3m to an overseas financial institution, as opposed to the overseas buyer. The overseas financial institution can use this money for loans to the individual overseas buyers to enable them to pay on cash terms for approved UK exports.

The UK exporter and overseas buyer can negotiate a commercial contract, knowing that up to 85% of the contract price can be lent to the buyer. Again, individual contracts for as little as US$25,000 can be financed in this way, with credit periods of two to five years.

20.5.4 Lines of credit to overseas banks

From the UK exporter's point of view, the differences between lines of credit to overseas banks and general- purpose lines of credit are merely academic.

From the point of view of the ECGD, the difference is that the ECGD is concerned solely with the repayment of the loan to the UK bank by the overseas financial institution. If the individual overseas buyer defaults on the loan from the overseas institution, the

ECGD is in no way liable. Thus, the ECGD can set up these facilities very quickly, because it does not need to see the individual commercial contracts.

20.6   Forfaiting

The forfaiting service provides finance to exporters who grant credit periods of between 180 days and seven years. Usually, the total minimum value of a forfaiting deal is £50,000 or the equivalent in foreign currency. Forfaiting deals, however, tend to be flexible and credit periods of ten years are seen.

20.6.1   How forfaiting operates

1. The importer finds a bank or other first-class institution that is willing to guarantee its liabilities. The institution is not resident in the exporter's country (and, in fact, is normally resident in the importer's country). When the buyer is resident in a developing country, however, the guarantor institution may well be a European bank.

2. The method of guarantee can take the following forms:

    - an aval, whereby the guarantor indorses bills of exchange drawn on the importer, thus becoming liable on them;

    - a separate form of guarantee of the importer's liabilities (this usually applies when promissory notes are signed by the importer, as opposed to bills of exchange being used);

    - when the guarantor is a US bank, the guarantee takes the form of a standby letter of credit whereby the US bank undertakes to honour bills of exchange drawn in the prescribed way.

3. The form of the guarantee is unimportant, provided that the guarantee is legally binding. What matters is the status of the guarantor institution.

4. Provided that the guarantor is undoubted, the exporter's bank, known as the 'forfaitist', will discount the bills or promissory notes (ie will pay the exporter the face value less the discount charge). If the importer is undoubted, then the forfait facility could be provided without the need of a guarantee from another institution. It is rumoured that a UK football club was able to obtain forfait finance for the transfer of a UK soccer star to Italy. The forfaitist did not require a guarantee because the Italian club was probably more creditworthy than its bank.

20.6.2   The benefits to the exporter of forfaiting

- The facility is flexible. The documentation can be set up in a matter of hours, whereas ECGD buyer credit facilities can take up to three months to arrange. In suitable cases, the forfait facility can cover the full amount of the contract price.

- The rate of discount applied by the forfaitist is fixed and subsequent changes in the general level of interest rates do not affect the discount.

- The finance is without recourse, so there is no need for any contingent liability on the exporter's balance sheet. Forfaiting does not affect any other facilities, eg any overdraft.

- All exchange risks, buyer risks and country risks are removed.

- The exporter receives cash in full at the outset.

- The finance costs can be passed on to the buyer if the exporter is in a strong bargaining position.

- Administration and collection problems are eliminated.

20.6.3 The disadvantages of forfaiting

- Costs can be high and there is no interest rate subsidy.

- It may be difficult to find an institution that will be prepared to guarantee the importer's liabilities. Sometimes, the guarantor institution may charge a high commitment fee if the buyer is not considered to be undoubted.

20.7 Leasing and hire purchase

Leasing of goods that are exported operates in much the same way as the leasing of goods traded within the domestic market. The leasing company (the 'lessor') buys the goods outright from the supplier and then leases them to the ultimate buyer, who has the use of the goods for an agreed period, subject to payment of the agreed rent to the lessor. There are various taxation complexities in connection with leasing, but these are not in the syllabus for this text.

The system can work in one of two ways:

- by arranging for a lessor in the exporter's country to buy the goods and to lease them to the overseas buyer – known as 'cross- border leasing';

- by arranging for a lessor in the buyer's country to act.

UK commercial banks all have subsidiary or associate leasing companies that can provide cross- border leasing facilities. These companies are also able to arrange for overseas lessors to act, where appropriate.

The benefit to the UK exporter is that the sale is, in effect, a cash sale and that there is no recourse unless it has defaulted on the commercial contracts.

Most forms of plant and machinery, vehicles or office equipment can be leased.

Hire purchase performs a similar function to leasing, but the buyer may be required to pay a deposit from its own resources. Once again, the legal differences between leasing and hire purchase are outside the scope of the syllabus.

20.8   The traditional roles of members of the British Exporters' Association

The organisations that are members of the British Exporters' Association are well-known firms in the City of London, which specialise in providing four main forms of service, as follows.

20.8.1   Export merchants

An 'export merchant' buys goods from a UK manufacturer and then sells them abroad. As far as the UK manufacturer is concerned, the sale is a domestic sale. All normal export risks are eliminated, because the manufacturer receives sterling payment from an undoubted UK organisation in accordance with the terms agreed. The disadvantage is that the UK manufacturer can tend to become out of touch with its market. In addition, the export merchant will pay a lower price than would be received if the manufacturer were to sell directly to the overseas buyer.

20.8.2   Manufacturers' export agents

In the case of 'manufacturers' export agents', a UK manufacturer employs the organisation to act as an agent for the purpose of obtaining overseas orders. A period of credit is agreed for the overseas buyer. The manufacturer then ships the goods and the export agent pays as soon as the goods have been despatched. The overseas buyer then pays the manufacturer's export agent in accordance with the agreed credit terms.

The finance is, in effect, without recourse, post- shipment finance. Although the sale contract is between the UK manufacturer and the importer, the manufacturer's export agent stands the credit risk.

20.8.3   Confirming houses

'Confirming houses' act in exactly the same way as manufacturers' export agents, but it is the buyer who employs them. Hence, a confirming house's fees are paid by the buyer, whereas a manufacturers' export agent's fees are paid by the exporter.

20.8.4   Export finance houses

'Export finance houses' provide finance for semi- capital or capital goods on a non-recourse basis. This will be supplied over the total period of credit granted to the importer, for up to 100% of the total amount due.

Export finance houses tend to be flexible in their outlook. Although their primary objective is to supply finance for large capital projects, they will also finance smaller deals. They will also arrange finance for bank consortia in relation to huge projects and joint ventures. Finance can be provided on a one- off basis or to cover a number of orders, or even through a line of credit arranged with an overseas bank in the importer's country.

Major UK banks have established subsidiaries that have infiltrated the traditional market of the export houses. New innovative services are continually being marketed by these companies. Students should therefore make enquiries as to how subsidiaries of their own banks have broken into this market and what services they currently offer.

20.9   Pre- shipment finance

The foregoing sections have all covered what is essentially post- shipment finance. Pre-shipment finance can be available from a number of sources:

- the assignment of documentary credit (see section 19.7);

- red clause documentary credit (see section 19.7);

- ECGD buyer credits generally provide post- shipment finance, but can be structured to include stage payments prior to actual physical export of goods, if the exporter's contract allows such payments;

- buyers may agree to avalise bills of exchange prior to shipment and these bills might then be discounted;

- the forfaiting of avalised bills that the buyer has made available prior to shipment, probably only for part of the contract value;

- an overdraft or loan, possibly secured by a debenture;

- a 'bridgeover' facility, whereby the bank provides pre- shipment finance, which will be cleared from, for example, post- shipment buyer credit or forfaiting. Much depends on the standing of the exporter, the ultimate buyer and the terms of the sale contract. Documentary credits can also be used by the exporter to persuade the bank to grant pre- shipment finance on a bridgeover basis.

Topic 21

Non- financial services for exporters

At the end of this topic, the student should be able to:

- describe the various types of travel facility available and understand their advantages and disadvantages;

- appreciate the considerations that a business must bear in mind when deciding whether or not to enter the export market;

- describe the non-financial services that banks can provide for new exporters;

- appreciate the services that are available to new exporters from sources other than banks;

- understand how joint ventures operate;

- appreciate how international licensing and international franchising can assist exporters.

21.1 Introduction

This topic will cover all of the non- financial services available to exporters, except for countertrade, bonds and standby letters of credit (which are covered in Topic 22).

21.2 Travel facilities

'Travel facilities' constitute a service that can be used by export sales people when they visit overseas countries on sales tours. For convenience, the travel facilities that apply to holidaymakers are also covered in this topic, because in many cases the needs and requirements of both export sales people and holidaymakers are very similar.

The main forms of travel facility, together with their advantages and disadvantages, are described below. These comments relate to travellers who are leaving the UK to travel abroad.

21.2.1   Sterling notes

There are no government restrictions on how much cash is taken out of the UK, but only relatively small amounts should be taken, to cover:

- sundry payments on board planes, ships or ferries and at UK airports;
- the payment of taxi fares and expenses for the homeward journey from the UK port or airport to home.

The disadvantages of relying entirely on sterling notes are:

- the danger of loss or theft;
- inconvenience as a result of bulk;
- that poor rates of exchange may be given for sterling notes;
- the traveller runs the exchange risk if they convert their sterling notes into local currency;
- there may be restrictions imposed by the overseas exchange controls on the amount of sterling notes allowed into, or – more vital still – out of, the country.

21.2.2   Foreign currency notes

It is a good idea to take a small number of foreign currency notes to meet initial expenses on arrival in the overseas country.

Once the traveller has acquired the notes, they have eliminated the exchange risk, unless they have surplus cash on their return, that has to be reconverted to sterling.

The disadvantages that apply if the traveller relies entirely upon taking foreign currency notes are:

- the danger of loss or theft;
- the inconvenience because of bulk;
- that the overseas government may impose exchange controls limiting the amount of cash a traveller can take into or out of the country;
- at the end of the trip, any surplus foreign coins cannot normally be converted into sterling;
- exchange risk applies to any surplus notes that are reconverted to sterling at the end of the trip.

21.2.3   Sterling traveller's cheques

Sterling traveller's cheques are purchased and paid for before the traveller leaves the UK, and they can be cashed at most banks throughout the world or can be used to pay bills in certain hotels, shops or restaurants.

The UK bank makes a charge when the traveller's cheque is first issued and a charge may be made by the organisation that cashes the cheque abroad.

The advantages of sterling traveller's cheques include that:

- there is a refund service available if the traveller's cheques are lost or stolen;
- they can be purchased in high denominations (eg £100) and hence may be less bulky than sterling or currency notes;
- the purchaser does not have to have an account to buy traveller's cheques from a bank (payment can be made in cash, if necessary);
- those issued by well- known banks can be used to make purchases in a variety of establishments, such as restaurants, shops and hotels;
- they have no expiry date.

The disadvantages of sterling traveller's cheques, however, include that:

- the traveller runs the same exchange risk as with sterling notes;
- sterling traveller's cheques are not always readily encashable abroad (for example, travellers should always take dollar traveller's cheques to the USA).

21.2.4 Foreign currency traveller's cheques

Foreign currency traveller's cheques have all of the advantages of sterling traveller's cheques and, in addition, the exchange risk is eliminated if the traveller's cheque is cashed in the country of the currency in which it is denominated. The traveller usually obtains a better rate of exchange if they buy their traveller's cheques in the UK.

The only disadvantage is that the traveller runs the same exchange risk as applies to foreign currency notes, ie any unused cheques will be reconverted to sterling at the end of the trip at the rate of exchange ruling on that date.

21.2.5 Credit cards

Credit cards operate abroad in much the same way as they operate domestically and the traveller can use them at any outlet displaying the appropriate symbol.

- Credit cards, as the name implies, give the holder the opportunity of enjoying a period of up to eight weeks' credit before paying off the amount owing on the card.
- A single plastic card will cover any number of transactions, provided that the traveller keeps within their credit limit.
- Credit card usage can help the holder to benefit from incentive schemes such as air miles or free travel insurance.
- They are widely accepted throughout the world in hotels, shops, restaurants, etc.
- They are subject to an exchange rate that is fixed by the card provider.

21.2.6   Debit cards or charge cards

Debit or charge cards, and travel and entertainment cards (such as American Express or Diners Club) operate in a similar way to credit cards except that:

- there may be an annual subscription;
- there is no period of credit allowed beyond the date of the account settlement, which must be made in full, usually by cheque, or by the favoured direct debit.

21.2.7   Open credit

Open credit involves a similar arrangement to a domestic UK open credit facility. The traveller's bank sends a specimen of the traveller's signature to a nominated bank branch abroad, and the overseas bank branch is instructed to cash the traveller's own personal cheques up to a stated amount.

The advantages of open credit are that:

- there is no risk of loss or theft;
- cash can be drawn as required and there is no loss of interest as applies to traveller's cheques and float time.

The disadvantage is that encashment is restricted to a named bank branch.

As a result of the wider usage of credit and debit cards, however, the use of open credits has diminished.

21.2.8   Company credit cards

Company credit cards are suitable for business customers who are limited companies, partnerships, associations, sole traders and other groups of particular individuals. The company is given an overall limit by the credit card company and it then issues company credit cards to individual employees who travel abroad. Each individual's card can have an individual limit programmed on it.

The advantages to the company include that:

- the credit cards can be used throughout the world – most airlines, restaurants and hotels accept payment by credit card;
- the scheme enables it to simplify its expense accounting system, yet still maintain a complete record of all transactions. Cash flow is improved, because expenses are debited once a month, instead of being debited at unpredictable times;
- the company receives a detailed statement for each executive together with a summary statement and payment invoice. Overseas transactions are converted and shown in sterling on the statements.

The advantages to the employee include:

- the fact that they have a company credit card can give them status in the eyes of their overseas counterparts;

- they are not required to use their own funds to meet company expenses, nor do they have the problem of claiming reimbursement from the company.

21.2.9 Emergency cash

If a traveller is unexpectedly without cash, money can easily be provided from their own bank, provided that there are sufficient funds available. Many banks now have dedicated helplines or fax numbers to help in emergencies, especially when these are caused by the loss or theft of a credit card or traveller's cheques.

The traveller will be asked to supply the following:

- full name;
- full address of where the traveller is currently residing;
- the amount of money required;
- if possible, the name and address of a local bank to which the funds should be remitted. Generally speaking, the funds will then be made available against passport identification.

Note: different banks tend to 'customise' travel facilities, so students should familiarise themselves with the facilities available from their own banks.

21.3 Should a business enter the export market?

A business must bear in mind the following considerations when deciding whether or not to enter the export market.

- Is there a market for the product?
- If there is a potential market, what selling price might be set?
- What additional costs must be incurred, for example in packaging, shipping and insurance?
- Is it possible to deliver the product overseas? Are there any import tariffs or quotas, or any onerous customs problems to solve? (Please refer to Topic 1 for details of how the GATT, the WTO and the SMP have reduced these problems.)
- How is the exporter to sell the goods? Does it require an agent or will the exporter sell directly to a distributor?
- The exporter will almost certainly need to visit the potential buyers, to ascertain whether there is any prospect of firm orders.
- The potential exporter must decide, in the light of the above, whether it would be profitable to export this product.
- Buyer and country risk.
- Exchange controls.
- Competition.

21.3.1   How the bank can help new exporters

The following list of services will help exporters to answer the questions posed in Section 21.3.

- **Status reports** on potential buyers and agents abroad.

- **Political and economic reports** on various overseas countries to help the exporter to decide upon the economic prospects and on the likelihood of country default.

- **Trade development departments** which give advice on technical problems affecting the export marketability of products. Some departments also offer a service that involves obtaining several contacts for an exporter in a particular market.

- Details of any **trade fairs** being held overseas, at which the customer might benefit from renting a stand. The bank may have its own representative present at such events and they may help to arrange on- the- spot introductions to the exporter.

- **Letters of introduction** to overseas banks, which may have detailed knowledge of the market and which could arrange introductions with buyers and agents. The UK bank could arrange for copies of the exporter's brochures and price lists to be forwarded.

- **Registers of potential buyers** for the customer's product.

- Recording the details of the exporter's' product on **registers** that are made available to potential overseas buyers.

- **Travel facilities** for export sales people on their travels abroad.

- Advice on general matters that affect the exporter, eg:

  - overseas documentary requirements, overseas tariffs, quotas and import requirements;

  - information on any exchange control restrictions on payments by overseas governments;

  - advice on the meaning and significance of Incoterms and arrangement of appropriate insurance for terms such as CIF;

  - advice on the significance of the various methods of payment for exports (open account, documentary collection, documentary credit, payment in advance), with an explanation of the risks and means of reduction of such risks (in areas such as the USA and the EU, open account trading is the usual method of payment);

  - advice on the exchange risk, together with appropriate methods of its reduction (forward contracts, currency borrowing, currency options and foreign currency accounts if there are receipts and payments in the same currency, bearing in mind that currency options may not be appropriate for **new** exporters);

  - the bank can recommend, without responsibility, a freight forwarder that will normally be a member of the British International Freight Association;

  - introduction to other providers of export services such as the Chamber of Commerce;

  - the bank can provide information on trade missions that are supported by UK Trade and Investment (see Section 21.4).

Note: normally, new exporters will be too small to become involved in the bank's confirming house operations.

21.5   Services available from non- bank sources

21.4.1   UK Trade and Investment

The UK government Trade and Investment website provides free information to help exporters and can be found at www.uktradeinvest.gov.uk.

The service brings together the work of the Foreign and Commonwealth Office and the Department for Business Enterprise and Regulatory Reform (BERR) in support of UK trade overseas. The service provides a series of commitments on behalf of the UK's firms, including:

- a special emphasis on helping smaller companies to develop their exporting skills and those that wish to grow their business internationally;

- a national information gateway to help firms to access the help available;

- identification of the markets and sectors in which government help can add most value to UK firms;

- customer feedback arrangements for firms to comment on performance;

   benchmarking of Britain's export services against those provided by some of its key international competitors.

The aim of the service is to help UK firms to take full advantage of overseas business opportunities, by providing support, information, advice and assistance throughout the exporting process.

Examples of the facilities available from this website include:

- free business leads – over 600 opportunities are published across all sectors and in over a hundred markets each month;

- sector and market reports;

- a self- evaluation questionnaire to assess whether a business is ready to export (details of products, turnover and other factors are input and the system provides an evaluation);

- an online overseas trade magazine;

- an export success newsfile; and

- an 'email us your question' facility.

These services continue to develop over time and students should visit the website to see what developments have arisen.

21.4.2   The British Chamber of Commerce

Chambers of Commerce usually specialise in the products of the local area. The Chambers often advise on the technical requirements of local products exported to particular markets and, in appropriate circumstances, the Chamber of Commerce can issue '**third- party inspection certificates**' showing that the exporter's goods meet the specifications of the importing country.

Most Chambers of Commerce now work within the Business Link system and can advise on how to access the various services of UK Trade and Investment.

Typical examples of the facilities available from a local Chamber of Commerce/Business Link system (in addition to those shown above) are:

- company information (financial and other) on potential buyers;
- directories and trade journals with details of potential customers and of new trends in the market;
- translation facilities;
- specialist help with technical documentation in areas such as those involving legal or medical terminology.

The aim of the Chamber of Commerce or Business Link system is to act as a local first point of contact for exporters. Where applicable, the full services of UK Trade and Investment can be accessed in this way.

The British Chamber of Commerce can be contacted via its website at www.chamberonline.co.uk.

21.4.3   Business libraries

Many business libraries can provide useful information: For example, details of the rate of inflation in Germany over the last five years, or details of the exchange rate changes between the sterling pound and US dollar over such a period of time. Such libraries often use Datastream or similar computer- based information sources.

21.5   Bank assistance for UK manufacturers that wish to set up joint ventures with overseas distributors

21.5.1   What is a 'joint venture'?

Sometimes, high import duties make the exporter's product uncompetitive in the overseas country. One means of avoiding such duties is to set up a '**joint venture**' with the local distributor. Such an operation can also overcome import quotas.

The UK exporter will usually take a small cash stake in the joint venture and will provide the expertise, and possibly some specialised plant and machinery, to help to set up the manufacturing operation. Once the operation is on stream, the UK manufacturer will provide some of the specialised components, but the joint venture company will assemble the product locally.

The product will then be sold in the overseas country and the UK exporter will be entitled to payment in accordance with agreed financial arrangements.

Joint ventures can be seen in reverse if we look at Japanese car operations in the UK.

21.5.2   How can a UK bank assist in a joint venture?

- The bank can provide travel facilities for executives who visit the overseas country (small amounts of local currency, traveller's cheques for short stays, and credit cards for longer journeys). Company credit cards can also be arranged.
- The bank, through the expertise of its international banking arm, can advise on:
    - whether an equity stake or a loan capital injection is better. Some overseas countries tax interest more favourably than dividends, and vice versa;
    - whether there are any overseas exchange controls that could affect remittance of dividends or capital back to the UK;
    - what is the likelihood of expropriation or country default (based on bank political and economic reports).
- If this information is not available at the international banking arm, it could obtain the details from the local office of the bank, if there is one in the area. Otherwise, a correspondent (agent) bank will be asked to assist.
- The bank will provide letters of introduction to:
    - a reputable local lawyer;
    - a reputable local accountant.
- All financial arrangements and other agreements should be drawn up, if possible, subject to English law.

21.5.3   Help with local banking arrangements when the joint venture begins

- The UK bank can open an account at the local branch of the bank if one exists. Failing that, it could provide a letter of introduction to a local correspondent bank.
- If there is a local branch office, the UK bank can arrange overdraft facilities.
- If a correspondent bank is used, the UK bank could agree to guarantee the joint venture's overdraft with it.

21.6   International licensing and international franchising

21.6.1   What are 'international licensing' and 'international franchising'?

'**International licensing**' is an arrangement whereby an exporter, who is the owner of exclusive rights gives permission for someone overseas to use the rights. The **rights** may be a brand name, a product, a process or a service.

The exporter, who is known as the '**master licensor**', will grant the overseas business, the **master licensee**, the right to use the product or service in a specified territory for a given period. The master licensee must pay a licence fee or royalty, or both.

'**International franchising**' is similar to licensing, but the overseas business, the 'franchisee', is subject to much stricter controls in the use of the product or service. The franchisee becomes, in effect, a controlled outlet of the 'franchisor'. Financial arrangements vary, but, usually, the franchisee pays a lump sum up front and then pays a royalty on subsequent sales.

21.6.2   Examples of products and countries that may be suitable for licensing or franchising

Any uniquely British products may be suitable for licensing or franchising, such as:

- specialist quality clothing;
- food and drink;
- specialist cosmetics (eg the Body Shop®).

Countries with a similar cultural background are most suitable, for example, Commonwealth countries, and those in Western Europe and North America. (Examples of franchising in reverse are McDonald's® and Wimpy®, in which the franchisor is American and the franchisee is in the UK.)

The product may need some amendment in the country of the franchisee: for example, fast food firms have deleted ham from their menus in the Middle East and have had to take into account the temperature problems with products such as frozen yoghurt. In addition, it is necessary to take account of any local labour laws, taxation policies and environmental regulations. Great care must be taken in drawing up legally binding agreements, especially in relation to intellectual property rights.

21.6.3   The advantages of franchising or licensing

From the point of view of a UK exporter, the advantages of franchising or licensing are that:

- there is greater commitment on the part of licensees than is found among traditional agents or distributors;

- there is greater control over presentation and pricing of products;
- there are lower start- up costs compared with joint ventures or traditional selling techniques;
- there is closer involvement with the overseas marketplace.

21.6.4   Bank assistance to UK exporters

Some banks already have specialist departments to provide assistance to UK exporters in relation to franchising and licensing. The bank can advise on:

- market research to test suitability;
- financial projections to cover cost of setting up the arrangements and the potential revenue;
- legal matters to ensure that the licensee is committed to payment of fees and the proper treatment of the product;
- exchange controls in overseas countries;
- promotions to find potential licensees and franchisees;
- differences between the home market and the overseas market.

Specialist advice is also available from the British Franchise Association at www.thebfa.org.

Note: Licensing applies only to well- established products or services. Do not suggest licensing or joint ventures for small firms just starting up. Joint ventures apply more to capital goods, whereas licensing or franchising is applicable mainly to consumer goods or services.

21.7   Types of agent and types of distributor

21.7.1   The difference between distributors and agents

On the one hand, the exporter may appoint a distributor, who is usually based in the importing country. The exporter sells goods to the distributor, who then sells these goods on its own account.

When an exporter appoints an agent, on the other hand, that agent may enter into a contract with the buyer on the exporter's behalf, or the agent may introduce the buyer to the exporter.

21.7.2   Sole agents and exclusive agents

21.7.2.1   Sole agents

When an agent is appointed on a 'sole' basis, the exporter cannot appoint another agent in the sole agent's agreed territory. The exporter may, however, obtain orders directly from buyers in the agreed territory without having to pay commission.

21.8.2.2   Exclusive agents

When the exporter appoints an 'exclusive agent' not only is the exporter barred from appointing another agent in the agreed territory, but the exporter is also barred from obtaining orders directly from that territory. If such orders are obtained, then commission must be paid to the exclusive agent.

Exporters should take specialist legal advice before appointing agents or distributors because there may be complex legal obligations involved.

Topic 22

Bonds, standby letters of credit and countertrade

On completion of this topic, the student should be able to:

- understand the role of bonds in international trade;
- describe the various types of bond;
- appreciate the function of a standby letter of credit and ISP98;
- distinguish between on demand and conditional bonds;
- describe the procedures for issuing bonds;
- appreciate the problems that bonds cause for exporters;
- understand how these problems can be reduced;
- describe the various forms of countertrade;
- appreciate the role of banks and others in promoting countertrade.

22.1   The role of bonds in international trade

A bond is issued by a guarantor, usually a bank or an insurance company, on behalf of an exporter. It is a guarantee to the buyer that the exporter will fulfil its contractual obligations. If these obligations are not fulfilled, the guarantor undertakes to pay a sum of money to the buyer in compensation. This sum of money can be anything from 1% to 100% of the contract value.

If the bond is issued by a bank, the exporter is asked to sign a counter-indemnity which authorises the bank to debit the exporter's account with any money paid out under the bond.

Bonds are usually required in connection with overseas contracts or with the supply of capital goods and services. When there is a buyer's market, the provision of a bond can be made an essential condition for the granting of the contract. Bonds are commonly required by Middle Eastern countries, but many other countries now also require them. Most international aid agencies, such as the World Bank, and most government purchasing organisations in the developing world, plus major purchasers of goods and services in the North Sea oil sector, now require bonds from sellers.

22.2   Types of bond

The various types of bond are as follows.

22.2.1   Tender or bid bonds

A 'tender bond' or 'bid bond' is usually for between 2–5% of the contract value, and will guarantee that the exporter will take up the contract if it is awarded. Failure to take up the contract results in a penalty for the amount of the bond. In addition, the tender bond usually commits the exporter and its bank to joining in a performance bond (see below) if the contract is awarded. Tender bonds serve to prevent the submission of frivolous tenders.

22.2.2   Performance bonds

'Performance bonds' guarantee that the goods or services will be of the required standard and a stated penalty is payable if they are not. The amount payable will be a stated percentage of the contract price: often, it is 10%, but sometimes more.

22.2.3   Advance payment bonds

Advance payment bonds undertake to refund any advance payments if the goods or services are unsatisfactory or if the goods or services are not provided.

22.2.4   Warranty or maintenance bonds

'Warranty bonds' or 'maintenance bonds' undertake that the exporter will maintain the equipment for a period of time.

22.2.5   Retention bonds

'Retention bonds' enable retention money, which would otherwise be held by the buyer beyond the completion of the contract, to be released early. These bonds guarantee the return to the buyer of such retention money in the event of non- performance of post-completion obligations by the exporter.

22.2.6   Recourse bonds

'Recourse bonds' are sometimes demanded by the Export Credits Guarantee Department (ECGD) to cover the potential recourse by the ECGD under buyer credits.

22.3　On demand bonds and conditional bonds

22.3.1　On demand bonds

'On demand' bonds, sometimes known as 'unconditional bonds', can be called at the sole discretion of the buyer. The bank must pay if called upon to do so, even in circumstances under which it may be clear to the exporter that the claim is wholly unjustified. UK courts have often ruled that the bank must honour claims under on demand bonds.

If the bank has to pay under the bond, it will debit the customer's account under the authority of the counter-indemnity. The exporter will then be left with the unenviable task of claiming reimbursement in the courts of the buyer's country.

It must be stressed that banks never become involved in contractual disputes. If payment is called for that conforms to the terms of the bond, the bank must pay.

22.3.2　Conditional bonds

'Conditional bonds' can be divided into two types:

- those requiring documentary evidence;
- those that do not require documentary evidence.

Conditional bonds requiring documentary evidence give maximum protection to the exporter. Payment can be called for by the buyer only against production of a specified document, such as a certificate of award by an independent arbitrator. Unfortunately, this type of conditional bond is often unacceptable, particularly in the case of Middle East buyers.

Conditional bonds that do not require documentary evidence are, however, little better than on demand bonds from the exporter's point of view. Such bonds often specify that payment must be made 'in the event of default or failure on the part of the contractor to perform its obligations under the abovementioned contract'. This terminology is so vague that banks are often obliged to pay a simple on demand claim if one is received.

22.4　The procedure for issuing bonds

If the UK bank is satisfied that joining in a bond is justified, it would prefer to issue its own bond direct to the importer. In certain countries, notably in the Middle East, local laws or customs prevent importers from accepting bonds issued directly by UK banks. In these circumstances, the UK bank will instruct a bank that is domiciled in the buyer's locality to issue a bond against the UK bank's own indemnity.

At the same time as the bond is issued, the exporter will complete the counter-indemnity to authorise the bank to debit the account with the cost of any payments under the bond. The bank will make a suitable charge for the service, usually a stated annual percentage of the bond's value. This percentage usually varies between 0.5%

and 1.5% a year, payable quarterly in advance. In addition, if a local bank is involved, it can charge up to 2% or more per annum.

22.5   The problems that bonds cause for exporters

22.5.1   The effect of bonds on the credit rating of the exporter

Banks treat the issue of bonds in exactly the same way as they would treat any lending facility. If payment is called for within the terms of the bond, the bank must pay, irrespective of whether its customer has funds to honour the counter- indemnity. Hence banks would normally wish to reduce a customer's maximum borrowing facilities pound for pound by the same amount as the bond.

Tender bonds involve the worst problems. The average success rate is often said to be one in eight for tenders, so the average contractor may, at any one time, have eight tenders outstanding. If each of these tenders involves a tender bond of, 2%, for example then the exporter's total potential borrowing facilities are reduced by 16% of its overall tender volume.

22.5.2   The unauthorised extension of bonds

Some countries, such as Syria, have laws that prevent the local bank from cancelling the bond without the importer's specific authority. This prohibition applies even if the bond contains an expiry date.

Sometimes, the local bank will threaten to call for payment unless the bond is formally extended. The usual result is that the local bank is able to persuade the UK bank to extend the bond and that the annual bank charges continue to be levied by both banks.

Sometimes, tender bonds are not cancelled, even when the contract has been awarded and a performance bond has been issued.

22.5.3   The unfair calling of bonds

The buyer may call for payment, even when such a call is unjustified. If the call conforms to the terms of the bond, the bank must pay and will debit the exporter's account under the terms of its counter- indemnity. The exporter can be left with the task of claiming reimbursement from the buyer via the overseas courts.

There is also a danger that advance payment or retention bonds could be called, even though the advance payment or retention money has never been paid over to the exporter in the first place.

In addition, political events in the overseas country might lead to the unfair calling of a bond.

22.6 How an exporter can overcome or reduce the problems of bonds

22.6.1 The effect of the bond on the exporter's credit rating

22.6.1.1 ECGD bond insurance policy (BIP)

If bonds have to be provided as part of a commercial contract, the ECGD bond insurance policy (BIP) can cover 100% of the liabilities involved. For 'on demand' bonds this cover also includes the unfair calling of bonds. In order to avail itself of the benefits of this policy, the exporter must already have some basic cover provided by ECGD, eg an export insurance policy or a buyer credit facility.

ECGD is normally willing to transfer the bond support from the exporter to the bank that issues the guarantee. This means that, from the bank's point of view, the issue of the bond is risk-free, because, in the event of a claim, the bank will pay out and be reimbursed by the ECGD. ECGD will only claim against the exporter if the bond has been called with justification and there will be no recourse if the bond has been called unfairly. Thus, whatever the justification for the claim, the bank will be reimbursed for the full amount by ECGD.

Note

- The ECGD BIP scheme does not provide cover for tender bonds.
- Any BIP cover must remain confidential between ECGD and the exporter.

22.6.1.2 Other insurers

Some private sector insurers, such as Atradius, may also be prepared to grant appropriate indemnities. The issue of bonds that are covered by such insurers' indemnities should not affect the bank's credit assessment, provided that the indemnity is assigned to the bank and provided that the insurer does not have recourse to the bank if the bond is called with justification. In many cases, however, private sector insurers will pay out only if the bond has been called unfairly. In such situations, the bank will only rely on the insurance as 'comfort' and will normally treat the bond as a credit facility.

22.6.2 The unauthorised extension of bonds

1. If the bond can be issued directly by the UK bank, standard wording can be incorporated to ensure that the bond has an expiry date and that the bond will be governed in accordance with English law. In such cases the bond cannot be extended without the exporter's agreement.

2. If 1) is not possible, the UK bank may agree to insert a clause in the counter-indemnity that specifies that the exporter's liability is limited to the period stated in the bond and that any extension must be approved by the exporter.

Obviously, this concession transfers the risk of an unauthorised extension from the exporter onto its bank and the bank will only agree to this for important customers.

3. When a tender bond stipulates that a performance bond must be issued if the contract is awarded, the performance bond should be worded so that it is only effective when the tender bond has been returned to the UK bank for cancellation.

22.6.3 The unfair calling of advance payment guarantees and retention money guarantee

The exporter should ensure that the bond incorporates a reduction clause. This should state that the guaranteed value can be reduced in line with performance of the contract. An operative clause should also be included. This will ensure that the bond is effective only on receipt by the exporter of the advance payment or retention money.

22.7   Other precautions that an exporter can take when required to provide bonds

In addition to the suggestions made earlier, the exporter can take the following precautions.

- The exporter should obtain the most detailed commercial and financial information on the prospective buyer and the market. Banks can assist in this matter, as can UK Trade and Investment or the Chamber of Commerce (see Topic 21).

- The exporter should consider employing a good local agent in relation to markets in which there are many contracts that require bonds. An agent can be particularly useful in obtaining the return of an expired bond so that formal cancellation can be effected. Many foreign banks continue to charge commission on bonds that have been issued against an indemnity from a UK bank even though the expiry date has passed; only on formal return and cancellation do they cease to charge. In addition, the UK bank must consider the contingent liability to continue to apply on such bonds, pending formal return of the document. Thus an agent who could obtain the return of a bond on its expiry date would be very useful in reduction of liabilities and charges.

- The cost of bonding can be built into the contract price. When tender bonds are required, a price escalation clause in the commercial contract could avoid situations in which the contract has become uneconomic due to delayed adjudication. If this arises, the exporter has the unenviable choice of completing an uneconomic contract or declining the contract and being made to pay under the tender bond.

- If the exporter acts purely as a subcontractor, it should ensure that any bond relates only to the part of the work for which it is subcontracted.

- The exporter should also consider ECGD or private sector insurance against unfair calling of the bond, where available.

22.8 ICC Uniform Rules for Demand Guarantees (URDG)

The ICC Uniform Rules for Demand Guarantees (URDG), Publication No 458, is a set of internationally accepted rules comprising 28 articles. They cover the practices relating to demand guarantees. They were designed primarily to control the unfair calling of guarantees while maintaining a fair status quo between the various interested parties.

The three major parties identified in these rules are as follows.

22.8.1 The beneficiary

The 'beneficiary' is the buyer of goods or services. They will wish to be safeguarded against the seller reneging on the terms of the underlying contract. At the outset, a demand guarantee would have been signed so that the beneficiary could be recompensed speedily in the event of the seller's default.

22.8.2 The principal

The 'principal' is the seller of the goods or services. The rules recognise the principal's right to expect just and equitable treatment in respect of receiving detailed written advice of any claim regarding any alleged contravention of the contract terms. It is believed that this should reduce spurious demands under guarantees by beneficiaries.

22.8.3 The guarantor

The 'guarantor' is the person or entity who will recompense the beneficiary under a demand guarantee. (This would normally be the principal's bank, which would take a counter-guarantee from the principal, so that it could be reimbursed in the event of it meeting a claim under the guarantee.)

The URDG stipulates that, in order for the rules to be able to apply, payment under the guarantee should not contain any onerous provisos: for example, the necessity of the guarantor judging whether the principal has, or has not, met its contractual obligations. The guarantee should be unambiguous and should merely call for the presentation of a written demand and any other specifically named documents. If such required documents upon presentation do not comply with the terms of the guarantee, the beneficiary will not be entitled to payment under the guarantee.

22.8.4 The provisions of URDG

A summary of the main provisions of URDG is as follows.

- **Article 2** confirms that guarantees are separate from the contracts on which they are based. Guarantors are therefore not legally tied by the underlying commercial agreements in any way.

- **Article 3** stipulates that the terms of guarantees should be transparent and accurate. They should also only contain relevant content. All guarantees should identify:

  - the principal;
  - the beneficiary;
  - the guarantor;
  - the relevant deal that necessitated the issuance of the guarantee;
  - the total amount payable and the currency involved;
  - the specific expiry date or expiry event of the guarantee;
  - the underlying terms for making demand for payment under the guarantee;
  - any proviso for the guaranteed amount to be reduced.

- **Article 4** prevents the beneficiary from assigning their right to make a demand under the guarantee to another person or entity. This article continues, however, by emphasising that a beneficiary can still assign the proceeds that may be due to them under the guarantee.

- **Article 5** states that guarantees and counter- guarantees are irrevocable.

- **Article 6** lays down that a guarantee is effective from its date of issue, unless it specifies otherwise.

- **Article 7** mentions that, if a guarantor is unable to issue a guarantee because law or statute prevents it from complying with the guarantee's terms, the guarantor should advise the party who gave it its instructions as quickly as possible, preferably by telecommunication.

  This article also confirms that a guarantor is under no obligation to issue a guarantee unless it wishes to do so.

- **Article 8** provides specific authority for the wording of a guarantee to allow the amount due to be reduced on (a) particular date(s) in the future upon presentation of specific documentation.

  This article is important to the principal because, if it is supplying goods or services during the period of the commercial contract, its liability on that contract will diminish in financial terms. Thus, the obligation under the guarantee could reduce pro rata in most cases When this occurs, it releases possible similar facilities with the principal's bank, should the bank be the guarantor, for the principal's use.

- **Article 9** specifies that, if documents are presented under the guarantee, including the demand for payment, the guarantor can refuse to pay when they appear to contain inconsistencies in relation to the terms of the guarantee.

- **Article 10** expressly gives the guarantor 'reasonable time' in which to examine a demand made under a guarantee before deciding whether to pay or not. The article is not specific on what constitutes 'reasonable time'.

  The article concludes by stating that, in the event of non- payment, the guarantor will immediately advise the beneficiary, preferably by teletransmission. Any documents presented to the guarantor should be kept at the disposal of the beneficiary.

- **Article 11** states that a guarantor or the principal's authorised agents (the latter are identified as 'instructing parties' in URDG) have no liability for any documents presented to them (or their contents) nor for the acts of others.

- **Article 12** exempts a guarantor or the principal's authorised agents from liability due to delay, loss or mutilation of letters, messages, demands or documents. Exemption also applies for the delay, mutilation or other mistakes linked to the transmission of any telecommunication. They also attract no liability for mistakes in translation or explanation of technical terms. In addition, they have the right to transmit any part of guarantee texts without translating them.

- **Article 14** absolves a guarantor or instructing party from any liability in the use of a third party's services in order to carry out the principal's instructions.

- It also provides for compensation from the principal to a guarantor or instructing party in respect of any liabilities or responsibilities incurred due to foreign laws or practices.

- **Article 15** stipulates that a guarantor or instructing party must act in good faith and with reasonable care if it is to benefit from the protections contained in articles 11, 12 and 14.

- **Article 16** limits the liability of a guarantor to the extent of the terms contained in the original guarantee or later amendments.

Articles 17–21 cover the rules relating to a demand being made under a guarantee.

- **Article 17** mentions that, notwithstanding Article 10, a guarantor should advise its principal (or, if applicable, the principal's instructing party) of a demand having been made without delay. This article can be coupled with **Article 21**, which states that the beneficiary's demand and any relevant documents must be transmitted without delay to the principal or its instructing party, where applicable.

- **Article 18** provides that, if a guarantor makes a payment under the guarantee, the amount due under it is reduced pro rata. If the full amount due under the guarantee has been paid, that guarantee is terminated.

- **Article 19** confirms that a demand must be made on, or before, the guarantee's expiry date (or before the expiry event – see **Article 22**) in agreement with the terms of the guarantee. Thus, any specific documentation required must be presented without discrepancies; otherwise the guarantor can refuse to meet the demand for payment.

- **Article 20** is very important in that it specifies the form in which a demand for payment must be made: such a demand must be in writing and be supported by a written statement of the details of the terms of the underlying contract that the principal has contravened or, similarly, in the case of a tender guarantee, the tender terms that the principal has breached.

  This article also covers the position regarding counter- guarantees, whereby, if a guarantor wishes to make demand under a counter- guarantee, it must be supported by a written statement that the guarantor has received a demand under the guarantee in accordance with the latter's terms and this article.

Articles 22–26 relate to the expiry provisions relating to guarantees.

- **Article 22** concerns when a guarantee is terminated. This can occur either upon a particular date (known as the 'expiry date') or when documents are presented to the guarantor for the purpose of terminating the guarantee (known as the 'expiry event'). If both an expiry date and expiry event are detailed in the guarantee, whichever happens first will determine when a guarantee expires.

- **Article 23** states that, notwithstanding any expiry instructions, a guarantee will be terminated when the guarantee is presented to a guarantor or when the beneficiary provides a written statement releasing a guarantor from liability.

- **Article 24** confirms that merely keeping possession of a guarantee after its cancellation does not give the beneficiary any rights under the guarantee.

- **Article 25** imposes upon the guarantor the obligation to advise the principal without delay of the termination of a guarantee or, if applicable, the relevant instructing party who, in turn, must advise the principal.

- **Article 26** concerns the granting of an extension to the validity term of a guarantee in place of making demand for payment under its terms. If such an extension is requested by the beneficiary, a guarantor must advise the party from which it receives its instructions without delay. The guarantor can then delay payment under the guarantee for a reasonable time while negotiations regarding the extension are taking place between the principal and beneficiary. Unless an agreement is reached over such an extension within this period, the guarantor must pay under the guarantee provided that the demand has no discrepancies. The beneficiary does not have to take any further steps.

  It must be remembered that, even if the principal agrees to an extension, it will not automatically occur unless the guarantor and any instructing party also condone such an extension.

- **Articles 27 and 28** relate to the law by which a guarantee or counter- guarantee will be governed and the courts that will deal with any dispute.

  This will normally be the country's law and the courts of the country in which the guarantor or the instructing party reside.

Full details of the relevant publication covering URDG can be obtained directly from the International Chamber of Commerce (ICC), Paris, France. It should be noted that, at the time of writing, the ICC had commenced a revision of the URDG458.

22.9   Standby letters of credit

22.9.1   Standby letters of credit as an alternative to bonds

An alternative to the bond is a 'standby letter of credit', issued in favour of the beneficiary, promising to pay a given amount against specified documents, usually a formal default claim.

There are various types of standby letters of credit, the main ones being linked to the various types of obligation covered by bonds. The main standby credits are therefore as follows:

- bid or tender bond standby credits;

- a counter standby (to support the issue of a performance standby if a commercial contract is awarded that had a bid or tender standby included);

- a performance standby;
- an advanced payment standby.

As a generalisation, the applicant of such a credit would be the equivalent of the person who applied for a bond or guarantee and the beneficiary would be the same as the beneficiary of a bond or guarantee. Thus, in the equivalent of a bid, counter and performance bond situation, the applicant would be the exporter or seller and the beneficiary would be the importer or buyer.

The use of standby credits is not, however, necessarily restricted to the above situations and there are many instances in which a documentary credit promising to pay a given amount against specified documents such as a formal default claim would be appropriate.

22.9.2 Standby letters of credit in support of debt obligations

A standby letter of credit can be used as support for trade debts. The debtor is the applicant and the creditor is the beneficiary of the credit.

For example, a business can be asked to provide a standby letter of credit to support its future payments on obligations such as leases, loans or responsibilities to freight forwarders and insurers. A standby letter of credit assures a potential creditor of the buyer's creditworthiness by guaranteeing that the debtor's bank will pay the creditor in the event of non- performance by the buyer.

The credit will specify what documents are required and the applicant will normally be required to deposit security for this contingent liability. The issuing bank will charge a fee and the advising bank may also require payment for its services.

The beneficiary can be located in the same country as the potential debtor, or the two parties can be located in different countries.

A simple application form for a trade debt standby letter of credit might be worded as in the following example.

Example 22.1   Specimen application for a standby letter or credit

---

APPLICATION FOR A STANDBY LETTER OF CREDIT AGREEMENT

To : Megabank plc : Office : Date

We request that you issue an irrevocable standby letter of credit on the following terms and conditions:

Full name and address of Applicant (Megabank's customer)

Full name and address of Beneficiary

Advising Bank (if left blank Megabank will choose its own advising bank)

Maximum Amount: Expiry Date: Details of who pays what charges

Documents required: (This could be a formal letter of demand from the beneficiary stating the amount of the debt, that the debt was properly incurred, and that the Applicant was in default)

Signature of Applicant:

Note: This standby letter of credit will be issued subject to International Standby Practices 1998 (ISP98).

22.9.3   International Standby Practices 1998 (ISP98)

The choice of which rules govern a standby letter of credit are determined by the applicant and/or the beneficiary. Standby letters of credit can be issued subject to the ICC Uniform Customs and Practice for Documentary Credits UCP 600; 2007 Revision (see Topic 18) or subject to ICC International Standby Practices (ISP98). The ISP98 rules are set out in Publication No 590.

ISP98 has the same purpose as UCP in that it aims to simplify and standardise the drafting and handling of standby letters of credit. Provided that the credit is stated to be 'subject to International Standby Practices Publication No 590' or 'subject to ISP98', these provisions will apply.

- Under **Rule 1.02**, it can be seen that these rules will supplement national laws, and so will apply unless there is anything in the law of the country concerned that contradicts them.

- Under **Rule 1.06**, it can be seen that the normal position on documentary credits applies, so that what determines whether payment can be enforced is whether the documents on the face of it conform to the terms of the credit.

- **Rule 9.01** states that all standby letters of credit must have an expiry date.

- Perhaps the key rule is **Rule 3**, which defines how documents are to be presented and authenticated. Specific provisions covering electronic generation and presentation are included here.

The rules have been carefully drafted to make them as 'watertight' as possible, because standby letters of credit can often apply in a dispute situation. The rules are written to provide guidance to judges and lawyers.

From a bank's point of view, a standby letter of credit is better than a bond, because it will be subject either to UCP 600 or to ISP98, instead of being subject to complex legalities. In addition, a standby letter of credit will always have a definite expiry date which can overcome one of the main problems for issuers of bonds. It is anticipated that the bulk of standby letters of credit in future will be issued subject to ISP98, because these rules are more appropriate than the traditional UCP for a bond type situation. These rules make standby letters of credit even more attractive as an alternative to bonds.

22.10   Countertrade

22.10.1   What is 'countertrade'?

There is no single accepted definition of 'countertrade' and the term is used by different specialists to describe different operations. Nevertheless, most participants would find the following definition acceptable:

Countertrade is an international trading transaction where export sales to a particular market are made conditional upon undertakings to accept imports from that market.

It is thus a form of bilateral trade that has continued to grow despite its condemnation by some international agencies because of its limiting effect on free trade and therefore on multilateral trade.

There are two basic reasons for the development of countertrade:

- some countries do not have the cash or credit facilities to pay for imports, so countertrade has become their only means of arranging deals;

- some developing countries wish to build up their manufacturing exports. Brazil, for example, one of the leading exponents of countertrade outside Europe, countertrades manufactured goods rather than raw materials, such as coffee or iron ore. The objective is not to help to dispose of the basic commodities, which can be sold on the world market (albeit for a low price), but rather to build up exports of manufactures.

In addition, it is common for restrictions to be placed on the markets in which the manufactured goods can be sold so as to achieve *additionality* of exports, rather than having the manufactures disposed of in markets in which cash buyers could be found independently of any countertrade deal.

22.10.2   Financial countertrade and industrial countertrade

There is, as ever, no firmly agreed definition of what constitutes 'financial countertrade' and what constitutes 'industrial countertrade'. Some might argue that one form of financial countertrade is a form of currency exchange whereby soft currencies with restrictions on conversion can still be converted into hard currencies.

Example 22.2

A UK exporter might sell some capital goods to a less developed country (LDC) in exchange for payment in the currency of the LDC. There may be LDC government restrictions, sometimes called 'exchange controls', which prevent the UK exporter from converting the LDC currency into sterling. The problem and a possible solution involving financial countertrade are set out below.

The problem

UK exporter	Goods sold	Problem for exporter
Sells capital goods to a less developed country (LDC)	Payment in the currency of the LDC	LDC government restrictions (exchange controls) that prevent the UK exporter from converting the LDC currency into sterling.

Possible solution

Subsequent action by UK exporter	How the sugar is disposed of
Uses LDC currency to buy sugar from an LDC producer (not that to which the goods were sold)	Sold to UK buyer for sterling

The capital goods exporter may well have no interest in sugar, but it uses the sugar as a legal means of circumventing the exchange controls of the LDC.

Another example of financial countertrade might be if a multinational bank that is owed money by an LDC firm were to agree to waive the debt in exchange for an equity stake in the project for which the money was originally lent. This procedure is sometimes called a 'debt–equity swap'.

22.10.2.1   Forms of industrial countertrade

- 'Counterpurchase' (also known as 'link purchase') is the most common form of countertrade, especially in Eastern European countries and in developing countries, such as Indonesia.

   The exporter agrees, as a condition of obtaining the order, to arrange for purchase of goods or services from the importer's country.

   The sequence of events is as follows.

   1.   The exporter obtains an order subject to arranging for the disposal of goods or services from the importing country.

   2.   Two parallel, but separate contracts are set up: one for the sale of goods to the importing country and one for the counterpurchase of goods from the importing country. The two contracts are separate, so there is no right of set- off between any money owed to the exporter under the order and any money owed for the sale of goods.

   The organisation directly responsible for the counterpurchase will not necessarily be the exporter itself, but could be some other trading house or trader. There is normally recourse to the original exporter if the counterpurchase obligations are not fulfilled.

- **Barter** involves a single contract for the simultaneous exchange of goods between two parties. An example would be UK exports of machinery to Zambia, paid for by a simultaneous shipment of wood or bitumen. Straightforward barter is popular with some African and Latin American countries, especially those with a shortage of hard currency, but pure barter deals are rare.

- **Compensation or buyback deals** are a form of barter that is favoured by some Eastern European countries under which suppliers of capital goods agree to be paid by the future output of the factory they are supplying. For example, a chemical company could sell a chemical processing plant and take part of the plant's future output of chemicals as payment.

- A typical example of **barter by means of trust accounts** would be the sale of trucks by a UK manufacturer to an African country, such as Kenya, with payment to come from the sale proceeds of local produce, eg coffee.

The sequence of events is as follows.

1. The coffee is shipped to the UK and the payment is retained in a UK bank in a 'trust account', also called an 'escrow account'.

2. The Kenyans arrange a documentary credit in favour of the UK truck manufacturer. The credit will be confirmed by the UK bank that maintains the escrow account, once there are sufficient funds from the sale of the coffee to cover the credit.

3. The credit is then advised to the UK manufacturer, which ships its goods and then presents the required documents to obtain payment.

- **Offset** is widely used in high- technology products. Export orders are given for items, such as aircraft, on condition that the exporter incorporates components or sub- assemblies manufactured in the importing country. There is often an agreement for technology transfer, possibly in the form of training given by the seller to workers in the buyer's country who are involved on the components or sub- assembly processes.

- **Switch trading** is best described by way of example: Colombia might sell coffee to Hungary and, instead of being paid, build up a credit balance. If Colombia were then to wish to import coal from Poland, arrangements could be made to use the credit balance from the coffee sales to pay for the coal. Hungary would thus settle with Poland.

A market is becoming established for dealing with such credit balances, presumably along the lines of the secondary market that is now developing in loans to developing countries.

- Companies with a significant level of continuing business in certain markets may be required to arrange for the counterpurchase of goods from that market. For example, a multinational company with a subsidiary in a developing country may be required to counterpurchase goods from that country to match the value of the subsidiary's import of raw materials. It may not be practical to balance this kind of trade item by item, so the company may maintain an **evidence account** of all transactions. Usually, this account must be kept in balance on a year- by- year basis.

Countertrade is becoming more innovative as it adapts to the changing international marketplace. In addition to the above, new forms of financial countertrade are emerging, such as debt–equity swaps, which have been pioneered by certain Latin

American countries. Also, many countries are adopting official countertrade policies, eg Thailand. This all seems a far cry from the predictions of a steep decline in countertrade operations following the break- up of the Soviet Union – particularly, in reality, because this event served to only increase countertrade deals and their international popularity.

22.10.3   The pitfalls of countertrade for the exporter

The main problems with countertrade that can arise for the exporter are:

- contractual commitments to purchase large quantities of unmarketable goods without any means of selling them;

- penalty payments, because the party to whom the counterpurchase has been committed has not honoured its obligations;

- loss of profits on the sale of the principal goods, because the costs of arranging the counterpurchase have not been considered;

- the discount between the face value of the goods taken in countertrade and the actual sale proceeds available.

   When the counterpurchase goods are raw materials or commodities such as soya beans, a discount of 2% may be sufficient to cover the exporter, but in the case of manufactured goods, a discount of 40–50% can sometimes arise.

   As a general rule, the nearer the counterpurchase goods are to commodities, the better;

- the costs involved in marketing counterpurchased goods is continually rising. Exporters are therefore seeking alternative methods of meeting their countertrade obligations, eg training the importer's employees.

22.10.4   Sources of help for the countertrade exporter

22.10.4.1   The bank

Banks have many advantages that make them highly suitable for countertrade operations:

- a massive computer database that is already used to match potential buyers and sellers;

- a huge customer base;

- expertise gained already from experience in arranging ECGD buyer credit facilities;

- the ability to innovate and to arrange an imaginative deal in the circumstances that apply. In particular, banks can advise the exporter on the premium to be included in the export price to offset the discount on counterpurchase goods;

- the ability to provide guarantees or bonds to cover the exporter's liability under a counterpurchase agreement.

Some banks have representative offices in cities such as Moscow, Hong Kong or Singapore.

22.10.4.2 The ECGD

The ECGD may provide insurance and financial guarantees for countertrade deals, but only in limited circumstances.

The most important proviso is that the payment obligation of the buyer (or borrower, in the case of buyer credit guarantees) must be totally independent of the provisions of the counterpurchase agreement. In other words, for ECGD support to be available, the covered transaction must have all of the characteristics and effect of a transaction to which no countertrade arrangements are related.

The ECGD is not prepared to involve itself in deals in which payment for the export sale depends on fulfilment of the counterpurchase obligation, largely because the risks are unquantifiable. In addition, the ECGD does not wish to be seen to contravene EU or World Trade Organization (WTO) agreements.

The ECGD will never become involved in insuring successful disposal of counterpurchase goods, although such insurance is available from specialist brokers or from countertrade specialists known as trading houses.

22.5   Specimen documents

Figure 2.2   Specimen tender guarantee

OUR GUARANTEE [GUARANTEE NUMBER]

We do understand that [APPLICANT'S NAME] ('the Applicant') [APPLICANT'S ADDRESS] are tendering for the [DESCRIPTION OF GOODS] under your invitation to Tender [TENDER/CONTRACT NUMBER ETC.] and that a Bank Guarantee is required for [AGREED PERCENTAGE OF CONTRACT] % of the amount of their tender.

We, BANK PLC, London HEREBY GUARANTEE the payment to you on demand of up to [AMOUNT IN FIGURES] (say, [AMOUNT IN WORDS]) in the event of your awarding the relative contract to the Applicant and of its failing to sign the Contract in the terms of its tender, or in the event of the Applicant withdrawing its tender before expiry of this guarantee without your consent.

This guarantee shall come into force on [COMMENCEMENT DATE] being the closing date for tenders, and will expire at close of banking hours at this office on [EXPIRY DATE] ('EXPIRY').

Our liability is limited to the sum of [AMOUNT IN FIGURES] and your claim hereunder must be received in writing at this office before Expiry accompanied by your signed statement that the Applicant has been awarded the relative contract and has failed to sign the contract awarded in the terms of its tender or has withdrawn its tender before Expiry without your consent, and such claim and statement shall be accepted as conclusive evidence that the amount claimed is due to you under this guarantee.

Claims and statements as aforesaid must bear the confirmation of your Bankers that the signatories thereon are authorised so to sign.

Upon Expiry this guarantee shall become null and void, whether returned to us for cancellation or not and any claim or statement received after Expiry shall be ineffective.

This guarantee is personal to yourselves and is not transferable or assignable.

This guarantee shall be governed by and construed in accordance with the Laws of England.

Figure 22.3   Specimen performance bond

OUR GUARANTEE [GUARANTEE NUMBER]

We understand that you have entered into a Contract [TENDER/CONTRACT NUMBER ETC.] (the Contract) with [APPLICANT'S NAME] [APPLICANT'S ADDRESS](the Applicant) for the [DESCRIPTION OF GOODS] and that under such Contract the Applicant must provide a Bank Performance Guarantee for an amount of [AMOUNT IN FIGURES] being [AGREED PERCENTAGE OF CONTRACT]% of the value of the contract.

We, BANK PLC, London, HEREBY GUARANTEE payment to you on demand of up to [AMOUNT IN FIGURES] (say, [AMOUNT IN WORDS]) in the event of the Applicant failing to fulfil the said Contract, provided that your claim hereunder is received in writing at this office accompanied by your signed statement that the Applicant has failed to fulfil the Contract. Such claim and statement shall be accepted as conclusive evidence that the amount claimed is due to you under this guarantee.

Claims and statements as aforesaid must bear the confirmation of your Bankers that the signatories thereon are authorised so to sign.

This guarantee shall expire at close of banking hours at this office on [EXPIRY DATE] ('EXPIRY') and any claim and statement hereunder must be received at this office before Expiry and after Expiry this guarantee shall become null and void whether returned to us for cancellation or not and any claim or statement received after Expiry shall be ineffective.

This guarantee is personal to yourselves and is not transferable or assignable.

This guarantee shall be governed by and construed in accordance with the Laws of England.

Figure 22.4   Specimen advance payment guarantee

OUR GUARANTEE [GUARANTEE NUMBER]

We understand that you have entered into a Contract [TENDER/CONTRACT NUMBER ETC.] with [APPLICANT'S NAME] (the Applicant) [APPLICANT'S ADDRESS] for the [DESCRIPTION OF GOODS] and that under the Contract the sum of [AMOUNT IN FIGURES] being [AGREED PERCENTAGE OF CONTRACT]% of the total contract value is payable in advance against a Bank Guarantee.

In consideration of your making an Advance Payment of [AMOUNT IN FIGURES] (the Advance Payment) to the Applicant we, BANK PLC, London, HEREBY GUARANTEE to refund to you on demand up to [AMOUNT IN FIGURES] (say, [AMOUNT IN WORDS]) in the event of the Applicant failing to fulfil the Contract.

Our maximum liability hereunder shall automatically reduce by [REDUCTION PERCENTAGE] of the value of [SERVICE/GOODS TO EFFECT REDUCTION] as evidenced by presentation to us by [PRESENTER FOR REDUCTION] of [DOCUMENTS FOR REDUCTION] showing the [EVIDENCE PRESENTED BY DOCUMENTS] which we shall be entitled to accept as conclusive evidence that the [CONCLUSIVE EVIDENCE OF] has been effected.

This guarantee shall remain valid until reduced to nil in accordance with the foregoing procedure or until close of banking hours at this office on [EXPIRY DATE] ('EXPIRY') whichever shall first occur. Any claim hereunder must be received in writing at this office before Expiry accompanied by your signed statement that the Applicant has failed to fulfil the Contract, and such claim and statement shall be accepted as conclusive evidence that the amount claimed is due to you under this guarantee.

Claims and statements as aforesaid must bear the confirmation of your Bankers that the signatories thereon are authorised so to sign.

This guarantee shall become operative upon issue of our amendment making it effective, which will be issued upon receipt by us of written confirmation from the Applicant that the latter has received the Advance Payment.

Upon Expiry, this guarantee shall become null and void, whether returned to us for cancellation or not and any claim or statement received after Expiry shall be ineffective.

This guarantee is personal to yourselves and is not transferable or assignable.

This guarantee shall be governed by and construed in accordance with the Laws of England.

* ALTERNATIVE

*This guarantee shall become operative automatically on receipt of the Advance Payment of [AMOUNT IN FIGURES] on the account of [APPLICANT'S NAME] at our [BRANCH] Branch.

Figure 22.5   Specimen progress payment guarantee

OUR GUARANTEE [GUARANTEE NUMBER]

We understand that you have entered into a Contract (the Contract) [TENDER/CONTRACT NUMBER ETC.] with [APPLICANT'S NAME] (the Applicant) [APPLICANT'S ADDRESS] for the [DESCRIPTION OF GOODS] and that under the Contract a Progress Payment of [AMOUNT IN FIGURES] being [AGREED PERCENTAGE OF CONTRACT]% of the total contract value is payable to the Applicant against a Bank Guarantee.

In consideration of your making a Progress Payment of [AMOUNT IN FIGURES] (the Progress Payment) to the Applicant we, BANK PLC, London, HEREBY GUARANTEE to refund to you to demand up to [AMOUNT IN FIGURES] (say, [AMOUNT IN WORDS]) in the event of the Applicant failing to fulfil the Contract.

Our maximum liability hereunder shall automatically reduce by [REDUCTION PERCENTAGE]% of the value of [SERVICE/GOODS TO EFFECT REDUCTION] as evidenced by presentation to us by [PRESENTER FOR REDUCTION] of DOCUMENTS FOR REDUCTION] showing the [EVIDENCE PRESENTED BY DOCUMENTS] which we shall be entitled to accept as conclusive evidence that the [CONCLUSIVE EVIDENCE OF] has been effected.

This guarantee shall remain valid until reduced to nil in accordance with the foregoing procedure or until the close of banking hours at this office on [EXPIRY DATE] ('EXPIRY'), whichever shall first occur. Any claim hereunder must be received in writing at this office before Expiry accompanied by your signed statement that the Applicant has failed to fulfil the Contract, and such claim and statement shall be accepted as conclusive evidence that the amount claimed is due to you under this guarantee.

Claims and statements as aforesaid must bear the confirmation of your Bankers that the signatories thereon are authorised so to sign.

This guarantee shall become operative upon issue of our amendment making it effective, which will be issued upon receipt by us of written confirmation from the Applicant that the latter has received the Progress Payment.

Upon Expiry this guarantee shall become null and void, whether returned to us for cancellation or not and any claim or statement received after Expiry shall be ineffective.

This guarantee is personal to yourselves and is not transferable or assignable.

This guarantee shall be governed by and construed in accordance with the Laws of England.

* ALTERNATIVE

*This guarantee shall become operative automatically on receipt of the Progress Payment of [AMOUNT IN FIGURES] on the account of [APPLICANT'S NAME] at our [BRANCH] Branch.

Figure 22.6   Specimen retention money bond

OUR GUARANTEE [GUARANTEE NUMBER]

We understand that under the terms of your Contract [TENDER/CONTRACT NUMBER ETC.] with [APPLICANT'S NAME] (the Applicant) [APPLICANT'S ADDRESS] for the [DESCRIPTION OF GOODS] you are retaining the sum of [AMOUNT IN FIGURES] being [AGREED PERCENTAGE OF CONTRACT]% of the Contract value by way of retention money (the Retention Money) and that you are prepared to release the said retention money against a Bank Guarantee.

In consideration of your releasing the sum of [AMOUNT IN FIGURES] to the Applicant we, BANK PLC, London HEREBY GUARANTEE repayment to you on demand of up to [AMOUNT IN FIGURES] (say, [AMOUNT IN WORDS]) in the event of the Applicant failing to fulfil the Contract.

This guarantee shall remain valid until close of banking hours at this office on [EXPIRY DATE] ('EXPIRY'). Any claim hereunder must be received in writing at this office before Expiry accompanied by your signed statement that the Applicant has failed to fulfil the Contract, and such claim and statement shall be accepted as conclusive evidence that the amount claimed is due to you under this guarantee.

Claims and statements as aforesaid must bear the confirmation of your Bankers that the signatories thereon are authorised so as to sign.

*This guarantee shall become operative upon issue of our amendment making it effective, which will be issued upon receipt by us of written confirmation from the Applicant that the latter has received the Retention Money.

Upon Expiry, this guarantee shall become null and void, whether returned to us for cancellation or not any claim or statement received after Expiry shall be ineffective.

This guarantee is personal to yourselves and is not transferable or assignable.

This guarantee shall be governed by and construed in accordance with the Laws of England.

* ALTERNATIVE

*This guarantee shall become operative automatically on receipt of the Retention Monies of [AMOUNT IN FIGURES] on the account of [APPLICANT'S NAME] at our [BRANCH] Branch.

Figure 22.7   Specimen overdraft guarantee

OUR GUARANTEE [GUARANTEE NUMBER]

In consideration of your granting advances by way of [TYPE OF BORROWING] on the account of [BORROWER] we hereby guarantee on demand being made to us in writing the due repayment of such advances in the event of [BORROWER] failing to repay such advances when required to do so by yourselves provided that the amount for which we shall be liable under his guarantee shall not exceed the sum of [AMOUNT IN FIGURES] (say, [AMOUNT IN WORDS]) *inclusive of interest and Bank charges.

Unless previously renewed by us, this guarantee is to be determined on [EXPIRY DATE] ('EXPIRY') subject to your right to cancel the facility prior to that date if you should think fit so to do, and to our right to determine our liability hereunder by giving notice in writing and upon receipt of such notice by you no further advances are to be made with recourse to us.

Claims under this guarantee must incorporate your declaration that the amount claimed represents outstanding advances by way of [TYPE OF BORROWING] on the account of [BORROWER] as aforesaid, *inclusive of interest and Bank charges, which have not been repaid by [BORROWER] as requested by you, and must be received by us at this office in writing or by authenticated SWIFT not later than 30 days after the above-mentioned expiry date, or not more than 40 days after the date of our prior notice of determination of liability, after which time this guarantee shall become null and void, whether returned to us for cancellation or not, and our liability hereunder shall terminate.

This guarantee is personal to yourselves and is not transferable or assignable.

This guarantee shall be governed by and construed in accordance with the Laws of England.

* ALTERNATIVE

* and in addition interest and Bank charges for a period not exceeding six months.

Figure 22.8   Specimen warranty bond

OUR GUARANTEE [GUARANTEE NUMBER]

We understand that you have entered into a Contract (the Contract) [TENDER/CONTRACT NUMBER ETC.] with [APPLICANT'S NAME] (the Applicant) [APPLICANT'S ADDRESS] for the [DESCRIPTION OF GOODS] and that under the Contract the Applicant must provide a Bank Warranty Bond for an amount of [AMOUNT IN FIGURES] being [AGREED PERCENTAGE OF CONTRACT]% of the value of the Contract.

We, BANK PLC, London, HEREBY GUARANTEE payment to you on demand of up to [AMOUNT IN FIGURES] (say, [AMOUNT IN WORDS]) in the event of the Applicant failing to fulfil the terms of the Warranty obligations under the Contract. Any claim hereunder must be received in writing at this office before Expiry accompanied by your signed statement that the Applicant has failed to fulfil the Warranty obligations under the Contract and such statement and claim shall be conclusive evidence that the amount claimed is due to you under the warranty.

Claims and statements as aforesaid must bear the confirmation of your Bankers that the signatories thereon are authorised so to sign.

This guarantee shall remain valid until close of banking hours at this office on [EXPIRY DATE] ('EXPIRY'). After Expiry this guarantee shall become null and void whether returned to us for cancellation or not and any claim or statement received after Expiry shall be ineffective.

This guarantee is personal to yourselves and is not transferable or assignable.

This guarantee shall be governed by and construed in accordance with the Laws of England.

Part V

Introduction

This final part of the book is concerned with two major aspects of the syllabus:

- bank services for importers, including all relevant aspects of documentary collections and documentary credits;
- transferable and back- to- back credits.

Topic 23

Inward documentary collections

On completion of this topic, the student should be able to:

- explain the difference between a clean and a documentary collection;
- understand and explain the responsibilities of all parties to a collection as stated in the ICC Uniform Rules for Collections (URC);
- explain the process of presenting a bill of exchange for payment or acceptance;
- explain what action must be taken when a bill of exchange is dishonoured;
- explain the procedure for dealing with goods consigned to the collecting bank;
- explain how offers of partial payment are handled under the URC and UK banking practice;
- appreciate the significance of 'avalisation' of inward bills for collection;
- explain how banks can help importers when bills of lading have gone missing;
- explain how the produce loan procedure can be used to provide finance to importers who buy on documents against payment terms.

23.1 An introduction to importing

Every vessel or aircraft arriving in the UK from a foreign departure point must report its arrival to the UK customs authorities, and all goods must be entered into customs on the prescribed form. There may be various levies, such as VAT and excise duties, to pay. Finally, it may be necessary to obtain an import licence for certain categories of goods, such as arms, drugs and livestock, but most goods imported into the UK fall under the category of 'open general licence', which means that no licensing formalities are required.

Importers must conform to the customs procedures, otherwise they cannot obtain possession of the goods. A detailed knowledge of customs regulations is, however, not required by this syllabus and questions on these matters do not appear on the exam papers.

Once customs formalities have been completed, the importer will present an original bill of lading (made out to order and blank indorsed) to the carrier, who will authorise the docks superintendent to release the goods. If waybills apply, the importer will present the waybill to the carrier with evidence of its identity, who will authorise the docks superintendent to release the goods, provided that the importer is named as consignee.

Similar procedures apply when the goods come by air, but, in this case, the transport document will be an air waybill.

23.2   General rules for the handling of inward collections

The handling of inward collections received by UK banks from their overseas correspondent banks is considered to be a very important service that, if not taken seriously, can result in monetary loss and can also damage a banking relationship.

A collection can be:

- 'clean' – ie a bill of exchange or cheque unsupported by documents;
- 'documentary' – ie documents supported (or unsupported) by a bill of exchange.

All documents sent for collection must be accompanied by a collection instruction giving complete and precise instructions. Banks are permitted to act only upon the instructions given in such collection instructions and in accordance with the underlying ICC – Uniform Rules for Collections, Publication No 522 (URC 522).

Any deviation from these instructions at the request of the drawee will be at the responsibility of the collecting bank.

The instructions of the remitting bank override the banking relationship, if any, between drawee and collecting bank.

Banks are to act in good faith, are to exercise reasonable care, must verify that the documents received appear to be as listed in the collection instruction and must immediately advise the party from whom the collection instruction was received of any documents that are missing. Banks have no further obligation to examine the documents.

All UK banks will act in accordance with the URC unless UK law or the collection instruction prevents this.

In the case of documents payable at sight, the presenting bank must make presentation for payment without delay and, in the case of documents payable at a tenor other than sight, the presenting bank must, if acceptance is called for, make presentation for acceptance without delay, and if payment is called for, make presentation for payment not later than the appropriate maturity date.

In relation to a documentary collection including a bill of exchange payable at a future date, the collection instruction should state whether the commercial documents are to be released to the drawee against acceptance (D/A) or against payment (D/P). In the absence of such statement, the commercial documents will only be released against payment.

23.3 The procedure for obtaining acceptance of a bill of exchange

Acceptance of a bill of exchange is an unconditional undertaking to pay the bill on maturity. The drawee should not, therefore, when accepting the bill, impose any conditions on payment. Acceptances citing, for example, a lesser amount and payable at a different date are referred to as 'qualified acceptances' and would not be acceptable to the remitting bank.

The bill may be accepted as payable at a place other than the acceptor's address, normally at its bank, ie 'Accepted payable at HSBC Bank plc'. This practice should be encouraged because the procedure for obtaining payment at maturity is greatly simplified: the bill needs only to be presented at the bank counters for payment.

The collecting bank is responsible for seeing that the form of the acceptance of a bill of exchange appears to be complete and correct, but is not responsible for the genuineness of any signature or for the authority of any signatory to sign the acceptance.

When the drawee is a customer, however, good banking practice dictates that the signature should be checked against the mandate.

Strict control must be maintained over an accepted bill, which must not be presented for payment at maturity through the post.

23.4 Action to be taken in the event of dishonour

A bill of exchange is dishonoured when a sight draft is unpaid on presentation or when a tenor draft is unaccepted on presentation or unpaid at maturity.

When an inward collection is dishonoured, the collecting bank must examine the collection order to see whether the bill is to be 'protested'. Protesting a bill provides legal evidence of dishonour that is acceptable to a court of law.

If protest is to be carried out, a Notary Public will personally call upon the drawee or acceptor and will demand payment or acceptance. If the payment or acceptance is not forthcoming, the Notary Public will draw up a 'deed of Protest' which will give the reasons stated for dishonour. A bill should be protested within one working day of dishonour, otherwise, under the Bills of Exchange Act 1882, s 51, all signatories are freed from liability on that bill.

23.4.1 Noting

Protesting is expensive and must be done within one working day of dishonour. To save money, it is possible to ask the notary public to 'note' the dishonour. At maturity of an accepted bill, the notary will present the bill either at the drawee's address or at the bank if payable there. If a bill is noted, the right to protest at a later date remains without any time limit.

23.4.2 Householder's protest

When a notary public is not available, a member of the bank staff can make a formal protest, known as a 'householder's protest'. Two ratepayers resident in the area of the drawee must witness the formal document. This is a valid form of protest.

Figure 23.1 Specimen form of householder's protest

SPECIMEN FORM OF HOUSEHOLDER'S PROTEST

Date:......................................

Know all persons that

I ....

householder of...

in the County of ....

in the United Kingdom, at the request of xxxxxx Bank plc, there being no Notary

Public available, did on the...day of ....20....

at ....

demand ....*Payment/Acceptance of the Bill of Exchange hereunder written

from..

to which demand answer was made ....

Wherefore I now in the presence of ....

and ....do protest the said Bill of Exchange.

*Delete as appropriate

Signature ....

Name..⎫

....⎪

Address ....⎪

....⎪

....⎬ Two Witnesses

....⎪

Name..⎪

....⎪

Address ....⎪

....⎪

....⎭

Copy of the Bill of Exchange

23.4.3 UK practice

Usual UK practice with inward documentary collections that are dishonoured is to note them if the collection order does not give any instructions regarding protest. This will retain the liability of all parties. This practice overrules article 24 of URC 522, which states that in the absence of specific instructions, there is no need to note or protest a dishonoured bill of exchange.

It is important that the remitting bank is kept fully informed of the situation in accordance with its instructions. If applicable, the case of need (see Topic 17) should also be advised, depending on their powers (article 25).

23.5   The protection of goods

Banks have no obligation to take any action in respect of the goods to which a documentary collection relates. Nevertheless, in the case that banks take action for the protection of the goods, whether instructed or not, they assume no liability or responsibility in relation to the fate and/or the condition of the goods, and/or for any acts and/or omissions on the part of any third parties entrusted with the custody and/or protection of the goods. Collecting banks must, however, immediately advise the bank from which the collection order was received of any such action taken.

Any charges and/or expenses incurred by banks in connection with any action for the protection of the goods will be for the account of the principal (exporter).

In practice, however, the collecting bank will take reasonable care when entrusting the goods to a warehouse agent.

23.6   Goods consigned to the collecting bank

Goods should not be despatched directly to the address of a bank or consigned to a bank without prior agreement on the part of that bank.

In the event of goods being despatched directly to the address of a bank or consigned to a bank for delivery to a drawee against payment or acceptance or upon other terms without prior agreement on the part of that bank, the bank has no obligation to take delivery of the goods, which remain at the risk and responsibility of the party despatching the goods (article 10).

In practice, great care is required when goods are consigned to the bank, because large losses have resulted from incorrect procedures being followed.

Quite often, goods consigned to the bank will arrive by air before the supporting documents have been received. At this stage, the banks will have little indication of the value of the collection other than the declared value of the goods for customs purposes. It is, therefore, important that a letter of release is handed only to the drawee who is undoubted and is prepared to sign an irrevocable undertaking to honour the documents upon presentation regardless of the terms of those documents.

Decisions of this nature will need to be made by a member of management.

23.7 The procedure for dealing with offers of partial payment

In relation to clean collections, partial payments may be accepted if, and to the extent to which and on the conditions on which partial payments are, authorised by the law in force in the place of payment. The documents will be released to the drawee only when full payment thereof has been received.

In relation to documentary collections, partial payments will be accepted only if specifically authorised in the collection order. Unless otherwise instructed, however, the presenting bank will release the documents to the drawee only after full payment has been received.

If a customer offers a part-payment after accepting a bill of exchange and taking control of the goods, it is UK banking practice to accept the payment (even though the collection order may state that part payments are not allowed), to note or protest the bill for dishonour and to hold the part-payment on a suspense account, pending further instructions from the remitting bank.

Note: The bill is protested, not the balance of the bill, because it is the bill that is dishonoured and not a part of the bill.

23.8 Charges

Banks may deliver documents against payment or acceptance without collecting charges unless the collection instruction specifically states that the documents must not be released unless charges are paid. If no specific instructions are given, the bank is in order to release the documents without collecting charges, which are for account of the remitting bank.

23.9 Settlement

Settlement of an inward collection must be carried out strictly in accordance with the instructions contained in the collection instruction. Students must be familiar with the requirements laid down in URC.

Some overseas countries have specific exchange control laws that insist on all payments firstly being paid in local currency and then being subject to an application to that country's central bank for conversion and remittance abroad. Where such laws exist, they will prevail over URC, but there are no such rules in the UK.

23.10 The avalisation of bills of exchange under inward collections

Let us briefly recall the parties to an inward collection in connection with imports to the UK:

- the principal – the overseas exporter;
- the remitting bank – the exporter's bank;
- the collecting or presenting bank – the importer's bank;
- the drawee – the importer.

From the point of view of inward collections, 'avalisation' can be defined as the addition of the presenting bank's name to a bill of exchange with the intention of guaranteeing payment at maturity. It will usually take the form of the following words being placed on the reverse of the bill of exchange:

Indorsed by way of aval (for the acceptor) for and on behalf of

.... Bank plc (ie UK presenting bank)

.... Authorised Signature

The practice of avalisation is not recognised within the UK Bills of Exchange Act 1882, but when a UK bank avalises a bill of exchange, that bank, in practice, guarantees payment.

Avalisation involves a contingent liability and a bank will consider the granting of such a facility in the same way as it considers any lending facility. In other words, the bank will consider the creditworthiness of its importer customer. If the bank avalises a bill of exchange, it will require the customer to complete an authority whereby the bank is irrevocably authorised to debit the customer's account upon presentation of the bill at maturity.

A brief comparison of avalisation and documentary credit facilities appears in Topic 24.

Note: Large losses have resulted from the failure to recognise the words 'aval', 'pour aval' and 'avalisation' appearing on inward collection schedules received from banks abroad – the documents being released to the drawee merely against its acceptance and without the bank's agreement to avalise the accepted bill of exchange.

23.11   How banks can help importers when bills of lading have gone missing

Any failure by the importer to remove its goods from the dockside within a specified time will result in 'demurrage' charges. Demurrage is a storage charge made by dock authorities on importers who fail to remove their goods.

One of the most common causes of a demurrage charge is the arrival of goods before the relevant bills of lading have reached the importer. A typical situation is set out at Example 23.1, which shows how a bank indemnity can solve the problem.

Example 23.1

A typical question might be set along the following lines.

Your customer telephones to say that a machine that it is importing has arrived in this country. It is unable, however, to take delivery because the bills of lading have not arrived.

The machine is incurring demurrage charges: how can the bank help the customer to obtain the machine and what precautions are involved?

Suggested answer to Example 23.1

An answer along the following lines is required.

- The bank could join in an indemnity to the shipping company (carrier) requesting the release of the machine without the bills of lading, and promising to reimburse the carrier if it suffered any loss.

- The customer must sign a counter-indemnity authorising the bank to pay any claims and debit the customer's account in reimbursement.

- The counter-indemnity will also promise that the importer will immediately send the missing bills of lading to the bank, should they come to hand.

- The bank will also ascertain whether the customer has paid for the machine, and, if not, what terms of payment have been agreed. If payment is by documentary collection, the customer must sign an irrevocable authority to honour the terms of the collection when presented. The bank could ask for the customer to place money on a suspense account earmarked to pay the collection, if the terms are D/P. Whether the bank insists on this will depend on the integrity and creditworthiness of the customer.

- The bank will issue the indemnity, provided that the customer is creditworthy and trustworthy. The amount of the indemnity will be similar to the value of the goods. It is not unknown for carriers to request up to 200% of the value of the goods. The indemnity must be in standard form so as not to impose any unreasonable obligations on the bank. The bank will consider the same principles as those that apply to consideration of the issue of bonds on behalf of a customer (see Topic 22).

- The bank will make a charge for the indemnity and can justify that charge by pointing out the saving on demurrage.

- If the missing bills of lading do subsequently come to hand, the bank will give them up to the carrier in exchange for cancellation of the indemnity.

Indemnities such as these represent a contingent liability on the part of the importer, because, at some future date, there could be a claim from the carrier. But most banks would regard the real risk as being very low or non-existent.

In practice, the bills of lading usually turn up and are surrendered in exchange for the cancelled indemnity. If they are not located, the indemnity is not normally released by the carrier until the passing of six years from the date of its issuance.

23.12   Produce loan procedure

Sometimes, importers buy goods on D/P collection terms for resale to a third party in the same country. It can happen that the importer requires finance to bridge the gap between payment of the sight draft and receipt of funds from the ultimate buyer.

In such cases, a 'produce loan' facility can enable the importer's bank to advance funds against the security of goods and/or their sale proceeds.

The procedure is as follows.

1. The bank will take a letter of pledge, from the customer. This will state that the documents and/or goods are pledged as security to the bank.

2. It will pay the bill of exchange in accordance with the instructions on the collection order.

3. It will debit a produce loan and credit the customer's current account with the agreed amount of the advance.

4. The documents will be retained by the bank. The bank will arrange with its agents to have the goods warehoused in the bank's name.

5. The goods must be insured at the customer's expense.

6. A 'status enquiry' will be made on the supplier of goods, to ensure that the goods should be of sound quality and on the ultimate buyer, to ensure that it will be able to pay for the goods.

7. The goods remain in the warehouse until the time comes for delivery to the ultimate buyer. When that time comes, the customer must sign a 'trust receipt'. The bank will then issue a delivery order to enable the customer to obtain the goods and take them to the ultimate buyer. The trust receipt states that the customer holds the goods as trustee for the bank.

   The bank has now lost physical control of the goods and relies on the customer to deliver them to the ultimate buyer.

8. The ultimate buyer pays directly to the bank and the proceeds are used to clear the produce loan, including interest and charges.

23.13   Special forms of finance for imports

Other than produce loans the main specialist forms of finance are as follows.

23.13.1   Factoring or invoice discounting

Factoring or invoice discounting applies when the goods are to be on- sold to other business organisations that are usually, but not necessarily always, located in the same country as the importer.

Note: UK factors will also provide finance to overseas exporters who have a good spread of UK debtors. The overseas exporter sends the invoices to the UK factor. The principles are the same as those described in Topic 19.

23.13.2 Acceptance credit facilities

Acceptance credit facilities apply when the goods are to be sold on.

Normally, the bank would lend unsecured, but it could conceivably require the security of the goods under a produce loan type facility.

The procedure is similar to that already described for exporters in Topic 19. The importer draws a bill of exchange (minimum £100,000) on the bank, the bank accepts the bill, and the importer discounts it. Provided that the tenor of the bill is below 180 days, it will be classed as a bank bill and thus can be discounted at fine rates.

23.13.3 Documentary credits payable after sight but which contain a negotiation clause

When the seller is in a strong enough bargaining position to insist on documentary credits, there can be a problem if the seller requires payment immediately on presentation of documents and the buyer requires credit terms.

One possible solution is a documentary credit that calls for term drafts, but which contains an authority for the nominated bank to negotiate against a complying presentation of documents. Provided that the applicant has agreed to be responsible for all discount costs, this credit will meet the requirements of the beneficiary.

From the importer's point of view, this facility is more generous than open account terms or documentary collection terms with overdraft or loan, or factoring or acceptance credit facilities to allow for payment to the supplier on shipment.

23.13.4 VAT deferment

In the absence of any arrangement to the contrary, importers will have to pay VAT on goods as they are cleared through customs. It is possible, however, for importers to arrange to open an account with the VAT authorities so that VAT is settled on a monthly basis. Usually, all VAT incurred in January would be settled on 15 February and all VAT incurred in February would be settled on 15 March, and so on.

The importer will require a bank indemnity in favour of HM Revenue & Customs (HMRC) to cover any non- payment of VAT incurred on the monthly settlement. The bank will apply normal credit criteria when deciding whether to grant the indemnity, will require a counter- indemnity from the importer and will charge a fee. These considerations will follow the principles described in Topic 22, concerning the issue of bonds on behalf of customers.

The importer must decide whether the cash flow gains, interest savings and convenience outweigh the bank's fee for the indemnity: the earlier in the month the goods clear customs, the greater the cash flow and interest benefits.

An additional means of legally avoiding VAT is available in connection with goods that are being brought into the UK from abroad and temporarily warehoused in the UK pending re- export. Such goods should be kept in a customs or bonded warehouse while in the UK. This will legally avoid the need to pay VAT, as long as the goods remain there until subsequent re- export. A variation of this method is the 'E'- type warehouse, which can be located at the importer's own premises. Provided that computerised stock control methods, backed up by periodic spot checks, show that the goods are accounted for separately, then there will be no VAT to pay as long as the goods are exported when they leave the control of the importer.

Figure 23.2

DELIVERY ORDER REQUEST

To: **HSBC Bank plc**
       International Branch
       London International Branch

Please issue a Delivery Order to: _____

                              Attn: _____

                              Fax: _____

Re Airway Bill No: _____ **or other Transport Doc:** _____

Goods Despatched by: _____ **(Name of Supplier)**

Goods Despatched From: _____ **(Name of Country)**

Currency and Amount: _____

          Invoice No: _____

Description of Goods: _____

          Marks: _____

          Weight: _____

          No of packages: _____

Documentary Credit No.
(If applicable)   :DC/DPCLDI _____

Goods to be Released to: _____
       (Leave blank if goods are to be released to yourselves)

Please forward original Delivery Order to: _____
       (Leave blank if this is not required)

In consideration of you, HSBC Bank plc, at our request issuing at your sole discretion the above Delivery Order ("the Delivery Order") in respect of the above-mentioned goods ("the Goods") to enable us or our named agent to take delivery of the Goods, we hereby irrevocably and unconditionally:

1. (a)   undertake and agree to indemnify you from and hold you harmless against any actions, damages, demands, costs, claims, losses and expenses (including legal costs on a full indemnity basis) which you may suffer or sustain arising out of or in connection with your issuing any Delivery Order or the exercise of your rights and powers hereunder;

   (b)   authorise you without reference to or further authority from us and despite any protests from us to make any payments and comply with any demands which may be claimed or made upon you under or in connection with your issuing the Delivery Order and agree that any such payment or demand shall be binding upon us and shall (in the absence of manifest error) be accepted by us as conclusive evidence of your liability to make any such payment or to comply with any such demand; and

   (c)   undertake and agree to provide to you on demand funds to meet any payments which you may make hereunder and that we will accept all documents presented for payment in connection with the Goods notwithstanding and discrepancies in the said documents whatsoever.

continued/

/continued

2. We irrevocably authorise you to debit the amount of any sum(s) of money due to you any payment(s) made by you hereunder to any account or accounts we maintain with you, including without limitation all or any demurrage, warehouse or airport charges which you may be called upon to pay, and for the purposes of effecting any such debit you may convert one currency into another at the spot rate of exchange (as conclusively determined by you) prevailing on such foreign exchange market as you shall decide.

3. We agree that the amount of any payment due hereunder may at your absolute discretion be deducted from the overall amount of any facility or financial accommodation provided to us by you despite any term to the contrary therein provided.

4. This undertaking authority and indemnity shall not be affected or impaired by any insufficiency or matter arising on delivery or inspection of the Goods or any documents, including any bills, relating thereto and, without limitation to the generality of the foregoing, any fault, insufficiency, dispute or protest on out part or any discrepancy in the Goods or any documents, including any bills, or any other matter.

5. We enclose with this request copies of:

    (a) Invoices
    (b) Transport Documents (air waybill/truck waybill).

6. We undertake to hold the Goods, any documents (including any documents of title) relating to the Goods, the proceeds thereof when sold any insurance proceeds thereof in trust for you on your account.

7. This undertaking is in addition to any other indemnity or security now or hereafter held by of made available to you.

8. This agreement shall be governed by the laws of England and Wales and we irrevocably submit to non-exclusive jurisdiction of the courts of England and Wales.

For and on behalf of: _____
(Customer name)

_____   _____
Authorised Signature (s) (as per Bank mandate)

Date: _____

Figure 23.3

WRIGHT KERR TYSON LTD.

since 1885

International Freight Forwarding Services

Registered in England 3065393

6 Sylvan Court
Sylvan Way
Southfields Business Park
Laindon, Basildon
Essex SS15 6TH
United Kingdom

Telephone: +44 (0) 1268 548888
Fax: +44 (0) 1268 548914
Website: www.wktuk.com
Email: operations@wktuk.com

WAREHOUSE RECEIPT – NUMBER WKT/MTC/321

Received for storage in good condition, unless as specified below*, at rates as agreed, for the account of and deliverable to

THE MAJOR TRADING COMPANY LIMITED, TONBRIDGE, KENT

Quantity	Type of Packages	Goods Description	Warehouse Location
500	BALES	COTTON GOODS	MALDON, ESSEX

- *Noted discrepancies* <u>NONE</u> ....

Signed _____   *Name* <u>JAMES SMITH</u>   *Date 3 October xxxx*

All goods are held at Clients risk and are not covered for Fire, Theft etc.

Wright Kerr Tyson Limited is a long standing Full Trading Member of the British International Freight Association (formerly the Institute of Freight Forwarders). As such we conduct our general freight forwarding business by the Association's Standard Trading Conditions (2005 Edition). As a Full Trading Member of the Association, we are entitled to print our Registered Number on all our letterheads and stationery.

Wright Kerr Tyson's Registered Number is 0285

Figure 23.4

HSBC ⟨X⟩

To: The Manager
HSBC Bank plc
Trade Services
_____ (Branch Address)

Dear Sir,

TRUST RECEIPT

I/We hereby acknowledge receipt for the sole purpose of obtaining delivery of and/or making delivery to purchasers of the goods therein described of the undermentioned documents of title listed in the Schedule hereto such goods as aforesaid being pledged to you as collateral security for the due performance of my/our obligations in respect of advances or accommodation made or given to me/us and/or due payment of drafts accepted by me/us as shown in the said Schedule and I/we undertake to hold the said documents of title the goods therein represented the proceeds thereof when sold and any insurance proceeds thereof in trust for you on your account and to deal with the same only upon the terms and conditions contained herein.

I/We undertake not to pledge the said goods as security for any other advances nor to part with control of them except to purchasers thereof in the ordinary course of business and further undertake in the event of the said goods or any part thereof being sold by me/us forthwith to pay you in full and without deduction of expenses the amount of my/our indebtedness to you out of the proceeds of sale immediately on my/our receipt thereof or any part thereof as the case may be (and if requested at any time by you forthwith to notify you of the terms of such sale) or to give you on request full authority directly to receive payment of and to give a good discharge for the amount of such indebtedness.

I/We further undertake not without your previous consent in writing to sell the said goods or any part thereof on credit terms of for less than the invoice price (or pro rata to the invoice price) as shown in the Schedule hereto.

I/We undertake until the said goods are sold to keep the same fully insured at my/our expense with such insurers as you may approve against usual marine risks fire and theft and against any such other risks as you may require to hold the policy or policies and other insurance instruments on your behalf to notify you forthwith of any circumstances likely to give rise to a claim under the insurances and to hand over to you or authorise the receipt by you of the amount of any recoveries under the insurances.

Your knowledge of any breach failure or omission in respect of any of my/our obligations hereunder shall not operate as a waiver of or otherwise detract from any of your rights hereunder and you may without notice to me/us at any time cancel the transaction evidenced by this Trust Receipt and in that event demand to be repossessed of the said documents of title or the goods represented thereby.

The undertakings given to you in this document shall be in addition to and not in substitution for any other rights and security I/we from time to time may give or have already given to you and this transaction shall be kept separate from all other transactions.

If two or more parties sign this Trust Receipt their obligations and liabilities shall be joint and several.

This Trust Receipt shall be construed and take effect in all respects according to English law.

Dated..

For and on behalf of
(customer name)

....
Authorised Signature(s)

1 of 2
p:\qualityme\HTVform\trustreceipt VER I 25/3/02 RH

SCHEDULE

No.	Description of Documents	Description of Goods	Name of Ship/ Warehouse etc.	Amount of Advance and/or Relative Bill	Invoice Price	Due Date

p:\qualityme\HTVform\trustreceipt VER1 25/3/02 RH

Topic 24

Documentary credits for imports

On completion of this topic, the student should be able to:

- appreciate the risks that a bank undertakes when issuing a documentary credit on behalf of an importer;

- explain how some of these risks can be reduced;

- understand and explain the technicalities that must be resolved to ensure that the documentary credit is logical and workable;

- understand and explain the effects of the ICC Uniform Customs and Practice for Documentary Credits (UCP) on the issuing of the credit, and the responsibilities of the applicant and issuing bank.

24.1   The risks that a bank runs when it issues a documentary credit

When a bank issues a documentary credit, it undertakes payment to the beneficiary (exporter) if the documents are presented in compliance with the terms and conditions of the credit. Normally, the issuing bank will obtain reimbursement from the customer (applicant) by debiting its account in accordance with the authority given at the time of issuance of the credit (see item 9 in the conditions of the specimen authority at Figure 24.1) or in a master agreement.

Figure 24.1   Specimen authority

HSBC ◆X◗

To: HSBC Bank plc (Bank) _____ Trade Service Centre

APPLICATION FOR IRREVOCABLE DOCUMENTARY CREDIT

[2]

Transferable? ☐ No ☐ Yes	DC Number	Date of application

Applicant (name and full address)	Beneficiary Name and Address (and telephone no, fax, no. Contact name within company, if known) [1]

Applicant's reference	Expiry Date.................................. [7] Place of Expiry.............................

Amount: Currency.................... Figures.................... [4]
  Words....................
  Acceptable variance in quantity of goods*/DC amount*: +/-..........................% (*Delete as appropriate)

Partial Shipment ☐ allowed ☐ not allowed	Transhipment ☐ allowed ☐ not allowed

Latest Shipment Date............................. [7]	Shipment/Despatch/Taking in charge From.................................... To......................................

Method of Advice: ☐ Full teletransmission   ☐ Airmail   ☐ Courier   [3]

☐   Drafts required drawn on Issuing Bank for full invoice value of the goods: ☐ At Sight: ☐ ....days after Sight:

☐   ....days after B/L, AWB, CMR.   ☐ ....days after Invoice Date.   ☐ Other..........................

Advising Bank/Routing Bank (if applicable) *(If left blank, DC will normally be advised through an HSBC Group Office)*	Instruct Advising Bank to add their confirmation ☐ Yes ☐ No If Yes, confirmation charges payable by ☐ Applicant ☐ Beneficiary

Documents to be presented within.............days after the date of   ☐ Shipment   ☐ Receipt but within validity of the
[7]   documentary credit

Trade term.............................   Place...
(e.g. FOB, FCA, CFR, CPT, CIF, EXW, DDU, DDP)

Goods (Brief description including quantity without excessive detail)

[6]

301-8A (0502 - UOT - IPK x 251

The issuing bank, however, must honour under the credit, irrespective of whether the applicant has funds in its account, provided that the terms and conditions of the credit have been complied with. As a result, the issuing bank treats the documentary credit in much the same way as any other lending facility and a limit will be marked on the account.

24.2 How the issuing bank can reduce its risks under documentary credits

As with any lending facility, the bank's prime considerations are the creditworthiness and integrity of its customer. An additional consideration is that the underlying goods can be used as security, provided that the correct formalities are observed.

Thus, the considerations additional to general creditworthiness and integrity are as follows.

- The nature of the goods– are they easily saleable if the bank has to sell them to cover its liability in the event of the applicant's default?

- Should the credit call for an inspection certificate issued by an independent party declaring that the goods are of a specific standard or quality? If such a document is called for and is produced, the goods should be of the required standard. If the document is not produced, the issuing bank is free of liability and will refuse payment because of a discrepancy due to the missing document.

- The beneficiary should be well known, or a good status report should be held regarding its commercial reliability and integrity.

- The bank needs to consider whether it should take cash cover from the applicant.

- The goods must be insured. If the credit calls for an insurance document (as would be the case if the underlying sale contract were CIF or CIP), then all is well; if the credit does not call for an insurance document (as would be the case with an ex- works, FOB or CFR sale), the bank must satisfy itself that the applicant has effected the necessary insurance.

- If air waybills are called for, the issuing bank must decide whether it wishes to be named as consignee. If the bank feels that it is necessary to retain control of the goods, the credit must stipulate that the air waybill shows the bank as consignee.

- If the goods are to be shipped by sea, it is in the interests of both bank and customer for the credit to call for a complete set of clean, shipped on board, bills of lading made out to order and blank indorsed or indorsed to the bank.

24.3 The authority that the applicant completes

Once an importer and exporter have agreed to deal on documentary credit terms, the importer must request its bank to arrange issuance of the credit. You will recall from Part III of the text that the importer is the applicant and its bank is the issuing bank.

From the specimen application form reproduced at Figure 24.1, you will see that the main details required are as follows.

1. Full name and address of beneficiary.

2. That the credit is irrevocable (article 3 of UCP 600). (UCP 600 only recognises irrevocable credits due to the fact that revocable credits are not as secure and are seldom issued.)

3. Whether the details are to be passed to the advising bank by teletransmission, airmail or courier.

4. The amount of the credit. If the word 'about' is used, then a 10% deviation either way will be allowed (article 30 of UCP 600).

5. The documents called for. These must be logical: for example, if the goods are to be despatched by air, it would be illogical to call for bills of lading.

6. The description of the goods is important, because, on presentation of documents, the invoice must describe the goods in a manner that corresponds to the description in the credit, whereas the transport document can describe the goods in general terms not conflicting with the description in the credit (article 18 – description on commercial invoice – and sub- article 14 (e) – description on other documents).

7. The latest date of shipment and the expiry date. It is not necessary to show a latest date of shipment, but if one is shown, it must not be later than the expiry date of the credit. If a latest date of shipment is shown and it is more than 21 calendar days before the expiry date, the documents must still be presented within the specified number of days (sub- article 14 (c)).

If the credit amount is expressed in a currency other than that of the country of the issuer and/or applicant, both the bank and the customer must decide whether it is necessary to cover the exchange risk.

Figure 24.2 Specimen application form

Documents Required: [5]

Original Invoice(s) signed plus..........................copies

For shipment by sea, full set of original clean "on board" ☐ bills of lading / ☐ multimodal or combined transport documents.

[5]
☐ made out to the shipper's order, blank endorsed and marked ☐ freight prepaid ☐ freight collect

and notify ....

☐ made out to order of..and marked ☐ freight prepaid ☐ freight collect

and notify ....

☐ Air waybill, marked "for the consignor/shipper", marked ☐ freight prepaid ☐ freight collect
and notify..bearing reference to this documentary credit number, showing actual date of despatch of goods including flight number and evidencing despatch of goods to..

☐ Original CMR/Truck waybill marked ☐ freight prepaid ☐ freight collect ☐ evidencing goods consigned to....................

☐ Other transport documents (please specify)..

☐ If CIF/CIP: insurance policy/certificate for full CIF/CIP value plus ☐ 10% ☐ ....% blank endorsed, covering institute cargo clauses 'A'/war/strike/other (please specify if required)..clauses

☐ If FOB etc: Insurance covered by applicant/buyer

Additional Documents

☐ Packing list in..........................copies ☐ Export licence/certificate in..........................copies ☐ Weight list in..........................copies

☐ GSP certificate form A in..................copies ☐ Certificate of ....origin in..................copies ☐ Other (please specify)

Special Instructions

Documents to be delivered in one lot unless otherwise specified to the Issuing Bank by ☐ Courier ☐ Registered Airmail

☐ Other (please specify)..........................

DC charges	Applicant	Beneficiary (see condition 13 below)
Within UK	☐	☐
Outside UK	☐	☐

☐ On receipt of documents in order, please debit our

Account number..

Sort code 40-..............-..............

Utilising Forward Contract No/Spot Rate..........................

Please debit DC opening commission, advising expenses to our

Account number..

Sort code 40-..............-..............

We request you to issue your irrevocable Documentary Credit for our account in accordance with the above instructions and subject to the conditions printed below:

....

signed on behalf of applicant in accordance with our mandate held by the Bank

Signature verified

In case of query, please telephone.. and ask for..

Conditions

1. Except so far as otherwise expressly stated, this Documentary Credit is subject to Uniform Customs and Practice for Documentary Credits (2007 Revision), International Chamber of Commerce Publication No 600.
2. We agree to take out in the manner and to the extent required by the Bank all insurance necessary for the full protection of the Bank's interest in the goods shipped under this Credit, and on behalf of the Bank and subject to its instructions to prosecute or to ensure the prosecution of any claim that may arise under any insurance and to pay the proceeds thereof to the Bank and to provide evidence of insurance if called upon to do so.
3. If this Credit is to be advised through an agency or correspondent bank in USA, you are authorised to accept at your sole discretion and under our responsibility American Institute clauses insurance policies.
4. You are authorised to make any additions to the documents specified under this Credit which you may consider necessary to ensure compliance with government regulations but you are not obliged to do so.
5. We certify that the import of goods described above is not prohibited or restricted and that we hold and undertake to exhibit to you a valid import licence where such licence is required.
6. The words "we", "our" and "us" shall be read as "I", "my" and "me" if this application is signed by or on behalf of an individual.
7. You are authorised at your sole discretion and without obligation to do so whenever you consider it advisable, customary or appropriate to waive or delete the following from the instructions contained on this form (whether completed by me/us or not), namely "Drafts required at sight/at days drawn on issuing bank for full invoice value of goods".
8. In the absence of any instructions to the contrary specified in "Special Instructions" above, you are authorised to instruct any bank or branch concerned to despatch any draft(s) and or any documents by one or more mails or other method of conveyance at your sole discretion.
9. We undertake on demand to reimburse you in respect of all payments and to indemnify you in respect of all liabilities, including legal costs, on a full indemnity basis and to discharge all liabilities which you may make or incur for us at our request or as a result of your allowing any drawer and or negotiating/confirming bank to obtain reimbursement before you have had the opportunity to inspect any documents in connection with this Credit and to pay interest from the date of the same having been made or incurred until repayment both before and after any demand made at the stipulated rate by you.
10. We are aware of the implications of article 34 of UCP 600 and acknowledge that where a bank claims to have paid/accepted (honoured) or negotiated under this Credit, its good faith and the fact of payment/acceptance (honour) or negotiation thereof shall be presumed in the absence of evidence to the contrary.
11. As continuing security for the payment of all sums for which we may from time to time be actually or contingently indebted or liable to you for any reason and on any account.
    (a) we hereby pledge and agree to pledge to you with full title guarantee firstly all bills, documents of title, transportation documents, insurance policies and other documents representing or relating to the goods shipped under this credit which goods and/or documents are in or come into your or your agent's actual or constructive possession or control and secondly, the goods represented thereby, and we warrant that such documents and goods shall not be subject to any lien, charge or other encumbrance in favour of any other person; and
    (b) we agree to ensure that all such documents are properly endorsed and delivered to you and you are hereby authorised to demand the same from any party on your behalf.
12. We furthermore agree that this Credit and any drawing(s) or advance(s) relating thereto shall be subject to the terms of any separate pledge (being in addition to that contained in Condition 11 above) where given to you.
13. Where charges are for the account of the beneficiary and are unpaid for any reason we undertake to reimburse you in full.

24.4 Reinstatement documentary credits

Re-instatement documentary credits are best explained through an example. The 'Flotsam and Jetsam Ltd' question provides a good illustration of the use of such techniques.

Question

Flotsam and Jetsam Ltd import a range of consumer items from many overseas countries. The directors have recently asked you to arrange an irrevocable letter of credit in favour of an overseas supplier to cover the company's imports for the next 12 months. Bank facilities are fully utilised and you are reluctant to issue an irrevocable letter of credit covering shipments valued in excess of £50,000 in any one month for the next 12 months. You are, however, prepared to issue an irrevocable letter of credit covering up to three months' shipments for a maximum of £150,000 (or the foreign currency equivalent), but you are not prepared to go beyond that limit. Nevertheless, the supplier has insisted that a bank undertaking should be issued in its favour, otherwise the company's source of supply will dry up.

1. Specify the banking instruments that would satisfy the customer's needs utilising irrevocable letters of credit, but which would not extend the bank facilities beyond the limit that you are prepared to sanction.

2. Briefly describe how these banking instruments would operate.

3. Make brief notes showing the explanation you would give to the directors describing the advantages and disadvantages to the company, and the beneficiary (its supplier), of each of the methods described in (a) and (b) above.

Suggested response

A documentary credit is a real liability to the issuing bank, because the bank must pay if the documents are presented in compliance with the terms and conditions of the credit.

The overseas supplier requires a documentary credit for a total sum of £600,000, which will allow part-shipment against pro rata drawings. The supplier then knows that payment of its full year's sales to Flotsam and Jetsam Ltd is guaranteed, provided that it conforms to the terms and conditions of the credit.

Our bank is, however, prepared to sanction only a maximum liability of £150,000 on behalf of Flotsam and Jetsam Ltd.

The supplier is in a strong bargaining position, so if Flotsam and Jetsam Ltd is to obtain the supplies, a documentary credit will be required.

Basically, the question asks what compromise is available whereby the supplier obtains a documentary credit, but our bank's liability is restricted to £150,000 maximum.

The questions can therefore be answered as follows.

1. A reinstatement letter of credit; or a standby letter of credit.

2a. In terms of the operation of a reinstatement documentary credit, the terms of the credit would be as follows:

- an expiry date in three months' time stating that, if the credit is reinstated for further amounts of £50,000, the expiry will be extended by an extra month;

- a maximum amount that may be drawn (£150,000, ie three months' shipments);

- that the credit will be issued for an initial sum of £50,000, stating that a maximum of £50,000 may be drawn in any one month;

- the credit will state that the value of any documents presented in accordance with the terms and conditions of the credit may be reinstated provided that Flotsam and Jetsam Ltd and the bank agree;

- the credit will state that Flotsam and Jetsam Ltd and/or the bank has the right to refuse reinstatement.

2b. In terms of the operation of a standby letter of credit:

- our bank is the issuing bank and Flotsam and Jetsam Ltd is the applicant;

- the credit would be for a maximum of £150,000;

- the credit will guarantee payment against presentation of a copy of an invoice and copy bill of lading, together with a signed certificate from the supplier certifying that payment for the goods shipped (as evidenced by the copy invoice and bill of lading) had not been made. Alternatively, payment could be guaranteed against a dishonoured, protested, bill of exchange drawn on Flotsam and Jetsam Ltd;

- the supplier would then trade on an open account basis, but would be able to claim under the standby letter of credit if Flotsam and Jetsam Ltd were not to pay. Alternatively, the supplier would trade on a documentary collection basis and, in the event of dishonour, would then use the standby credit to obtain payment.

Note: the standby letter of credit could state 'issued subject to the Uniform Customs and Practice for Documentary Credits (2007 revision) – UCP 600' or it could be stated to be 'issued subject to ISP98'. The differences between the rules have been fully covered in Topic 21 and the reader is invited to refer back to that topic for any further examination of this aspect. For the purposes of the points illustrated above, it is not necessary to consider which rules might apply.

3. The advantages of a reinstatement documentary credit for Flotsam and Jetsam Ltd (the importer or applicant) are as follows:

- The bank regards this facility as a liability of £150,000, rather than £600,000, hence borrowing facilities are at a much lower level and bank charges are reduced.

- Flotsam and Jetsam Ltd and the bank have the right to refuse to authorise reinstatement of any amount drawn under the credit. Thus, Flotsam and Jetsam Ltd and the bank are committed only to three months' purchases or liability and might cancel the facility if alternative supplies were to become available.

- The credit is subject to UCP 600 and so payment can only be made against stipulated documents.

4. The disadvantage of a re-instatement documentary credit for Flotsam and Jetsam Ltd is, as with all documentary credits, that payment is made against documents, not against goods. Hence, payment will be made against the presentation of complying documents even if the goods prove to be faulty.

5. The advantages of a reinstatement documentary credit to the supplier or beneficiary is that, as with all documentary credits, payment of the amount (£150,000) is guaranteed against presentation of complying documents.

6. The disadvantages of a reinstatement credit for supplier and beneficiary is that only three months' sales are guaranteed, not 12, because Flotsam and Jetsam Ltd or the bank could refuse to reinstate drawings.

Note: importers prefer to issue credits, which can be extended or increased by amendment rather than by an automatic mechanism built into the credit, while the opposite can be said for exporters.

24.5 A comparison of avalisation and documentary credit facilities from the point of view of the importer's bank

The similarities between avalisation and documentary credit facilities, from the point of view of the importer's bank are that each facility involves the bank in guaranteeing the indebtedness of the customer. Therefore, the facilities are available only to good customers.

The differences, meanwhile, are as follows.

*   Avalisation is usually unsecured, in that the collection is clean or documents are released on acceptance.

*   The issuing bank can gain a measure of protection by calling for suitable documents under a documentary credit (eg an inspection certificate issued by an independent party). Such protection is not available for avalisation.

*   Documentary credits can be issued on any mutually agreed terms between the bank and the applicant. Avalisation is normally confined to bills of exchange of minimum amounts of £10,000.

*   Avalisation facilities can be agreed quickly; documentary credits can take more time to set up.

*   In the UK, there is no statutory recognition of avalisation. Thus, the UK bank will require a specific indemnity from its customer to authorise reimbursement of any money paid by the bank to the presenter of the bill.

Topic 25

Transferable and back- to- back letters of credit

On completion of this topic, the student should be able to:

- understand and explain the nature of transferable credits;
- differentiate between transferable and back-to-back credits;
- appreciate the differences between transferable credits, back-to-back credits, red clause credits and produce loans.

25.1 The transferable credit and situations in which it can be used

A '**transferable credit**' is defined in article 38 of the ICC Uniform Customs and Practice for Documentary Credits (2007 Revision) (UCP 600). Under UCP 600, a credit is transferable only if it is expressly designated to be transferable by the issuing bank. Any other terms or descriptions such as 'divisible', 'assignable', 'transmissible' and 'fractionable' do not render a credit transferable.

A transferable credit is used when the supplier of goods sells them through a middleman and does not deal directly with the ultimate buyer. If the supplier is in a strong bargaining position, it may insist that a documentary credit be set up in its favour.

The middleman may not wish to arrange a documentary credit itself, and its bankers may, in any case, may not be willing to issue a credit on its behalf. Thus the middleman will approach the ultimate buyer and ask it to arrange for the issuance of a transferable documentary credit in the middleman's favour. The middleman is known as the 'first beneficiary' of the credit.

The credit will be designated transferable and will allow the first beneficiary to request the bank authorised to honour (ie to pay, to incur a deferred payment undertaking or to accept) or negotiate, or, in the case of a freely available credit, to request the bank specifically authorised in the credit as the transferring bank to make the credit available to one or more third parties who are known as 'second beneficiaries'. Thus the supplier of the goods is known as the 'second beneficiary'.

An example of a transfer request form that would be sent to a first beneficiary is shown at Figure 25.1.

Figure 25.1 Specimen transfer request form

HSBC ◀X▶   Request for Transfer of Documentary Credit

TO: **HSBC Bank plc** _____ Trade Services Centre

Date: _____

Documentary Credit No: _____

Issuing Bank: _____

As beneficiary of the above-mentioned transferable credit, we request that you make this credit available to:

(1)

upon the same terms and conditions as the original credit with the exception of the following:

(2) Amount: _____ (Words _____)

(3) Quantity (if part shipments allowed): _____ Unit price: _____

(4) Valid in _____ until: _____

(5) Latest shipment date: _____

(6) Period for presentation in accordance with UCP600 Article 14 (c): _____ Days.

(7) The percentage of insurance cover required (if applicable) under the transferred credit is increased to _____ %.

(8) We request you to notify the transferee by: ☐ Airmail   ☐ Courier   ☐ Teletransmission

(9) We ☐ intend   ☐ do not intend   to substitute our own invoices and drafts (if any) for those of the transferee.

(10) In accordance with UCP600 sub-article 38(c), amendments to the original credit

☐ require   ☐ do not   require our consent before being advised to the above-mentioned second beneficiary.

(11) Any irregularities in documents presented ☐ must   ☐ need not   be referred to us before you take any action.

(12) Disclosure of the parties to this transaction ☐ must   ☐ need not   be avoided.

(13) Disclosure of our profit margin ☐ must   ☐ need not   be avoided.

The transferred credit will be subject to the Uniform Customs and Practice for Documentary Credits (2007 Revision) International Chamber of Commerce Publication No. 600

For and on behalf of
(Insert customer name) _____

_____

Authorised Signature(s)

Contact Name _____   Bank: _____

Telephone No. _____

Fax No. _____   Signature Verified: _____

20206-4 (05.07 : UOI = 1 x PD50)

Note: The following requirements must also be fulfilled before any advice of transfer is issued by HSBC Bank plc.

- All Requests for Transfer must be accompanied by the original L/C advice, together with any attachements and amendments.

- Receipt by the Bank of the company's remittance (cleared funds) in respect of our charges as follows:

  – Transfer commission caluculated at the rate of 0.5% of the amount transferred (Minimum £125)
  – And any other applicable charges

- This form must be signed by an authorised official(s) of your company and the signature(s) verified by your Bankers.

NOTES ON COMPLETION OF TRANSFER FORM

(1) Complete this area with the full name and address of the company to which you require the credit to be transferred; this information can include the contact point(s) within the company. If the transfer is to be in favour of a company outside the UK, provide details of their banker, if known.

(2) This is the amount that you require to be transferred. The amount must be in the same currency as the original credit.

(3) The goods description must remain the same as that in the original credit. The unit price(s) however, may be altered.

(4) The expiry date must not be after the expiry date of the original credit.

(5) The latest shipment date must not be after the latest shipment date of the original credit.

(6) The period for presentation may be shorter than that quoted in the original credit.

(7) Amount of insurance cover may be increased to cover the value of your invoice(s).

(8) Signify the manner in which the transferred credit is to be advised.

(9) Tick the appropriate box dependent upon whether your own invoices will be substituted or not. The name of the original applicant must appear in any documents (other than the invoice) if it is a specific requirement of the original credit. We will assume (unless informed otherwise) that you require your name to be substituted for that of the applicant.

(10) Tick the appropriate box dependent upon whether you wish to provide separate instructions to amend the transfer credit, or whether we are authorised to amend this credit simultaneously with the original.

(11) Tick the appropriate box dependent upon whether you require notification of document discrepancies before we revert to the transferee.

(12) Tick the appropriate box dependent upon whether disclosure of the identity of the original applicant and/or the transferee to the other party must be avoided.

(13) Tick the appropriate box dependent upon whether disclosure of your profit margin to the original applicant and/or the transferee must be avoided.

We are obliged by the Uniform Customs and Practice for Documentary Credits ICC No 600 to issue the transfer credit on the same terms and conditions as the original credit with the exception of those points made above; you should therefore consider very carefully the terms of the credit to ensure that any information that you do not wish to be passed on to either the Applicant or Transferee is handled by way of amendment prior to the transfer instruction being completed.

25.1.1   The terms on which the first beneficiary can authorise transfer of its rights under the credit to a second beneficiary

The transferring bank is under no obligation to transfer the credit, unless it agrees to do so and on terms to which they are agreeable. Unless the original credit states otherwise, a transferable credit can be transferred only once, thus the second beneficiary or beneficiaries cannot transfer their rights to a third beneficiary.

The transfer will be in accordance with the terms of the original credit except that:

- the name and address of the first beneficiary will be shown instead of that of the applicant, except where a transfer for 100% of the original credit value is made and/or no substitution of documents is to occur by the first beneficiary;

- the amount of the credit and unit price may be reduced to allow for the middleman's profit;

- the expiry date, presentation period and the latest date for shipment (if one is stipulated) may be curtailed to be earlier than on the original credit;

- the percentage for which insurance cover must be effected may be increased to provide the amount of cover stipulated in the original credit.

It is the transferring bank, acting on the instructions of the first beneficiary, that will advise the credit to the second beneficiary.

The first beneficiary must inform the transferring bank of the conditions under which it may advise any subsequent amendments to the second beneficiary.

25.1.2 The operation of a transferable credit when the second beneficiary has shipped the goods and presented the documents

The second beneficiary will present the required documents, usually via its own bankers, to the transferring bank. The invoice and bill of exchange will usually be for less than the amount stated in the credit that was advised to the first beneficiary. On receipt of the documents, the transferring bank will examine them for compliance and request the first beneficiary to provide its substitute invoices and draft (if any). Upon receipt, the transferring bank will substitute the invoice and bill of exchange (if any) of the first beneficiary for those of the second beneficiary.

The transferring bank will then forward the documents to the issuing bank and obtain reimbursement, if it has not done so already by virtue of any reimbursement instructions that may be contained in the original credit. On receipt of the funds, the amount claimed by the second beneficiary will be paid to it and the difference, less any bank charges, will be paid to its middleman as profit. If, for any reason, the first beneficiary fails to present his own invoices and draft (if any), the transferring bank may send the documents of the second beneficiary to the issuing bank, including the second beneficiary's invoices and drafts for a lesser amount, without further responsibility to the first beneficiary.

25.1.3 The ICC Uniform Customs and Practice for Documentary Credits (UCP 600)

Students should note the following points in addition to the UCP 600.

- The content of UCP 600 applies to all credits in which it is expressly stated that the rules are applicable to that transaction, except to the extent that the terms and conditions of the credit modify or exclude one or more of those rules.

- All requests for issuance of a credit and letters of credit themselves should indicate '**subject to UCP 600**' or '**UCPLATESTVERSION**'.

- Transferable credits are covered in article 38.

- A credit can be transferred only if it is expressly stated to be transferable.

- The first beneficiary can only request the transferring bank to transfer. The bank is not obliged to do so.

- The first beneficiary must pay all charges in relation to the transfer and the bank need not effect the transfer until such charges are paid.

- The credit can be transferred only on the terms and conditions specified in the original credit, except for the amount, unit price, expiry date, date of shipment, period for presentation, all of which may be reduced or curtailed. The first beneficiary can request that the second beneficiary provide the full amount of insurance, based on the price paid by the applicant.

- Under article 39, the fact that a credit is not stated to be transferable shall not affect the beneficiary's right to assign any proceeds to which it may become entitled under the credit (see Topic 18).

25.1.5 Transferable credits: flow charts

25.1.5.1 The arrangements for setting up the credit

Figure 25.2

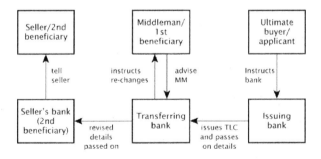

Changes in details when the transferring bank issues their advice of the credit:

- first beneficiary's name substituted for applicant's;

- lower amount;

- earlier expiry date.

Note: only credits that expressly say they are transferable can be transferred (article 38 UCP 600).

25.1.5.2 Presentation of documents under a transferred letter of credit

Figure 25.2

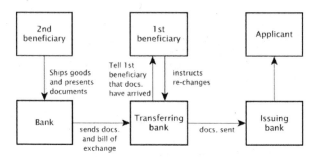

Changes in documents when transferring bank sends them to the issuing bank:

- substitute first beneficiary's invoices, which will normally be for a higher amount;
- substitute first beneficiary's bill of exchange for the full amount of the invoice or according to credit terms (credit may indicate drafts drawn for a percentage of the invoice value);

25.1.5.3 Payment under a transferred letter of credit to first and second beneficiaries (ignoring the complexities of nostro or vostro accounts)

Figure 25.3

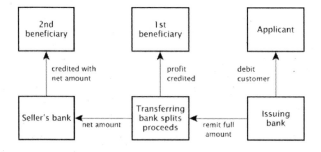

Note: goods shipped direct from seller's country to ultimate buyer's country.

25.2 Back- to- back credits and situations in which they can be used

'**Back- to- back credits**' consist of two entirely separate documentary credits, but one credit may act as security for issuance of the other. They apply in transactions when original suppliers and ultimate buyers deal through a middleman. In fact, back- to- back credits are used in the same situations as transferable credits, but the rights and obligations of the parties differ with the two types of credit.

If the supplier insists on a documentary credit, the middleman may apply to its bankers for them to issue one on its behalf. If the middleman's bankers are satisfied as to its creditworthiness, they will issue the credit in the normal way and no other formalities will apply. The 'back- to- back' aspect comes into play if the middleman's bankers insist that the middleman obtains a documentary credit in its favour from the ultimate buyer as security for that which the middleman has applied for in favour of the seller.

Only the middleman and its bankers need know of the back- to- back aspect and only they are concerned with the back- to- back aspect. The other parties – that is the ultimate buyer, the original supplier and their bankers – are not affected in any way whatsoever by the back- to- back aspect.

25.2.1 Procedures for arranging back- to- back credits

The procedure for arranging back- to- back credit when the middleman's bankers require a documentary credit as security for a credit that they are asked to issue is as follows.

1. The middleman asks the ultimate buyer to arrange a documentary credit in its favour. This is known as the 'first credit'.

2. The middleman then requests its bankers to issue a credit in favour of the supplier of the goods. This is known as the 'second credit' and the middleman is the applicant for the second credit. The second credit will not be issued until the first one has been advised. The middleman's bankers may insist that the first credit be confirmed by them so as to bestow rights under the UCP 600 to the bank.

3. The second credit must at least require the same documents as the first credit and must have an earlier expiry date and be for a lower amount than the first credit.

The procedure when the original supplier ships its goods and presents the documents in accordance with the second credit is as follows.

1. The documents are presented via the supplier's bank or directly to the issuing bank, which is the bank of the middleman. This issuing bank pays the supplier, debiting the middleman by way of a separate loan.

2. The middleman's bankers, who will be the advising bank of the first credit, substitute the middleman's invoices for those of the supplier. The bill of exchange will be for a higher amount and will agree with the amount on the new invoices.

3. The middleman's bankers, then, as advising bank of the first credit, present the documents to the issuing bank.

4. The issuing bank of the first credit pays in accordance with the terms, debiting the cost to the ultimate buyer.

5. On receipt of the proceeds of the first credit, the middleman's bankers clear the loan account in the name of the middleman and any surplus represents the middleman's profit.

It is also possible that the terms of the second credit can be aligned in such a way that payment under both credits occurs at the same time, ie a fixed or determinable due date for payment (90 days after bill of lading date, etc).

25.2.2 The liabilities of the parties to a back- to- back credit

The credits are entirely separate instruments and thus the middleman and its bank are responsible for paying the second credit, irrespective of whether payment is subsequently received under the first credit.

The second credit must have an earlier expiry date than the first, otherwise the documents required to procure payment under the first credit would not be available in time. It is a good precaution to make the second credit expire in the place of issue otherwise the issuing bank is in the hands of the postal authorities, and delayed receipt of documents may mean non- payment under the first credit.

25.3   A comparison of the differences between transferable and back- to- back credits

- With transferable credits, the ultimate buyer is aware that it is dealing with a middleman; with back- to- back credits, it is not.

- With transferable credits, the middleman and its bankers have no additional liability; with back- to- back credits, they are fully liable on the second credit.

25.4   The positions when the first credit calls for an insurance document

When the first credit calls for an insurance document, but the second credit does not, the middleman's bankers must make sure that their customer has insured and can produce the appropriate document in time for presentation under the first credit.

When both the first and second credits call for an insurance document, care must be taken to stipulate that the amount of insurance evidenced by the document required by the second credit is sufficient to meet the amount of insurance required by the first credit.

This may seem self- evident, but it must be remembered that the amount of cover is generally based on the amount of the invoice. Because the invoice value of the second credit is less than that of the first credit, the second credit must specify a *sufficiently high amount of cover.*

Note: there are no special rules in UCP 600 with which to deal with back- to- back credits. Each credit stands on its own merits.

25.5 Cash flow from the point of view of the middleman

25.5.1 Transferable credits

In relation to transferable credits, there are no debits to the account of the middleman at all. When the funds are paid to its bank, the middleman credits its account with the 'profit' and pays the balance to the second beneficiary. The only entry on the middleman's bank account will be a credit for the profit.

25.5.2 Back- to- back credits

In relation to back- to- back credits, the middleman is the applicant for the second credit and the beneficiary of the first credit. The second credit has the earlier expiry date and so the middleman will be debited with the full amount of the second credit. Shortly afterwards, it will be credited with payment of the full amount of the first credit (unless, as mentioned above, the second credit is structured in such a way that the settlement under both credits occurs on the same date).

There will be two separate entries on the account:

- a debit for the amount of the second credit;
- a credit for the amount of the first credit.

Topic 26

Facility letters, covenants and other considerations

At the end of this topic, the reader should be able to:

- understand the significance of facility letters and the covenants found in them, and how they might trigger default situations;

- recognise the importance of clarity concerning jurisdiction and choice of law;

- anticipate the effects of other counties' exchange control regulations on the ability of overseas clients to make payment for purchases.

26.1 Facility letters

As can be seen from the previous topics, many of the facilities made available by banks to clients engaged in international trade are subject to the bank agreeing credit facilities for the customer. For example, the bank will wish to mark a covering limit on an account enjoying foreign currency forward contracts, to cover the risk of needing to debit the account in a close-out situation. Import documentary credits opened by banks on behalf of clients will need a covering limit marking on the account, because the bank has entered into a conditional guarantee on behalf of the customer to pay out funds at a future date if the correct documents are presented. Advances against outward documentary collections will need covering limits in the same way as will any other overdraft or loan facility granted by banks. Guarantees, bonds and other undertakings issued by banks on behalf of clients will involve prior agreement by the banks on the amount and period of such engagements. Limits will be marked to cover such liabilities so that the banks can monitor their exposure to risk on behalf of their customers.

Whenever banks agree facilities for their clients, it is customary for the bank to issue to the customer a 'facility letter' or 'loan agreement document' setting out the terms of the facility being granted. The client must sign agreement to such terms before being allowed to start using the facilities.

These letters or agreement forms will cover such matters as:

- the type of facility or facilities being granted;

- the maximum amounts of the facilities;

- the currency, or currencies, of the facilities;

- the interest rates and charges to be paid for the facilities;

- the expiry date of the facilities, or the date on which they must be renewed or reviewed;
- when and where the facilities may be drawn down;
- details of any security (collateral) to be lodged with the bank to cover the facilities;
- details of which laws should cover the agreement and in what areas legal action should be taken, if required when the bank and borrower are subject to different legal jurisdictions;
- any covenants with which the bank requires the client to comply.

It is very important that facility letters are clearly drafted and that their contents are fully understood by all parties to reduce, as far as possible, any misconceptions about the conditions on which the facility has been granted. It is vital that all parties fully understand their duties, rights and responsibilities under such agreements before the facility is put into effect. Banks should ensure that facility letters are written in easy- to-understand terminology and they should take extra time to explain fully to their clients, especially to new clients, exactly what the terms in the facility letters actually mean.

26.2 Covenants in facility letters and the considerations that may apply

26.2.1 Types of covenant

A '**covenant**' in a bank facility letter is an agreement by the client to operate within certain parameters and to provide for the bank specified information, financial or otherwise, at stated future times.

The types of covenant found in facility letters vary depending on the individual circumstances of the client and the facilities being provided. The usual role of covenants is to help reduce the risk to the bank and/or to help the bank to monitor the progress of the customer using the facility. The extent of the covenants must be realistic, however, in relation to the client's size and circumstances.

Covenants may be specifically tailored to cover the individual client or bank circumstances, but typical covenants seen in facility letters include:

- a 'negative pledge', which is an agreement that the client will not borrow more from, or give any extra security to, other lenders (see below);
- a 'debtor maintenance' clause whereby the client agrees to maintain the total value of debtors of the business at a certain margin, over the agreed facility limit (for example, a margin of 25%, would mean that that debtors must represent at least 125% of the total borrowing);
- a 'gearing restriction', limiting the amount that the client can borrow relative to net worth (please refer back to Topic 8 for the position regarding covenants and translation exposure);
- a 'minimum level of net tangible assets clause' (relating to the net value of the client's assets, after deducting intangible assets such as goodwill and brands) aims to provide protection to the bank against losses or reduction in capital or reserves as a result of asset write- offs;

- an 'interest cover covenant', involving agreeing a formula under which interest must be covered by profit before tax and interest at an agreed multiplier. Two or three times interest cover is a typical requirement. Alternatively, these covenants may stipulate interest cover in terms of cash flow to interest. This is to ensure that interest payments are not vulnerable to a reduction in profits or cash flows;

- a 'change of control clause', agreeing that ownership of the borrowing client will not change for the duration of the bank facility. This is particularly important if the borrower is part of a larger group and may be spun off from the group in future.

Clients and borrowers must scrutinise any covenants that may appear in the facility letter and some key considerations are shown below.

26.2.1.1 Negative pledge

One of the most important clauses can be the negative pledge clause. The purpose of such a clause is to ensure that no other creditor of the company is put in a better position than the lending bank. The borrower should take care to negotiate any exceptions it might need and should consider obtaining exclusions from the negative pledge clause for:

- any existing security given to other lenders;

- any existing or future security given for asset based finance such as equipment leasing or hire purchase;

- any future security over assets that are to be purchased (similar thinking to the leasing or hire purchase situation above);

- liens and pledges arising in the ordinary course of business, for example in connection any import or export finance facilities, such as documentary credits or the purchase of goods on retention of title terms.

26.2.1.2 Financial ratio clauses

If there are any financial covenants that relate to ratios or cover and if these ratios or cover are to be calculated by the methods used for published financial accounts, it is essential to make it clear that any such calculations will continue to be carried out on the basis of the generally accepted accounting practice (GAAP) that existed at the time the facility letter was signed. Failure to have such clarity may mean that the financial ratios are calculated on a different basis if GAAP changes in future, with potentially damaging consequences.

Once the documentation has been completed and the facilities have been drawn down, the bank providing the facilities will require the client or borrower to provide financial or other information at pre-set dates to help the bank monitor compliance with the covenants in the facility letter. This will usually involve the provision of reliable monitoring figures to the bank on a regular basis, usually monthly or quarterly, within one or two weeks of the end of the period concerned. Indeed, a covenant to this effect will often be included in the facility letter.

On receipt of the figures the bank will check them to ensure that none of the covenants has been breached, because breach of covenants means that technically the client is in default of the loan agreement.

26.2.1.3 Events of default clauses

'Events of default' are events that give the lender the right to demand repayment and to cancel any obligation to make any future advances. Many facility letters include a clause that states that breach of any covenants set out in the documentation constitutes an event of default. Borrowers with large numbers of subsidiaries will try to limit the application of these clauses to material subsidiaries only.

A major event of default happens when a client enjoying bank facilities applies for liquidation if a limited company, or files for bankruptcy or an individual aoluntary arrangement (IVA) if a sole trader or partnership. The winding up of a partnership or the dissolution of a company, or the death of a sole trader, would normally be treated as an event of default, unless the bank has accepted proposals to repay or refinance facilities that it has granted.

One potential events of default clause that needs careful consideration is the 'cross-default' clause. This clause gives the lending bank the right to demand repayment of its facility if any other debt of the borrower to any other creditor is unpaid when due.

The borrower should, if possible, try to limit the scope of the cross default clause by rewording to the effect that:

- it should only apply to 'financial indebtedness' as opposed to trade debt;
- it should not apply to debts that are in dispute;
- it should not apply to amounts below a specified amount;
- it should not apply if the debt has become overdue because of changes in law or changes in tax provisions.

Other typical events of default could include:

- a failure to repay capital or interest on the due date;
- a cross- default clause (see above);
- changes in control of a company;
- any material adverse change in the financial condition of the company.

The 'material adverse change' clause can be controversial: borrowers may well argue that any such material adverse change will have caused breach of one the existing financial covenants anyway, so such a clause is superfluous; others may argue that the legal process of defining and proving 'material adverse change' can be long and costly. Nevertheless, such clauses continue to appear in loan documentation.

As with all contracts, the precise nature of the covenants and events of default clauses in the facility letter will be a matter of negotiation and bargaining power. At times of low interest and low default rates, such as that which existed just prior to the 2007 summer 'credit crunch', borrowers could often negotiate less onerous covenants and events of default clauses. Indeed, there was much publicity in early 2007 about the 'covenant- lite' facility letters granted to private equity borrowers to finance takeovers. At the time of writing (January 2008), however, credit conditions are much tighter and it is likely that banks will insist on strongly worded covenant or events of default clauses in their facility letters. It is sometimes said that when credit conditions are easy, it is bank relationship managers who win internal arguments on covenants, but when credit conditions tighten then it is bank credit departments that become the decision makers in facility letter wording.

26.2.1.4   The sanctions that a bank can invoke for breach of events of default clauses

The breach of any event of default clause will leave a variety of options open to the bank that provides facilities to the defaulter. The ultimate sanction will be for the bank to cancel all facilities and demand repayment of all outstanding loans, usually within seven or 14 days, but many of the trade finance facilities granted by banks are long-term or ongoing facilities, such as import documentary credits or bonds and guarantees from which the bank cannot speedily extricate itself. Another course might be for the bank to realise security held to cover the facility and use the cash raised to reduce its exposure to the client.

Other options open to the bank include the following.

- With gearing restrictions or debtor margin covenants, for example, the bank could give the client notice to take action to bring the figures back within the parameters agreed in the covenants within a certain period of time. This process would be tightly monitored by the bank and further action taken if were not complied with.

- The bank can insist on extra security being lodged if facilities are to continue at present levels.

- The bank could reduce the facilities being made available to the client to levels with which it is more comfortable under the new circumstances.

- The bank could increase the interest that it charges on the facilities until the covenants are again being complied with.

- The bank could apply an enforced regular reduction programme on the account, eg by increasing regular repayments into the loan account.

- The bank could restructure the facilities granted in an attempt to reduce risk. One example might be to transfer overdraft borrowing to a factoring facility.

- If the client is a limited company and the bank holds a floating charge as part of its security, as is often the case, it could appoint a receiver to act in its interests by running the company or winding it up.

It is worth bearing in mind that, because of the ongoing and often long-term nature of bank facilities in international trade, it is usually in the interests of the bank and its client for the client to continue trading. Thus, the bank may well be tolerant of temporary breaches of covenants. This applies especially when the breaches are of a technical nature: for example, when a company breaches a maximum gearing covenant because of a different calculation due to changes in GAAP. If problems do manifest themselves, however, the bank will watch the situation much more closely, perhaps by requiring more regular monitoring figures, and may even insist on calling in investigating accountants to report back to the bank on the state of affairs in the client's business. This is a costly affair and the bank would not do this lightly.

26.3   Choice of law and jurisdiction

With most banks trading internationally, it is almost certain that some of their clients for international trade services will be from other countries. It is therefore important when entering into contracts for any services that the documentation makes it perfectly clear in what jurisdiction the contract is signed and under which law disputes should be resolved. UK banks are big enough, in most cases, to stipulate in their contracts and facility letters that facilities are granted under UK jurisdiction, are subject to English or Scottish law, and that in the case of dispute, action may be taken only in UK courts.

If this is not made clear in the facility letter, or if no facility letter is issued, then many factors come into play in deciding where resolution must be played out in case of disputes. The domicile of the defendant is important, as is the place with which any of the parties claim closest connection. The Contracts (Applicable Law) Act 1990 gives guidance on such matters, but it is better to agree a specific law and jurisdiction at the very beginning, and to write it into facility letters before contracts are entered into and facilities granted, than to risk expensive international litigation later.

In an effort to avoid full and expensive litigation in courts, alternative dispute resolution methods may first be used, and mediation and conciliation services or formal arbitration – for example, by trade bodies – are much cheaper and often quicker than litigation. These can also be stipulated up front in agreements with clients.

Even if cases do proceed to court and the bank wins an award in a foreign court or jurisdiction, it may still have problems enforcing such awards in other arenas and arbitration awards may still be difficult to enforce internationally if the other party is reluctant to comply. Even within the European Union, courts in some countries vary in their efficiency in enforcing awards from other countries. The longer these processes take, the higher the costs.

To sum up, banks should always ensure that, wherever possible, they specify clearly in all documentation before making facilities available which jurisdiction and courts will prevail should problems arise.

26.6   Exchange controls

Not very long ago, many countries around the world had in place strict exchange control regimes – legislation that meant that citizens or businesses in those countries could not freely transfer funds to other countries or access foreign currencies. All incoming foreign currency or other foreign assets had to be changed into local currency at authorised banks immediately upon receipt and government or central bank permission was required to take or transfer foreign currency or other assets out of the country.

These rules were often put in place by governments of economically weak countries to prevent rapid outflows of 'hard' currencies, but other governments, often with stronger economies, used them simply to control the movement of their citizens.

Governments in countries with weak economic fundamentals felt the need to strictly control the inflow and outflow of non- domestic currencies so that sufficient foreign currency could be conserved within the country for the purchase of essential imports. These governments maintained exchange controls on foreign exchange transactions to prevent the bulk of available hard currency in the country from being transferred abroad. The motivation for owners of funds to transfers them out of the countries with weak economic fundamentals was and is safety and value conservation. By switching into hard currencies in bank accounts outside the country, the fund owner would hope to avoid the risk of rapid devaluation due to high local inflation rates (cf Zimbabwe in 2007–08) or even government appropriation.

Different rules applied in different countries. Some countries ran two exchange rates: one for day- to- day trade transactions and the other for capital transactions involving purchases of overseas assets. Other countries had 'official rates' at which tourists and government officials could exchange currencies, with extortionate black market rates prevailing for other, less fortunate citizens. Others, often in Comecon (Eastern Bloc) countries in the old Soviet Union days, insisted that tourists change a set amount of 'hard' currency for every day of their stay into nearly worthless local currencies, with which there was nothing to buy. Needless to say, any surplus local currency could not be changed back to hard currency on leaving the country.

Under exchange control regimes, the control of regular trading transactions was often delegated to state banks (or commercial banks, if they existed). These banks were responsible for ensuring that outward payments were only allowed for genuine trade transactions. For inward hard currency receipts, the banks had a duty to ensure that the amounts officially recorded related to the full value of genuine underlying goods or services and that these hard currencies were exchanged for local currency immediately. In some countries, citizens travelling abroad had to apply to the central bank, via their own banks, for specific permission to take funds abroad if they wished to take more than the very limited amounts (which were as low as £50 per person in the UK during the 1960s, increased to £300 in the late 1970s). Local banks had delegated authority to check and confirm that the rules had been applied. Application for approval by the central bank was required for other types of overseas expenditure (for example, foreign study or overseas medical treatment). Investment and capital purchase overseas also needed special applications and were often refused. Holding accounts in foreign currencies was forbidden, so they could not be used for currency hedging purposes.

Today, only a few countries in the world have strict exchange control regulations still in force. These are mostly small, poor and lesser developed countries, although some, such as Cuba and North Korea, are bigger and better developed.

Where countries still do have exchange controls, this can be a problem for those who export to them. Exchange controls can create difficulty in the transfer of funds to the exporters, even though the importer may wish to do so and may have sufficient *local* funds to cover the payment.

The proceeds of export documentary collections to such areas will be slowed down because of the need for remittances to be approved and may not be forthcoming if not approved. Some exporters in the past have been known to open accounts in local currencies in such countries (if permitted) into which their buyers can pay local currency, for (hopefully) later transfer to the seller's country in hard currency.

We saw in Topic 22 how countertrade is often used to circumvent exchange control regulations, with payment in goods rather than currency. If payment for exports is offered by documentary credit, the bank should ensure that it is irrevocable, designated in hard currency and confirmed by a bank in the exporter's country.

Foreign investment into such countries with weak economic fundamentals is usually welcomed by the host government, but repatriation of profits or dividends to parent businesses may prove to be impossible or difficult, and withdrawing the investment funds at a later date may well be problematical. Often, the rules covering such matters change regularly, depending on the whims of local leaders, so long-term planning for such investments can be very difficult.

Many countries still have some restrictions on the import and export of large amounts of foreign currencies, but these are now mainly part of local rules to prevent money laundering. And although exchange controls are gradually disappearing, occasionally, they can make a comeback, as in the case of Malaysia, which reintroduced exchange controls on capital transfers following the South East Asian financial turmoils of 1997.

Appendix 1

Uniform rules for collections (1995 revision)

A. General provisions and definitions

Article 1

Application of URC 522

a)   The Uniform Rules for Collections, 1995 Revision, ICC Publication No 522, shall apply to all collections as defined in Article 2 where such rules are incorporated into the text of the 'collection instruction' referred to in Article 4 and are binding on all parties thereto unless otherwise expressly agreed or contrary to the provisions of a national, state or local law and/or regulation that cannot be departed from.

b)   Banks shall have no obligation to handle either a collection or any collection instruction or subsequent related instructions.

If a bank elects, for any reason, not to handle a collection or any related instructions received by it, it must advise the party from whom it received the collection or the instructions by telecommunication or, if that is not possible, by other expeditious means, without delay.

Article 2

Definition of Collection

For the purposes of these Articles:

a)   'Collection' means the handling by banks of documents as defined in sub- Article 2(b), in accordance with instructions received, in order to

i)   obtain payment and/or acceptance,

or

ii)   deliver documents against payment and/or against acceptance,

or

iii)   deliver documents on other terms and conditions.

b)   'Documents' means financial documents and/or commercial documents:

   i)   'Financial documents' means bills of exchange, promissory notes, cheques, or other similar instruments used for obtaining the payment of money;

   ii)   'Commercial documents' means invoices, transport documents, documents of title or other similar documents, or any other documents whatsoever, not being financial documents.

c)   'Clean collection' means collection of financial documents not accompanied by commercial documents.

d)   'Documentary collection' means collection of:

   i)   Financial documents accompanied by commercial documents;

   ii)   Commercial documents not accompanied by financial documents.

Article 3

Parties to a Collection

a)   For the purposes of these Articles the 'parties thereto' are:

   i)   the 'principal' who is the party entrusting the handling of a collection to a bank;

   ii)   the 'remitting bank' which is the bank to which the principal has entrusted the handling of a collection;

   iii)   the 'collecting bank' which is any bank other than the remitting bank, involved in processing the collection;

   iv)   the 'presenting bank' which is the collecting bank making presentation to the drawee.

b)   The 'drawee' is the one to whom presentation is to be made in accordance with the collection instruction.

B. Form and structure of collections

Article 4

Collection Instruction

a)   i)   All documents sent for collection must be accompanied by a collection instruction indicating that the collection is subject to URC 522 and giving complete and precise instructions. Banks are permitted to act only upon the instructions given in such collection instruction, and in accordance with these Rules.

   ii)   Banks will not examine documents in order to obtain instructions.

   iii)   Unless otherwise authorized in the collection instruction, banks will disregard any instructions from any party/bank other than the party/bank from whom they received the collection.

b)   A collection instruction should contain the following items of information, as appropriate:

   i)   Details of the bank from which the collection was received including full name, postal and SWIFT addresses, telex, telephone, facsimile numbers and reference.

ii) Details of the principal including full name, postal address, and if applicable telex, telephone and facsimile numbers.

iii) Details of the drawee including full name, postal address, or the domicile at which presentation is to be made and if applicable telex, telephone and facsimile numbers.

iv) Details of the presenting bank, if any, including full name, postal address, and if applicable telex, telephone and facsimile numbers.

v) Amount(s) and currency(ies) to be collected.

vi) List of documents enclosed and the numerical count of each document.

vii) a) Terms and conditions upon which payment and/or acceptance is to be obtained.

      b) Terms of delivery of documents against:

         1) payment and/or acceptance

         2) other terms and conditions

It is the responsibility of the party preparing the collection instruction to ensure that the terms for the delivery of documents are clearly and unambiguously stated, otherwise banks will not be responsible for any consequences arising therefrom.

viii) Charges to be collected, indicating whether they may be waived or not.

ix) Interest to be collected, if applicable, indicating whether it may be waived or not, including:

    a. rate of interest

    b. interest period

    c. basis of calculation (for example 360 or 365 days in a year as applicable).

x) Method of payment and form of payment advice.

xi) Instructions in case of non- payment, non- acceptance and/or noncompliance with other instructions.

c) i) Collection instructions should bear the complete address of the drawee or of the domicile at which the presentation is to be made. If the address is incomplete or incorrect, the collecting bank may, without any liability and responsibility on its part, endeavour to ascertain the proper address.

  ii) The collecting bank will not be liable or responsible for any ensuing delay as a result of an incomplete/incorrect address being provided.

C. Form of presentation

Article 5

Presentation

a) For the purposes of these Articles, presentation is the procedure whereby the presenting bank makes the documents available to the drawee as instructed.

b) The collection instruction should state the exact period of time within which any action is to be taken by the drawee.

Expressions such as 'first', 'prompt', 'immediate' and the like should not be used in connection with presentation or with reference to any period of time within which documents have to be taken up or for any other action that is to be taken by the drawee. If such terms are used banks will disregard them.

c) Documents are to be presented to the drawee in the form in which they are received except that banks are authorized to affix any necessary stamps at the expense of the party from whom they received the collection unless otherwise instructed, and to make any necessary endorsements or place any rubber stamps or other identifying marks or symbols customary to or required for the collection operation.

d) For the purpose of giving effect to the instructions of the principal, the remitting bank will utilize the bank nominated by the principal as the collecting bank. In the absence of such nomination, the remitting bank will utilize any bank of its own, or another bank's choice in the country of payment or acceptance or in the country where other terms and conditions have to be complied with.

e) The documents and collection instruction may be sent directly by the remitting bank to the collecting bank or through another bank as intermediary.

f) If the remitting bank does not nominate a specific presenting bank the collecting bank may utilize a presenting bank of its choice.

Article 6

Sight/Acceptance

In the case of documents payable at sight the presenting bank must make presentation for payment without delay.

In the case of documents payable at a tenor other than sight the presenting bank must, where acceptance is called for, make presentation for acceptance without delay and where payment is called for, make presentation for payment not later than the appropriate maturity date.

Article 7

Release of Commercial Documents

Documents Against Acceptance (D/A) *v.* Documents Against Payment (D/P)

a) Collections should not contain bills of exchange payable at a future date with instructions that commercial documents are to be delivered against payment.

b)   If a collection contains a bill of exchange payable at a future date, the collection instruction should state whether the commercial documents are to be released to the drawee against acceptance (D/A) or against payment (D/P).

In the absence of such statement commercial documents will be released only against payment and the collecting bank will not be responsible for any consequences arising out of any delay in the delivery of documents.

c)   If a collection contains a bill of exchange payable at a future date and the collection instruction indicates that commercial documents are to be released against payment, documents will be released only against such payment and the collecting bank will not be responsible for any consequences arising out of any delay in the delivery of documents.

Article 8

Creation of Documents

Where the remitting bank instructs that either the collecting bank or the drawee is to create documents (bills of exchange, promissory notes, trust receipts, letters of undertaking or other documents) that were not included in the collection, the form and wording of such documents shall be provided by the remitting bank, otherwise the collecting bank shall not he liable or responsible for the form and wording of any such document provided by the collecting bank and/or the drawee.

D. Liabilities and responsibilities

Article 9

Good Faith and Reasonable Care

Banks will act in good faith and exercise reasonable care.

Article 10

Documents *v* Goods/Services/Performances

a)   Goods should not be despatched directly to the address of a bank or consigned to or to the order of a bank without prior agreement on the part of that bank.

Nevertheless, in the event that goods are despatched directly to the address of a bank or consigned to or to the order of a bank for release to a drawee against payment or acceptance or upon other terms and conditions without prior agreement on the part of that bank, such bank shall have no obligation to take delivery of the goods, which remain at the risk and responsibility of the party despatching the goods.

b)   Banks have no obligation to take any action in respect of the goods to which a documentary collection relates, including storage and insurance of the goods even when specific instructions are given to do so. Banks will take such action only if, when, and to the extent that they agree to do so in each case.

Notwithstanding the provisions of sub- Article 1(c), this rule applies even in the absence of any specific advice to this effect by the collecting bank.

c) Nevertheless, in the case that banks take action for the protection of the goods, whether instructed or not, they assume no liability or responsibility with regard to the fate and/or condition of the goods and/or for any acts and/ or omissions on the part of any third parties entrusted with the custody and/ or protection of the goods. However, the collecting bank must advise without delay the bank from which the collection instruction was received of any such action taken.

d) Any charges and/or expenses incurred by banks in connection with any action taken to protect the goods will be for the account of the party from whom they received the collection.

e) i) Notwithstanding the provisions of sub- Article 10(a), where the goods are consigned to or to the order of the collecting bank and the drawee has honoured the collection by payment, acceptance or other terms and conditions, and the collecting bank arranges for the release of the goods, the remitting bank shall be deemed to have authorized the collecting bank to do so.

ii) Where a collecting bank on the instructions of the remitting bank or in terms of sub- Article 10(e)i arranges for the release of the goods, the remitting bank shall indemnify such collecting bank for all damages and expenses incurred.

Article 11

Disclaimer For Acts of an Instructed Party

a) Banks utilizing the services of another bank or other banks for the purpose of giving effect to the instructions of the principal, do so for the account and at the risk of such principal.

b) Banks assume no liability or responsibility should the instructions they transmit not be carried out even if they have themselves taken the initiative in the choice of such other bank(s).

c) A party instructing another party to perform services shall be bound by and liable to indemnify the instructed party against all obligations and responsibilities imposed by foreign laws and usages.

Article 12

Disclaimer on Documents Received

a) Banks must determine that the documents received appear to be as listed in the collection instruction and must advise by telecommunication or, if that is not possible, by other expeditious means, without delay, the party from whom the collection instruction was received of any documents missing, or found to be other than listed.

Banks have no further obligation in this respect.

b) If the documents do not appear to be listed the remitting bank shall be precluded from disputing the type and number of documents received by the collecting bank.

c) Subject to sub- Article 5(c) and sub- Articles 12(a) and 12(b) above, banks will present documents as received without further examination.

Article 13

Disclaimer on Effectiveness of Documents

Banks assume no liability or responsibility for the form, sufficiency, accuracy, genuineness, falsification or legal effect of any document(s), or for the general and/ or particular conditions stipulated in the document(s) or superimposed thereon; nor do they assume any liability or responsibility for the description, quantity, weight, quality, condition, packing, delivery, value or existence of the goods represented by any document(s), or for the good faith or acts and/or omissions, solvency, performance or standing of the consignors, the carriers, the forwarders, the consignees or the insurers of the goods, or any other person whomsoever.

Article 14

Disclaimer on Delays, Loss in Transit and Translation

a)   Banks assume no liability or responsibility for the consequences arising out of delay and/or loss in transit of any message(s), letter(s) or document(s), or for delay, mutilation or other error(s) arising in transmission of any telecommunication or for error(s) in translation and/or interpretation of technical terms.

b)   Banks will not be liable or responsible for any delays resulting from the need to obtain clarification of any instructions received.

Article 15

Force Majeure

Banks assume no liability or responsibility for consequences arising out of the interruption of their business by Acts of God, riots, civil commotions, insurrections, wars, or any other causes beyond their control or by strikes or lockouts.

E. Payment

Article 16

Payment Without Delay

a)   Amounts collected (less charges and/or disbursements and/or expenses where applicable) must be made available without delay to the party from whom the collection instruction was received in accordance with the terms and conditions of the collection instruction.

b)   Notwithstanding the provisions of sub- Article 1(c) and unless otherwise agreed, the collecting bank will effect payment of the amount collected in favour of the remitting bank only.

Article 17

Payment in Local Currency

In the case of documents payable in the currency of the country of payment (local currency), the presenting bank must, unless otherwise instructed in the collection instruction, release the documents to the drawee against payment in local currency only if such currency is immediately available for disposal in the manner specified in the collection instruction.

Article 18

Payment in Foreign Currency

In the case of documents payable in a currency other than that of the country of payment (foreign currency), the presenting bank must, unless otherwise instructed in the collection instruction, release the documents to the drawee against payment in the designated foreign currency only if such foreign currency can immediately be remitted in accordance with the instructions given in the collection instruction.

Article 19
Partial Payments

a)   In respect of clean collections, partial payments may be accepted if and to the extent to which and on the conditions on which partial payments are authorized by the law in force in the place of payment. The financial document(s) will be released to the drawee only when full payment thereof has been received.

b)   In respect of documentary collections, partial payments will be accepted only if specifically authorized in the collection instruction. However, unless otherwise instructed, the presenting bank will release the documents to the drawee only after full payment has been received, and the presenting bank will not be responsible for any consequences arising out of any delay in the delivery of documents.

c)   In all cases partial payments will be accepted only subject to compliance with the provisions of either Article 17 or Article 18 as appropriate.

Partial payment, if accepted, will be dealt with in accordance with the provisions of Article 16.

F. Interest, charges and expenses

Article 20

Interest

a)   If the collection instruction specifies that interest is to be collected and the drawee refuses to pay such interest, the presenting bank may deliver the document(s) against payment or acceptance or on other terms and conditions as the case may be, without collecting such interest, unless sub- Article 20(c) applies.

b)   Where such interest is to be collected, the collection instruction must specify the rate of interest, interest period and basis of calculation.

c) Where the collection instruction expressly states that interest may not be waived and the drawee refuses to pay such interest the presenting bank will not deliver documents and will not be responsible for any consequences arising out of any delay in the delivery of document(s). When payment of interest has been refused, the presenting bank must inform by telecommunication or, if that is not possible, by other expeditious means without delay the bank from which the collection instruction was received.

Article 21

Charges and Expenses

a) If the collection instruction specifies that collection charges and/or expenses are to be for account of the drawee and the drawee refuses to pay them, the presenting bank may deliver the document(s) against payment or acceptance or on other terms and conditions as the case may be, without collecting charges and/or expenses, unless sub- Article 21(b) applies.

Whenever collection charges and/or expenses are so waived they will be for the account of the party from whom the collection was received and may be deducted from the proceeds.

b) Where the collection instruction expressly states that charges and/or expenses may not be waived and the drawee refuses to pay such charges and/or expenses, the presenting bank will not deliver documents and will not be responsible for any consequences arising out of any delay in the delivery of the document(s). When payment of collection charges and/or expenses has been refused the presenting bank must inform by telecommunication or, if that is not possible, by other expeditious means without delay the bank from which the collection instruction was received.

c) In all cases where in the express terms of a collection instruction or under these Rules, disbursements and/or expenses and/or collection charges are to be borne by the principal, the collecting bank(s) shall be entitled to recover promptly outlays in respect of disbursements, expenses and charges from the bank from which the collection instruction was received, and the remitting bank shall be entitled to recover promptly from the principal any amount so paid out by it, together with its own disbursements, expenses and charges, regardless of the fate of the collection.

d) Banks reserve the right to demand payment of charges/and expenses in advance from the party from whom the collection instruction was received, to cover costs in attempting to carry out any instructions, and pending receipt of such payment also reserve the right not to carry out such instructions.

G. Other provisions

Article 22

Acceptance

The presenting bank is responsible for seeing that the form of the acceptance of a bill of exchange appears to be complete and correct, but is not responsible for the genuineness of any signature or for the authority of any signatory to sign the acceptance.

Article 23

Promissory Notes and Other Instruments

The presenting bank is not responsible for the genuineness of any signature or for the authority of any signatory to sign a promissory note, receipt, or other instruments.

Article 24

Protest

The collection instruction should give specific instructions regarding protest (or other legal process in lieu thereof), in the event of non- payment or non- acceptance.

In the absence of such specific instructions, the banks concerned with the collection have no obligation to have the document(s) protested (or subjected to other legal process in lieu thereof) for non- payment or non- acceptance.

Any charges and/or expenses incurred by banks in connection with such protest, or other legal process, will be for the account of the party from whom the collection instruction was received.

Article 25

Case- of- Need

If the principal nominates a representative to act as case- of- need in the event of non-payment and/or non- acceptance the collection instruction should clearly and fully indicate the powers of such case- of- need. In the absence of such indication banks will not accept any instructions from the case- of- need.

Article 26

Advices

Collecting banks are to advise fate in accordance with the following rules:

a)   Form of advice

All advices or information from the collecting bank to the bank from which the collection instruction was received, must bear appropriate details including, in all cases, the latter bank's reference as stated in the collection instruction.

b)   Method of advice

It shall be the responsibility of the remitting bank to instruct the collecting bank regarding the method by which the advices detailed in (c)i, (c)ii and (c)iii are to be given. In the absence of such instructions, the collecting bank will send the relative advices by the method of its choice at the expense of the bank from which the collection instruction was received.

c)   i)   Advice of payment

The collecting bank must send without delay advice of payment to the bank from which the collection instruction was received, detailing the amount or amounts collected, charges and/or disbursements and/or expenses deducted, where appropriate, and method of disposal of the funds.

  ii)   Advice of acceptance

The collecting bank must send without delay advice of acceptance to the bank from which the collection instruction was received.

  iii)   Advice of non- payment and/or non- acceptance

The presenting bank should endeavour to ascertain the reasons for nonpayment and/or non- acceptance and advise accordingly, without delay, the bank from which it received the collection instruction.

The presenting bank must send without delay advice of non- payment and/or advice of non- acceptance to the bank from which it received the collection instruction.

On receipt of such advice the remitting bank must give appropriate instructions as to the further handling of the documents. If such instructions are not received by the presenting bank within 60 days after its advice of nonpayment and/or non- acceptance, the documents may be returned to the bank from which the collection instruction was received without any further responsibility on the part of the presenting bank.

Appendix 2

– UCP 600 –
Uniform Customs and Practice for Documentary Credits (2007 revision)

Article 1

Application of UCP

The *Uniform Customs and Practice for Documentary Credits, 2007 Revision*, ICC Publication No. 600 ("UCP") are rules that apply to any documentary credit ("credit") (including, to the extent to which they may be applicable, any standby letter of credit) when the text of the credit expressly indicates that it is subject to these rules. They are binding on all parties thereto unless expressly modified or excluded by the credit.

Article 2

Definitions

For the purpose of these rules:

Advising bank means the bank that advises the credit at the request of the issuing bank.

Applicant means the party on whose request the credit is issued.

Banking day means a day on which a bank is regularly open at the place at which an act subject to these rules is to be performed.

Beneficiary means the party in whose favour a credit is issued.

Complying presentation means a presentation that is in accordance with the terms and conditions of the credit, the applicable provisions of these rules and international standard banking practice.

Confirmation means a definite undertaking of the confirming bank, in addition to that of the issuing bank, to honour or negotiate a complying presentation.

Confirming bank means the bank that adds its confirmation to a credit upon the issuing bank's authorization or request.

Credit means any arrangement, however named or described, that is irrevocable and thereby constitutes a definite undertaking of the issuing bank to honour a complying presentation.

Honour means:

a.   to pay at sight if the credit is available by sight payment.

b.   to incur a deferred payment undertaking and pay at maturity if the credit is available by deferred payment.

c.   to accept a bill of exchange ("draft") drawn by the beneficiary and pay at maturity if the credit is available by acceptance.

Issuing bank means the bank that issues a credit at the request of an applicant or on its own behalf.

Negotiation means the purchase by the nominated bank of drafts (drawn on a bank other than the nominated bank) and/or documents under a complying presentation, by advancing or agreeing to advance funds to the beneficiary on or before the banking day on which reimbursement is due to the nominated bank.

Nominated bank means the bank with which the credit is available or any bank in the case of a credit available with any bank.

Presentation means either the delivery of documents under a credit to the issuing bank or nominated bank or the documents so delivered.

Presenter means a beneficiary, bank or other party that makes a presentation.

Article 3

Interpretations

For the purpose of these rules:

Where applicable, words in the singular include the plural and in the plural include the singular.

A credit is irrevocable even if there is no indication to that effect.

A document may be signed by handwriting, facsimile signature, perforated signature, stamp, symbol or any other mechanical or electronic method of authentication.

A requirement for a document to be legalized, visaed, certified or similar will be satisfied by any signature, mark, stamp or label on the document which appears to satisfy that requirement.

Branches of a bank in different countries are considered to be separate banks.

Terms such as "first class", "well known", "qualified", "independent", "official", "competent" or "local" used to describe the issuer of a document allow any issuer except the beneficiary to issue that document.

Unless required to be used in a document, words such as "prompt", "immediately" or "as soon as possible" will be disregarded.

The expression "on or about" or similar will be interpreted as a stipulation that an event is to occur during a period of five calendar days before until five calendar days after the specified date, both start and end dates included.

The words "to", "until", "till", "from" and "between" when used to determine a period of shipment include the date or dates mentioned, and the words "before" and "after" exclude the date mentioned.

The words "from" and "after" when used to determine a maturity date exclude the date mentioned.

The terms "first half" and "second half" of a month shall be construed respectively as the 1st to the 15th and the 16th to the last day of the month, all dates inclusive.

The terms "beginning", "middle" and "end" of a month shall be construed respectively as the 1st to the 10th, the 11th to the 20th and the 21st to the last day of the month, all dates inclusive.

Article 4

Credits v. Contracts

a. A credit by its nature is a separate transaction from the sale or other contract on which it may be based. Banks are in no way concerned with or bound by such contract, even if any reference whatsoever to it is included in the credit. Consequently, the undertaking of a bank to honour, to negotiate or to fulfil any other obligation under the credit is not subject to claims or defences by the applicant resulting from its relationships with the issuing bank or the beneficiary.

   A beneficiary can in no case avail itself of the contractual relationships existing between banks or between the applicant and the issuing bank.

b. An issuing bank should discourage any attempt by the applicant to include, as an integral part of the credit, copies of the underlying contract, proforma invoice and the like.

Article 5

Documents v. Goods, Services or Performance

Banks deal with documents and not with goods, services or performance to which the documents may relate.

Article 6

Availability, Expiry Date and Place for Presentation

a. A credit must state the bank with which it is available or whether it is available with any bank. A credit available with a nominated bank is also available with the issuing bank.

b. A credit must state whether it is available by sight payment, deferred payment, acceptance or negotiation.

c. A credit must not be issued available by a draft drawn on the applicant.

d. i. A credit must state an expiry date for presentation. An expiry date stated for honour or negotiation will be deemed to be an expiry date for presentation.

    ii. The place of the bank with which the credit is available is the place for presentation. The place for presentation under a credit available with any bank is that of any bank. A place for presentation other than that of the issuing bank is in addition to the place of the issuing bank.

e. Except as provided in sub- article 29 (a), a presentation by or on behalf of the beneficiary must be made on or before the expiry date.

Article 7

Issuing Bank Undertaking

a. Provided that the stipulated documents are presented to the nominated bank or to the issuing bank and that they constitute a complying presentation, the issuing bank must honour if the credit is available by:

    i. sight payment, deferred payment or acceptance with the issuing bank;

    ii. sight payment with a nominated bank and that nominated bank does not pay;

    iii. deferred payment with a nominated bank and that nominated bank does not incur its deferred payment undertaking or, having incurred its deferred payment undertaking, does not pay at maturity;

    iv. acceptance with a nominated bank and that nominated bank does not accept a draft drawn on it or, having accepted a draft drawn on it, does not pay at maturity;

    v. negotiation with a nominated bank and that nominated bank does not negotiate.

b. An issuing bank is irrevocably bound to honour as of the time it issues the credit.

c. An issuing bank undertakes to reimburse a nominated bank that has honoured or negotiated a complying presentation and forwarded the documents to the issuing bank. Reimbursement for the amount of a complying presentation under a credit available by acceptance or deferred payment is due at maturity, whether or not the nominated bank prepaid or purchased before maturity. An issuing bank's undertaking to reimburse a nominated bank is independent of the issuing bank's undertaking to the beneficiary.

Article 8

Confirming Bank Undertaking

a. Provided that the stipulated documents are presented to the confirming bank or to any other nominated bank and that they constitute a complying presentation, the confirming bank must:

i. honour, if the credit is available by

    a) sight payment, deferred payment or acceptance with the confirming bank;

    b) sight payment with another nominated bank and that nominated bank does not pay;

    c) deferred payment with another nominated bank and that nominated bank does not incur its deferred payment undertaking or, having incurred its deferred payment undertaking, does not pay at maturity;

    d) acceptance with another nominated bank and that nominated bank does not accept a draft drawn on it or, having accepted a draft drawn on it, does not pay at maturity;

    e) negotiation with another nominated bank and that nominated bank does not negotiate.

ii. negotiate, without recourse, if the credit is available by negotiation with the confirming bank.

b. A confirming bank is irrevocably bound to honour or negotiate as of the time it adds its confirmation to the credit.

c. A confirming bank undertakes to reimburse another nominated bank that has honoured or negotiated a complying presentation and forwarded the documents to the confirming bank. Reimbursement for the amount of a complying presentation under a credit available by acceptance or deferred payment is due at maturity, whether or not another nominated bank prepaid or purchased before maturity. A confirming bank's undertaking to reimburse another nominated bank is independent of the confirming bank's undertaking to the beneficiary.

d. If a bank is authorized or requested by the issuing bank to confirm a credit but is not prepared to do so, it must inform the issuing bank without delay and may advise the credit without confirmation.

Article 9

Advising of Credits and Amendments

a. A credit and any amendment may be advised to a beneficiary through an advising bank. An advising bank that is not a confirming bank advises the credit and any amendment without any undertaking to honour or negotiate.

b. By advising the credit or amendment, the advising bank signifies that it has satisfied itself as to the apparent authenticity of the credit or amendment and that the advice accurately reflects the terms and conditions of the credit or amendment received.

c. An advising bank may utilize the services of another bank ("second advising bank") to advise the credit and any amendment to the beneficiary. By advising the credit or amendment, the second advising bank signifies that it has satisfied itself as to the apparent authenticity of the advice it has received and that the advice accurately reflects the terms and conditions of the credit or amendment received.

d. A bank utilizing the services of an advising bank or second advising bank to advise a credit must use the same bank to advise any amendment thereto.

e. If a bank is requested to advise a credit or amendment but elects not to do so, it must so inform, without delay, the bank from which the credit, amendment or advice has been received.

f. If a bank is requested to advise a credit or amendment but cannot satisfy itself as to the apparent authenticity of the credit, the amendment or the advice, it must so inform, without delay, the bank from which the instructions appear to have been received. If the advising bank or second advising bank elects nonetheless to advise the credit or amendment, it must inform the beneficiary or second advising bank that it has not been able to satisfy itself as to the apparent authenticity of the credit, the amendment or the advice.

Article 10

Amendments

a. Except as otherwise provided by article 38, a credit can neither be amended nor cancelled without the agreement of the issuing bank, the confirming bank, if any, and the beneficiary.

b. An issuing bank is irrevocably bound by an amendment as of the time it issues the amendment. A confirming bank may extend its confirmation to an amendment and will be irrevocably bound as of the time it advises the amendment. A confirming bank may, however, choose to advise an amendment without extending its confirmation and, if so, it must inform the issuing bank without delay and inform the beneficiary in its advice.

c. The terms and conditions of the original credit (or a credit incorporating previously accepted amendments) will remain in force for the beneficiary until the beneficiary communicates its acceptance of the amendment to the bank that advised such amendment. The beneficiary should give notification of acceptance or rejection of an amendment. If the beneficiary fails to give such notification, a presentation that complies with the credit and to any not yet accepted amendment will be deemed to be notification of acceptance by the beneficiary of such amendment. As of that moment the credit will be amended.

d. A bank that advises an amendment should inform the bank from which it received the amendment of any notification of acceptance or rejection.

e. Partial acceptance of an amendment is not allowed and will be deemed to be notification of rejection of the amendment.

f. A provision in an amendment to the effect that the amendment shall enter into force unless rejected by the beneficiary within a certain time shall be disregarded.

Article 11

Teletransmitted and Pre- Advised Credits and Amendments

a. An authenticated teletransmission of a credit or amendment will be deemed to be the operative credit or amendment, and any subsequent mail confirmation shall be disregarded.

If a teletransmission states "full details to follow" (or words of similar effect), or states that the mail confirmation is to be the operative credit or amendment, then the teletransmission will not be deemed to be the operative credit or amendment. The issuing bank must then issue the operative credit or amendment without delay in terms not inconsistent with the teletransmission.

b. A preliminary advice of the issuance of a credit or amendment ("pre- advice") shall only be sent if the issuing bank is prepared to issue the operative credit or amendment. An issuing bank that sends a pre- advice is irrevocably committed to issue the operative credit or amendment, without delay, in terms not inconsistent with the pre- advice.

Article 12

Nomination

a. Unless a nominated bank is the confirming bank, an authorization to honour or negotiate does not impose any obligation on that nominated bank to honour or negotiate, except when expressly agreed to by that nominated bank and so communicated to the beneficiary.

b. By nominating a bank to accept a draft or incur a deferred payment undertaking, an issuing bank authorizes that nominated bank to prepay or purchase a draft accepted or a deferred payment undertaking incurred by that nominated bank.

c. Receipt or examination and forwarding of documents by a nominated bank that is not a confirming bank does not make that nominated bank liable to honour or negotiate, nor does it constitute honour or negotiation.

Article 13

Bank- to- Bank Reimbursement Arrangements

a. If a credit states that reimbursement is to be obtained by a nominated bank ("claiming bank") claiming on another party ("reimbursing bank"), the credit must state if the reimbursement is subject to the ICC rules for bank- to- bank reimbursements in effect on the date of issuance of the credit.

b. If a credit does not state that reimbursement is subject to the ICC rules for bank- to- bank reimbursements, the following apply:

i. An issuing bank must provide a reimbursing bank with a reimbursement authorization that conforms with the availability stated in the credit. The reimbursement authorization should not be subject to an expiry date.

ii. A claiming bank shall not be required to supply a reimbursing bank with a certificate of compliance with the terms and conditions of the credit.

iii. An issuing bank will be responsible for any loss of interest, together with any expenses incurred, if reimbursement is not provided on first demand by a reimbursing bank in accordance with the terms and conditions of the credit.

iv. A reimbursing bank's charges are for the account of the issuing bank. However, if the charges are for the account of the beneficiary, it is the responsibility of an issuing bank to so indicate in the credit and in the reimbursement authorization. If a reimbursing bank's charges are for the account of the beneficiary, they shall be deducted from the amount due to a claiming bank when reimbursement is made. If no reimbursement is made, the reimbursing bank's charges remain the obligation of the issuing bank.

c. An issuing bank is not relieved of any of its obligations to provide reimbursement if reimbursement is not made by a reimbursing bank on first demand.

Article 14

Standard for Examination of Documents

a. A nominated bank acting on its nomination, a confirming bank, if any, and the issuing bank must examine a presentation to determine, on the basis of the documents alone, whether or not the documents appear on their face to constitute a complying presentation.

b. A nominated bank acting on its nomination, a confirming bank, if any, and the issuing bank shall each have a maximum of five banking days following the day of presentation to determine if a presentation is complying. This period is not curtailed or otherwise affected by the occurrence on or after the date of presentation of any expiry date or last day for presentation.

c. A presentation including one or more original transport documents subject to articles 19, 20, 21, 22, 23, 24 or 25 must be made by or on behalf of the beneficiary not later than 21 calendar days after the date of shipment as described in these rules, but in any event not later than the expiry date of the credit.

d. Data in a document, when read in context with the credit, the document itself and international standard banking practice, need not be identical to, but must not conflict with, data in that document, any other stipulated document or the credit.

e. In documents other than the commercial invoice, the description of the goods, services or performance, if stated, may be in general terms not conflicting with their description in the credit.

f. If a credit requires presentation of a document other than a transport document, insurance document or commercial invoice, without stipulating by whom the document is to be issued or its data content, banks will accept the document as presented if its content appears to fulfil the function of the required document and otherwise complies with sub- article 14 (d).

g. A document presented but not required by the credit will be disregarded and may be returned to the presenter.

h. If a credit contains a condition without stipulating the document to indicate compliance with the condition, banks will deem such condition as not stated and will disregard it.

i. A document may be dated prior to the issuance date of the credit, but must not be dated later than its date of presentation.

j. When the addresses of the beneficiary and the applicant appear in any stipulated document, they need not be the same as those stated in the credit or in any other stipulated document, but must be within the same country as the respective addresses mentioned in the credit. Contact details (telefax, telephone, email and the like) stated as part of the beneficiary's and the applicant's address will be disregarded. However, when the address and contact details of the applicant appear as part of the consignee or notify party details on a transport document subject to articles 19, 20, 21, 22, 23, 24 or 25, they must be as stated in the credit.

k. The shipper or consignor of the goods indicated on any document need not be the beneficiary of the credit.

l. A transport document may be issued by any party other than a carrier, owner, master or charterer provided that the transport document meets the requirements of articles 19, 20, 21, 22, 23 or 24 of these rules.

Article 15

Complying Presentation

a. When an issuing bank determines that a presentation is complying, it must honour.

b. When a confirming bank determines that a presentation is complying, it must honour or negotiate and forward the documents to the issuing bank.

c. When a nominated bank determines that a presentation is complying and honours or negotiates, it must forward the documents to the confirming bank or issuing bank.

Article 16

Discrepant Documents, Waiver and Notice

a. When a nominated bank acting on its nomination, a confirming bank, if any, or the issuing bank determines that a presentation does not comply, it may refuse to honour or negotiate.

b. When an issuing bank determines that a presentation does not comply, it may in its sole judgement approach the applicant for a waiver of the discrepancies. This does not, however, extend the period mentioned in sub- article 14 (b).

c. When a nominated bank acting on its nomination, a confirming bank, if any, or the issuing bank decides to refuse to honour or negotiate, it must give a single notice to that effect to the presenter.

The notice must state:

i. that the bank is refusing to honour or negotiate; and

ii. each discrepancy in respect of which the bank refuses to honour or negotiate; and

    iii. a) that the bank is holding the documents pending further instructions from the presenter; or

        b) that the issuing bank is holding the documents until it receives a waiver from the applicant and agrees to accept it, or receives further instructions from the presenter prior to agreeing to accept a waiver; or

        c) that the bank is returning the documents; or

        d) that the bank is acting in accordance with instructions previously received from the presenter.

d. The notice required in sub- article 16 (c) must be given by telecommunication or, if that is not possible, by other expeditious means no later than the close of the fifth banking day following the day of presentation.

e. A nominated bank acting on its nomination, a confirming bank, if any, or the issuing bank may, after providing notice required by sub- article 16 (c) (iii) (a) or (b), return the documents to the presenter at any time.

f. If an issuing bank or a confirming bank fails to act in accordance with the provisions of this article, it shall be precluded from claiming that the documents do not constitute a complying presentation.

g. When an issuing bank refuses to honour or a confirming bank refuses to honour or negotiate and has given notice to that effect in accordance with this article, it shall then be entitled to claim a refund, with interest, of any reimbursement made.

Article 17

Original Documents and Copies

a. At least one original of each document stipulated in the credit must be presented.

b. A bank shall treat as an original any document bearing an apparently original signature, mark, stamp, or label of the issuer of the document, unless the document itself indicates that it is not an original.

c. Unless a document indicates otherwise, a bank will also accept a document as original if it:

    i. appears to be written, typed, perforated or stamped by the document issuer's hand; or

    ii. appears to be on the document issuer's original stationery; or

    iii. states that it is original, unless the statement appears not to apply to the document presented.

d. If a credit requires presentation of copies of documents, presentation of either originals or copies is permitted.

e. If a credit requires presentation of multiple documents by using terms such as "in duplicate", "in two fold" or "in two copies", this will be satisfied by the presentation of at least one original and the remaining number in copies, except when the document itself indicates otherwise.

Article 18

Commercial Invoice

  a. A commercial invoice:

    i. must appear to have been issued by the beneficiary (except as provided in article 38);

    ii. must be made out in the name of the applicant (except as provided in sub-article 38 (g));

    iii. must be made out in the same currency as the credit; and

    iv. need not be signed.

  b. A nominated bank acting on its nomination, a confirming bank, if any, or the issuing bank may accept a commercial invoice issued for an amount in excess of the amount permitted by the credit, and its decision will be binding upon all parties, provided the bank in question has not honoured or negotiated for an amount in excess of that permitted by the credit.

  c. The description of the goods, services or performance in a commercial invoice must correspond with that appearing in the credit.

Article 19

Transport Document Covering at Least Two Different Modes of Transport

  a. A transport document covering at least two different modes of transport (multimodal or combined transport document), however named, must appear to:

    i. indicate the name of the carrier and be signed by:

      - the carrier or a named agent for or on behalf of the carrier, or

      - the master or a named agent for or on behalf of the master.

    Any signature by the carrier, master or agent must be identified as that of the carrier, master or agent.

    Any signature by an agent must indicate whether the agent has signed for or on behalf of the carrier or for or on behalf of the master.

    ii. indicate that the goods have been dispatched, taken in charge or shipped on board at the place stated in the credit, by:

      - pre- printed wording, or

      - a stamp or notation indicating the date on which the goods have been dispatched, taken in charge or shipped on board.

    The date of issuance of the transport document will be deemed to be the date of dispatch, taking in charge or shipped on board, and the date of shipment. However, if the transport document indicates, by stamp or notation, a date of dispatch, taking in charge or shipped on board, this date will be deemed to be the date of shipment.

    iii. indicate the place of dispatch, taking in charge or shipment, and the place of final destination stated in the credit, even if:

a) the transport document states, in addition, a different place of dispatch, taking in charge or shipment or place of final destination, or

b) the transport document contains the indication "intended" or similar qualification in relation to the vessel, port of loading or port of discharge.

iv. be the sole original transport document or, if issued in more than one original, be the full set as indicated on the transport document.

v. contain terms and conditions of carriage or make reference to another source containing the terms and conditions of carriage (short form or blank back transport document). Contents of terms and conditions of carriage will not be examined.

vi. contain no indication that it is subject to a charter party.

b. For the purpose of this article, transhipment means unloading from one means of conveyance and reloading to another means of conveyance (whether or not in different modes of transport) during the carriage from the place of dispatch, taking in charge or shipment to the place of final destination stated in the credit.

c. i. A transport document may indicate that the goods will or may be transhipped provided that the entire carriage is covered by one and the same transport document.

ii. A transport document indicating that transhipment will or may take place is acceptable, even if the credit prohibits transhipment.

Article 20

Bill of Lading

a. A bill of lading, however named, must appear to:

i. indicate the name of the carrier and be signed by:

- the carrier or a named agent for or on behalf of the carrier, or

- the master or a named agent for or on behalf of the master.

Any signature by the carrier, master or agent must be identified as that of the carrier, master or agent.

Any signature by an agent must indicate whether the agent has signed for or on behalf of the carrier or for or on behalf of the master.

ii. indicate that the goods have been shipped on board a named vessel at the port of loading stated in the credit by:

- pre- printed wording, or

- an on board notation indicating the date on which the goods have been shipped on board.

The date of issuance of the bill of lading will be deemed to be the date of shipment unless the bill of lading contains an on board notation indicating the date of shipment, in which case the date stated in the on board notation will be deemed to be the date of shipment.

If the bill of lading contains the indication "intended vessel" or similar qualification in relation to the name of the vessel, an on board notation indicating the date of shipment and the name of the actual vessel is required.

iii. indicate shipment from the port of loading to the port of discharge stated in the credit.

If the bill of lading does not indicate the port of loading stated in the credit as the port of loading, or if it contains the indication "intended" or similar qualification in relation to the port of loading, an on board notation indicating the port of loading as stated in the credit, the date of shipment and the name of the vessel is required. This provision applies even when loading on board or shipment on a named vessel is indicated by pre- printed wording on the bill of lading.

iv. be the sole original bill of lading or, if issued in more than one original, be the full set as indicated on the bill of lading.

v. contain terms and conditions of carriage or make reference to another source containing the terms and conditions of carriage (short form or blank back bill of lading). Contents of terms and conditions of carriage will not be examined.

vi. contain no indication that it is subject to a charter party.

b. For the purpose of this article, transhipment means unloading from one vessel and reloading to another vessel during the carriage from the port of loading to the port of discharge stated in the credit.

c. i. A bill of lading may indicate that the goods will or may be transhipped provided that the entire carriage is covered by one and the same bill of lading.

ii. A bill of lading indicating that transhipment will or may take place is acceptable, even if the credit prohibits transhipment, if the goods have been shipped in a container, trailer or LASH barge as evidenced by the bill of lading.

d. Clauses in a bill of lading stating that the carrier reserves the right to tranship will be disregarded.

Article 21

Non- Negotiable Sea Waybill

a. A non- negotiable sea waybill, however named, must appear to:

i. indicate the name of the carrier and be signed by:

- the carrier or a named agent for or on behalf of the carrier, or

- the master or a named agent for or on behalf of the master.

Any signature by the carrier, master or agent must be identified as that of the carrier, master or agent.

Any signature by an agent must indicate whether the agent has signed for or on behalf of the carrier or for or on behalf of the master.

ii. indicate that the goods have been shipped on board a named vessel at the port of loading stated in the credit by:

- pre- printed wording, or

- an on board notation indicating the date on which the goods have been shipped on board.

The date of issuance of the non- negotiable sea waybill will be deemed to be the date of shipment unless the non- negotiable sea waybill contains an on board notation indicating the date of shipment, in which case the date stated in the on board notation will be deemed to be the date of shipment.

If the non- negotiable sea waybill contains the indication "intended vessel" or similar qualification in relation to the name of the vessel, an on board notation indicating the date of shipment and the name of the actual vessel is required.

iii. indicate shipment from the port of loading to the port of discharge stated in the credit.

If the non- negotiable sea waybill does not indicate the port of loading stated in the credit as the port of loading, or if it contains the indication "intended" or similar qualification in relation to the port of loading, an on board notation indicating the port of loading as stated in the credit, the date of shipment and the name of the vessel is required. This provision applies even when loading on board or shipment on a named vessel is indicated by pre- printed wording on the non- negotiable sea waybill.

iv. be the sole original non- negotiable sea waybill or, if issued in more than one original, be the full set as indicated on the non- negotiable sea waybill.

v. contain terms and conditions of carriage or make reference to another source containing the terms and conditions of carriage (short form or blank back non- negotiable sea waybill). Contents of terms and conditions of carriage will not be examined.

vi. contain no indication that it is subject to a charter party.

b. For the purpose of this article, transhipment means unloading from one vessel and reloading to another vessel during the carriage from the port of loading to the port of discharge stated in the credit.

c. i. A non- negotiable sea waybill may indicate that the goods will or may be transhipped provided that the entire carriage is covered by one and the same non- negotiable sea waybill.

ii. A non- negotiable sea waybill indicating that transhipment will or may take place is acceptable, even if the credit prohibits transhipment, if the goods have been shipped in a container, trailer or LASH barge as evidenced by the non- negotiable sea waybill.

d. Clauses in a non- negotiable sea waybill stating that the carrier reserves the right to tranship will be disregarded.

Article 22

Charter Party Bill of Lading

a. A bill of lading, however named, containing an indication that it is subject to a charter party (charter party bill of lading), must appear to:

i. be signed by:
- the master or a named agent for or on behalf of the master, or
- the owner or a named agent for or on behalf of the owner, or
- the charterer or a named agent for or on behalf of the charterer.

Any signature by the master, owner, charterer or agent must be identified as that of the master, owner, charterer or agent.

Any signature by an agent must indicate whether the agent has signed for or on behalf of the master, owner or charterer.

An agent signing for or on behalf of the owner or charterer must indicate the name of the owner or charterer.

ii. indicate that the goods have been shipped on board a named vessel at the port of loading stated in the credit by:

- □ pre- printed wording, or

- □ an on board notation indicating the date on which the goods have been shipped on board.

The date of issuance of the charter party bill of lading will be deemed to be the date of shipment unless the charter party bill of lading contains an on board notation indicating the date of shipment, in which case the date stated in the on board notation will be deemed to be the date of shipment.

iii. indicate shipment from the port of loading to the port of discharge stated in the credit. The port of discharge may also be shown as a range of ports or a geographical area, as stated in the credit.

iv. be the sole original charter party bill of lading or, if issued in more than one original, be the full set as indicated on the charter party bill of lading.

b. A bank will not examine charter party contracts, even if they are required to be presented by the terms of the credit.

Article 23

Air Transport Document

a. An air transport document, however named, must appear to:

i. indicate the name of the carrier and be signed by:

- – the carrier, or

- – a named agent for or on behalf of the carrier.

Any signature by the carrier or agent must be identified as that of the carrier or agent.

Any signature by an agent must indicate that the agent has signed for or on behalf of the carrier.

ii. indicate that the goods have been accepted for carriage.

iii. indicate the date of issuance. This date will be deemed to be the date of shipment unless the air transport document contains a specific notation of the actual date of shipment, in which case the date stated in the notation will be deemed to be the date of shipment.

Any other information appearing on the air transport document relative to the flight number and date will not be considered in determining the date of shipment.

iv. indicate the airport of departure and the airport of destination stated in the credit.

v.   be the original for consignor or shipper, even if the credit stipulates a full set of originals.

vi.   contain terms and conditions of carriage or make reference to another source containing the terms and conditions of carriage. Contents of terms and conditions of carriage will not be examined.

b.   For the purpose of this article, transhipment means unloading from one aircraft and reloading to another aircraft during the carriage from the airport of departure to the airport of destination stated in the credit.

c.   i.   An air transport document may indicate that the goods will or may be transhipped, provided that the entire carriage is covered by one and the same air transport document.

ii.   An air transport document indicating that transhipment will or may take place is acceptable, even if the credit prohibits transhipment.

Article 24

Road, Rail or Inland Waterway Transport Documents

a.   A road, rail or inland waterway transport document, however named, must appear to:

i.   indicate the name of the carrier and:

- be signed by the carrier or a named agent for or on behalf of the carrier, or
- indicate receipt of the goods by signature, stamp or notation by the carrier or a named agent for or on behalf of the carrier.

Any signature, stamp or notation of receipt of the goods by the carrier or agent must be identified as that of the carrier or agent.

Any signature, stamp or notation of receipt of the goods by the agent must indicate that the agent has signed or acted for or on behalf of the carrier.

If a rail transport document does not identify the carrier, any signature or stamp of the railway company will be accepted as evidence of the document being signed by the carrier.

ii.   indicate the date of shipment or the date the goods have been received for shipment, dispatch or carriage at the place stated in the credit. Unless the transport document contains a dated reception stamp, an indication of the date of receipt or a date of shipment, the date of issuance of the transport document will be deemed to be the date of shipment.

iii.   indicate the place of shipment and the place of destination stated in the credit.

b.   i.   A road transport document must appear to be the original for consignor or shipper or bear no marking indicating for whom the document has been prepared.

ii.   A rail transport document marked "duplicate" will be accepted as an original.

iii.   A rail or inland waterway transport document will be accepted as an original whether marked as an original or not.

c.   In the absence of an indication on the transport document as to the number of originals issued, the number presented will be deemed to constitute a full set.

d. For the purpose of this article, transhipment means unloading from one means of conveyance and reloading to another means of conveyance, within the same mode of transport, during the carriage from the place of shipment, dispatch or carriage to the place of destination stated in the credit.

e.   i. A road, rail or inland waterway transport document may indicate that the goods will or may be transhipped provided that the entire carriage is covered by one and the same transport document.

    ii. A road, rail or inland waterway transport document indicating that transhipment will or may take place is acceptable, even if the credit prohibits transhipment.

Article 25

Courier Receipt, Post Receipt or Certificate of Posting

a. A courier receipt, however named, evidencing receipt of goods for transport, must appear to:

  i. indicate the name of the courier service and be stamped or signed by the named courier service at the place from which the credit states the goods are to be shipped; and

  ii. indicate a date of pickup or of receipt or wording to this effect. This date will be deemed to be the date of shipment.

b. A requirement that courier charges are to be paid or prepaid may be satisfied by a transport document issued by a courier service evidencing that courier charges are for the account of a party other than the consignee.

c. A post receipt or certificate of posting, however named, evidencing receipt of goods for transport, must appear to be stamped or signed and dated at the place from which the credit states the goods are to be shipped. This date will be deemed to be the date of shipment.

Article 26

"On Deck", "Shipper's Load and Count", "Said by Shipper to Contain" and Charges Additional to Freight

a. A transport document must not indicate that the goods are or will be loaded on deck. A clause on a transport document stating that the goods may be loaded on deck is acceptable.

b. A transport document bearing a clause such as "shipper's load and count" and "said by shipper to contain" is acceptable.

c. A transport document may bear a reference, by stamp or otherwise, to charges additional to the freight.

Article 27

Clean Transport Document

A bank will only accept a clean transport document. A clean transport document is one bearing no clause or notation expressly declaring a defective condition of the goods or their packaging. The word "clean" need not appear on a transport document, even if a credit has a requirement for that transport document to be "clean on board".

Article 28

Insurance Document and Coverage

a. An insurance document, such as an insurance policy, an insurance certificate or a declaration under an open cover, must appear to be issued and signed by an insurance company, an underwriter or their agents or their proxies.

   Any signature by an agent or proxy must indicate whether the agent or proxy has signed for or on behalf of the insurance company or underwriter.

b. When the insurance document indicates that it has been issued in more than one original, all originals must be presented.

c. Cover notes will not be accepted.

d. An insurance policy is acceptable in lieu of an insurance certificate or a declaration under an open cover.

e. The date of the insurance document must be no later than the date of shipment, unless it appears from the insurance document that the cover is effective from a date not later than the date of shipment.

f. i. The insurance document must indicate the amount of insurance coverage and be in the same currency as the credit.

   ii. A requirement in the credit for insurance coverage to be for a percentage of the value of the goods, of the invoice value or similar is deemed to be the minimum amount of coverage required.

   If there is no indication in the credit of the insurance coverage required, the amount of insurance coverage must be at least 110% of the CIF or CIP value of the goods.

   When the CIF or CIP value cannot be determined from the documents, the amount of insurance coverage must be calculated on the basis of the amount for which honour or negotiation is requested or the gross value of the goods as shown on the invoice, whichever is greater.

   iii. The insurance document must indicate that risks are covered at least between the place of taking in charge or shipment and the place of discharge or final destination as stated in the credit.

g. A credit should state the type of insurance required and, if any, the additional risks to be covered. An insurance document will be accepted without regard to any risks that are not covered if the credit uses imprecise terms such as "usual risks" or "customary risks".

h. When a credit requires insurance against "all risks" and an insurance document is presented containing any "all risks" notation or clause, whether or not bearing the heading "all risks", the insurance document will be accepted without regard to any risks stated to be excluded.

i. An insurance document may contain reference to any exclusion clause.

j. An insurance document may indicate that the cover is subject to a franchise or excess (deductible).

Article 29

Extension of Expiry Date or Last Day for Presentation

a. If the expiry date of a credit or the last day for presentation falls on a day when the bank to which presentation is to be made is closed for reasons other than those referred to in article 36, the expiry date or the last day for presentation, as the case may be, will be extended to the first following banking day.

b. If presentation is made on the first following banking day, a nominated bank must provide the issuing bank or confirming bank with a statement on its covering schedule that the presentation was made within the time limits extended in accordance with sub- article 29 (a).

c. The latest date for shipment will not be extended as a result of sub- article 29 (a).

Article 30

Tolerance in Credit Amount, Quantity and Unit Prices

a. The words "about" or "approximately" used in connection with the amount of the credit or the quantity or the unit price stated in the credit are to be construed as allowing a tolerance not to exceed 10% more or 10% less than the amount, the quantity or the unit price to which they refer.

b. A tolerance not to exceed 5% more or 5% less than the quantity of the goods is allowed, provided the credit does not state the quantity in terms of a stipulated number of packing units or individual items and the total amount of the drawings does not exceed the amount of the credit.

c. Even when partial shipments are not allowed, a tolerance not to exceed 5% less than the amount of the credit is allowed, provided that the quantity of the goods, if stated in the credit, is shipped in full and a unit price, if stated in the credit, is not reduced or that sub- article 30 (b) is not applicable. This tolerance does not apply when the credit stipulates a specific tolerance or uses the expressions referred to in sub- article 30 (a).

Article 31

Partial Drawings or Shipments

a. Partial drawings or shipments are allowed.

b. A presentation consisting of more than one set of transport documents evidencing shipment commencing on the same means of conveyance and for the same journey, provided they indicate the same destination, will not be regarded as covering a partial shipment, even if they indicate different dates of shipment or different ports of loading, places of taking in charge or dispatch. If the presentation consists of more than one set of transport documents, the latest date of shipment as evidenced on any of the sets of transport documents will be regarded as the date of shipment.

A presentation consisting of one or more sets of transport documents evidencing shipment on more than one means of conveyance within the same mode of transport will be regarded as covering a partial shipment, even if the means of conveyance leave on the same day for the same destination.

c. A presentation consisting of more than one courier receipt, post receipt or certificate of posting will not be regarded as a partial shipment if the courier receipts, post receipts or certificates of posting appear to have been stamped or signed by the same courier or postal service at the same place and date and for the same destination.

Article 32

Instalment Drawings or Shipments

If a drawing or shipment by instalments within given periods is stipulated in the credit and any instalment is not drawn or shipped within the period allowed for that instalment, the credit ceases to be available for that and any subsequent instalment.

Article 33

Hours of Presentation

A bank has no obligation to accept a presentation outside of its banking hours.

Article 34

Disclaimer on Effectiveness of Documents

A bank assumes no liability or responsibility for the form, sufficiency, accuracy, genuineness, falsification or legal effect of any document, or for the general or particular conditions stipulated in a document or superimposed thereon; nor does it assume any liability or responsibility for the description, quantity, weight, quality, condition, packing, delivery, value or existence of the goods, services or other performance represented by any document, or for the good faith or acts or omissions, solvency, performance or standing of the consignor, the carrier, the forwarder, the consignee or the insurer of the goods or any other person.

Article 35

Disclaimer on Transmission and Translation

A bank assumes no liability or responsibility for the consequences arising out of delay, loss in transit, mutilation or other errors arising in the transmission of any messages or delivery of letters or documents, when such messages, letters or documents are transmitted or sent according to the requirements stated in the credit, or when the bank may have taken the initiative in the choice of the delivery service in the absence of such instructions in the credit.

If a nominated bank determines that a presentation is complying and forwards the documents to the issuing bank or confirming bank, whether or not the nominated bank has honoured or negotiated, an issuing bank or confirming bank must honour or negotiate, or reimburse that nominated bank, even when the documents have been lost in transit between the nominated bank and the issuing bank or confirming bank, or between the confirming bank and the issuing bank.

A bank assumes no liability or responsibility for errors in translation or interpretation of technical terms and may transmit credit terms without translating them.

Article 36

Force Majeure

A bank assumes no liability or responsibility for the consequences arising out of the interruption of its business by Acts of God, riots, civil commotions, insurrections, wars, acts of terrorism, or by any strikes or lockouts or any other causes beyond its control.

A bank will not, upon resumption of its business, honour or negotiate under a credit that expired during such interruption of its business.

Article 37

Disclaimer for Acts of an Instructed Party

a. A bank utilizing the services of another bank for the purpose of giving effect to the instructions of the applicant does so for the account and at the risk of the applicant.

b. An issuing bank or advising bank assumes no liability or responsibility should the instructions it transmits to another bank not be carried out, even if it has taken the initiative in the choice of that other bank.

c. A bank instructing another bank to perform services is liable for any commissions, fees, costs or expenses ("charges") incurred by that bank in connection with its instructions.

    If a credit states that charges are for the account of the beneficiary and charges cannot be collected or deducted from proceeds, the issuing bank remains liable for payment of charges.

A credit or amendment should not stipulate that the advising to a beneficiary is conditional upon the receipt by the advising bank or second advising bank of its charges.

d. The applicant shall be bound by and liable to indemnify a bank against all obligations and responsibilities imposed by foreign laws and usages.

Article 38

Transferable Credits

a. A bank is under no obligation to transfer a credit except to the extent and in the manner expressly consented to by that bank.

b. For the purpose of this article:

Transferable credit means a credit that specifically states it is "transferable". A transferable credit may be made available in whole or in part to another beneficiary ("second beneficiary") at the request of the beneficiary ("first beneficiary").

Transferring bank means a nominated bank that transfers the credit or, in a credit available with any bank, a bank that is specifically authorized by the issuing bank to transfer and that transfers the credit. An issuing bank may be a transferring bank.

Transferred credit means a credit that has been made available by the transferring bank to a second beneficiary.

c. Unless otherwise agreed at the time of transfer, all charges (such as commissions, fees, costs or expenses) incurred in respect of a transfer must be paid by the first beneficiary.

d. A credit may be transferred in part to more than one second beneficiary provided partial drawings or shipments are allowed.

A transferred credit cannot be transferred at the request of a second beneficiary to any subsequent beneficiary. The first beneficiary is not considered to be a subsequent beneficiary.

e. Any request for transfer must indicate if and under what conditions amendments may be advised to the second beneficiary. The transferred credit must clearly indicate those conditions.

f. If a credit is transferred to more than one second beneficiary, rejection of an amendment by one or more second beneficiary does not invalidate the acceptance by any other second beneficiary, with respect to which the transferred credit will be amended accordingly. For any second beneficiary that rejected the amendment, the transferred credit will remain unamended.

g. The transferred credit must accurately reflect the terms and conditions of the credit, including confirmation, if any, with the exception of:

- the amount of the credit,
- any unit price stated therein,
- the expiry date,
- the period for presentation, or
- the latest shipment date or given period for shipment,

- any or all of which may be reduced or curtailed.

The percentage for which insurance cover must be effected may be increased to provide the amount of cover stipulated in the credit or these articles.

The name of the first beneficiary may be substituted for that of the applicant in the credit.

If the name of the applicant is specifically required by the credit to appear in any document other than the invoice, such requirement must be reflected in the transferred credit.

h. The first beneficiary has the right to substitute its own invoice and draft, if any, for those of a second beneficiary for an amount not in excess of that stipulated in the credit, and upon such substitution the first beneficiary can draw under the credit for the difference, if any, between its invoice and the invoice of a second beneficiary.

i. If the first beneficiary is to present its own invoice and draft, if any, but fails to do so on first demand, or if the invoices presented by the first beneficiary create discrepancies that did not exist in the presentation made by the second beneficiary and the first beneficiary fails to correct them on first demand, the transferring bank has the right to present the documents as received from the second beneficiary to the issuing bank, without further responsibility to the first beneficiary.

j. The first beneficiary may, in its request for transfer, indicate that honour or negotiation is to be effected to a second beneficiary at the place to which the credit has been transferred, up to and including the expiry date of the credit. This is without prejudice to the right of the first beneficiary in accordance with sub-article 38 (h).

k. Presentation of documents by or on behalf of a second beneficiary must be made to the transferring bank.

Article 39

Assignment of Proceeds

The fact that a credit is not stated to be transferable shall not affect the right of the beneficiary to assign any proceeds to which it may be or may become entitled under the credit, in accordance with the provisions of applicable law. This article relates only to the assignment of proceeds and not to the assignment of the right to perform under the credit.

Appendix 3

Uniform Rules for Bank- to- Bank Reimbursements under Documentary Credits

A. General provisions and definitions

Article 1

Application of URR

The Uniform Rules for Bank- to- Bank Reimbursements under Documentary Credits ('Rules'), ICC Publication No. 525, shall apply to all Bank- to- Bank Reimbursements where they are incorporated into the text of the Reimbursement Authorization. They are binding on all parties thereto, unless otherwise expressly stipulated in the Reimbursement Authorization. The Issuing Bank is responsible for indicating in the

Documentary Credit ('Credit') that Reimbursement Claims are subject to these Rules.

In a Bank- to- Bank Reimbursement subject to these Rules, the Reimbursing Bank acts on the instructions and/or under the authority of the Issuing Bank.

These Rules are not intended to override or change the provisions of the ICC Uniform Customs and Practice for Documentary Credits.

Article 2

Definitions

As used in these Rules, the following terms shall have the meanings specified in this Article and may be used in the singular or plural as appropriate:

a) 'Issuing Bank' shall mean the bank that has issued a Credit and the Reimbursement Authorization under that Credit.

b) 'Reimbursing Bank' shall mean the bank instructed and/or authorized to provide reimbursement pursuant to a Reimbursement Authorization issued by the Issuing Bank.

c) 'Reimbursement Authorization' shall mean an instruction and/or authorization, independent of the Credit, issued by an Issuing Bank to a Reimbursing Bank to reimburse a Claiming Bank, or, if so requested by the Issuing Bank, to accept and pay a time draft(s) drawn on the Reimbursing Bank.

d) 'Reimbursement Amendment' shall mean an advice from the Issuing Bank to a Reimbursing Bank stating changes to a Reimbursement Authorization.

e) 'Claiming Bank' shall mean a bank that pays, incurs a deferred payment undertaking, accepts draft(s), or negotiates under a Credit and presents a Reimbursement Claim to the Reimbursing Bank. 'Claiming Bank' shall include a bank authorized to present a Reimbursement Claim to the Reimbursing Bank on behalf of the bank that pays, incurs a deferred payment undertaking, accepts draft(s), or negotiates.

f) 'Reimbursement Claim' shall mean a request for reimbursement from the Claiming Bank to the Reimbursing Bank.

g) 'Reimbursement Undertaking' shall mean a separate irrevocable undertaking of the Reimbursing Bank, issued upon the authorization or request of the Issuing Bank, to the Claiming Bank named in the Reimbursement Authorization, to honour that bank's Reimbursement Claim provided the terms and conditions of the Reimbursement Undertaking have been complied with.

h) 'Reimbursement Undertaking Amendment' shall mean an advice from the Reimbursing Bank to the Claiming Bank named in the Reimbursement Authorization, stating changes to a Reimbursement Undertaking.

i) For the purposes of these Rules branches of a bank in different countries are considered separate banks.

Article 3

Reimbursement Authorization Versus Credits

A Reimbursement Authorization is separate from the Credit to which it refers, and a Reimbursing Bank is not concerned with or bound by the terms and conditions of the Credit, even if any reference whatsoever to the terms and conditions of the Credit is included in the Reimbursement Authorization.

B. Liabilities and responsibilities

Article 4

Honour of a Reimbursement Claim

Except as provided by the terms of its Reimbursement Undertaking a Reimbursing Bank is not obligated to honour a Reimbursement Claim.

Article 5

Responsibilities of the Issuing Bank

The Issuing Bank is responsible for providing the information required in these Rules in both the Reimbursement Authorization and Credit and is responsible for any consequences resulting from non- compliance with this provision.

C. Form and notification of authorizations, amendments and claims

Article 6

Issuance and Receipt of a Reimbursement Authorization or Reimbursement Amendment

a) All Reimbursement Authorizations and Reimbursement Amendments must be issued in the form of an authenticated teletransmission or a signed letter. When a Credit, or an amendment thereto that has an effect on the Reimbursement Authorization, is issued by teletransmission, the Issuing Bank hould advise its Reimbursement Authorization or Reimbursement Amendment to the Reimbursing Bank by authenticated teletransmission. The teletransmission will be deemed the operative Reimbursement Authorization or the operative Reimbursement Amendment and no mail confirmation should be sent. Should a mail confirmation nevertheless be sent, it will have no effect and the Reimbursing Bank will have no obligation to check such mail confirmation against the operative Reimbursement Authorization or the operative Reimbursement Amendment received by teletransmission.

b) Reimbursement Authorizations and Reimbursement Amendments must be complete and precise. To guard against confusion and misunderstanding, Issuing Banks must not send to Reimbursing Banks:

i) a copy of the Credit or any part thereof or a copy of an amendment to the Credit in place of, or in addition to, the Reimbursement Authorization or Reimbursement Amendment. If such copies are received by the Reimbursing Bank they shall be disregarded.

ii) multiple Reimbursement Authorizations under one teletransmission or letter, unless expressly agreed to by the Reimbursing Bank.

c) Issuing Banks shall not require a certificate of compliance with the terms and conditions of the Credit in the Reimbursement Authorization.

d) All Reimbursement Authorizations must (in addition to the requirement of Article 1 for incorporation of reference to these Rules) state the following:

i) Credit number;

ii) currency and amount;

iii) additional amounts payable and tolerance, if any;

iv) Claiming Bank or, in the case of freely negotiable credits, that claims can be made by any bank. In the absence of any such indication the Reimbursing Bank is authorized to pay any Claiming Bank;

v) parties responsible for charges (Claiming Bank's and Reimbursing Bank's charges) in accordance with Article 16 of these Rules.

Reimbursement Amendments must state only the relative changes to the above and the Credit number.

e) If the Reimbursing Bank is requested to accept and pay a time draft(s), the Reimbursement Authorization must indicate the following, in addition to the information specified in (d) above:

i) tenor of draft(s) to be drawn;

ii) drawer;

iii) party responsible for acceptance and discount charges, if any.

    Reimbursement Amendments must state the relative changes to the above.

    Issuing Banks should not require a sight draft(s) to be drawn on the Reimbursing Bank.

f) Any requirement for:

i) pre- notification of a Reimbursement Claim to the Issuing Bank must be included in the Credit and not in the Reimbursement Authorization;

ii) pre- debit notification to the Issuing Bank must be indicated in the Credit.

g) If the Reimbursing Bank is not prepared to act for any reason whatsoever under the Reimbursement Authorization or Reimbursement Amendment, it must so inform the Issuing Bank without delay.

h) In addition to the provisions of Articles 3 and 4, Reimbursing Banks are not responsible for the consequences resulting from non- reimbursement or delay in reimbursement of Reimbursement Claims, where any provision contained in this Article is not followed by the Issuing and/or Claiming Bank.

Article 7

Expiry of a Reimbursement Authorization

Except to the extent expressly agreed to by the Reimbursing Bank, the Reimbursement Authorization must not have an expiry date or latest date for presentation of a claim except as indicated in Article 9.

Reimbursing Banks will assume no responsibility for the expiry date of Credits and if such date is provided in the Reimbursement Authorization it will be disregarded.

The Issuing Bank must cancel its Reimbursement Authorization for any unutilized portion of the Credit to which it refers, informing the Reimbursing Bank without delay.

Article 8

Amendment or Cancellation of Reimbursement Authorizations

Except where the Issuing Bank has authorized or requested the Reimbursing Bank to issue a Reimbursement Undertaking as provided in Article 9 and the Reimbursing Bank has issued a Reimbursement Undertaking:

a) The Issuing Bank may issue a Reimbursement Amendment or cancel a Reimbursement Authorization at any time upon sending notice to that effect to the Reimbursing Bank.

b) The Issuing Bank must send notice of any amendment to a Reimbursement Authorization that has an effect on the reimbursement instructions contained in the Credit to the nominated bank or, in the case of a freely negotiable Credit, the advising bank. In the case of cancellation of the Reimbursement Authorization prior to expiry of the Credit, the Issuing Bank must provide the nominated bank or the advising bank with new reimbursement instructions.

c) The Issuing Bank must reimburse the Reimbursing Bank for any Reimbursement Claims honoured or draft(s) accepted by the Reimbursing Bank prior to the receipt by it of notice of cancellation or Reimbursement Amendment.

Article 9

Reimbursement Undertakings

a) In addition to the requirements of sub- Article 6(a), (b) and (c) of these Rules, all Reimbursement Authorizations authorizing or requesting the issuance of a Reimbursement Undertaking must comply with the provisions of this Article.

b) An authorization or request by the Issuing Bank to the Reimbursing Bank to issue a Reimbursement Undertaking is irrevocable ('Irrevocable Reimbursement Authorization') and must (in addition to the requirement of Article 1 for incorporation of reference to these Rules) contain the following:

   i) Credit number;

   ii) currency and amount;

   iii) additional amounts payable and tolerance, if any;

   iv) full name and address of the Claiming Bank to whom the Reimbursement Undertaking should be issued;

   v) latest date for presentation of a claim including any usance period;

   vi) parties responsible for charges (Claiming Bank's and Reimbursing Bank's charges and Reimbursement Undertaking fee) in accordance with Article 16 of these Rules.

c) If the Reimbursing Bank is requested to accept and pay a time draft(s), the Irrevocable Reimbursement Authorization must also indicate the following, in addition to the information contained in (b) above:

   i) tenor of draft(s) to be drawn;

   ii) drawer;

   iii) party responsible for acceptance and discount charges, if any.

   Issuing Banks should not require a sight draft(s) to be drawn on the Reimbursing Bank.

d) If the Reimbursing Bank is authorized or requested by the Issuing Bank to issue its Reimbursement Undertaking to the Claiming Bank but is not prepared to do so, it must so inform the Issuing Bank without delay.

e) A Reimbursement Undertaking must indicate the terms and conditions of the undertaking and:

   i) Credit number and Issuing Bank;

   ii) currency and amount of the Reimbursement Authorization;

   iii) additional amounts payable and tolerance if any;

   iv) currency and amount of the Reimbursement Undertaking;

   v) latest date for presentation of a claim including any usance period;

   vi) party to pay the Reimbursement Undertaking fee, if other than the Issuing Bank. The Reimbursing Bank must also include its charges, if any, that will be deducted from the amount claimed.

f) If the latest date for presentation of a claim falls on a day on which the Reimbursing Bank is closed for reasons other than those mentioned in Article 15, he latest date for presentation of a claim shall be extended to the first following day on which the Reimbursing Bank is open.

g) i) An Irrevocable Reimbursement Authorization cannot be amended or cancelled without the agreement of the Reimbursing Bank.

ii) When an Issuing Bank has amended its Irrevocable Reimbursement Authorization, a Reimbursing Bank that has issued its Reimbursement Undertaking may amend its undertaking to reflect such amendment. If a Reimbursing Bank chooses not to issue its Reimbursement Undertaking Amendment it must so inform the Issuing Bank without delay.

iii) An Issuing Bank that has issued its Irrevocable Reimbursement Authorization Amendment shall be irrevocably bound as of the time of its advice of the Irrevocable Reimbursement Authorization Amendment.

iv) The terms of the original Irrevocable Reimbursement Authorization (or an Authorization incorporating previously accepted Irrevocable Reimbursement Authorization Amendments) will remain in force for the Reimbursing Bank until it communicates its acceptance of the amendment to the Issuing Bank.

v) A Reimbursing Bank must communicate its acceptance or rejection of an Irrevocable Reimbursement Authorization Amendment to the Issuing Bank. A Reimbursing Bank is not required to accept or reject an Irrevocable Reimbursement Authorization Amendment until it has received acceptance or rejection from the Claiming Bank to its Reimbursement Undertaking Amendment.

h) i) A Reimbursement Undertaking cannot be amended or cancelled without the agreement of the Claiming Bank.

ii) A Reimbursing Bank that has issued its Reimbursement Undertaking Amendment shall be irrevocably bound as of the time of its advice of the Reimbursement Undertaking Amendment.

iii) The terms of the original Reimbursement Undertaking (or a Reimbursement Undertaking incorporating previously accepted Reimbursement Authorizations) will remain in force for the Claiming Bank until it communicates its acceptance of the Reimbursement Undertaking Amendment to the Reimbursing Bank.

iv) A Claiming Bank must communicate its acceptance or rejection of a Reimbursement Undertaking Amendment to the Reimbursing Bank.

Article 10

Standards for Reimbursing Claims

a) The Claiming Bank's claim for reimbursement:

i) must be in the form of a teletransmission, unless specifically prohibited by the Issuing Bank, or an original letter. A Reimbursing Bank has the right to request that a Reimbursement Claim be authenticated and in such case the Reimbursing Bank shall not be liable for any consequences resulting from any delay incurred. If a Reimbursement Claim is made by teletransmission, no mail confirmation is to be sent. In the event such a mail confirmation is sent, the Claiming Bank will be responsible for any consequences that may arise from a duplicate reimbursement;

ii) must clearly indicate the Credit number and Issuing Bank (and Reimbursing Bank's reference number, if known);

iii) must separately stipulate the principal amount claimed, any additional amount(s) and charges;

iv) must not be a copy of the Claiming Bank's advice of payment, deferred payment, acceptance or negotiation to the Issuing Bank;

v) must not include multiple Reimbursement Claims under one teletransmission or letter;

vi) must, in the case of a Reimbursement Undertaking, comply with the terms and conditions of the Reimbursement Undertaking.

b) In cases where a time draft is to be drawn on the Reimbursing Bank, the Claiming Bank must forward the draft with the Reimbursement Claim to the Reimbursing Bank for processing, and include the following in its claim if required by the Credit and/or Reimbursement Undertaking:

   i) general description of the goods and/or services;

   ii) country of origin;

   iii) place of destination/performance;

   and if the transaction covers the shipment of merchandise

   iv) date of shipment;

   v) place of shipment.

c) Claiming Banks must not indicate in a Reimbursement Claim that a payment, acceptance or negotiation was made under reserve or against an indemnity.

d) Reimbursing Banks assume no liability or responsibility for any consequences that may arise out of any non- acceptance or delay of processing should the Claiming Bank fail to follow the provisions of this Article.

Article 11

Processing Reimbursement Claims

a) i) Reimbursing Banks shall have a reasonable time, not to exceed three banking days following the day of receipt of the Reimbursement Claim, to process claims. Reimbursement Claims received outside banking hours are deemed to be received on the next banking day.

   If a pre- debit notification is required by the Issuing Bank, this pre- debit notification period shall be in addition to the processing period mentioned above.

   ii) If the Reimbursing Bank determines not to reimburse, either because of a non- conforming claim under a Reimbursement Undertaking, or for any reason whatsoever under a Reimbursement Authorization, it shall give notice to that effect by telecommunication or, if that is not possible, by other expeditious means, without delay, but no later than the close of the third banking day following the day of receipt of the claim (plus any additional period mentioned in sub- Article (i) above). Such notice shall be sent to the Claiming Bank and the Issuing Bank and, in the case of a Reimbursement Undertaking, it must state the reasons for non- payment of the claim.

b) Reimbursing Banks will not process requests for back value (value dating prior to the date of a Reimbursement Claim) from the Claiming Bank.

c) Where a Reimbursing Bank has not issued a Reimbursement Undertaking and a reimbursement is due on a future date:

   i) The Reimbursement Claim must specify the predetermined reimbursement date.

ii) The Reimbursement Claim should not be presented to the Reimbursing Bank more than ten (10) of its banking days prior to such predetermined date. If a Reimbursement Claim is presented more than ten (10) banking days prior to the predetermined date, the Reimbursing Bank may disregard the Reimbursement Claim. If the Reimbursing Bank disregards the Reimbursement Claim it must so inform the Claiming Bank by teletransmission or other expeditious means without delay.

iii) If the predetermined reimbursement date is more than three banking days following the day of receipt of the Reimbursement Claim, the Reimbursing Bank has no obligation to provide notice of nonreimbursement until such predetermined date, or no later than the close of the third banking day following the receipt of the Reimbursement Claim plus any additional period mentioned in (a)(i) above, whichever is later.

d) Unless otherwise expressly agreed to by the Reimbursing Bank and the Claiming Bank, Reimbursing Banks will effect reimbursement under a Reimbursement Claim only to the Claiming Bank.

e) Reimbursing Banks assume no liability or responsibility if they honour a Reimbursement Claim that indicates that a payment, acceptance or negotiation was made under reserve or against an indemnity and shall disregard such indication. Such reserve or indemnity concerns only the relations between the Claiming Bank and the party towards whom the reserve was made, or from whom, or on whose behalf, the indemnity was obtained.

Article 12

Duplications of Reimbursement Authorizations

An Issuing Bank must not, upon receipt of documents, give a new Reimbursement Authorization, or additional instructions, unless they constitute an amendment to, or a cancellation of an existing Reimbursement Authorization. If the Issuing Bank does not comply with the above and a duplicate reimbursement is made, it is the responsibility of the Issuing Bank to obtain the return of the amount of the duplicate reimbursement. The Reimbursing Bank assumes no liability or responsibility for any consequences that may arise from any such duplication.

D. Miscellaneous provisions

Article 13

Foreign Laws and Usages

The Issuing Bank shall be bound by and shall indemnify the Reimbursing Bank against all obligations and responsibilities imposed by foreign laws and usages.

Article 14

Disclaimer on the Transmission of Messages

Reimbursing Banks assume no liability or responsibility for the consequences arising out of delay and/or loss in transit of any message(s), letter(s) or document(s), or for delay, mutilation or other errors arising in the transmission of any telecommunication. Reimbursing Banks assume no liability or responsibility for errors in translation.

Article 15

Force Majeure

Reimbursing Banks assume no liability or responsibility for the consequences arising out of the interruption of their business by acts of God, riots, civil commotions, insurrections, wars or any other causes beyond their control, or by any strikes or lockouts.

Article 16

Charges

a) The Reimbursing Bank's charges should be for the account of the Issuing Bank. However, in cases where the charges are for the account of another party, it is the responsibility of the Issuing Bank to so indicate in the original Credit and in the Reimbursement Authorization.

b) When honouring a Reimbursement Claim, a Reimbursing Bank is obligated to follow the instructions regarding any charges contained in the Reimbursement Authorization.

c) In cases where the Reimbursing Bank's charges are for the account of another party, they shall be deducted when the Reimbursement Claim is honoured.

Where a Reimbursing Bank follows the instructions of the Issuing Bank regarding charges (including commission, fees, costs or expenses) and these charges are not paid or a Reimbursement Claim is never presented to the Reimbursing Bank under the Reimbursement Authorization, the Issuing Bank remains liable for such charges.

d) Unless otherwise stated in the Reimbursement Authorization, all charges paid by the Reimbursing Bank will be in addition to the amount of the Authorization provided that the Claiming Bank indicates the amount of such charges.

e) If the Issuing Bank fails to provide the Reimbursing Bank with instructions regarding charges, all charges shall be for the account of the Issuing Bank.

Article 17

Interest Claims/Loss of Value

All claims for loss of interest, loss of value due to any exchange rate fluctuations, revaluations or devaluations are between the Claiming Bank and the Issuing Bank, unless such losses result from the non-performance of the Reimbursing Bank's obligation under a Reimbursement Undertaking.

Index

References in this index are to heading numbers.